P9-CQY-729

Feminism and International Relations

Feminist International Relations (IR) scholarship recently celebrated its twentieth anniversary. Over those years, feminist researchers have made substantial progress concerning the question of how gender matters in global politics, global economics, and global culture. The progress has been noted both in the academic field of IR and, increasingly, in the policy world.

Celebrating these achievements, this book constructs conversations about the history, present state of, and future of feminist IR as a field across subfields of IR, continents, and generations of scholars. Providing an overview and assessment of what it means to "gender" IR in the twenty-first century, the volume has a unique format: it features a series of intellectual conversations, presenting cutting-edge research in the field, with provocative comments from senior scholars. It examines issues including global governance, the United Nations, war, peace, security, science, beauty, and human rights and addresses key questions including:

- What does viewing the diverse problems of global politics through gendered lenses look like in the twenty-first century?
- How do feminisms accommodate differences in culture, race, and religion?
- How do feminist theoretical and policy analyses fit together?

These conversations about feminist IR are accessible to non-specialist audiences and will be of interest to students and scholars of Gender Studies, Feminist Politics, and IR.

J. Ann Tickner is a Professor in the School of International Relations at the University of Southern California. Her principle areas of research include international theory, peace and security, and feminist approaches to international relations.

Laura Sjoberg is Assistant Professor of Political Science at the University of Florida. Her research is in the area of gender and security, with foci on just war theorizing and women's violence.

Feminism and International Relations

Conversations about the past, present and future

Edited by
J. Ann Tickner and Laura Sjoberg

Routledge
Taylor & Francis Group

LONDON AND NEW YORK

First published 2011
by Routledge
2 Park Square, Milton Park, Abingdon, Oxon, OX14 4RN

Simultaneously published in the USA and Canada
by Routledge
711 Third Avenue, New York, NY 10017

Routledge is an imprint of the Taylor & Francis Group, an informa business

© 2011 J. Ann Tickner and Laura Sjoberg, selection and editorial matter;
the contributors their contributions.

The right of J. Ann Tickner and Laura Sjoberg to be identified as editors of
this work has been asserted by them in accordance with the Copyright,
Designs and Patent Act 1988.

All rights reserved. No part of this book may be reprinted or reproduced or
utilised in any form or by any electronic, mechanical, or other means, now
known or hereafter invented, including photocopying and recording, or in
any information storage or retrieval system, without permission in writing
from the publishers.

British Library Cataloguing in Publication Data
A catalogue record for this book is available from the British Library

Library of Congress Cataloging in Publication Data
Feminism and international relations: conversations about the past,
present, and future / edited by J. Ann Tickner & Laura Sjoberg.
    p. cm.
    1. Feminism–Political aspects. 2. Feminism–International cooperation.
3. International relations. I. Tickner, J. Ann. II. Sjoberg, Laura, 1979–
    HQ1236.F4455 2011
    327.1082–dc22   2010047163

ISBN13: 978-0-415-58457-9 (hbk)
ISBN13: 978-0-415-58460-9 (pbk)
ISBN13: 978-0-203-81681-3 (ebk)

Typeset in Times New Roman
by Taylor & Francis Books

Printed and bound in Great Britain by
TJ International Ltd, Padstow, Cornwall

To the family of feminist scholars of IR/global politics, without whom this would be unimaginable.

Contents

Acknowledgments

The genesis of this volume was a conference entitled "Twenty Years of Feminist International Relations," organized by the editors of this volume together with Jane Jaquette. Collectively we are thankful to the University of Southern California's Center for International Studies for their generous support and hosting of the conference. We also wish to thank the other conference sponsors – USC's School of International Relations, the College of Letters, Arts and Sciences and the Center for Feminist Research. Indira Persad at the Center for International Studies did an amazing amount of logistical work, without which we could not have hosted the conference.

In addition to the authors of the essays in this volume, Jane Bayes, Carol Cohn, Christina Gray, Laura Hebert, Yesim Ince, Philippa Levine, Daniel Lynch, Nicholas Onuf, Patricia Owens, and Carola Weil participated in the conference, which was also attended by a number of students and faculty members at the USC who provided important feedback on the papers and asked interesting questions. A number of people read part, or all, of this book as we were preparing it for publication, including its contributors (Brooke Ackerly, Soumita Basu, Eric Blanchard, Catia Confortini, Maya Eichler, Cynthia Enloe, Sandra Harding, Jane Jaquette, Angela McCracken, Jessica Peet, V. Spike Peterson, Abigail Ruane, Brent Steele, and Jacqui True), Amy Eckert, Caron Gentry, Jennifer Lobasz, and two anonymous reviewers. Additionally, Jon Whooley and Isabella Woodley read the whole book in the last weeks before submission, providing many useful edits. From the beginning of the project, we have enjoyed working with Hannah Shakespeare and Heidi Bagtazo at Routledge. Any mistakes, of course, remain our own.

In addition to the attendees at this particular conference, we gratefully acknowledge the rich theoretical and empirical exchanges we have had with members of the feminist theory and gender studies community in International Relations (generally and in the Feminist Theory and Gender Studies section of the International Studies Association) over the past decades. This book also builds on conversations at, and research generated by past conferences similar to this one, such as the 1989 conference at USC and the 1990 conference at Wellesley College, both of which helped to launch the field of feminist IR. A second conference at USC in 2001 looking retrospectively at and forward from feminist IR's first decade. The participants in these conferences, as well as the work of the feminist IR community as a whole, were our inspiration for this book.

J. Ann Tickner

I owe an enormous debt of gratitude to Laura Sjoberg who, in her usual style, has contributed more than her fair share of writing and editing this volume. Laura is a prodigious worker, a thoughtful scholar, and superb intellectual partner. I am proud to be able to claim her as my student although most of her success is due to her remarkable intellectual capabilities, hard work, boundless energy, and unflagging enthusiasm.

A special word of thanks also to Jane Jaquette who provided much needed support and advice on planning and executing the conference out of which this volume emerged. My only regret is that the conference could only include a small number of those who have created and contributed to what is now widely recognized as the sub-discipline of feminist IR. I am forever indebted to the broader feminist community worldwide, too numerous to name individually, who have supported and nurtured me with ideas and friendship throughout this remarkable twenty-year journey that we have taken together.

Laura Sjoberg

I would first and foremost like to express gratitude to my co-editor, J. Ann Tickner. Ann has served as my mentor (formally as my Ph.D. advisor and informally on a continuing basis), as a personal and professional example of strength, fortitude, and success, and as a colleague on a number of exciting collaborative projects. If my work (in this volume or elsewhere) has any value, it is entirely attributable to my debt to Ann. At the conference, we talked a little bit about feminist International Relations as a family. To many, including myself, Ann is a crucial member of that family. In this volume, Eric Blanchard, Catia Confortini, Angela McCracken, Abigail Ruane and I are all J. Ann Tickner's students; Jessica Peet (my student) is Ann's grand-student.

In addition to Ann, a number of the founding scholars in feminist IR, including but not limited to Carol Cohn, Jindy Pettman, Sara Ruddick, Anne Sisson Runyan, Judith Stiehm, Christine Sylvester, and Cindy Weber have been amazing mentors and friends who I am lucky to have been able to know and work with; my work here is inspired by and guided by their mentorship.

I would not have been able to do the work I have done on this book without the institutional and financial support of the University of Florida Department of Political Science, and without the professional support of my mentor there, Sammy Barkin, to whom I am hopelessly indebted. In doing the editing work for this book, my constant companions have been my Chihuahuas: April, who, when I am bored and working on the bibliography, can be convinced that a banker's lamp is the sun; Gizmo, who will sit in my office chair and stare at the computer and accomplish about as much as I do; and Max, who actually ate a draft of this book's introduction.

Notes on contributors

Brooke A. Ackerly is Associate Professor of Political Science at Vanderbilt University. Her research interests include democratic theory, feminist methodologies, human rights, and social and environmental justice. She integrates into her theoretical work empirical research on activism. Her publications include *Political Theory and Feminist Social Criticism* (Cambridge Unbiversity Press, 2000), *Universal Human Rights in a World of Difference* (Cambridge University Press, 2008), and *Doing Feminist Research* with Jacqui True (Palgrave, 2010). She is currently working on the intersection of global economic, environmental, and gender justice.

Soumita Basu is Hayward R. Alker Postdoctoral Fellow at the Center for International Studies, USC. She holds a Ph.D. in International Politics from the University of Wales, Aberystwyth. Her doctoral dissertation examined emancipatory security praxis with respect to Security Council Resolution 1325. She has worked with Women in Security, Conflict Management and Peace (New Delhi) and Women's International League for Peace and Freedom (New York). Her research interests include critical security studies, feminist International Relations, historical materialism, and the United Nations. She published a chapter on SCR 1325 in *The Gender Imperative: Human Security vs State Security*, edited by Betty A. Reardon and Asha Hans (Routledge, 2010).

Eric M. Blanchard is a Lecturer in the School of International Relations at the University of Southern California in Los Angeles, California, where he completed his doctorate. His research interests include international security, International Relations theory, East Asian politics, international ethics, qualitative research methods, and gender. He participated in the "Gender in International Relations" conference at USC in 2001. His work has appeared in *International Studies Quarterly*, *Signs: Journal of Women and Culture in Society*, and *Review of International Studies*.

Catia C. Confortini holds a Ph.D. from the University of Southern California's School of International Relations. Her dissertation, entitled "Imaginative Identification: Feminist Critical Methodology in the Women's International

League for Peace and Freedom (1945–75)," received the 2009 Peace and Justice Studies Association's Best Dissertation of the Year Award. Her work on feminist peace studies is published in *Peace and Change*, *Gender, War and Militarism*, edited by Laura Sjoberg and Sandra Via (Prager, 2010), the *International Studies Association's Encyclopedia*, and *Peace and Freedom*, the magazine of the US section of Women's International League for Peace and Freedom. She is currently a visiting lecturer for the Peace and Justice Studies Program at Wellesley College.

Maya Eichler is a postdoctoral fellow in Gender and International Security at Harvard University's Kennedy School of Government. She received her Ph.D. in Political Science from York University and held the Hayward R. Alker postdoctoral fellowship – on the theme of Gender in Global Issues – at the Center for International Studies, University of Southern California. Her areas of specialization are International Relations, gender studies, and Russian politics. She has published in the *International Feminist Journal of Politics* and several edited volumes, and co-edited a special issue of the *Austrian Journal of Political Science* on "Counter/Terror/Wars: Feminist Perspectives" (no. 2, 2008). She is currently completing a book manuscript entitled *Militarizing Men: Gender, Conscription, and War in Post-Soviet Russia*, as well as conducting research on gender and the privatization of military security.

Cynthia Enloe is Research Professor of International Development and Women's and Gender Studies at Clark University. She received her Ph.D. in Political Science from University of California, Berkeley and has been awarded an Honorary Doctorate by the University of London. Among her books are *Bananas, Beaches and Bases* (University of California Press, 1989), *Maneuvers* (University of California Press, 2000), *The Curious Feminist* (Rowman & Littlefield, 2004) and *Nimo's War, Emma's War: Making Feminist Sense of the Iraq War* (University of California Press, 2010).

Sandra Harding is the author or editor of 15 books on issues in epistemology, philosophy of science, and feminist and postcolonial theory. She teaches in the Department of Education at University of California, Los Angeles and co-edited *Signs: Journal of Women in Culture and Society* (2000–2005). Her most recent books are *Science and Social Inequality* (University of Illinois, 2006), *Sciences From Below: Feminisms, Postcolonialities and Modernities* (Duke, 2008), and *After Postcolonial Theory: A Science and Technology Studies Reader* (Duke, forthcoming).

Jane S. Jaquette is Teaching Professor Emerita in the departments of Politics and Diplomacy and World Affairs at Occidental College. She has published over fifty articles and edited several books on a range of issues in feminist IR: comparative women's political participation and democracy, with an emphasis on Latin America; women/gender and development; and the relevance of Machiavelli and Hobbes to contemporary feminist thought. Her most recent book is *Feminist Agendas and Democracy in*

Latin America (2009). She and V. Spike Petersen co-chaired the 1989 USC conference on gender and IR, "Women, the State, and War."

Angela McCracken received her Ph.D. from the School of International Relations at the University of Southern California, where she also received a Graduate Certificate in Gender Studies. She is a gender advisor to non-profits, and has published her scholarship on gender, globalization, and nuclear proliferation in edited volumes. She is completing a book manu-script on intersections between the global political economy of beauty, traditional gender norms, and youth in Mexico.

Jessica L. Peet is a doctoral candidate at the University of Florida with a B.A. from Ohio State University in Political Science and minors in Women's Studies and International Studies. Her research interests include feminist international relations, gender studies, security studies (broadly defined), human trafficking, and the impact of language and discourse on the con-struction of identity. She was recently invited to participate in a conference on state policies concerning sex trafficking in Calcutta. She is also a member of the Gainesville Human Trafficking Taskforce.

V. Spike Peterson is a Professor in the School of Government and Public Policy at the University of Arizona. In 1988–89 she was a fellow at the University of Southern California and co-organized, with Jane Jaquette, the first 'feminist IR' conference in the United States. She edited *Gendered States* (Lynne Rienner, 1992), and is co-author with Anne Sisson Runyan of the third (renamed) edition of *Global Gender Issues in the New Millen-nium* (Westview Press, 2010/1999/1993). Her book *A Critical Rewriting of Global Political Economy: Reproductive, Productive and Virtual Economies* (Routledge, 2003) examined intersections of ethnicity/race, class, gender and national hierarchies in the context of globalization, and she is currently researching informalization, intersectionality, and global insecurities.

Abigail E. Ruane is a 2010 Ph.D. graduate of the University of Southern California's School of International Relations. Her dissertation developed a feminist constructivist approach to pursuing more inclusive interests and behavior, illustrated using historical negotiations over women's human rights in the United Nations. She has published articles in *International Studies Perspectives*, has one forthcoming in the *International Feminist Journal of Politics*, and is currently working to finalize a book co-authored with Patrick James entitled *The International Relations of Middle-earth: Learning from the Lord of the Rings*. She was awarded the International Studies Association's 2009 Misty Gerner Teaching Award with Patrick James for work on this project and ISA's 2011 Kenneth Boulding Award for an earlier version of her chapter in this volume.

Laura Sjoberg holds a Ph.D. in International Relations and a Gender Studies Certificate from the Culture, Gender, and Global Society Program in the

School of International Relations at the University of Southern California. She is Assistant Professor of Political Science at the University of Florida, where her research is on gender and security. She is the author of *Gender, Justice, and the Wars in Iraq* (Lexington Books, 2006) and (with Caron E. Gentry) *Mothers, Monsters, Whores: Women's Violence in Global Politics* (Zed Books, 2007), and editor of *Gender and International Security: Feminist Perspectives* (Routledge, 2010) and (with Amy Eckert) *Rethinking the 21st Century: New Problems, Old Solutions* (Zed Books 2009).

Brent J. Steele is an Associate Professor of Political Science and International Relations at the University of Kansas. He is the author of *Ontological Security in International Relations* (Routledge, 2008), and *Defacing Power: The Aesthetics of Insecurity in Global Politics* (University of Michigan Press, 2010). He is also the co-editor with Eric Heinze of *Ethics, Authority and War: Non-State Actors and the Just War Tradition* (Palgrave, 2009). His research has most recently appeared in *International Studies Review, Millennium, Cambridge Review of International Studies, International Political Science Review, International Relations, International Studies Quarterly,* and *Journal of International Relations and Development,* and has forthcoming articles in *Review of International Studies* and *Journal of International Political Theory.* He teaches courses on International Relations theory, international ethics, United States foreign policy, and critical security studies.

J. Ann Tickner is Professor in the School of International Relations and former director of the Center for International Studies at the University of Southern California. She is also a past president of the International Studies Association. She is the author of *Gendering World Politics* (Columbia University Press, 2001) and *Gender in International Relations* (Columbia University Press, 1992), as well as many articles on feminist International Relations theory.

Jacqui True received her Ph.D. at York University, Canada and was a post-doctoral fellow in the Centre for International Studies at the University of Southern California in 2000–2001. She is a Senior Lecturer in International Relations at the University of Auckland, New Zealand. Her research interests include feminist methodologies, international political economy, gender mainstreaming, and global governance. She is author and editor of several books, and has most recently published a book with Brooke Ackerly, *Doing Feminist Research in Political and Social Sciences* (Palgrave, 2010). Her forthcoming book and current research project is *The Political Economy of Violence Against Women* (Oxford). She is currently the chair of the Feminist Theory and Gender Studies Section of the International Studies Association, one of four editors of International Studies Perspectives, and a member of the founding and organizing committee for the Oceanic Conference in International Studies (OCIS). OCIS IV was held in Auckland June 30–July 2, 2010 featuring J. Ann Tickner as keynote speaker.

1 Introduction

International Relations through feminist lenses

Laura Sjoberg and J. Ann Tickner

In 2010, women comprised only about 19 percent of the world's parliamentarians. This was true despite the increasing popularity of gender quotas (especially in newly drafted constitutions) and even though most states have no sex-exclusionary rules about running for political office.[1] There is surprisingly little difference between women's representation in the parliaments of some western, liberal democracies (after the 2008 election, only 18 percent of members of the United States Congress were women) and some Islamic states, understood to be conservative and backwards, especially on women's rights (such as the United Arab Emirates where women are 22.5 percent of their parliament, and Pakistan where women are 22.2 percent). Some of the "leaders" in women's representation (such as Sweden, Norway, and Denmark) are unsurprising, while others (such as Rwanda and Cuba) are puzzling to analysts who associate women's rights with modernity, progress, and western liberal values. Feminist analysis suggests that, while the formal exclusion of women from office still may occur in some cases, the relative lack of women in high political office is usually the result of disguised forms of exclusion. Gendered norms and assumptions define masculinity as the standard to which all office-holders must aspire, regardless of their biological sex.

Assumptions about gender shape a wide range of events in global politics. In 2003, the Iraqi military took its first group of United States prisoners of war, a supply battalion that had been involved in an accident in their Humvee when they were lost in the desert. Several of the American soldiers had been injured in the accident, and several more were injured or killed in the gunfire as the Americans attempted to resist capture. Of the five survivors, three had either bullet wounds or serious, bleeding wounds from the car accident. The Iraqi military imprisoned two of the injured U.S. soldiers, and two others who had been captured, and engaged in practices generally understood to be torture in terms of international law. The fifth, however, was taken to a hospital and treated, and the Iraqi military unsuccessfully tried to return her to the United States military. When, a few days later out of military necessity, they abandoned the hospital, the Iraqi military left that prisoner, Jessica Lynch, in the hospital with medical care. While we do not have a first-hand account of why the Iraqi military treated Jessica Lynch differently, feminist analysis suggests that the Iraqis had some understanding of the gender, race, and class dynamics that made young, blonde Jessica Lynch more valuable to the United States military than the three men and one African American single mother who were (mis)treated as "normal" prisoners of war (see Sjoberg 2007).

These examples suggest gender is mapped in global politics in complicated, surprising, and multilayered ways. They provide just two of literally hundreds of empirical puzzles that feminist researchers in International Relations (IR) have analyzed, theoretically and empirically, to look both for how gender matters and for the contingent, contextual ways in which it manifests itself in global politics.

This is because, in Cynthia Enloe's (2010) words, "making feminist sense" of global politics is a big task, which requires endless, careful research and thinking (not to mention rethinking) about people, parts of the world, and processes that are difficult to investigate because they fall outside the purview of what is traditionally understood as the proper research concerns of the discipline of IR. While IR studies issues such as the effect of regime types on states' propensity for war, competitive power-balancing, and international trade and investment, feminist theorists have shown that understanding global politics relies as much on seeing the dynamics of marriages, of sexual relationships, of masculine expectations of men and feminine expectations of women, and of household-level political economies as it does on IR's "traditional" issues. Feminist scholars have argued, therefore, that it is not possible to separate making "feminist sense" of global politics from making sense of global politics more generally; in the relatively short history of the subfield, IR feminists have sought to ask where women and gender are in global politics and what such research reveals that was previously unseen.

This book was compiled as feminist research in IR enters its third decade. Conferences in the late 1980s and one in 1990, together with a special issue of the journal *Millennium* titled "Women in International Relations," published in 1988, are generally seen to have played a significant role in founding the subfield, which has drawn inspiration from feminist work in women's studies, sociology, psychology, history, and the philosophy of science.[2] Feminist IR scholars applied feminist thinking in these disciplines, (as well as other new feminist theorizing), to the problems of interest to IR theorists, while at the same time, by demonstrating the relevance (and indeed necessity) of gender theorizing they tried to broaden the spectrum of problems IR finds interesting. Recently, as feminist IR "turned 20," a number of events, panels, and discussions were held to celebrate and discuss the contributions that feminist IR has made to thinking about global politics more generally as well as the contributions that it could, as a research program, make in the future. As IR feminists reflect on the past 20 years, they are asking questions such as: What have we learned about how women are a part of global politics and how they impact global politics? What have we learned about gendered expectations about people, states, and organizations in the global political arena, and how are political processes dependent on these expectations?

One such event, the "Twenty Years of Feminist IR" conference held at the University of Southern California in April 2010, generated the chapters, comments, and discussions for this book.[3] Hosted by the book's editors and Jane Jaquette, the conference asked veteran scholars in the field, as well as newer researchers, to reflect on these questions and their implications for the past, present, and future of feminist contributions to knowing, understanding, and "making sense" of global politics.[4] The conference, and this edited volume, took the idea of "conversations" seriously, intentionally putting in conversation some of the founding voices in feminist theorizing in IR and some recent entrants into the field who have used, expanded on, employed, or critiqued their work.

The remainder of this introduction serves two purposes. First, it is a guide to the contents of the book for those generally familiar with the field, engaging those members of our readership in conversations about where feminist IR has been and where it is going. Second, it is an introduction to the field of feminist IR for those whose feminist curiosity about global politics is newer. It begins with a discussion of some of the terms and concepts that are critical to feminist IR and the contexts in which they emerged. It then introduces the concept of "conversations," a concept that is important both for feminist IR generally and for this book specifically. The next section talks about some of the past conversations in feminist IR, particularly the founding moments of the subfield, which remain substantively important but can also be seen as inspiration for feminist thinking twenty years later. The final section fast forwards to the compilation of this book, exploring, through a discussion of the individual chapters, what feminist IR looks like today, and foreshadowing some of the concluding discussions at the conference about where the subfield is going and how we might better understand (gender and) global politics in the next two decades of feminist IR research.

Feminist International Relations

This book is about the conversations between, and contributions of, those who view international relations with a "feminist curiosity" or through "gendered lenses." Most of the early feminists in IR were IR theorists, researchers, and policy practitioners before they were feminist theorists, researchers, and practitioners. Many of them attended graduate programs in political science where there were few women, read syllabi full of scholarly articles by mainly or only men, and experienced IR as a scholarly place often hostile to women and femininity.

These scholars began looking for gender, in the politics of IR as a discipline and in global politics more generally. To appreciate what this means, we begin with definitions of the terms "sex" and "gender," and controversies around these definitions. Well into the twentieth century, sex and gender were understood to be synonymous: people were biologically male (and therefore masculine) or female (and therefore feminine); household roles, economic benefits, and social dynamics were structured around people's sex/gender. Feminist scholars (among others), however, suggested a distinction between "sex" and "gender" to address what had come to be understood as "essentialist" thinking about women and men based on biology, where how men and women were treated (and what was expected of them) was based on their sex. For these scholars, "sex" refers to biological maleness or femaleness whereas gender refers to the personality traits and conceptions of self that we expect people to have on the basis of their sex, where masculinities are associated with maleness and femininities with femaleness.[5] Characteristics such as strength, rationality, independence, protector, and public life are associated with masculinity while characteristics such as, weakness, emotional, interdependence, the need for protection, and domesticity are associated with femininity. While men can be feminine, women can be masculine, and men and women can be hybrids of these traits, masculinity is expected of men, and femininity is expected of women. However, there is not just one, but a number of masculinities and femininities.

For example, a masculinity that was salient in early twenty-first century United States culture was "metro," a word used to refer to heterosexual men who combined an interest in women and chivalry with modern, sophisticated traits often associated with gay men, like the ability to cook and the decision to dress fashionably. "Metro" was contrasted to "Rambo" or "macho" masculinities, which emphasized a rough-and-tumble sort of manliness that was more concerned with toughness than finesse.

Masculinities and femininities are not just differences; they are differences that have hierarchical power implications. Feminist theorists have talked about an ideal-typical masculinity sitting on top of the hierarchy of gender tropes, contrasted at the other end of the spectrum to a subordinated femininity that is a necessary "other" to the powerful, hegemonic masculinity (Connell 1995). Other, middling gender tropes like subordinated masculinities are placed in a hierarchy. While the content of the hegemonic masculinity varies across time, place, and culture, feminist political scientists, sociologists, historians, and anthropologists have observed that gender hierarchies shape social and political interactions in most societies. This means that we cannot think of just one "gendered" experience (much less just one men's experience or just one women's experience) because genders are lived and performed differently and in different contexts. Nonetheless, gendered power relations are salient in almost every area of social and political life.

If "sex" is biological, and "gender" is social, "gender hierarchies" are socially constructed hierarchies based on gendered expectations of individuals, states, and other actors in global politics. Recently, feminist theorists have come to question whether the sex/gender dichotomy is as simple as it appears. These theorists suggest that the body is not something that we can ignore when thinking about how we come to read gender onto sex (in other words, genders do not just come out of thin air), and that bodies are not something that are just "out there" independent of social influence and construction. Anne Fausto-Sterling suggests that "we look at the body as a system that simultaneously produces and is produced by social meanings" and sex and gender as necessarily co-constituted (2005, 2).

IR feminists are increasingly taking this latter approach to gender. However, it is important to ask not just what we mean by "sex" and "gender" but also what we mean by feminism. Some people (erroneously) associate feminism with being anti-men, or even man-hating, and as advocacy for women at the expense of men in political and social life. This is not accurate generally, and not how it is used in feminist IR or in this book. Feminism consists of two interlinked phenomena. First, feminism was (and remains) a political movement interested primarily in women's rights and gender emancipation. Second, and distinctly if relatedly, feminism is a scholarly approach that looks through gender lenses to understand not only more about women and gender, but also how seeing women and gender helps us learn more about the world in general. Feminists have described their work as being "neither just about women, nor the addition of women to male-stream constructions" (Peterson 1992, 205). Instead, it is about what we see in global politics by looking at and for women and gender, and what those things tell us about how the world works.

So what does looking for women and gender in global politics tell us about how the world works? While we realize that an adequate answer to this question cannot be contained in one book, much less in its introduction, we will offer a few observations on some of the different ways that looking for sex and gender can help us to see global politics in new ways. We recognize that there are many feminist approaches to thinking about local and global politics and that some feminist thinkers have understood these feminisms as fundamentally in tension. Instead, we are drawn to John Hoffman's view that these differences should be seen "as one river with numerous currents rather than as a series of rivers flowing in different and even contradictory directions" (2001, 48). This view maintains a critical understanding of feminist theory and practice while remaining committed to an inclusive ethic of scholarship. In this spirit, we now provide a short introduction to various feminisms in IR.

While IR feminists share an interest in gender emancipation, as noted above, they often approach the journey towards emancipation differently. Liberal feminists believe that women's equality can be achieved by removing legal and other obstacles that have denied them the same rights as men; their primary interest is in integrating women into global politics at all levels. Liberal feminists in IR often use gender (and usually they mean "sex") as an explanatory variable in security and foreign policy analysis, arguing that including women would be net beneficial to achieve policy goals (e.g., Caprioli and Boyer 2001). While the approach of integrating women into the governance and economic structures of the existing order is useful, some feminists see it as limited.

Many other IR feminisms question an approach that tries to provide women equal opportunities within the political, social, economic, educational, and professional structures created by men for men; they claim that it is not only inadequate to the task of ending gender subordination, but that it is misguided because it reifies masculine models of citizenship and political processes. These feminist theorists note that gender inequalities continue to exist, even in societies that have long since been committed to giving women the same opportunities as men; they also see deeper problems in the gendered structures and functions of global politics. Constructivist feminists focus on the ways that ideas about gender shape and are shaped by global politics, seeing gender subordination as the dynamic result of social processes and suggests that, therefore, changing norms about masculinity and femininity is essential to redressing it (e.g., Prügl 1999; Locher and Prügl 2001). Critical feminism explores the ideational and material manifestations of gendered identities and gendered power with an interest in changing the gendered (im) balance of global politics (e.g., Steans 1998). Poststructuralist feminism is particularly concerned with performative and linguistic constructions and manifestations of genders, asking how and why gender-based dichotomized linguistic constructions, such as strong/weak, rational/emotional, and public/ private, serve to empower masculinities and devalorize femininities (e.g., Hooper 2001; Shepherd 2008a). Postmodern feminisms critically interrogate the naturalness of the categories of "woman" and "gender," and correspondingly, the ways that they map onto global politics, looking for creative and critical ways to deconstruct gender hierarchies (e.g., Sylvester 1994). Postcolonial feminists are particularly interested in critically interrogating the nature of relations of domination and subordination under imperialism, and imperialistic moves that can plague the relationship between western feminists and non-western women (e.g., Chowdhry and Nair 2002; Mohanty 2003). Postcolonial feminists look to understand and redress gender subordinations in particular cultural and sociopolitical contexts, rather than relying on some universal understanding of women's needs.[6]

There are other axes of difference that cut across these various feminist approaches to understanding global politics. One is the often-rehearsed debate in the field of IR between "positivists" and "postpositivists." Positivist scholars believe in the existence of objective knowledge independent of the experiences of the knower; they generally rely on some version of the scientific method of hypothesis testing and data analysis to arrive at this objective knowledge. Postpositivist scholars reject the possibility that knowledge can be legitimate without recognizing the relationship between the knower and the known; they pursue reflexive research that acknowledges both its perspectival nature and its political content.

Most, though not all, IR feminists are postpositivists who see traditional IR theorizing as privileging knowledge of the select few (usually privileged men) and share a political commitment to understanding the world from the perspectives of those who are marginalized and/or feminized in global social and political life. A related, though not identical, tension is the question of "quantitative" versus "qualitative" research. While some scholars in IR generally and feminist IR specifically associate quantitative (mostly statistical) research with positivism, and qualitative research with postpositivism, that map does not provide a perfect guide to the field. Some scholars employ statistical and even mathematical methods with a political, emancipatory, reflexive, and even radical purpose; others use case studies and other qualitative methods towards positivist ends. Still, regardless of the ends to which statistical methods are used, some feminist scholars question the inherent countability of sex, gender, and sexuality, while others insist that these factors must be counted, lest they be rendered invisible.

In addition to these "first order" debates, IR feminist theorists deal with differences between feminisms in a variety of ways. Some search for unity, some look to value and maintain diversity, and some express an interest in solidarity. Each of these approaches to what "feminisms" are influences scholars' research trajectories and scholarly self-identifications. Still, in feminist IR, many researchers have come to see feminist methodology as an intellectual process guiding feminism that is flexible in terms of its tools but in (broad) agreement about the intellectual and political goals of feminist theorizing (Ackerly et al. 2006, 4).

This is how this book and its authors view feminisms: inclusive, yet critically oriented. The authors in this book employ many different methodological strategies (including but not limited to theoretical analysis, discourse analysis, process tracing, structured interviews, unstructured interviews, and models), and approach theorizing gender from a number of the different feminist perspectives outlined above, sometimes combining them. The diversity of the scholarship in this book is not meant to silence these debates or differences. Rather, it is meant to include them as a regular part of conversations between and among (feminist) scholars of global politics.

Conversations

The organization of this book as conversations, interlinked and layered at different levels, is not just stylistic but substantive. Lucinda Peach (1994, 153) once noted that the "emphasis on collaboration in feminist theorizing" means that feminist articles, books, and other research products might look different from other scholarship, given the tendency of feminists and feminisms to work in dialogue and conversation. This tendency is not incidental; it is fundamental – feminisms' concerns for the relationship between positionality and knowledge and for understanding relationships of domination and subordination in politics suggest that dialogue is one of the most appropriate ways to approach theorizing, analyzing, and practicing global politics.

Feminist research generally, and this book specifically, draws a distinction between "communicating to" an audience (where the researcher as the authorial voice gathers correct information and informs the audience of that information) and "communicating with" an audience where knowledge is discovered in conversation with diverse others. Floya Anthias (2002, 282) has characterized the moment of communicating as a "dialogical moment," where "effective dialogue requires an already formulated mutual respect, a common communication language, and a common starting point in terms of power." It also assumes the goodwill of all the partners in the dialogue (Anthias 2002, 282). Mutual respect, common language, goodwill, and common starting points in terms of power can, of course, never be perfectly achieved. And even finding this rare and excellent combination of qualities between researchers (or practitioners in the policy world) does not guarantee success. Instead, conversations are difficult, and it is hard to avoid coming into the dialogue convinced that one's own argument is correct and those of others are flawed. Feminist conversations, then, are ideal-types, to be aspired to if never perfectly achieved.

Recognizing these limitations, "dialogue and diversity are seen as strengths" in feminist theorizing (Ackerly et al. 2006, 5). Engaging in dialogues that aspire to approximate the communicative ideal-type described above is not only an exercise in theoretical methodology, it is itself theorizing. Marysia Zalewski (1996) tells us that theory can be understood as explanation, critique, or practice; feminist conversations are an exercise in theorizing feminist politics through practice.

This is the standard to which this book aspires. Rather than writing a traditional book about how the substance of feminist IR is in the conversations between feminisms, we have elected to demonstrate the substance of feminist IR through actual conversations between feminists and feminisms. This book is a conversation in a number of ways. First, as noted above, it is a conversation that took place among the book's 16 authors and the rest of the attendees at the "Twenty Years of Feminist International Relations" conference. Both in the chapters themselves and in our Conclusion to the book, we have attempted to show the interaction between the substance presented by paper-writers and commentators, questions from the audience, and questions of grave import for the past, present, and future of feminist IR.

Second, the remainder of this book is separated into eight "chapters." However, since each chapter has two authors (or, in the case of a co-authored piece, three), they differ from standard chapter format. The initial authors, Catia Confortini, Abigail Ruane, Jacqui True, Soumita Basu, Maya Eichler, Eric Blanchard, Laura Sjoberg, Jessica Peet, and Angela McCracken, have written journal-article-length original research contributions to the field of feminist IR. However, the authors were asked to think about their work in dialogue with the work of some of the early or founding scholars in the field or with scholarship that had influenced the development of the field, and to write their articles with an eye towards adopting the work that they found most inspiring for their own research programs. Where possible, we asked one of the scholars who had been inspirational to the article-writer or a scholar working in a tradition that had been crucial to the research to serve as a commentator on the article, in conversation with someone who had written in conversation with their work. The commentators, Cynthia Enloe, Laura Sjoberg,

Brent Steele, V. Spike Peterson, Sandra Harding, Jane Jaquette, Brooke Ackerly, and J. Ann Tickner, were asked to comment on each piece with an eye towards two conversations: one between the article-writer's work and their own, and the other between the article-writer's work and the past, present, and future of feminist IR. These multilevel dialogues structure the text of this book. Another layer of conversation is evident in the book's Conclusion, which creates a dialogue out of some of the reflections from the conference's concluding session, the question and answer periods in each individual session, and the authors' commentaries on each other's work during the process of bringing their contributions from conference papers and commentaries to a book manuscript.

We hope that these multi-layer conversations between the scholars in this book will not end at its printing, and will be extended to other scholars and students in the field. None of the work in this book is meant to be a definitive statement, either of the goals, aims, and products of feminist research in IR or of feminist contributions to a particular empirical question or project. Instead, this book and its individual parts, like feminist IR more broadly, is itself a growing, changing dialogue, in which the reader plays an active part. To this end, we hope that this text, and the conversations in it, inspire more debates and conversations, rather than standing on their own terms as *the* conversation about the past, present, and future of feminist IR. In the spirit of situating this book as a part of the larger project of feminist theorizing in IR and of global politics, the remainder of this chapter thinks about feminist IR in terms of past and present, and then, through brief summaries of the individual chapters, foreshadows some of the discussions about the future that are taken up in its conclusion.

... About the past

Feminist theories entered the IR discipline in the late 1980s and early 1990s, at a time of general ferment in the field. Around the time that the Cold War ended, many scholars faulted neorealism, the paradigmatic approach dominant at the time, for having been unable to predict the end of the Cold War (both generally and in terms of how it happened). Scholars began to question the usefulness of IR's traditional concepts for analyzing the post-Cold War world. This questioning is generally referred to as the "third debate," and has been delineated in a number of ways (see Lapid, 1989). Perhaps the most well-known is Robert Cox's (1986) distinction between "problem-solving" and "critical" theory, where problem-solving theory, which is not explicitly normative, takes the world as given and looks to explain how it came to be that way. Critical theory, however, looks to understand the world (and particularly its injustices) for the purpose of changing it for the better. The third debate has also been described as a debate between "positivism" and "postpositivism" in the terms described above, or between "positivism" and "pluralism" or methodological diversity.[7]

Regardless of how we define this moment in IR history, the acceptable range of theorizing seemed to be broadening, creating more space for "critical" theorizing. Feminist research was generally situated on the "critical" side of the critical/problem-solving divide. Early IR feminists challenged the discipline to think about how its understandings of global politics might be improved if attention were paid to women's experiences; it claimed that only by introducing gender analysis could the differential impact of the state system and the global economy on women's lives be fully understood.

As we mentioned above, in 1988, the journal *Millennium* published a special issue on "Women and International Relations," now widely seen as the beginning of feminist IR's research program. In that issue, J. Ann Tickner (1988, 429) claimed that "international relations is a man's world, a world of power and conflict in which warfare is a privileged activity." Some IR scholars reacted by acknowledging the promise of feminist approaches for seeing global politics differently. Robert Keohane characterized feminist IR as "likely to fundamentally change IR's greatest debates" (1989, 246).

In 1989 and 1990, two of the inaugural conferences introducing feminist theorizing in IR took place, at the University of Southern California in Los Angeles, and at Wellesley College in Wellesley, Massachussetts. The 1989 USC conference, also hosted by the Center for International Studies, was entitled "Women, the State and War: What Difference Does Gender Make?" The close to seventy conference participants came from a variety of social science disciplines; most were feminist scholars, others were IR scholars with little exposure to gender analysis. Aiming to show the scope and significance of potential feminist critiques of IR's core concepts, the conference theme focused on examining neorealist Kenneth Waltz's (1959) three levels of analysis, the individual, the state and the anarchic international system. Some of the questions addressed by participants included: Why has gender not previously been addressed in IR theory? Are the "individual" and the "state" gendered? Is Waltz's emphasis on the anarchic state *system* as leading to war – rather than individuals of types of states – a gendered construction? In what ways does feminist scholarship share, contribute to, and/or transform existing critiques of realism? (Peterson 1989). In the concluding words of conference co-organizer Jane Jaquette, the conference "opened a dialogue we hope to continue" (Peterson, 1989: 26).

In 1990, a conference sponsored by the Ford Foundation, entitled "Gender in International Relations" was held at Wellesley College. In this case, most of the participants were IR scholars; some, but not all, were feminist scholars also. This conference produced papers that were published in the volume *Gendered States: Feminist (Re)Visions of International Relations Theory,* edited by V. Spike Peterson, one of the conference co-organizers (see Peterson, 1992). Using feminist lenses, authors deconstructed, critiqued and reframed some of the major concepts in the field such as the state, sovereignty, anarchy, political identity and security. In Peterson's words, they saw gender as constitutive of, not merely coincidental with, international relations

(Peterson, 1992: 24). We turn now to a discussion of the extent to which revisioning IR and opening up conversational spaces, aspirations expressed at both conferences, have been successful.

... In the present

Following its 20th anniversary, the story of feminisms in IR is one of both successes and continuing struggles. Feminist research programs have grown and flourished intellectually; a global community of scholars interested in looking at IR through gendered lenses has been established. Some gender analysis has now been incorporated into mainstream research. Feminist work, as we will discuss briefly below, has produced a number of theoretical developments and empirical results that tell us important things about global politics. Thinking about gender has become an important element of the policy strategies of a number of governments and international organizations. Accountability for women's oppression and other gender issues is increasingly discussed in the "real world" of global politics.

Still, the productivity of conversations between feminists and other IR scholars has been more mixed than early conversations at the conferences described above might suggest. The dialogue at the 1989 conference between feminist and other IR scholars has not continued, at least on the same scale. As IR feminists began to build their own bodies of scholarship, subsequent conferences were more often conversations among feminist scholars, or between academic feminists, policymakers and/or activists.[8] Some IR feminists have come to question the utility of attempting to maintain ties to a(n) (increasingly) narrow IR discipline, based largely in United States political science departments. Although some attempts to relate to and with IR have been fruitful, others have produced "awkward silences and miscommunications" that feminist scholars have associated with a "gendered estrangement" (Tickner 1997). In order to set up a discussion of the potential for the subfield in the future, the remainder of this section will address the accomplishments of, and barriers to (and debates within), feminist theorizing in IR.

As we mentioned above, most feminists looking at global politics share a normative and empirical concern that the international arena is gender-hierarchical, and that this gender hierarchy is reflected and reproduced in IR scholarship. Feminists' normative concern is that the gender hierarchy in global politics is inherently unjust. Their empirical concern is that theories that do not take account of this gender hierarchy are partial because of their neglect of it; this, they claim, handicaps theorists' explanatory power and practitioners' range of policy options and expected results. Feminists have argued that gender lenses are necessary in three ways: conceptually, for understanding the meanings of global politics; empirically, for seeing realities, understanding causes, and predicting outcomes; and normatively, for promoting positive change.

Feminist theorists of IR have looked at these questions from a number of different perspectives, and in a number of different contexts, providing both theoretical depth and empirical richness. While recognizing that we cannot do justice to the vast amount of interesting and varied research, we will discuss a couple of examples in order to demonstrate the diversity and depth of this research. Early feminist works, such as V. Spike Peterson's edited volume *Gendered States* (1992), mentioned earlier, focused on identifying the gendered elements of a number of the concepts commonly used in IR, such as the state, sovereignty, international anarchy, and deterrence. Work that has been characterized as "second generation" research applied these theoretical insights to different contexts, at the same time as it expanded its theoretical reach. For example, Katherine Moon's *Sex Among Allies* (1997) demonstrated that individual women's lives were both the subject and object of "high" security politics between the United States and South Korea during the Cold War, and drew implications from Korean camptown prostitutes' experiences to better understand security theorizing and practice. Jacqui True's (2001) *Gender, Globalization, and Post-Socialism* showed how global politics are shaped by and shape gender relations in families, and challenged the conventional understanding of gender relations in post-socialist transitions. Elisabeth Prügl (1999) showed us what home-based work can tell us about global political economy and women's lives, and what gendered ideologies and constructions can tell us about home work.

Although, as we mentioned earlier, in recent years, feminist IR and the IR discipline more generally have had strained conversations, feminist work has become more visible. This increased visibility has raised a number of questions, tensions, and new puzzles. Where do violent women fit? How does feminism accommodate differences in culture, race, and religion? What would examining global politics through gendered lenses really look like? How do feminist theoretical and policy analyses fit together?

These puzzles have been addressed, in part, by work that challenges the boundaries of feminist theorizing in IR such as Marysia Zalewski and Jane Parpart's explorations of the "Man Question" (1998, 2008), research on women's violence in (e.g., Sjoberg and Gentry 2007), and research questioning the role of colonialism and imperialism in feminist IR (e.g., Agathangelou and Ling 2009). A growing tradition of Feminist Security Studies (FSS) includes both theoretical and empirical work that challenges, interrogates, and looks to transform the boundaries of Security Studies (e.g., Shepherd 2008; Sjoberg 2010b). Another growing tradition of feminist Global Political Economy (GPE) sees gender as fundamental to the production and reproduction of political economies around the world, and offers rich theoretical analyses and empirical evidence. While some scholarship looks to "mainstream" gender in the discipline of IR (e.g., Steans 2003; Sjoberg 2009b), other work questions whether IR is really the right home for feminist scholarship, or whether it is by definition too constraining (e.g., Weldes and Squires 2007).

Looking back at two decades of feminist IR and forward towards the third, there is no easy ending to the sentence "feminist IR is. ... " that will give the reader a sense of certainty and an ability to rehearse a coherent one-sentence definition. Rather, feminist IR is a diverse, vibrant, growing tradition, where researchers can disagree on fundamental questions of epistemology and disciplinary relations while journeying together towards understanding the existence, consequences, and pragmatic reactions to gender hierarchy in global politics.

... And the future?

Looking forward to the future of feminist theorizing in IR is both a complex and exciting task. It is complex because it is part challenge, part aspiration. The challenges include dealing with some of the hard questions that have been raised both in this introduction and throughout the chapters of this book: How comfortable or uncomfortable is IR as a home for feminist theorizing about global politics? What epistemologies and methods are appropriate for feminist analyses of global politics? What do we mean by "sex" and "gender," and what are the complexities of their overlaps? How do we navigate the real salience of masculinities and femininities in global politics without taking an essentialist approach to what men and women are? How do we effectively take account of the intersectionality of race, gender, culture, class, and religion in an increasingly diverse world? How do we take account of security, political economy, and rights-based claims in increasingly complex situations in global politics? How do feminist theoretical and empirical academic studies translate to relevance for the policy world and advice to policymakers?

These questions will be recurring challenges throughout this book, and, we expect, in the coming years of scholarship in the tradition we have come to know as feminist IR. At the same time that looking forward requires engaging some of these challenges, it also involves aspirations: What do we want feminist IR to be when we revisit these questions again 20 years from now? What work needs to be done to make those visions realizable? While acknowledging the limits of feminist theorizing and/in IR, the chapters in this book address both the challenges and hopes facing feminist theorizing in the future.

Looking back, looking forward: outline of conversations in feminist IR

As we mentioned above, the body of the book is composed of eight "chapters" with two parts in each. The first part is a substantive, article-length essay exploring new avenues in the field but based on the development of previous scholarship. The second part is commentators' engagements, which discuss, situate, contextualize, and critique these essays and bring them into dialogue with other chapters as well as with the discipline at large. Where possible, the commentators are scholars who have been involved in the founding or evolution of a particular aspect of the field with which the essay-writers are engaging; commentators were asked to comment not only on the work itself, but also on its use of their work, and its implications for the past, present, and future of feminist IR.

Each of the chapters uses gender analysis, in the sense we defined it earlier, to shed light on a variety of political and economic global issues. Drawing from a number of theoretical approaches, all the authors move beyond liberal explanations of women's subordination, to reveal gendered structures that contribute, not only to the subordination of women and other marginalized groups, but that also have an effect on global politics more generally. While the methodologies they employ may be different, all the authors are post-positivist in the sense in which we defined positivism above. Many build on, or are critically engaged with, IR constructivism broadly defined. The chapters support Ackerly et al.'s (2006) claim that dialogue and diversity are strengths in feminist theorizing. Dialogue occurs, not only with the commentators and their work, but is a method that several of the authors use for their own research and/or in conversation with their research subjects. The chapters cover a broad range of topics; some, such as security and war, are topics that have been central to IR. Introducing gender into their analyses, these chapters look at these issues in new ways; other topics, such as body politics examined through the norms of beauty, have never been part of the discipline. Some of the authors begin their conversation through engagement with the broader IR discipline and then move to feminist theoretical reformulations; others begin with these feminist reformulations. Since, as we said earlier, feminism emerged out of political movement committed to social change, emancipation is a thread that runs through many of the chapters. Some of the authors indicate, either explicitly or implicitly, how their work can be useful to activists and/or policymakers.

Chapter 2, "Reclaiming agency for social change: feminism, International Relations, and the Women's International League for Peace and Freedom, 1945–75," is an analysis of the Women's International League for Peace and Freedom (WILPF), an International Non Governmental Organization (INGO) and one of the oldest women's peace organizations. In conversation with feminist Brooke Ackerly, on whose work she draws to develop her theoretical framework, Catia Confortini examines the work of WILPF in three areas – disarmament, decolonization, and the conflict in Israel/Palestine – from 1945 to 1975. Confortini's contribution also engages with and critiques constructivist IR, with which she proposes a conceptually tighter and concretely more substantial relationship with feminist IR. Specifically, the chapter addresses the agent–structure problem in constructivism and provides a feminist critical methodology that could help in promoting emancipatory social change. It also suggests a reformulation of the relationship between feminist IR and peace studies that advances theoretical arguments about peace and gender. Consistent with constructivist claims, the chapter suggests that the WILPF's understanding of "peace" depended on the organization's ideologies, which were the product of both the historical context within which the WILPF operated as well as its members' agency. To the extent that the WILPF was able to challenge the political, economic and social milieu in which it operated, the WILPF women's agency asserted itself vis-à-vis structural constraints through a self-reflective feminist methodology. Confortini takes inspiration from and elaborates on the methodology of feminist social criticism, developed by Brooke Ackerly and from IR feminist Christine Sylvester's notion of empathetic cooperation. She shows that this critical feminist methodology opens spaces for actors to challenge structural constraints. In conversation with Confortini's contribution, Brooke Ackerly engages in a discussion of what feminist method in IR entails, the tools for feminist theory and practice in global politics, and what Confortini's work does to advance our thinking on these methodological issues. Ackerly also calls attention to Confortini's use of imaginative identification, or what WILPF chairman Dorothy Hutchinson called intelligent compassion, a compassion that is concrete and informed by experiential knowledge. Ackerly notes that even though this term has not been used before in feminist IR, intelligent compassion is an essential tool for feminism.

Although she is working from a different theoretical framework and uses very different language, Abigail Ruane, in conversation with Brent Steele, is also talking about empathy and compassion as she investigates how negotiators could frame their conversations in ways which are inclusive and value others as equals. In Chapter 3, "Pursuing inclusive interests, both deep and wide: women's human rights and the United Nations," Ruane shifts the focus from an INGO to an International Governmental Organization (IGO), the United Nations. Drawing on a discussion of gender norms as they have developed in United Nations' conventions, resolutions and policy statements on women's human rights broadly defined, Ruane asks how it is possible to pursue more inclusive behavior in international affairs when we look through gender lenses. She argues that there are at least two kinds of "inclusiveness": "inclusive roots" (a broad basis for group interests) and "inclusive borders" (broad membership for group interests, but a potentially elite definition of those interests). Also using IR constructivism as her introductory framework, Ruane draws on a Gramscian conception of hegemony and a current version of psychology's Social Identity Theory (SIT) to develop a broader path to inclusive behavior than that suggested by Wendtian constructivism. She argues that, under conditions of perfect ideological hegemony, dominant narratives based on "friend" rather than "bully" models facilitate inclusive borders. Under conditions of perfect ideological choice, defining members of newly defined groups as like the self facilitates inclusive borders. Under more typical conditions of imperfect ideological hegemony/choice, where both friend and bully models exist, inclusive borders are possible by either conforming to "friend" narratives or making relational metanarratives explicit and reacting against "bully" narratives. Ruane explores the development of negotiations over women's rights in the United Nations during the past century in terms of the level of inclusiveness of the roots and borders of rights concepts. Ruane's research is also emancipatory. She offers her chapter as providing concrete standards and strategies that could be useful in the pursuit of more inclusive women's human rights. Bringing Ruane's work into dialogue with questions of interest to contemporary critical IR theorizing, Brent Steele finds tools in it, such as narrative, identity, security, and power, useful to the critical evaluation of (gender and) security. Interested in the question of the role of language in (feminist) IR work, Steele argues that Ruane's model is vital for rewriting and reinterpreting rights discourses in global politics, and asks how to use, recycle, and deconstruct the gendered traditions that Ruane and other feminists have uncovered in Western security practices.

In Chapter 4 Jacqui True, in conversation with Jane Jaquette, continues to engage the theme of the development of norms within the context of the United Nations and other IGOs. In her contribution, "Feminist problems with international norms: gender mainstreaming in global governance," True claims that, from her feminist perspective, the diffusion and internalization of international norms is a problem of global power and inequality rather a panacea for a more just and peaceful world order. Offering a less benign reading of the impact of the United Nations' norm-setting agenda than Ruane, and arguing against much of the IR constructivist literature on the diffusion of norms, True suggests that the process of taking for granted particular embodied ideas and relationships, or the normalization of norms, can be directly linked to the reproduction of violence and oppression. Taking a more critical stance toward IR constructivism more generally than Confortini and Ruane, True challenges the assumption that feminism and constructivism share a middle ground or common ontological worldview.[9] True's contribution goes on to explore how gender identities and power relations are embedded in global governance organizations. She investigates "gender mainstreaming" as the increasingly dominant language of bureaucratic politics through which policymakers worldwide understand women and men and engage with the politics of the global – be it global security, development, poverty, or trade. In certain IGOs, such as the United Nations, mainstreaming can be seen as an attempt to normalize gender. Moreover, True shows how processes of diffusion and socialization that position international organizations as teachers of norms do not just face (internal and external) resistance but may end up reinforcing dominant gender identities and international power relations. In conversation with True's contribution, Jane Jaquette discusses the tensions between her views and True's as important windows into the increasing complexity of promoting gender equality on a global scale in theory and in practice. While acknowledging its limitations, Jaquette, a scholar who has also worked in the policy world, offers a more positive view of gender mainstreaming as it has been implemented in various international organizations and national governments.

Chapter 5, "Security as emancipation: a feminist perspective," is a more direct engagement with IR theory—specifically with critical security studies. Cross-pollinating ideas about rights and security, issues that are addressed also in the preceding chapters, Chapter 5 is a conversation between Soumita Basu and Laura Sjoberg about the relationship between feminist theorizing and human emancipation as it is used in the subfield of Critical Security Studies. Basu's contribution is a feminist reinterpretation of security as emancipation (SAE) as it is defined and developed by critical security scholars, Ken Booth and Richard Wyn Jones. Basu reviews both the literature in Feminist Security Studies (FSS) and the writings of Booth and Wyn Jones. Consistent with SAE, Basu defines security more broadly than the conventional focus on emergencies, and links security to human emancipation. Basu argues that this perspective provides a richer analysis of global security because it reveals to the discerning eye a previously unseen array of actors— both who merits security and who is to provide it—and issues. Following from this, Basu notes that security discourses can be used to benefit people outside of the traditional structure of power in politics. Exploring ways in which SAE can be studied and practiced, Basu examines two particular aspects of this conceptualization—referents of security and attainment of security (and the process thereof). She proposes we stop thinking of security in terms of two autonomous agents –}one who makes a threat to another's security, and that other who is made insecure by the threat. Using gender as a relational, transformative category, the attainment of security is identified as progressive transformations in these relations. In engagement with Basu's piece, Laura Sjoberg further expands on some of the potential affinities between SAE approaches and feminist approaches (particularly the emancipatory politics of both approaches) as well as on some remaining areas of potential tension, including questions of the "referent" of FSS, who defines what emancipation is, and what feminist praxis really means.

Chapter 6, "Russian veterans of the Chechen wars: a feminist analysis of militarized masculinities," moves our focus from how to achieve security broadly defined to the issue of violence and war, a topic that has been of central concern to scholars of IR since the founding of the discipline at the beginning of the twentieth century. However, it does so through an engagement with the concept of masculinity, a concept often used in feminist work, but one that has never been used by the discipline more generally. In conversation with Cynthia Enloe, Maya Eichler applies the concept of "militarized masculinity," developed by scholars of feminist IR, to an examination of veterans of the Russian–Chechen wars. The wars offer a fascinating case study that illuminates the complicated relationship between masculinities, militarism, and state violence. Eichler's analysis shows that the Russian–Chechen wars resulted in serious challenges to the militarized-masculine ideal of the heroic warrior. The wars revealed men who were unwilling to fight, men who used excessive force, and veterans who experience psychological, economic, and social difficulties upon their return to civilian life ("Chechen syndrome"). Eichler argues that the inherent fragility of militarized masculinity became heightened under the conditions of post-communist crisis. The chapter concludes with a discussion of efforts by government and parts of civil society to counter the challenges to militarized masculinity by emphasizing a representation of Chechen veterans as patriotic heroes. As Eichler notes, it is important to pay close attention to how men and masculinities become de- and re-militarized, rather than assume a natural link between men and militarism. In conversation with Eichler's piece, Cynthia Enloe discusses the importance and challenges of theorizing masculinities in feminist IR theorizing and the nuances of feminist research and feminist listening.

Chapter 7 also uses feminist tools to engage with issues of war and violence. Drawing on feminist science studies, Chapter 7 is a conversation between Eric Blanchard and Sandra Harding over Blanchard's contribution, "The technoscience question in feminist International Relations: unmanning the U.S. war on terror." Blanchard notes that information technology, seen in the virtual economic and security networks that cross military, social, economic, and political realms, presents challenges to which IR has devoted relatively little attention. This is despite the prevalence of high-speed communication in our everyday "domestic" worlds and the importance of asymmetrical, technologically-enabled insurgencies attributed to non-western enemies in our "international" worlds. The U.S. military campaigns in Afghanistan and Iraq, launched in response to the 9/11 attacks, represented a new stage in the maturation of computer-aided global systems of military violence. Blanchard sees some relevant questions: Can academic practices and activisms successfully critique such systems? How can attention to gender help us understand the reach and impact of this transformation on the future of world politics? Building on feminist theorist Sandra Harding's scholarship on science, method, modernity, and culture's role in the production of knowledge, the chapter offers a framework with which to understand the intersection of technological and gender systems as they relate to international relations, while inquiring into the possibilities of subjecting this sector of science and technology studies to scrutiny and transformation in a feminist mode. Like Eichler, Blanchard makes use of the concept of masculinity; suggesting that the use of computer-guided drone missiles, fired from safe locations inside the United States, problematizes our image of warrior masculinity, Blanchard asks us to consider the implications of "unmanning warfare." Harding, in conversation with Blanchard's piece and his use of her framework, engages the question of the relationship between militarism and scientific development, discusses the social construction of science and the scientific method, and explores the use of feminist standpoint methodologies for addressing questions of global development, global security, and global politics.

One of the rationales for the development of hi tech weapons, such as drone missiles, is their potential for limiting civilian casualties. Yet, as Blanchard suggests, drone warfare raises ethical issues about punishing foreign non-combatants while protecting one's own military forces. In conversation with

J. Ann Tickner, Laura Sjoberg and Jessica Peet continue the discussion of civilian casualties in Chapter 8 entitled "Targeting civilians in wars: feminist contributions," Sjoberg and Peet note that, while the non-combatant immunity principle has been phrased in various ways with various "lines in the sand," its basic claim is that civilians should not be killed in wars. Nevertheless, states do attack civilians, intentionally and strategically. Referring to a recent scholarly debate that asks why, Sjoberg and Peet critically evaluate the civilian victimization debate through feminist lenses, asking how gender weighs into belligerents' decisions to intentionally target civilians. After exploring feminist contributions to the debate about the non-combatant immunity principle, Sjoberg and Peet introduce a theoretical approach to civilian victimization in war, inspired by feminist thinking about the gendered nature of war and militarism, which argues that states use "civilian" as a proxy for "women" as signifier of nation as a Clausewitzian center of gravity. Belligerents attack civilians to attack women to attack the essence of the enemy. Sjoberg and Peet then offer empirical evidence in two forms: statistical work on the relationship between sex, gender, and other variables in the civilian victimization literature, and an illustrative case study about World War I. Their contribution argues that belligerents do not attack a gender-neutral category of "civilians" but, instead, they attack women instrumentally as state and nation. In conversation with Sjoberg and Peet's contribution, J. Ann Tickner frames the issue of civilian casualties within the wider IR debate about the behavior of democracies in war – whether democracies are less likely to kill civilians than other types of regimes. She also discusses the question of the utility of quantitative methods for feminist IR work, the effectiveness of different strategies for engaging "mainstream IR" from a feminist perspective, and the importance of theorizing both masculinities and femininities in complicated dialogue for a fuller picture of the influence of gender and IR.

We have chosen to conclude the substantive section of the book with a conversation between Angela McCracken and V. Spike Peterson around McCracken's contribution, "Beauty and the *quinceañera*: reproductive, productive, and virtual dimensions of the global political economy of beauty." We do this because McCracken's research takes up an issue that is relatively new to feminist IR and one which points to some possible new directions. Using intersectional analysis, she draws on feminist literature on the gendering of bodies to talk about the construction of gendered and racial ideals of beauty. Such literatures are just beginning to be incorporated into IR feminist analysis and are ones that are likely to receive more attention in the future. The story about the American soldier Jessica Lynch with which we began this introduction points to some interesting new ways in which theories about beauty and gendered bodies can be useful even for helping us understand issues about war and conflict.

In Chapter 9, McCracken claims that there is a global political economy of beauty that shapes and is shaped by the personal production of beauty. The politics of this global economy of beauty favor historically gendered hierarchies, but also evidence some openness to the transformation of gender and racial inequality in Mexico. The production of beauty in the fiesta de quince años in Guadalajara, Mexico, serves as a site to explore the mutual construction of personal beauty and the global political economy of beauty through dress, dance, and cosmetics. This case study employs V. Spike Peterson's reproductive, productive, and virtual framing of the global political economy and extends out from the production of Mexican youth's beauty ideals and practices into the global dimensions of market, household, and symbolic exchanges involved in producing gender ideals in dress, dance, and cosmetics in the fiesta. As seen through the production of beauty and fashion in the *fiesta de quince años*, McCracken finds that the global political economy of beauty has both diversifying and reinforcing effects on traditional gendered norms. Increasing individualization and commercialization of the fiesta tradition enables and encourages diverse approaches to the celebration of the 15-year milestone. The importance of global symbolic exchange has increased the diversity of images and ideals of beauty in Mexico. However, the globalization of the beautifying industries is successful in large part due to gendered production, reproduction, and consumption. Therefore, McCracken sees that the global political economy of beauty tends to reinforce religious- and patriarchal family-based norms of hierarchy. Using the comparison of the *quinceañera* and wedding traditions, V. Spike Peterson engages with McCracken's work empirically, while at the same time discussing the implications of McCracken's feminist theorizing about the political economy of beauty and feminist theorizing about gendered political economies more generally, for understanding international politics and international economics.

Our conversations conclude in Chapter 10, which is written out of dialogue between the contributors to this book and other scholars in the feminist IR community, who attended the "Twenty Years of Feminist IR" conference at USC in 2010. Addressing questions about the appropriateness of IR as a disciplinary home for feminist theorizing about global politics, the question of the relationship between sex and gender, the salience of masculinities and femininities in global politics, and the increasing need for intersectional and cross-cutting analyses of global politics, this chapter looks forward to some of the challenges and potential directions of feminist theorizing in IR over the next 20 years.

Notes

1 This data can be found from the Inter-Parliamentary Union, at http://www.ipu.org/wmn-e/world.htm.
2 It is striking the degree to which similar feminist critiques of IR were springing up independently at the same time in different geographical locations – in Australia, Europe and the United States – and also in International Law. See, for example, Charlesworth et al. (1991), and Pettman (1993).

3 All of the attendees have, or have in the past had, some affiliation with USC – as faculty, graduate students, post-doctoral fellows or co-organizers of, or attendees at, previous conferences, or, in Jessica Peet's case, as a student of a former USC graduate student.

4 Two of the original conferences, at USC in 1989 and Wellesley College in 1990, were co-organized by Jane Jaquette and J. Ann Tickner respectively

5 Recognizing that almost 1% of the world's population is born neither clearly biologically male nor female, increasingly, sex refers to other biological sexes, such as intersex and trans.

6 For examples of each of these approaches, see Tickner and Sjoberg (2010).

7 The term "third debate" is somewhat ambiguous. In European IR it is usually referred to as the "fourth debate," and rarely has there been critical engagement between the different schools of thought.

8 Marking ten years of feminist scholarship, two conferences were held, at Wellesley College in 2000 and USC in 2001, both also funded by the Ford Foundation. The theme of these conferences was "Gender in International Relations From Seeing Women and Recognizing Gender to Transforming Policy Research." Participants included individuals from the academy, and the policy and activist worlds.

9 The claim that feminism and constructivism share a middle ground was made by Birgit Locher and Elisabeth Prügl (2001) in their article entitled "Feminism and Constructivism: Worlds Apart or Sharing the Middle Ground?"

2 Reclaiming agency for social change

Feminism, International Relations and the Women's International League for Peace and Freedom, 1945–75

Catia C. Confortini

The Women's International League for Peace and Freedom (WILPF) was born in the midst of World War I, when over 1,200 women from the warring countries met at the Hague in 1915; its goals, claiming a political voice for women and stopping the war were ambitious ones. Though their efforts did not end the conflict, they are thought to have influenced Woodrow Wilson's attempt to implement liberal ideals in the international realm in his famous 14-point post-war arrangement proposal. Today, WILPF has a leading role in feminist peace advocacy internationally: together with a number of other Non-Governmental Organizations (NGOs), it has been instrumental in bringing about the UN Security Council Resolutions on Women, Peace and Security.[1] While remaining faithful to its liberal internationalist origins, and in spite of being an organization made up of primarily of white, middle-to-upper-class Western women, WILPF has evolved into a leading critic of militarism, racism, sexism, environmental destruction, and unfettered capitalism, emphasizing the connection between all forms of oppression and exclusion. As an insider in the liberal system, it is stretching its boundaries, thereby contributing to incremental emancipatory social change. Much of this transformation happened following the two World Wars and, in particular, during the 30 years after World War II. Learning how WILPF made itself an agent of social and institutional change can be of theoretical and practical help for understanding the possibilities of emancipatory agency.

Starting from a constructivist understanding of agents and structures as co-constituted, this chapter outlines the elements of a feminist critical methodology for emancipatory social change, taking the example of WILPF's policies from 1945 to 1975. As a political subject, WILPF was embedded in the hegemonic structure of liberal modernity,[2] which shaped its understanding of "peace," grounding it in the principles and ideologies of political and, to a lesser extent, economic liberalism. Using examples taken from a more extensive research project on WILPF's work (Confortini 2009), I argue that changes in those policies reflected the gradual development of a critique of the historical and political context of liberalism, as the foundational ideology of liberal modernity. Further, I argue that, to the extent that WILPF challenged these hegemonic forces, it was able to do so thanks to a set of theoretically informed practices, which I call feminist critical methodology. WILPF's women's intentionality (agency) intersected with the constitutive presence of liberal modernity (structure) to open spaces for emancipatory social change.

The chapter begins with an analysis of feminist contributions to a theory of agency in constructivist IR theory, followed by the articulation of a feminist methodology for social change. I then draw on some examples from WILPF's history to illustrate my argument. Finally I put forward my argument's implications for international relations theory and social movements interested in emancipatory social change.

Constructivism, critical theory, and feminism

Of the many approaches to International Relations (IR), constructivism theorizes structure and agency co-constitution.[3] For constructivists structures are understood as seemingly enduring patterns of relations and rules reflecting specific historical and social contexts and guiding expectations of behavior (Klotz and Lynch 2007, Chapter 2). Constructivism holds that individuals' thinking and behavior are conditioned by structures, but not determined by them. Individuals retain, with a certain degree of agency the ability to change the rules and expectations that make up structures and thereby effect social change. Birgit Locher and Elisabeth Prügl call this an "ontology of becoming": constructivists "describe the world not as one that is, but as one that is in the process of becoming"(Locher and Prügl 2001, 114). This ontology allows constructivism to theorize social change without falling into the trap of rigid behaviorism (Checkel 2006).

Among constructivists, critical theorists are specifically concerned with social change: their purpose is to historicize and denaturalize the social order in order to transform it (Cox 1981). Though this normative element is not necessarily shared by other constructivists (Tickner 2005, 2006; Zalewski 2006), it is what makes critical theory akin to feminism (Ackerly and True 2006). However, as a number of feminists have claimed, critical theory has generally not paid sufficient attention to gender in their understanding of social change (Whitworth 1994; Chin 1998; Prugl 1999; True 2003). Brooke Ackerly and Jacqui True challenge critical theory's own theorizing: defining methodology as "guiding self-conscious reflections on epistemological assumptions, ontological perspective, ethical responsibilities, and method choices" (Ackerly et al. 2006, 6), they propose a feminist methodology conducive to better (more critical) IR theory (Ackerly and True 2006). I am similarly concerned about identifying a set of theoretical practices to facilitate the expression of an agency that is conscious and critical of the structural constraints that define it and under which it operates. To the extent that such a methodology can be made explicit, it forms the basis for a critical constructivist theory of agency.

Feminism, social change and emancipation

Feminism offers distinct contributions to constructivist critical theory, which need to be taken seriously in order to pursue a theory of agency.

Gender as power

A feminist understanding of power as gendered leads feminists to be especially concerned about the ways in which the "gender order" creates, supports and perpetuates relations of domination at all levels, from the domestic to the international. Moreover, given the invisibility of women in many areas of public life, feminists claim that silences and exclusions are essential to the works of gendered power (Enloe 1996). Feminist insights suggest then that, in order to be able to transform the world, actors need first to be able to identify actual and potential forms of oppression and exclusion and their connection to each other. Without this ability a methodology of social change cannot be fully emancipatory, because it would continue to hide systems of gendered power.

Where are the women?

The awareness of women's exclusion from theory production as well as from public life leads feminism to ask for women's right to speak and be heard (Harding 1993).[4] It also points to the impossibility of feminist thought divorced from women's lived experiences both as a source of inspiration and as a normative meter (Eschle 2001; Ackerly and True 2006). Specifically, feminist normative commitments are grounded in a "political ethics of care," which "starts from the position that the giving and receiving of care is a vital part of all human lives, and that it must therefore be a normative guide in the creation of decent societies" (Robinson 2006, 222).[5]

The connection between theory, practice and the ethics of care leads to the importance of drawing insights from women's lives and feminist activism for developing a set of practices conducive to emancipatory social change. It also forces continual re-evaluation of one's theory in terms of its impact on those affected by it. The import of these principles for a critical constructivist theory of agency is the realization that, in order to be able to transcend structural constraints, actors need a method that would compel the continual interpellation of the entire community for an evaluation of the impact of any decision. The dialogue thus engendered needs to be aware of power differentials within the community and also between the community and outside critics.

Power and the identity of the knower

The basic constructivist ontology of co-constitution leads feminists to an awareness that the theorist's agency and identities are conditioned by the particular normative-historical context in which s/he operates (Locher and Prügl 2001). Therefore, knowledge production itself risks reinforcing structures of oppression. To avoid this pitfall feminism borrows from post-structuralists the insight that any knowledge claims need necessarily be provisional, contextual and not absolute or general (Ackerly and True 2006). However, feminism retains a normative commitment to the concept of eman-cipation as a principle of judgment (Locher and Prügl 2001; Prügl 1998), while being aware of emancipation's own historicity (Hutchings 2001).[6]

This has important implications for a theory of agency. The question of how we know whether a decision leads to emancipatory social change cannot be completely answered unless we (1) continually scrutinize the degree to which our very definitions of emancipation and social change are structurally conditioned and contribute to perpetuating oppression; and (2) our practices are themselves exclusionary or oppressively assimilationist (Hutchings 2004) At the same time, doing away with or sidelining normative precepts does not help us answer the practical question of how to effect social change.

Postmodern political scientist Kevin Olson borrows from the Foucauldian notion of governmentality the consideration that government (structure) pro-duces a particular kind of political subject and proposes "reflexive democ-racy" as a form of government that "allow[s] people to set some of the terms of their own subject formation" (Olson 2008, 47). In discussing the possibility of conversation between the multiple schools of IR, Lily Ling describes the history of interactions between cultures/worlds as a "constant process of hybrid world making to ensure survival." In this process new, hybrid sub-jectivities are created that compel the recognition that the "Other exists in part *within* the ... Self" (Ling 2002, 286). Similarly, Kimberly Hutchings suggests that cross-cultural encounters need "an attentiveness and openness in relation to the other through which both self and other may be transformed" beyond simple information-gathering or even understanding (Hutchings 2004, 254, interpreting Spivak). A critical theory of agency needs a method that (1) compels actors to question their very existence as political subjects, thus providing tools for identifying and remedying actual or potential exclusionary and oppressive ideas and practices; and (2) enables them to re-define their identities as hybrid-in-the-making.

Summary

From feminist methodological contributions I draw four requirements for a critical constructivist theory of agency. In order to be able to transcend structural constraints and effect emancipatory social change, actors need a method that:

1 compels critical self-reflection over their own assumptions, language and embeddedness in a particular historical and ideological context;
2 guides them toward inclusivity and opens them to input and ideas from (potentially) all members of society;

3   allows them to identify and remedy actual or potential forms of oppression
     and exclusion in society *and* in their own practice;
4   enables the recurrent evaluation of their practices and ideas.

the next section will draw and expand on Brooke Ackerly's theory of Third
World feminist social criticism (TWFSC) to suggest a methodology for
emancipatory social change. I concur with Ackerly and define this methodology as "feminist" because it has been used by feminist activists all over the
world. Activists can be called feminist when they "are engaged in activism …
organized by women to transform themselves and their world" (Ackerly 2000,
31). My research intends to confirm and extend Ackerly's findings in feminist
activism. I extend her and Jacqui True's argument that feminist methodology
and feminist theoretical methods make for "more critical, critical IR theory and
practice" (Ackerly and True 2006, 244), and propose that to the extent that a
feminist critical methodology as I outline is employed by activists, it opens up
the possibility for challenging and dismantling the structural conditions of their
existence as political actors. Thus feminist critical methodology is itself a tool
for emancipatory social change.

Third World feminist social criticism

Starting her observations from within a group of Bangladeshi women activists, Brooke Ackerly develops a model of social criticism that improves deliberative democratic theory. Ackerly faults theorists of deliberative democracy
for severely underplaying exclusions and inequalities in all societies. On the
one hand, deliberations and collective decision-making are important to
achieve a more broad-based and inclusive collective knowledge. On the other
hand, deliberative democrats need strategies for enabling citizens to practice
democracy in the presence of inequality. Moreover, in order to effectively
challenge inequalities and exclusions, deliberative democracy needs mechanisms for self-criticism. Ackerly draws from Third World women (and a variety
of other feminist) activists a method that makes up for deliberative democratic theory's shortcomings. The practice, which she labels "Third World
feminist social criticism," employs three main tools.

First, guiding criteria are "a list of minimum standards that critics use to
challenge existing values, practices, and norms" (Ackerly 2000, 31). They help
critics evaluate "competing claims to oppression" and direct their criticisms
of values, practices and norms (Ackerly 2000, 116). Ackerly's own list is
derived from women's human rights activism and standards, but in different
contexts and with different goals in mind political actors draw up their own
list. Because they can be arbitrary and are bound to be limited and defined by
the structure within which actors are embedded, guiding criteria need to be
constantly revised and assessed. In Ackerly's theory, the "corrective" to
imperfect guiding criteria are deliberative inquiry and skeptical scrutiny.
Second, deliberative inquiry is "the practice of generating knowledge through

collective questioning, exchange of views, and discussion among critics and members of society" (Ackerly 2000, 10). Deliberation ideally promotes inclusive and collective learning through thoughtful reflection and discussion among social critics and members of society. Ackerly works under the constructivist assumption that the material conditions and circumstances under which the social critic operates, her identities, her subjectivities and her communities all contribute to shape the knowledge she produces. But as part of her feminist methodology, Ackerly argues that knowledge needs to be worked out in a collective process, through formal or informal discussions, actions, evaluations and reevaluations. It needs to be constantly partial and evolving, yet pragmatic and action-oriented, specifically oriented to the solution of problems identified by the community as problems. Deliberation does not necessarily mean that only the collective is responsible for final decisions and only the collective can guide practical behavior. It does, however, mean that a continuous interpellation of the collective is necessary for democracy to work in the presence of inequalities.

However, the fact that all are invited at a deliberative forum, even a loosely structured and informal one, does not guarantee that all will attend and be heard or listened to. In fact, Ackerly recognizes that the rules, language, and site of deliberation (the operation of power) could all work in favor of some and not other members of the collectivity. She engages both feminist and non feminist deliberative democracy theorists and faults them ultimately for requiring equality as a condition for participation in democracy, which is ideally supposed to promote equality.[7]

Finally, Ackerly's solution to the problems of effective communication without exclusions in deliberative situations is the strategy of skeptical scrutiny. According to Ackerly, "skeptical scrutiny is an attitude toward existing and proposed values, practices, and norms that requires one to examine their existing and potentially exploitable inequalities" (Ackerly 2000, 75). Skeptical scrutiny, used in conjunction with deliberative inquiry and guiding criteria, is a tool that allows critics to continually scout for actual and potential inequalities and how they work to silence voices. Skeptical scrutiny allows actors to question society's practices, values, and norms *and also* their own. Within the TWFSC model, social critics represent essential facilitators of society's self-examination and provoke the examination of their own methods, roles, qualifications, and conclusions. Because no one person or group can fully assess the extent to which power inequalities and structural constraints work to the detriment of the less powerful, a variety of critics are necessary. Critics from inside or outside of the community, and critics that can navigate between that community and the outside are all necessary to promote deliberative opportunities and inquiry.

TWFSC's three elements make the practice "conducive to incremental, informed, collective, and uncoerced social change" (Ackerly 2000, 14) toward a "more democratic society (however envisioned)" (Ackerly 2000, 6). Ackerly cautions that TWFSC does not *guarantee* such change and points at structural impediments to its achievement: "[s]uccessful social change depends on a broad range of conditions determined by the familial, social, political, and economic context of the criticism and activism" (Ackerly 2000, 122). In other words, marginalized groups within a society may offer better, more informed proposals for social change by following the prescriptions of TWFSC. But whether society adopts such proposals depends on whether those groups or individuals are themselves recognized as deliberative partners. Because she draws this method from the experiences of feminist activists in particularly marginalized contexts, Ackerly is acutely aware of the numerous limitations their political actions face from the outside. But Ackerly underestimates TWFSC's potential: with a prescription for making silent voices intelligible and compelling to dominant groups, TWFSC becomes effectively a theory of emancipatory social change.

Imaginative identification: a feminist critical methodology for social change

TWFSC ideally enables deliberation and political participation for the less powerful, for those who have been silenced and/or marginalized (Ackerly 2000, 234). But those who are at the centers of (political, economic or social) power can be trapped in and blinded by the historical, ideological, and political context they inhabit. As previously observed, unhampered communication requires a method for social interactions that enables both the questioning of the conditions of one's own existence and the creation of new hybrid subjectivities. I propose that this dual objective can be facilitated by extending TWFSC's tool box with a strategy which I call "imaginative identification." Its articulation is inspired by WILPF's practice but it is part of feminists' ethical/methodological repertoire.[8]

At WILPF's 1968 Congress, outgoing International Chair Dorothy Hutchinson described this strategy as follows:

> Jane Addams's greatness lay in her rare combination of two qualities … These are Intelligence—the mental capability which sets man [sic] apart, and Compassion—the emotional capability which enables Man [sic], by an effort of his imagination, to feel suffering which is not his own, so acutely that he is compelled to act to relieve it. … The function of the WILPF has always been to study public policy, to make moral judgments based on imaginative identification with those who are victimized by inhuman public policies, and to educate ourselves and others for effective political action to change these policies.
>
> (Hutchinson 1968, 7–8)[9]

"Imaginative identification" requires the interrogation of actors' own subjectivities and the constant alertness to the possibility that empathetic efforts could involve hegemonic or imperialist moves. This makes "imaginative identification" necessary for a theory of emancipatory social change: in the next section I will show that, where imaginative identification failed, guiding criteria, deliberative inquiry and skeptical scrutiny were not enough to bring about changes in WILPF's policies and ideas between 1945 and 1975. In concert, guiding criteria, deliberative inquiry, skeptical scrutiny and imaginative identification provide a *feminist critical methodology* that is conducive to emancipatory social change.

Feminist critical methodology in WILPF

Liberalism and WILPF

The women of WILPF paid particular attention to the interplay between their decision-making processes, methods, and policy positions (methodology) from the very beginnings of the organization. In her study of the relationship between British feminism and pacifist transnationalism immediately after World War I, Jo Vellacott draws a difference between the militant and non-militant British suffrage organizations. According to her it was not coincidental that the British women's peace movement (and within it the British section of WILPF) was born from the latter during World War I, as they stressed nonviolence and more democratic decision-making procedures (Vellacott 1988, 1993). Vellacott claims that a thoughtful and intentional commitment to the congruence between goals (women's suffrage) and methods (local, regional, and national networks of collective decision-making) helped the non-militant suffragists reflect on the violent and militaristic foundations of a system that denied political equality to women (Vellacott 1993). Similarly, WILPF's deliberate, if implicit, application of a feminist critical methodology helped the organization overcome the limitations imposed by the ideological and historical context which defined the very possibility of its agency.

As a transnational organization, WILPF owed its existence to a particular configuration of liberal modernity, which in effect created the organization as a political subject. Its characteristics, its institutional make-up, and its working procedures owed their form to the historical conditions that made them possible. The women of WILPF, as members of the organization, were equally shaped as political subjects by the ideologies of liberal modernity. Finally, their understandings of "peace" (their guiding criteria) were also embedded in (and thus defined and delimited by) this historical and ideological structure. For WILPF the preconditions and elements of a just peace centered around: (1) freedom (loosely identified with the establishment of liberal democracy); (2) self-determination (an element of freedom); (3) total and universal disarmament; (4) economic development and prosperity to satisfy human needs. WILPF's idea of peace thus rested on liberal ideals, on the essentially liberal belief in the institutionalization of liberal norms of social, political, and economic cooperation and governance, based on liberal values, shared norms, and legal frameworks that would guarantee the rights and needs of people (Richmond 2008). But because dependent on liberalism, WILPF's guiding criteria also depended on liberalism's partially exclusionary and oppressive ideologies and practices.

However, between 1945 and 1975 WILPF's ideas of peace, as expressed in their policies on several issues underwent a number of changes, which reflected a departure from their entrenchment in the kind of hegemonic liberalism that characterized the post-war West. For example, WILPF's policies on disarmament reflected two different understandings of peace. Initially and for roughly a couple of decades, WILPF believed that disarmament would follow peace. This, in turn, would be established with the help of a set of rational laws and consensual agreements among states that would make the resort to war unnecessary. Science and technology, guided by rationality and reason, had the ability to guide humanity toward progress and tame nuclear energy for peaceful uses. Though it was important to have an avenue like WILPF where women could speak out on matters of international politics and in favor of disarmament, peace, and the rational, peaceful utilization of nuclear energy, WILPF thought that women had no special knowledge, or a special interest in peace.[10] These positions reflected liberal modern understandings about the nature of law, reason, and science and WILPF's adherence to the normative and ideological framework that was shaping the creation of the post-war international order.[11] WILPF gradually worked its way out of these constraints, while not entirely abandoning the liberal principles that guided it. The organization eventually came to understand peace as an outcome of disarmament (or disarmament as a prerequisite of peace), which would follow the establishment of a human-needs-based and just economic order. Its economic critique of the international system brought WILPF to question the profit-driven nuclear and military industry as inextricably linked to weapons production. Finally, WILPF came to see disarmament and a just economy to be of special interest to women; it began to view peace work as a task for which women had developed useful skills; and it started to understand militarism and the arms race as incompatible with the goals and principles of feminism as a political movement for people's equality and well-being and, ultimately, for peace. Similar changes can be seen in WILPF's policies on decolonization, where an initial cautious optimism toward the decolonization process, the Trusteeship system and the future of world community in the wake of decolonization was replaced with a consensus in support of struggles for independence, and the denunciation of a "system of exploitation, privilege and profit" as the ultimate source of (structural) violence (WILPF IEC 1972).

Likewise, specific geo-political areas of WILPF's work saw gradual yet radical ideological and policy shifts. Such is the case with WILPF's positions on the conflict in Israel/Palestine, where WILPF's embeddedness in Orientalism as a peculiarly modern and liberal ideology translated into the marginalization and silencing of Arab/Palestinian narratives, which resulted in a timid support of the creation of Israel and its domestic and international policies. From the beginning, Israel was posited as the "Western" "modern" thus more peaceful state in contrast with a "backward" "bellicose" Other (the Arabs, Arab states, and the Palestinians). Arab (particularly Muslim) women were taken as the symbol of this backwardness and their "liberation" as a justification for the establishment of a Western democracy (Israel) in the region. In a gradual and non-linear process, WILPF's feminist critical methodology allowed a challenge to these ideological constructions and a reshaping of the ideological context in which WILPF was situated. As a consequence, WILPF formulated new policies and new views about "peace" in the Middle East, which recognized the legitimacy of both Jewish and Palestinian aspirations to nationhood. These policy shifts reflected an ideological shift, a critique of the liberal principles that had guided WILPF for many decades and ultimately represented a different understanding of peace, one which expanded the boundaries of the historical and ideological context that had shaped the organization.

WILPF's methodology

By tracing the historical trajectory of these policy and ideational changes and the practices that underpinned them, I find that the women of WILPF practiced both deliberative inquiry and skeptical scrutiny. However, several instances show that imaginative identification was a necessary complement for those practices to lead to policy changes.

As a primarily Western organization, whose membership was organized according to nation-states, WILPF was not well-equipped for inclusivity in deliberations. As an organization with consultative status with the United Nations, it had access to a variety of views, but only to the extent that these views were represented at the UN. Before the 1960s the UN was itself hardly a mirror of the world's population, and after decolonization was completed its state-centered liberal framework also limited inclusive deliberative possibilities.

Nevertheless, many of WILPF's leaders were conscious of the implications of these limitations and consistently sought out input from a variety of sources. For example, a Rome seminar on Women and Public Life in 1966 prompted a leader of WILPF to harshly criticize WILPF's sections for having lost the ability to communicate and interact with women like the ones that were represented in Rome, women whom she described as "people outside their social circle." She added: "this kind of contacts are [sic] the stimulus and enrichment which is now completely lacking in our own WILPF International. This is one of the many other reasons why we circle around our tiny circles, alas!" (Baer 1966, 1).

The mid-1960s marked the beginning of a change in WILPF's practices in regards to cooperation with other organizations. Whereas WILPF had earlier maintained only loose forms of association on disarmament questions with umbrella organizations, for instance, it progressively favored and practiced a more sustained and consistent effort at coordination with several peace organizations. Increased participation in NGO meetings and increased involvement in joint activities with other organizations meant increased contacts with outside critics, especially people whose views would not otherwise be represented in WILPF. Occasions for such contacts were rarer in the 1950s, though WILPF had been in touch with several Japanese women and organizations since the war.

For example, US WILPF was among the first organizations to seek contacts with Vietnamese women in the 1960s. Those contacts and the input of African American members brought about a critique of the Vietnam War[12] as connected to racial and economic injustice in the US. WILPF thus emphasized both the adverse consequence of war for women and their moral responsibility to bring about peace (Hutchinson 1966). In fact, the argument, which was clearly indebted to and expanded Martin Luther King Jr.'s, had not been entirely clear to non-US WILPF members whose requests for clarifications at the 1967 International Executive Committee Meeting spurred yet another moment of deliberative inquiry (Hutchinson 1967; WILPF International Office 1970).

The second half of the 1960s also marked heightened efforts at engaging in discussions on how WILPF's own structure, methods, and ideology hampered the participation of women outside the traditional geographical, racial, and class limitations of WILPF's member base (Boulding 1968). Specifically, WILPF started debating the effectiveness of its continuous reliance on "methods of reason and persuasion" (Hutchinson 1967), on public diplomacy efforts and on government lobbying especially in the context of international government organizations. Some favored more direct forms of action and public protest, particularly those younger WILPFers who had participated in Women Strike for Peace (WSP) since the early 1960s.

This movement was born on November 1, 1961, when thousands of U.S. housewives in 60 cities refused to work for one day and called for an end to the arms race. WSP was one of the first to protest against the Vietnam War and initiate contacts with Soviet and Vietnamese women. While this movement employed maternalist rhetoric to call for disarmament (at least this was true in the US), it had also very deliberatively developed a horizontal, non-hierarchical "un-structure" that later feminists emulated (Swerdlow 1993; Wittner 1997). So it was those younger members who became in the 1960s the most ardent critics of both WILPF's methods and the constraints and limitations of liberalism (Bussey 1980; Foster 1989). The dialogue about the organization's effectiveness had also brought to the fore the criticism that WILPF had compromised its principles by diluting its critiques of the capitalist system, the abolishment of which was the only hope to create "the economic conditions necessary for both peace and freedom" (Hutchinson 1967).

Direct protest and cooperation with other NGOs, as forms of deliberative inquiry, represented methodological choices that helped change ideologies and policies. Choosing these forms of political action was made possible by a changing historical context, but it also had an effect on WILPF's ideology. More inclusive deliberative inquiry by itself, however, could only cause a change of ideas and policies as a consequence of WILPF's willingness to put into question both those ideas and the organization's methods.

The debates over whether or not to cooperate with other organizations are an example of the use of skeptical scrutiny as applied to WILPF's own methods. In 1972 French member Yvonne Sée described the strengths and weaknesses of WILPF's modus operandi. While she stressed elements of continuity in WILPF's work, she also considered it a strength that WILPF "re-evaluate and ... adjust to new situations." Thus, she saw WILPF work as focused both on the objectives enshrined in its constitution, as well as continually in progress, and critical of established knowledge; recurrent self-reflection was embedded in WILPF's methodology. Sée particularly expressed skepticism toward ideologies (which she saw "as brainwash in order to serve the establishment") and the "universal status quo (boundaries, political and national ideologies)" and the need to "not feel bound to a particular viewpoint" (Sée 1972).

Deliberative inquiry in the 1960s and 1970s favored the expression of skeptical scrutiny of WILPF's thoughts on several areas of its work. For instance, the unstated assumptions of the 1940s and 1950s, which led to WILPF's uncritical support of the Trusteeship Council were challenged through skeptical scrutiny. However, only when the late 1960s brought a critical mass of new members, committed to listening to the voices of outside and multi-sited critics to partially make up for the chronic scarcity of institutionalized inclusive deliberations, did WILPF radically change its views about peace, insofar as they related to questions of decolonization. The ideological and policy changes of the 1960s were facilitated by some members' commitment to subject the organization's methods to skeptical scrutiny, thus bringing to the fore how the absence of adequate representation of voices outside WILPF's traditional constituencies influenced WILPF's ideologies and policies. But while increasingly inclusive deliberative opportunities favored WILPF's reflection about the intersection between race, gender, economic justice, and peace, alone they were not enough to provoke institutional or personal change. To the extent that WILPF women were willing to subject their unstated assumptions about race, liberal political thought, and the international economic system to a self-reflexive process (hence exercising skeptical scrutiny), they also felt compelled to challenge and modify their interpretation of their guiding criteria. Skeptical scrutiny further reinforced the awareness of the need to expand deliberative opportunities.

For instance, in 1968 U.S. member Dorothy Steffens pointed out that it was "symptomatic of the problems" of WILPF that "a white woman from North America" like herself should be asked to speak to WILPF's International Congress about "new ways of working in Africa" (Steffens 1968).[13] In Steffens' view, the League was failing to be relevant to most women, and especially to women in the developing world, due to both organizational weaknesses and to inadequate program priorities. Organizationally, WILPF was lacking in mechanisms to guarantee the continuity of contacts between Congresses, to cultivate the leadership of younger women, and to increase and maintain contacts and cooperation with women's groups in countries not yet represented in WILPF. She was unsure whether it was appropriate or timely for WILPF to try to expand its membership to the continent, but she felt very strongly that any work done there had to be done in such a way as to respect and encourage the expression of local knowledge, skills, and cultures.

Programmatically, Steffens opined that WILPF had lost its original dual focus on both peace and freedom: recalling Jane Addams' beginnings as a social worker, she criticized WILPF's apparent disdain for "'Social-Work' type of activities." Steffens added that it was not by chance that the U.S. section was the most rapidly growing national section, and it had begun to grow after it had re-prioritized its work on domestic issues, as well as the U.S. involvement in Vietnam (Steffens 1968). The issues raised by the Steffens' 1968 report resonated in the discussions of the Commission on Future Directions of WILPF which, partly reflecting Steffens' recommendations, proposed the implementation of organizational reforms and programmatic studies. Among these, the Commission encouraged WILPF to "think out afresh the ways in which we relate to revolutionary movements which espouse violence in the pursuit of peace and freedom" (Boulding 1968). Subjecting methods themselves to skeptical scrutiny allowed the organization to correct (though not eliminate) methodological obstacles to wider organizational reach.

However, several instances show that deliberative inquiry and skeptical scrutiny were not always sufficient to lead to policy and ideational changes. The lack of representation made it imperative that skeptical scrutiny be complemented by imaginative identification lest marginalized voices were not understood or listened to. Whenever the women of WILPF met with outside critics they often applied this practice. My interview with Elise Boulding (WILPF's International Chair from 1968 to 1971), who recalled the first meetings with Soviet women, illustrates this:

> in 1961 WILPF was invited to participate in hosting a group of Soviet women ... And so that was an extraordinary occasion because we came to see the real heroism of these women who had all survived the war under great, great difficulties, and seen very, very much suffering. And they had violence, more than we in the United States. We hadn't really seen that kind of violence. We hadn't been overseas. And they spoke with such—they had such a strong sense of their role and what they had to do and their calling to build a peaceful society. And they were so open to listening. We were all learning from each other.
>
> (Elise Boulding, interview by the author, May 21, 2005)

Those meetings, as well as earlier meetings with Japanese women and the late 1960s and 1970s encounters with Vietnamese women, produced lasting changes in WILPF.

There were also numerous occasions on which imaginative identification was used together with deliberative inquiry and skeptical scrutiny to make better-informed judgments about the Palestine/Israel conflict. For example, deliberative inquiry and imaginative identification guided the members of a fact-finding mission to the Middle East in 1975, who approached their trip with the understanding that the situation in Israel/Palestine was better evaluated through an empathetic view of the insiders' perspectives:

> the League could make a unique contribution to understanding in the area if the Mission studied the problems Arab and Israeli women face in the current conflict situation and in gaining a better knowledge of their status in society, their activities and their aspirations.
>
> (Frank 1975)

Only through this method, they believed, could the League come to an agreement and take a definite policy stand on some "significant international issues, even on those that are the most controversial" (Ballantyne 1975, 20). Libby Frank, one of the two members of that expedition, recalls that a breakthrough moment in her understanding of Palestinian–Israeli relations happened during a discussion she had with Siba Fahoum, one of the Lebanese section members, while on a plane trip together in 1975:

> I had a book, which was anti-Semitic. It was ostensibly put out by the PLO, ... and I showed it to her, we were sitting together on the plane and I would say: Siba, look at this. How could they put out something like this? And she looked at it and she said: "we didn't do that. The PLO didn't do that." And I said: "what do you mean?" It showed a picture of a huge Arab, a huge Arab ogre wanting to devour tiny little Israel. ... What the booklet indicated was that the Arabs wanted to destroy Israel and she said: "we don't, never, that's not how we portray that situation." She said: "we Palestinians and Arabs, we show Israel as a big ogre, and they are the military strength and they are trying to defeat us." ... It was very interesting. It was very enlightening.
>
> (Libby Frank, interview by the author, May 10, 2004)

By reading the booklet with skeptical eyes *and* practicing an empathetic understanding of the concerns and interpretation of her interlocutor, Fahoum and Frank together arrived at the conclusion that the booklet was part of pro-Israeli government's propaganda. Thus a willingness to subject her interpretation of a racist pamphlet to skeptical scrutiny and to imaginatively identify with a different interpretation, Frank revisited her assumptions about a supposedly peaceful Israel and a belligerent (Arab/Palestinian) other.

Assessment

Changes in the international context alone are not enough to understand or explain how WILPF's positions changed in the course of thirty years. The international context of the 1960s (with the surge of citizens' protests, second-wave feminism, and the non-aligned movement) provided the opportunity for increased input from outside and multi-sited critics,[14] who promoted more inclusive deliberative processes and the critique of WILPF's often unstated assumptions and practices. But WILPF in the 1960s joined other organizations in formulating wider reaching understandings of peace; it did not *follow* others. For example, rather than adopting an entirely horizontal and non-hierarchical structure (which was characteristic of some of the organizations and movements with which WILPF cooperated) WILPF maintained its essentially liberal organizational framework and formal decision-making procedures. Optimally, within those spaces it practiced "a horizontal, participatory, inclusive, responsible, educative and nurturing way of doing things—a way that some would claim as feminist" (Cockburn 2008), though this was not always so. WILPF's policy changes did not represent an adaptation to a changing political and economic environment. Rather, WILPF's is a story among many of organizations and social movements that brought about some changes in the international realm.

The literature on the role of social movements in effecting international change illustrates this point (for example Cortright 1993, 2008). Ian Welsh claims that "[o]ne measure of movement success [can be] the extent to which the cultural artefacts of movements, as opposed to their knowledge claims, are adopted within a particular social formation" (Welsh 2000, 29). In this sense, anti-nuclear and anti-militarist movements of the Cold War enabled the formation of contemporary social movements and influenced their structures, cultures and methods. Thus their reach extended beyond their actual or perceived impact on the nuclear policies of nation-states.

The 1970s saw the rise of neoliberalism which, as an extremely individualist ideology, subordinated the state to the market, promoted the deregulation and privatization of the economy, the minimization of the state and the consequent elimination of the institutions of welfare (Richardson 2001; Richmond 2008), at the national and (through international financial and trade organizations) at the global level. WILPF was further radicalized by proposing a strong critique of liberalism's very foundations, which were also its own. Between 1975 and 1985 the West experienced a resurgence of anti-Communist paranoia and accusations of Communism were leveled against WILPF, as they had been in the 1930s and 1950s. This time WILPF did not go on the defensive; rather it continued and intensified its critique of the international order.

WILPF was a Western liberal middle-class white women's organization, which stretched the boundaries of the liberal context within which it was inscribed and from which it both drew inspiration and tried to break free. WILPF came out of this period as a different kind of organization, one that showed a more intentional and more intensive effort at becoming a truly international organization, rather than a Western organization guided by liberal internationalist principles. So while WILPF operated within a liberal modern zeitgeist, it also pushed liberalism and internationalism toward a more inclusive, less hegemonic form.

Conclusions

Between 1945 and 1975 WILPF's understanding of peace as expressed in its policies underwent several changes. Such changes were made possible by a feminist critical methodology that allowed WILPF's self-reflection on its own embeddedness in structures of oppression and exclusion. This awareness allowed the delivery of a critique of those structures, to expand their boundaries hence effecting social change. The story of WILPF offers a further contribution to the agent–structure question in constructivism by showing how a group of women peace activists advanced, through the practice of a feminist critical methodology, a critical constructivist theory of agency. As activists, WILPF's women practiced a theoretically-informed methodology whenever, during the course of making policy decisions, they reflected on the relationship between their views about the world (ontology), their understanding of how they knew what they (thought they) knew about the world (epistemology), their ethical stances about world problems and the issue of peace, and the ways they chose to act on them (methods). In the theoretical methods applied by WILPF I identified the possibility for a political agency that is conscious and critical of structural limits and is therefore useful for activists and social movements interested in emancipatory social change.

Like Ackerly's model of feminist social criticism from which it derives, feminist critical methodology moves forward the agent–structure debate in international relations by pointing out that methodological choices affect the ability of actors to effect social change. Further, feminist critical methodology points to the need for social and self-reflection about actors' own embeddedness into a structure for actual structural change to be made possible. Imaginative identification, a feminist discipline practiced by WILPF, complements TWFSC as a critical constructivist theory of agency. Together, TWFSC and imaginative identification make up a feminist critical methodology used by WILPF to question its very identity as a liberal organization, its ideological foundations and notions about gender, race, and class relations inscribed in those foundations. Imaginative identification guarantees the enactment of a feminist ethics of care and the creation of hybrid subjectivities, both of which are necessary to fully compel the skeptical scrutiny of entrenched ideas, thus enabling an agency that challenges structural constraints.

Notes

1 UNSCR 1325, adopted in October 2000, was the first of such resolutions. It calls for the equal participation of women in post-conflict peace-building and reconstruction efforts. It was followed by UNSCR 1820, 1888 and 1889 (on violence against women in war and their inclusion at all stages of the peace process).

2 Robert Latham has defined liberal modernity as the hegemonic "mode of fashioning and sustaining aspects of social and political existence" through "practices, principles and institutions associated with liberal governance, rights, markets, and self-determination" (Latham 1997, 14–15). Borrowing Fernand Braudel's terms, Latham views the post-war liberal order as a *conjuncture* within the *longue durée* of liberal modernity. The "liberal moment" represented the "convergence of specific historical developments, constructions of agency, and configurations of ... violence and military power" in the immediate aftermath of World War II (Latham 1997, 41).

3 Following Audie Klotz and Cecelia Lynch, I group into the label "constructivist" a variety of scholars who may differ on ideological and epistemological grounds, but who share three common ontological principles: (1) the need for contextualizing the issues under analysis; (2) the belief that the social world is, for some important part, made up of intersubjective understandings; (3) the insistence on the co-constitution of structure and agency (Klotz and Lynch 2007).

4 For a discussion of the difference between epistemic authority and epistemic privilege and their relation to feminist standpoint epistemology, see Janack 1997.

5 Sara Ruddick's much misinterpreted "maternal thinking" similarly stems from a *practice* grounded in preservative love and sustaining a care-giving ethics that runs counter to militaristic (and I would extend oppressive) enterprises (Ruddick 1989). Linda Alcoff has offered a compelling postmodern tribute to Ruddick's work in Alcoff 2003. Kimberly Hutchings recuperates the value of Ruddick's ethic of care for international politics in Hutchings 1999.

6 Elsewhere Hutchings claims that critical theory and poststructuralism maintain a Kantian-derived artificial distinction between morality and politics, which condemns the theorist "either to raise contingency and historicity to the level of a static and timeless absolute, or to judging the international in terms of an abstract and ungrounded reading of history as progress," hence failing to move beyond the unsatisfactory political dilemma "between the pragmatism of the strategist, and the idealism of the moral philosopher" (Hutchings 1992, 62).

7 Mouffe (2000), Feldman (2004), Benhabib (2004), and Besson and Martí (2006) among others have drawn attention to this paradox in deliberative democratic theory, that the preconditions for deliberation are at the same time the desired outcome of the deliberative mode.

8 I believe that the suggestions that follow are entirely consistent with Ackerly's theory and intentions. In my interpretation, imaginative identification is sometimes implicit in TWFSC's skeptical scrutiny. My purpose here is to make it an explicit part of a feminist critical methodology for emancipatory social change, separate from skeptical scrutiny and fulfilling different tasks.

9 One obviously cannot ignore the use of the masculine noun to refer to humanity, indicative of structural (patriarchal) conditionings to identity and language.

10 Verta Taylor has developed the concept of abeyance to describe the organizational and cultural processes that allowed the women's movements of the 1940s and 1950s in the West to survive through a hostile political environment. and eventually make possible the flourishing of "second-wave" feminism (Taylor 1989). Though Taylor is specifically concerned with women's movements organized around feminist goals, social movements' abeyance can help understand the reasons why WILPF found it irrelevant to undertake feminist analyses of peace and militarization in this period.

11 For feminist critiques of enlightenment rationality, law, and science, see Keller 1982; Pateman 1988; Haraway 1989; Tickner 1992; Keller and Longino 1996; and Sylvester 2002.
12 An African American member of WILPF, Flemmie Kittrell, was on WILPF's International Executive Committee of WILPF between 1959 and 1962 and, together with Gertrude Baer and Indian member Sushila Nayar, part of the official WILPF delegation to the Second United Nations' Conference of Nongovernmental Organizations on the Eradication of Prejudice and Discrimination in Geneva in 1959 (WILPF IEC 1959). Several African American women served in position of leadership within the US WILPF from after World War II and into the 1970s. Their numbers dwindled considerably after that decade (Blackwell 2004).
13 With this observation Steffens anticipated feminist theoretical debates on the problems and questions of speaking on behalf of marginalized groups. See Roof and Wiegman 1995.
14 In Ackerly's model social critics represent essential facilitators of society's self-examination and provoke the examination of their own methods, roles, qualifications, and conclusions. In order to do this effectively a variety of critics who offer multiple perspectives (inside, outside, and from multiple sites) are necessary to collectively foster the ongoing and self-reflective model of social criticism (Ackerly 2000).

Intelligence and compassion, the tools of feminists

An engagement with Catia Confortini

Brooke A. Ackerly

Students often ask, "What are *feminist* methods?" Generally, I answer that there are not specifically feminist methods, but that feminism makes the use of any method more rigorous by being more broadly politically and theoretically informed. That is, there are feminist methodologies which are ways of approaching research and social change politics that are informed by the political concerns feminists have raised and the theoretical lenses they have used to clarify them. I return to this question afresh with every research project and Catia Confortini's project inspired me to revisit it again. By reflecting on the activism of a women's organization for peace with a long and variegated history of political lenses and transnational alliances, Confortini offers us a form of activism that integrates two feminist commitments that often become disaggregated by academic feminism: intelligence and compassion.

In this essay, after a brief summary of the theory Confortini develops in her scholarship, I celebrate her insight about the importance of compassion for social change. A leader of the Women's International League for Peace and Freedom (WILPF) defines the key for guiding this compassion toward empowering political change (and not merely charity) as "imaginative identification." I then argue that for social-change-oriented activism and the scholarship that enables us to comprehend its politics, Confortini's feminist constructivist methodology is preferable to the poststructuralist's imaginary, though that does have something to teach us too. Finally, I illustrate the importance of deliberative opportunities for enabling imaginative identification to yield new learning. Confortini's recovering of a particular form of compassion—imaginative identification, which is a way of understanding across profound differences—is an important resource for social-change activism and scholarship of social change because the global contexts of this work require deep attention to difference. However, as Confortini and WILPF show, this form of compassion alone is not a basis for social change or research on social change; it needs to be complemented by a form of intelligence that is informed by a broad range of experience, made comprehensible through sustained deliberative modes of learning with one another. This aspiration has made feminist IR scholars particularly interested in questions of method—our own as researchers and the methods and strategies of feminist activists.

A third way for feminist social criticism

The connection between Catia Confortini's project and mine in *Political Theory and Feminist Social Criticism* is obvious from her argument: Confortini turns a methodology for social criticism into a methodology for social change. She argues that by developing the tools of social criticism, the ambitions of social criticism can include social change. Whereas I read women's activism for its theoretical insight, she read it for its sociological insight.[1] She asks, what should activists with feminist normative commitments do to bring about change consistent with those commitments? Confortini enhances my account of social criticism with an insight from a women's peace organization, WILPF, that social change depends not only on the passion to have a positive impact in the world, but also the willingness to educate oneself carefully, deeply, and broadly about the diverse best ways to bring that about. Intelligent compassion is WILPF's guiding principle. Confortini brings this to life in WILPF's work and uses it to illustrate the need for compassion and educative deliberation in policy advocacy.

The basic argument of *Political Theory and Feminist Social Criticism* is that political theorists need to pay attention to the struggles and wishes of the age when we formulate our theories about those struggles and about the issues at stake in those struggles as well as the concepts and institutions that are useful for addressing them. Following the inspiration of the nonaligned movement during decolonization, I argue that this approach maps a "third way" that neither echoes modern liberalism's unfailing return to universals even while being critical of their false universality, nor echoes post-structuralism's rejection of the generalizing narratives that are useful for giving accounts of injustice that follow the patterns of hierarchy within societies. In recognition of the third way, outlined by the African and Asian leaders of the non-aligned movement during decolonization and the Cold War, I called this approach "Third World feminist social criticism." Naively, I thought that we could reclaim the political intent behind non-aligned political leaders' assertion that they were the authors of the meaning of their politics. Instead of the political affirmation from post-colonial leaders themselves which it was, global elites have suggested that "Third World" is pejorative language and that instead we should discuss geopolitics in the "neutral" language of "global North" and "global South."

I offered these insights from women's activism as a development of critical theory's view of social criticism:

1 Social critics must follow a methodology intended to be sensitive to the reality of an imperfect world where power inequalities enable coercion and potential exploitation to silence some within a society and to impede social criticism and social change.
2 The social critic must criticize the values, practices, and norms of a society. This may require being a critical voice as a representative of silent voices,

facilitating the social criticism of others (possibly by creating a safe place for those who are excluded or exploited), or contributing to social criticism directly.

3   There are no constraints on the origins or qualities that qualify one to be a social critic; social criticism requires multiple critics from a variety of origins and critical perspectives.

Confortini focuses on the first of these, the methodology, which is made up of three parts: guiding criteria, skeptical scrutiny, and deliberative inquiry. For social change, the other dimensions of the theory which outline who should be a critic (everyone) and what their responsibilities should be (to promote critical learning with others) are equally important. I will return to these in the last section.

Confortini's contribution to feminist critical methodology

Confortini draws on the work of WILPF to contribute an important complementary insight to the theory of social criticism. She introduces the concept by quoting at length from a speech by Dorothy Hutchinson in 1968 at the WILPF International Congress. Hutchinson describes the strategy as celebrating two values that characterized Jane Addams:

> Intelligence—the mental capability which sets man apart, and Compassion—the emotional capability which enables Man, by an effort of his imagination, to feel suffering which is not his own, so acutely that he is compelled to act to relieve it.[2]

There are two elements of social change being celebrated here: compassion as a guide for "imaginative identification with those who are victimized by inhuman public policies"; and intelligence as a guide for educating ourselves and others. Together, Hutchinson calls these "intelligent compassion" (1968, 7).

Confortini's essay makes visible the importance of imaginative identification in WILPF's work and for compassionate intelligence as a practice behind social-change advocacy. According to Confortini, Third World feminist social criticism's methodology needs the compliment of imaginative identification to be the compassionate intelligence of WILPF and of feminist social change more generally.

Why imaginative identification is better than poststructuralist imaginative distance

While imagination is very important to challenging our "knowing" and inspiring our learning, we cannot rely on our imagination to provide useful information. Consider a recent survey in which 52 percent of nondisabled

Americans—disproportionately with higher incomes and higher levels of education—claim that they would rather be dead than disabled.[3] One way to read this survey is that more than half of nondisabled Americans *imagine* that disability is worse than death. While we might want to reflect on what this means for the meaning in their lives, I want to emphasize what this means for our imaginations: we cannot trust our imaginations. A large percentage of the nondisabled population cannot imagine the lives, joys, loves, angers, struggles, and fulfillment that persons with disabilities enjoy. Compassionate intelligence depends on imaginative identification *and* imaginative analysis. If we cannot know something through our own experience, then we need tools of inquiry and analysis that can enable us to know it.

Hutchinson has a diagnosis for this failure of imagination: "Our imaginations are not only stunted by our insulation form actual contact with the misery of our brothers, but we are also dehumanized by modern social and political complexities which make us feel remote from national decision making and helpless to affect it" (1968, 7). On this view, we awaken our imaginations through learning. Hutchinson elaborates:

> Added to the indignities to which human beings are subjected and their cruel struggle for the necessities of life, there is the dehumanizing affect of ignorance. Knowledge is essential for developing the full human potential of the individual and as a basis for group judgments regarding political, social and economic values. No society should make these value judgments for another. Therefore, education should never be the imposition of political, social or economic dogmas but rather preparation for making free and informed choices as to political organization, population control, industrialization, etc. compatible with each society's culture and traditions. "Full sharing in human knowledge is a human right."
>
> (Hutchinson 1968, 6)

For activists, as Hutchinson says, "Unless we find means for expressing and implementing *our* intelligent compassion, we become as frustrated and impotent as those who need our help" (1968, 7).

In Confortini's and Hutchinson's view, intelligent compassion is concrete and concretely informed by experiential knowledge from within particular contexts. While we have not used this language as we have been developing the field over the last 20 years, it is an essential tool of feminist IR. It is the methodology behind the work of curious feminists in their exploration of so many puzzles—puzzles themselves that were obscure to the field of IR twenty years ago (Peterson 1992; Tickner 1992; Zalewski and Parpart 1998; Enloe 2004).

When Christine Sylvester developed the idea of "empathetic cooperation," she sought to spark such imaginative reflection. This reflection would be essential among allies, but more importantly it was a tool for understanding differences among those in conflict as well. However, Sylvester's account has had a limited effect on the field because it is descriptive and yet hypothetical. One illustration comes from another theorist's hypothetical construction (Sylvester 1994a, 97; (1994b, 321–22). The more concrete illustrations render invisible the differences, disagreements, and conflicts among activists (1994b, 330–33). In Sylvester's account of empathetic cooperation, there is greater emphasis on the "empathy" than on the "cooperation" across difference. Empathetic cooperation functions in 1994 as a stance toward the other, whereas in activism and in the development Confortini provides, feminist IR requires a tool for social change, one that respects the concerns to which a stance of empathetic cooperation is a response and yet is as dynamic in its implications as the activists and self-advocates who deploy it.

Confortini's discussion of imaginative identification is grounded in the 20-year tradition of feminist IR which has developed a profound interest in exploring differences among women and across contexts (Zalewski 2000; Chowdhry and Nair 2002; Zalewski 2007).[4] Her approach is also guided by feminist constructivists' commitment to examining the ways in which power is internal to processes of construction (Locher and Prugl 2001). In Confortini's discussion imaginative identification is concrete and emphasizes empathy (where possible) *and* cooperation (where possible). Confortini does more than put forward an argument in favor of deploying an empathetic stance. She offers a methodological illustration of its deployment in struggles for peace, particularly in the struggles of a network of women working to envision and promote peace together despite vast differences. I will now highlight what Confortini teaches us about cooperation for social criticism and social change by looking at WILPF over three decades. In order for this to be a contribution to a theory of social criticism and social change we need to glean from the work of activists in struggle, not mere description, but rather a methodology for use in other contexts, not just by academics, but by activists themselves as they work through differences, disagreements, and conflicts. Confortini shows us such a methodology.

WILPF's imaginative identification and learning through deliberative opportunities

As Confortini shows through a review of the learning by WILPF members and by WILPF as an organization over three decades, imaginative identification is not a state of mind, but a strategy and practice in struggle (and a hard one to carry out at that). We are good at pointing out *other's internalized hegemonies* (Grewal and Kaplan 1994; Chan-Tiberghien 2004; Jabri 2004), but not necessarily our own. How do we resist our internalized hegemonies? Not within *hypothetical* deliberative opportunities, but in *real* ones.

According to Confortini in the 1960s, WILPF joined local and global trends around the world—civil rights movements, *dalit* movements, indigenous rights movements, and decolonization movements—in rethinking the building blocks of liberalism—freedom and equality—and what they mean for nation-building and international relations. In the critical democratic vision of the 1960s and 1970s, basic needs, a just economic order, and popular participation become important building blocks of liberal democracy in the eyes of many on the political left.[5]

WILPF self-reflectively challenged itself to develop member and organizational capacity to care about women and peace in an ever-broadening range of contexts and to appreciate what the hybrid subjectivity of their diverse membership and the diverse contexts in which women struggle for peace means for individual and shared work for peace. To do this they created a range of ways of developing individual and collective capacity for imaginative identification. There are two dimensions of these initiatives: creating opportunities to know and deliberate about the import of the range of peace struggles in which women are engaged; and broadening the range of women participating in and concerns raised in these deliberative opportunities.

WILPF created increased opportunities for deliberation by triennial Congresses, by holding conferences, and by arranging meetings with women from countries whose governments are in conflict: Lebanon, the Soviet Union, and Vietnamese. Many participated in these contexts with an eye to making these non-hierarchical deliberative spaces where the values of the organization are practiced, not merely discussed.

While some of these engagements took place only once, WILPF sought sustained cooperation with NGOS outside of their familiar circles. Those familiar circles included those networked through their UN consultative status, but also were understood by some WILPF members as defined by class. Many WILPF members were aware of what they did not know and blamed the narrowness of their circle. In their view, the hegemony of ideas comes from the power of the status quo and the particularity of individual viewpoints. In order to broaden their knowledge base they cultivated new members and new partnerships. They sought out the perspectives of "outsiders" and "other" women. They sought out "input from a variety of sources" (cite Confortini this volume).

In addition, as illustrated by Steffen's self-criticism as an expert on Africa, they were self-conscious about their own situatedness and the inappropriateness of any of them to speak as women for all women (see p. 33).

In short, WILPF offers an example of how a feminist organization from the global North developed the tools for practicing compassionate intelligence through imaginative identification. They set up deliberative opportunities with outsiders. This was not merely an aesthetic goal. They made institutional change that strengthened young leadership, and they approached listening as a sustained enterprise (cite Confortini this volume). They were continually confronting themselves with insights about their own blind spots—be these ones from their past or ones from their present. By creating and enriching deliberative contexts for a range of participants and directing critical attention to that inclusiveness, WILPF exhibited a practice of feminist social criticism.

Conclusion: WILPF, Third World feminist social criticism, and social change

Even with its roots in the global North, WILPF exhibits many of the strategies of what I have called Third World feminist social criticism. WILPF was seeking a third way. Illuminating this ambition—and WILPF's struggles and successes with it—are important contributions of Confortini's work. In the latter half of the 1960s, WILPF paid attention to its own internal democratic process, methods, and policy positions. For WILPF walking the talk was an important contribution to the peace movement (Vellacott 1993). On my reading, WILPF saw that compassion alone was not going to get them anywhere. They needed "intelligence" which as Hutchinson described it, is based on critical learning across profound differences. Such critical learning required real challenging engagement, a demanding form of listening, and an openness to rethinking everything.

Willing to change, WILPF tried to remake itself with new membership and young leadership. However, as Confortini notes, the normative and political context in which they operated is not conducive to this transformation. Imaginative identification is an individual tool. As Confortini notes with examples, individual members changed their point of view as a result of engagement with outsiders and developing a multi-sited critical perspective (cf. Ackerly 2000). However, the broader liberal modern context constrained the change that was possible for the organization.

This is one reason why Confortini's constructivist lens is valuable. Whether theorists, empiricists, or activists, when we work toward compassionate intelligence, we may be inclined to forget that a commitment to compassionate intelligence does not change the challenges to which constructivists draw our attention. The complex forces of social, economic, and political power, which Hutchinson cautioned could dehumanize us with complacency and conformity, can make the most zealous do-gooders among us blind with frustration. WILPF did not bring about world peace. The criticisms of war that were "obvious" to Hutchinson and her audience in 1968 bear repeating to a contemporary ear: "Ours is a time of dizzyingly rapid change. Whether it is to be a transition to catastrophe or to a world of unprecedented peace and plenty may depend on relatively few people with vision and courage" (Hutchinson 1968, 11). In her view, WILPF and allied activists, not political leaders, are the relatively few with vision, "privileged in this crucial time to guide the course of history into an era of unparalleled hope." The opportunity is clear: "Never before in history has mankind had the technological capability to provide a decent standard of living for all. This is not possible if only men will devote their attention and their resources to life rather than to death" (Hutchinson 1968, 11). The constructivist lens can put this aspiration and its failure in context. Compassionate intelligence gives us the ability to notice the power dynamics at work within social processes themselves, that is, even within an organization working toward world peace to define and refine its work.

Notes

1 Even before Confortini's dissertation, let alone this chapter, took shape our conversations on the methodology in *Political Theory and Feminist Social Criticism*
 informed my work. *Universal Human Rights in World of Difference* includes a
 more detailed sociological discussion of women's human rights strategies (Ackerly
 2008a: 283–301). In that book, I use those insights, developed with Bina D'Costa,
 as an outline for considering how the theoretical work of women's human rights
 activists can guide the improvement of their practice. Confortini's chapter illustrates
 why the relationship between empirics and theory is so important for feminist IR
 (Ackerly 2008b, 2009).
2 Dorothy Hutchinson, Chairman's Keynote Address, "The Right to be Human,"
 1968, pp. 7–8, box 25, 16th International Congress Report 1966 and 17th International Congress Report 1968, WILPF SCPC Accession, University of Colorado at
 Boulder Archives. See above where Confortini sites more extensively from the
 speech
3 "Disaboom Survey Reveals 52 Percent of Americans Would Rather be Dead than
 Disabled," *PR Web Press Release Newswire* (Denver, CO, 2008). I thank Stacy
 Clifford for drawing my attention to this study and other issues related to disability,
 particularly cognitive disability.
4 For reviews see (Ackerly and Attanasi 2009) and (Ackerly and True 2010).
5 Political theorists joined this conversation as well (Rawls 1958; Pateman 1970;
 Shue [1980] 1996).

3 Pursuing inclusive interests, both deep and wide

Women's human rights and the United Nations

Abigail E. Ruane

Bartolomé de las Casas, a sixteenth-century Spanish Dominican priest who worked toward a more equitable colonial society in the "New World," found a way of pursuing inclusive interests in a way which recognized others' difference yet valued them equally. Hayward Alker argues that this was only possible after a journey of experiences which changed him "from Conquistador, to caring colonialist, to other-respecting, anti-colonial, intercultural communicator" (Alker 1996, 174). Rather than arguing, like his colleague Sepulveda, that others who were different must be less important (lower on a social hierarchy), or suggesting, like Columbus, that others must be the same to be equal, las Casas affirmed the possibility that others could be both different and equal (see Todorov 1992; Alker 1996).

Provoked by the las Casas story, this chapter aims at contributing to International Relations (IR) theory by developing and illustrating a feminist constructivist model for how to pursue more just and inclusive interests, in order to create the foundation for more just and inclusive behavior. This responds to J. Ann Tickner's (1997) call for a "renewed conversation" between feminism and IR scholarship despite difficulties due to ontological and epistemological differences. It also builds on the window of opportunity in this endeavor highlighted by Birgit Locher and Elisabeth Prügl (2001); they note that "constructivism shares ontological grounds with feminism and thus provides a unique window of opportunity for understanding" (112). Agreeing with Locher and Prügl (2001), and highlighting shared interests in power by Onufian constructivists and feminists, this chapter seeks to contribute to IR theory by developing and illustrating a feminist constructivist model for how to construct more inclusive identities as the basis for more just and inclusive interests and behavior.

Overall, I argue that pursuing substantively, rather than seductively, inclusive interests is possible under imperfect conditions of ideological hegemony. This can happen through a two-step process: I describe this as first expanding interests' "borders" and then deepening their "roots." This enables interests to be conceptually redefined, at first seductively, but second, more substantively, because it moves from a narrow and more colonial definition of interests (which are defined narrowly but may be extended broadly) to a richer more democratic definition of those interests (which are defined broadly). I ground this argument within the context of narrating identities under varying conditions of ideological hegemony; particularly, I suggest that because dominant narratives create the building blocks which construct particular narrative identities, both high and low levels of ideological hegemony restrict how creatively particular narrative identities can be defined. After developing this model, I use the case of women's human rights discourse in the United Nations (1948–2008) to illustrate it and suggest how more inclusive interests can be possible.

As a whole, this contributes both to constructivist and feminist IR theory, as well as social theory in general. Within IR, it suggests that constructivist theorizing by Alexander Wendt and Nicholas Onuf can be developed by highlighting the relationship between identity and power. It also suggests that feminist theorizing by Brooke Ackerly can be complemented with a standard of inclusiveness not tied to elite perspectives. More broadly, it suggests that discussion of "the common good" must be held to explicit standards, since the "common good" is often less "common" than may at first appear. Finally, it supports Tickner's (1997) argument for the valuing of difference, and suggests a two-step process by which more inclusive interests can be pursued.

Pursuing more inclusive interests: the case of women's human rights

This chapter focuses on the case of women's human rights to illustrate its conceptual model for how to pursue more inclusive interests as a basis for inclusive behavior. This case usefully highlights how to pursue rights which recognize "difference" but still allow for "equality"—concerns critical both from gendered and cultural perspectives. It also suggests how more inclusive ideas can begin to translate meaningfully into more inclusive behavior.

In the feminist literature the question of how to pursue more substantive and inclusive equality in a world of difference has been addressed in the "equality/difference" debate (evident primarily in the early to mid-twentieth century), which has historically been framed as between two competing perspectives over whether women should have "equal" or identical rights to men, or whether they should be "protected" because they are "different" (see Whitworth 1994). Although current discussions have moved beyond this simplistic and dichotomous framing, this debate usefully illustrates a false choice: it suggests rights must *either* be equal (identically applicable) *or* different (differently applicable because of different experience). It does not recognize (as some current scholarship does), that rights are *both* based on particular experience (different for some than others) *and* potentially applicable to various groups. As such, levels of "equality" apply both to the *definition* of rights (whose experience they are based in) and the *extension* of those rights (which groups they are applied to).

In the human rights literature similar issues have been addressed in the "universalism/relativism" debate (especially evident in the second half of the twentieth century), which is historically framed as between two competing perspectives over whether human rights are "universal" (e.g., in terms of overlapping conceptual basis, popular support, and commonly shared cultural, religious, and legal justification) or "relative" (e.g., in terms of particular—elite, Western, male—basis, interpretation, and prioritization of rights) (see, on the one hand, Donnelly 1982, 2007; Pannikar 1982; Simma and Alston 1989; Twiss 1998, 56–59; and, on the other hand, Charlesworth 1994; Sen 1997). Like with the "equality/difference" debate, the extremes caricaturized here have begun to be overcome in recent scholarship (e.g., An-Na'im 1995; de Sousa Santos 2002; Ackerly 2008b; see also Renteln 1988). However, this dichotomous framing again usefully illustrates the false choice between difference and equality: particularly, it suggests that rights are *either* universally applicable (universal) *or* rooted in particular perspectives (relative). However, it does not recognize how rights are *both* rooted in particular perspectives *and* potentially extendable to different groups. This suggests that rights rooted in elite (e.g., western, male) experience may be formally universal because they can be extended to all human beings. However, more substantively, universal rights must be rooted and defined by a more inclusive and universal set of experience.

Opportunities for inclusive interests: constructivism

How is it possible to pursue inclusive interests which recognize "difference" but allow for "equality"? Constructivist research which analyzes how interests are defined provides a useful basis to address this question. However, existing constructivist analysis of inclusion is limited by a lack of intersection between the fruitful but relatively distinct discussions of inclusiveness (especially by Alexander Wendt) and power (especially by Nicholas Onuf). As a result, questions which feminist theory suggests are critical to consider—including addressing whose interests are involved, and whose interests are prioritized—remain limited.

Wendt and inclusiveness

First, Wendt suggests that states can act more inclusively to reduce the "recurrence and repetition" of the international system by redefining other states as "friends" rather than "enemies" or "rivals." Drawing on early Social Identity Theory (SIT) in social psychology, Wendt assumes that because actors seek positive interpretations of their ingroups, the extent state actors share interests with others depends on the extent to which they define others as being in their ingroup (Zehfuss 2002, 15; see also Wendt 1996, 52; Wendt 1999, 106, 229, 241–43 and Chapter 7). Wendt argues that, as Maja Zehfuss so lucidly paraphrases, "[s]elf-interested identities lie at the heart of the self-help system and [state] identity change is the way to get out" (Zehfuss 2002, 15; see also Wendt 1999); this is why "anarchy is what states make of it" (Wendt 1992). As such, "[id]entities provide the basis for interests which are defined in the process of conceptualising situations" (Zehfuss 2002, 14; see also Wendt 1992, 298; 1999, 122). State identities are defined in terms of their overlapping identification with broader groups (e.g., international society, NATO, ASEAN, the West, the South, democracies, autocracies). These social identifications generate behavior prioritizing the interests of groups with whom actors identify (e.g., as "friends"), rather than those with whom actors do not identify (e.g., as "rivals" or "enemies"). They provide scripts for action which suggest, but do not determine, paths of behavior: actors can identify with and draw on multiple group and subgroup scripts at any given time, each with potentially different sources of interests.

Despite important insights, Wendt's discussion of inclusiveness is limited by an inadequate consideration of power relations both within and between groups. He asks "whether states are capable ever of ... expanding the boundaries of the Self to include Others" (1999, 241). And he defines this expansion in terms identification with a particular role—that of a "friend" (the Kantian approach), rather than that of an "enemy" (the Hobbesian approach) or "rival" (the Lockean approach) (Wendt 1999, 258–59). However, he does not recognize how expanding the boundaries of the self can be seductively—rather than substantively—inclusive, because it does not also expand the basis for *defining* the interests of the self. This is most clearly evident in Wendt's discussion of "friendship" where he states that "mutual aid against outsiders could be accompanied by force within the relationship (as in the 'care' of the husband who beats his wife but protects her from other men)" (1999, 299). Here, Wendt normalizes violence within a group, even while focusing on the group (of "friends" rather than "rivals" or "enemies") lowest on the scale of "use of violence" between groups. Because Wendt inadequately addresses asymmetric power relations, he cannot guarantee that increasing boundary inclusiveness by expanding the ingroup is not colonizing or oppressing, rather than empowering by rooting ingroup interests more deeply in a broader experience.

Onuf and power

Second, Onuf does not directly address inclusiveness but develops a sophisticated analysis of power which is highly relevant to this issue in his classic argument that "rules yield rule" (see Onuf 1989). According to Onuf, agents meaningfully construct the world using rules—statements that tell people what they should do (Onuf 1998, 59). However, because resources available to different agents vary, "some agents exercise greater control over the content of those rules, and over their success in being followed, than other agents do" (1998, 75). As a result, such agents can "use rules to exercise control and obtain advantages over other agents" (1998, 63) more than others. Consequently, "rules yield rule"—not just *patterned* relations, but *asymmetrically patterned* relations (1998, 75, 63). Furthermore, while degree of domination within social relations varies in degree, intentionality, and visibility depending on the kind of rules most in evidence (see Onuf 1998, 75–77), Onuf argues that some level of social asymmetry is always present because agents' lack of *autonomy* (freedom to act) requires some form of *domination* (asymmetrical relations).

Onuf's framework of "rules yielding rule" usefully illustrates how groups can be structured by internal and external power hierarchies. However, his assumption that lack of autonomy requires domination conflates inclusive membership with exclusive definition of group interests, and consequently is unnecessarily limited. As such, while his framework rightly points out the limitations of inclusiveness which merely expands group membership (in this case, of putative rule-makers) without deepening the basis of group interests, his assumption that elite (rule-maker) interests are necessarily defined at the expense of non-elites (a zero-sum assumption) does not necessarily follow. Particularly, in the case where the interests of rule-makers are *not* defined at the expense of rule-followers, it should be possible for rules to yield *patterned relations*, rather than *asymmetrically patterned relations*. As such, more rootedly inclusive or "win-win" interests supporting such rules may be possible in situations structured by empowering—rather than dominating—relationships, such as when multiple perspectives are valued and used to inform rule-maker interests. Although it may be the case that such practical conditions are rare, it remains useful to consider at least a theoretical spectrum of inclusiveness assuming patterned, but not necessarily asymmetrically patterned, behavior.

Taken together, constructivist research by Wendt and Onuf suggests that understanding how relationships of power influence discussions of whose interests are involved and whose interests are prioritized is critical to pursuing more inclusive interests. However, this research is limited in addressing opportunities for inclusive roots, rather than just inclusive borders, because of either a limited understanding of power (for Wendt), or an assumption of some level of relational domination (for Onuf). However, feminist research which recognizes egalitarian "empowering" as well as dominating forms of power suggests alternative paths where interests with more inclusive roots, as well as borders, can be pursued.

Constraints on inclusive interests: understanding and valuing self and other

How is it possible to pursue more conceptually inclusive interests in international affairs? Feminist scholarship suggests that at least two issues must be navigated in this process. First, because pursuing inclusive interests involves both "us" and "them," understandings of *whose interests are included* are critical. Second, because relationships between "us" and "them" entail relations of power, *whose interests are prioritized* are also key.

First, in pursuing more inclusive interests, *whose* interests are included? Active exclusion of certain interests is one obstacle. However, even good faith efforts to pursue more inclusive interests can be limited. As feminist standpoint research suggests, all perspectives are partial and rooted in particular experience, rather than "objective" knowledge (e.g., Hartsock 1983; Harding 1998). This can significantly limit efforts at inclusion, not because of bad faith, but because of lack of imagination or an inability to relate. Iris Marion Young (1994) argues that we may never really be able to "walk in someone else's shoes"; but instead, may only project our experience onto others in frequently inappropriate ways. However, even if it is possible to walk in each other's shoes, this may only be possible to a limited extent, or under certain circumstances—for example, by drawing on minority perspectives, multiple perspectives, "'world'-travelling" to see with the eyes of the other, putting oneself in a situation of exchange with related others, or empathetically cooperating (e.g., Lugones 1987; Collins 1989; Crenshaw 1991; Sylvester 1994; Yuval-Davis 1997, Ackerly 2000, 2008b). Consequently, even efforts to include "everyone" can be limited by interpretations of who "everyone" is.

Second, in pursuing more inclusive interests, whose interests are *prioritized*? Even when diverse interests are recognized and included, certain (often elite) interests are often prioritized as more important than others.[1] Feminists suggest that interests may not necessarily be "objectively" of greater or lesser importance, but may instead be valued based on the perspective and relative influence of the viewer: consequently, the interests of individuals in dominant positions tend to be seen as more important than the interests of those in subordinate positions. Feminist discussions of power which differentiate collaborative forms of power ("power-to" or "power-with") from dominating forms of power ("power-over") (see Allen 2008) also highlight divergent assumptions over whether existing interests are seen as competing or potentially complementary: On the one hand, dominating power assumes a "zero-sum game" where the interests of some come at the expense of others. On the other hand, empowering power assumes the possibility of a "positive-sum game" where "win-win" solutions incorporating interests of multiple parties are possible. Overall, feminist scholarship on power suggests that empowering relationships which recognize "win-win" solutions facilitate more substantively inclusive interests, whereas dominating relationships which define the interests of one as more important than and at the expense of others restrict inclusive goals.

In addition to relational power hierarchies existing *within* groups or issue areas, such hierarchies also exist *between* them: consequently, it is not enough to critique "internal" hierarchies (e.g., supporting a focus on men rather than women in development), it is also important to critique broader ranging hierarchies which exist across multiple-level "games" (e.g., those prioritizing "state security" over "human security" or "women's rights"). Overall, hierarchies from relational structures within families, to among social groups (such as defined by ethnicity or class), to among states (such as defined by developed or developing status) and otherwise are all at risk of exclusionary interests and behavior because of reliance on dominating rather than egalitarian relational structures.

Opportunities for inclusive interests: curb cut feminism

What do these interpretations of power mean for pursuing inclusive interests which recognize "difference" but allow for "equality"? Brooke Ackerly (2008b) provides an excellent example of what this could look like in her development of a universal theory of human rights which tries not to involve cultural imperialism. Ackerly navigates the issues raised by the "equality/difference" and "universalism/relativism" debate by pursuing an inclusive ideal (universal human rights) in a way that tries not to tie that ideal to particular elite interests (e.g., Western, male, or other priorities). She does this by rejecting particular "standards" of inclusiveness (e.g., "fundamental" rights as defined by divine authority or "enlightened" reasoning) as always based in certain perspectives. She argues that "[a]ny principle, even inclusion, can be exclusive" and consequently that "A non-ideal theory of human rights needs an immanent source of justification that can be applied within and across cultures, one that is not a principle, nor itself an exercise of potentially exploitable power" (2008b, 202–3).

Instead of a standard of inclusiveness, Ackerly chooses a method.[2] Her "curb cut feminism" methodology assumes that we live in a "non-ideal" world and consequently gives precedence to attentive deliberations in "domains of continued dispute." It involves attentive dialogue (listening as well as speaking) among critical people with different perspectives (e.g., insiders, outsiders, multi-sited critics, and silent or silenced critics). Ackerly argues that this allows for more "inclusive accountability" (2008b, 35) because it allows participants to "challenge unreflective ways of knowing in order to reveal forms of power concealed in institutions and habituated practices" (27) with a "destabilizing epistemological perspective" (35). She suggests that this focus on inclusive process over inclusive principles enables more substantively inclusive consideration of rights because it minimizes sources of potentially exploitable power based in particular or elite interpretation or application of human rights principles.

Despite its overall excellence, Ackerly's approach is limited by reliance on "deliberation" without standards of inclusiveness. Although I agree with her that "[t]hrough collaboration we become increasingly attentive to the invisible among us ... and the invisible outside of 'us'" (2008b, 245), I am not convinced that increased visibility of complex memberships will guarantee equal valuing of diverse perspectives. Even if deliberations involve different perspectives (e.g., insiders, outsiders, multi-sited critics, and silent or silenced critics), there will always be those who cannot be at the table, and concerns which are not always adequately (or at all) addressed or prioritized in discussion. Consequently, discourse among those who do participate will likely remain limited by unequal recognition or prioritization.

Accordingly, while attentive deliberation among diverse critics in "domains of continued dispute" is an excellent starting point in pursuing more inclusive interests—especially in recognizing difference in the pursuit of equality and utilizing feminist insights about power—more is needed. To meet this need, this chapter develops and illustrates a standard of inclusiveness not tied to any particular perspective, which can be used to evaluate the inclusiveness if such "deliberations." This standard creates the basis for evaluating the justice and inclusiveness of particular interests and behavior. In doing so, this highlights how pursuing inclusive interests requires recognizing ideological power—something supported much more by Onuf than Wendt in constructivist theory. This also highlights how doing so makes it possible to, first, recognize and evaluate the extent to which inclusive goals are pursued— something that develops Ackerly's feminist deliberative method with a standard of evaluation; and, second, to pursue those goals more extensively— through a two-step process of expanding borders and then deepening roots.

A feminist constructivist model of inclusiveness

Building on feminist and constructivist research, I now develop a conceptual model for how to pursue inclusive identities and interests as the basis for inclusive behavior in international affairs. My main argument is that pursuing more inclusive interests is possible by pursuing more inclusive identities. However, more substantive inclusiveness is possible under different conditions and can be pursued with different strategies than formal inclusiveness. This draws on a Gramscian understanding of hegemony, a narrative model of identity, and a current understanding of social psychology's Social Identity Theory. I illustrate this using the discourse over women's human rights from the founding of the United Nations to the present (1948–2008).

Key terms

Let me first clarify my conceptual framework. First, I assume a relatively broad understanding of *interests*: as Wendt (1999) suggests, "interests are beliefs about how to meet needs" (Wendt 1999, 130, quoting McCullagh 1991). This creates more room to "expand the pie" by focusing on why goals are pursued than by focusing on particular ways to fulfill those goals (Lax and Sebenius 1986; Fisher et al. 1991).

Second, I focus on interests as informed by actors' narrations of their identities. Adapting Dan McAdams's development of William James' (1963) differentiation between the self as knower ("I") and known ("me") by incorporating the understanding that actors can identify either in personal (idiosyncratic) or social (group) terms, I assume that *identity is the story that I tell about me or us* (see McAdams 1993, 62, quoted in Smith and Sparkes 2006, 175). As such, "identity" refers to the story that I tell about either "me" (personal identity) or "us" (group identity).

Third, I focus on *conceptual* rather than *implementation* obstacles to inclusion. Because actors draw on dominant cultural narratives in narrating their identities and defining their interests, *ideological hegemony* critically circumscribes opportunities for inclusion. According to Gramsci, a "hegemony of ideas"—or combination of intellectual and moral leadership ("consent") and domination ("force");—naturalizes the rule of certain historical blocs (see Germino 1990, 256). From this perspective, popular ideologies limit the creativity of the narratives of actors who draw on them; however, they are even more constraining because they frequently naturalize forces of domination through what Marx and some feminists have called "false consciousness" and what Bourdieu called "misrecognition": by disguising coercion so people can go along with it, all the while believing that they are consenting of their own free will (see Friedman 2005, 242–43; see also Gramsci 1985, 130; Ives 2002, 330). Despite this, because "consent" (intellectual and moral leadership) is separate from "force" (domination), I argue that ideologies which are *dominant* do not necessarily have to be *dominating*.[3]

Fourth, (building on insights from the "equality/difference" and "universalism/relativism" debates), I must clarify that "inclusive" interests can refer to at least two different things: I describe these as "inclusive roots" and "inclusive borders." I will elaborate here to be as clear as possible: On the one hand, interests with *inclusive roots* draw on diverse experiences from a broad range of group members, rather than being defined by elites: groups which treat the viewpoints of all group members are as equally viable and equally address those viewpoints in defining group goals have *inclusive* roots; however, groups which exclude, minimize, or discount viewpoints of certain group members have *exclusive* roots (e.g., "groupthink"[4]). On the other hand, interests which have *inclusive borders* apply to a broad membership: big groups have *inclusive* borders; small groups have *exclusive* borders.

Inclusive roots and borders are not theoretically incompatible. For example, big groups can have inclusive roots as well as borders to some degree (e.g., democracies: for the people and by the people). And small, elite groups frequently have explicitly exclusive roots and borders (e.g., "white-only" men's clubs: for a white male membership but about a subset of racist white males). However, they do not always overlap. For example, small groups (with exclusive borders) can have inclusive roots (e.g., non-hierarchical, co-actively led, or consensus-based, feminist groups). And relatively big groups (with inclusive borders) can have exclusive roots (e.g., fundamentalist religious groups which claim that particular religious interpretations apply to all religious members or all people). Furthermore, feminist scholars demonstrate that big groups which claim to be inclusive (e.g., democracies) often have inclusive borders but exclusive roots: for example, groups including both women and men are frequently based on a "male model" that prioritizes interests based in elite men's (rather than women's) experiences (e.g., Charlesworth 1994; Okin 1999).

Overall, it is important to recognize that pursuing interests with more inclusive borders can only go so far in pursuing a more just world: Expanding membership does not guarantee that group interests will be defined by experience with a broad, rather than narrow (idealized and homogenous ingroup) basis. As such, interests with more inclusive borders do not guarantee more inclusive roots.

Conceptual model

A clearer understanding of the opportunities for interests with both inclusive roots and inclusive borders is possible by considering a context of ideological hegemony in conjunction with recent social psychological insights supporting feminist research differentiating empowering from dominating forms of power. First, current social psychological insights are important because they contradict Wendt's assumption (based in earlier, and now outdated, social psychology) that pursuing more inclusive interests requires defining others as part of an expanded (and homogenized) ingroup, an ingroup which is affirmed as valuable only *relative* to a denigrated outgroup (for a related critique, see Rumelili 2002, 2004). Instead, current insights differentiate ingroup affirmation from outgroup denigration; this suggests that substantively or rootedly inclusive interests are possible by affirming the self independently from others, and affirming others as equally valuable, but different from, the self (see Hewstone et al. 2002; Otten 2002).

Second, insights from Gramscian and social psychological traditions suggest that inclusiveness can be understood to be limited in different ways under different conditions of ideological hegemony (see Ruane 2010). On the one hand, high levels of ideological hegemony restrict creative reinterpretation of existing narratives; consequently, they limit the extent to which existing narratives which assume hierarchical relationships can be reinterpreted. On the other hand, low levels of ideological hegemony (high levels of ideological choice) lack developed narratives; consequently, they limit the extent to which alternative experiences can be understood and related to. In between these two extremes, there is a broader variety of narratives available to be drawn on, and the limiting factor is primarily the interpretation of existing narratives as well as their number, value, accessibility and framing (e.g., the relative availability and perceived value of various relational models).

Dominant cultural narratives are important because they circumscribe the way actors define both who they are and what their interests involve. In a Western context, two such culturally common stories which foreground issues of relational power and parallel the paths are, Otten (2002) suggests, those of "bully" and "friend."

Bullies and friends

"Bully" model and "friend" models are both metaphors and stories which can be understood as foundational to how people define and act in their lives, in many contexts. They are stories in that they refer to particular iconic narratives about mythologized roles of bullies and friends (e.g., about a schoolyard bully or a childhood friend). However, they are metaphors in that they are applied in multiple contexts (e.g., romantic to business relationships, but also interpersonal to interstate relationships) by different kinds of actors (individuals and groups) as the basis for meaningfully interpreting and acting in their situations. Furthermore, they provide two completely different models of relational power distributions.

On the one hand, a bully lives by what Weinhold (2000) calls a "dominator value system" supporting violence. Bullies repeatedly take physical or verbal action (such as violence, threats, and intimidation) "to gain power over or to dominate another person" by exploiting those who they see as having less power, status, or influence, without regard for their rights or needs (Weinhold 2000, 4). "Bully" stories assume a relationship of threat between ingroup and outgroup, and consequently require self-protection, typically through outgroup denigration.

On the other hand, an ideal friend can be understood as the opposite of a bully: someone who lives by a "humanistic or democratic value system" (Eider 1987 quoted in Weinhold 2000, 2). They "[s]eek equalitarian relationships based on mutual respect, trust, and caring," and draw on shared norms and non-violent conflict resolution to look for win-win solutions for all. The story of egalitarian relationships creates a strong position for potential friends, who can expect a reward, benefit, balance, and support from voluntary relationships with others who are often nearby, seen consistently, and who appropriately and reciprocally engage in self-disclosure (see Glover 2009) .

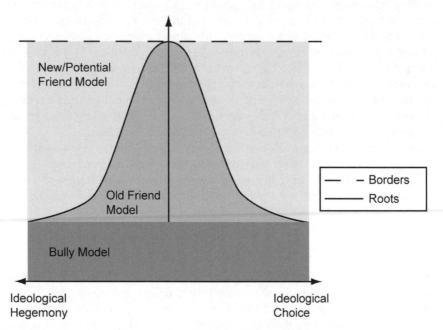

Figure 3.1 Conceptual limits to inclusion under ideological hegemony

Of course, such "ideal" friendships do not always occur in everyday life, where friendships can involve different levels of relational hierarchy. However, this ideal remains useful: it suggests possibilities for new or "potential" friends; in addition, the experience of more egalitarian friendships may be more evident in certain friendships. Some relationships have been recognized as particularly egalitarian, involving not only exchanges of "monologues" which alternate mirroring the other's experience with projection of one's own experience, but also involving each friend exploring and interpreting their experience in different ways and consequently being able to relate more complexly and more deeply to the experiences of others—especially certain friendships among women (see, e.g., Coates 1997). As such, interests with inclusive borders are facilitated by "potential friend" models which define others as equally valuable as and similar to the ingroup ("like me" or "like us")—such narratives affirm the self independently from affirmed others (rather than relative to denigrated others). Furthermore, interests with inclusive roots may be facilitated by "old friend" models which define others as equally valuable as, but also different from, the independently affirmed ingroup ("us")—such narratives affirm the self independently but recognize and value difference, rather than assimilating others (as "like me" or "like us") in the process.

Of bullies and friends under ideological hegemony

What are the major constraints to pursuing inclusive interests under varying conditions of ideological hegemony involving narratives of relational power (e.g., bully or friend)? First, pursuing interests with inclusive borders is possible across the board: egalitarian "potential friend" relational models facilitate *inclusive* borders, while hierarchical "bully" relational models facilitate *exclusive* borders: "potential friend" models apply from individual to group, and from ideological hegemony to ideological choice. They involve defining others as either "like me" (under conditions of ideological choice, or where groups are newly or as yet undefined) or "like us" (under conditions of ideological hegemony, or where groups are characterized by more rigid, stereotypical narratives).

Second, pursuing interests with inclusive roots is difficult both under ideological hegemony and ideological choice, but for different reasons: ideological hegemony limits group imagination (e.g., due to particular narrative dominance) while ideological choice limits individual imagination (e.g., the lack of clearly structured narrative options from which to draw). The greatest opportunity for inclusive roots lies under conditions of imperfect ideological hegemony/choice, where actors can draw on existing narratives in ways more creative than constrained. Here, inclusive roots can be facilitated by drawing on an "old friends" model which increases identity complexity and value, so individuals can define themselves both as part of an ingroup and different from its hegemonic, caricaturized, ideal type. Social psychological discussions of intergroup bias suggest that such tactics might include increasing the value of (possibly previously devalued) subgroup contributions (the "jigsaw classroom"), defining subgroup members both within their subgroup and as a part of an overarching but complex superordinate group identification ("dual identity"), or focusing on subgroup members as part of the main group in some ways, but separate in other ways ("crossed identities") (see, e.g., Hewstone et al. 2002; Ruane 2010).

Overall, this suggests that pursuing interests with more inclusive roots may be possible as part of a two-step process: first, by pursuing interests with more inclusive borders, and second, by using that as a foundation to redefine interests more substantively. This does not mean either that increasing root inclusiveness is impossible as a first step, or that increasing border inclusiveness guarantees increasing root inclusiveness (neither is true). However, it does mean that inclusive roots may be more likely to follow inclusive borders than to arise independently. This is the case for multiple reasons: because expanding borders is possible across a broader range of conditions (from ideological hegemony to choice) than deepening roots (only under limited ideological hegemony); because affirming of "us" without denigrating of "them" is a critical (though limited) step toward valuing difference; and, finally, because comparing "potential friend" to "old friend" relational models suggest that certain kinds of friendship can both value and recognize difference.

Implications for women's human rights

What are the implications of this feminist constructivist model of inclusion for the case of women's human rights? In general, it suggests that pursuing women's human rights with more inclusive roots as well as borders can be facilitated by first expanding the borders of rights (e.g., extending "men's rights" to women), and then redefining those rights to be rooted more broadly in women's experience (e.g., redefining "women's rights as human rights"). As a review of women's human rights in the United Nations (1948–2008) suggests, these implications are supported by this case.

Women's human rights in the United Nations: historical trends

Since the founding of the United Nations, women's rights discourse has evolved in stages where governmental and activist actors tend to choose increasingly *valued* discursive frameworks over time as an often strategic method of increasing the attention paid to women's human rights. At the same time, this trend is moderated by another trend in which actors *redefine* existing frameworks increasingly inclusively by both extending their application and rooting them more and more in different women's lives. Although each discursive frame includes its own conceptual baggage, as well as benefits, this dual approach has over time enabled the conceptualization of women's human rights in ways which are both increasingly valued and increasingly inclusive of women with a diversity of experiences and concerns.[5] Below, I review these historical trends.

First, before the founding of the United Nations, discourse over women's rights was highly restricted because interference with "women's rights" was seen as a violation of centrally important state sovereignty. The "human rights" language introduced to address women's rights in the early twentieth century increased the importance of women's rights enough so that "state sovereignty" concerns were no longer able to immediately trump concerns about women's rights, as previously. Once women's rights concerns were on the table, they were then fleshed out more extensively. Discourse on "equality" recognized that women's role in childbearing did not preclude their work outside the home and expanded women's access to rights that were previously restricted to "protect" them.

Next, during the 1970s, women's rights again gained importance when the Commission on the Status of Women strategically reframed the debate using the popular language of economic development by focusing on "integrating women in development" rather than the relatively unpopular previous frame of women's rights. Again, once women's concerns were on the table, they were developed. Discourse expanded from "women in development" (WID) who had to be "integrated" into men's worlds, to "gender and development" (GAD) which recognized women's work as consistently "invisible, ignored, and undervalued" and institutions as needing to change extensively, rather than just including women in unchanged institutional structures ("adding women and stirring").

During the 1990s, the level of importance of women's rights stayed relatively flat (neither increasing nor decreasing in value) with the campaign for "women's rights as human rights", articulated alongside a continuing discourse on "development." The "women's rights as human rights" framework again developed women's rights based on women's experience: it moved from defining women's equality as being "on the basis with men" (relying on a male standard), to defining women's equality *as women*. This expanded women's rights by moving beyond the equality/difference debate, which required women to either have formal but not substantive equality in the form of identical rights, or to accept inequality and second-class citizenship because of social and biological differences with men; instead it suggested women could be "different but equal" by introducing a female, rather than male, reference point. This recognized that "equality" must be a two-way street: for example, not only must women have the right to participate equally in the "public sphere," but men must have the right and incentive to participate equally in an equally valued "private sphere."

Finally, at the turn of the millennium, women's rights again gained importance with the transition to a "women in peace and security" framework which framed women's rights as a basis for maintaining international peace and security. Since this framework is relatively recent, efforts to deepen conceptualizations of women's rights within it are only in their initial stages. However, the history of women's human rights discourse suggests there is room here to grow.

Overall, this analysis of women's human rights discourse clearly illustrates my conceptual model. Women's rights historically have evolved by drawing on alternative frameworks (e.g., sovereignty, human rights, development, security) when existing frameworks prove themselves overly restrictive for advocates' goals. Each new frame created the opportunity for increasingly inclusive borders of women's rights by creating a new understanding of who the women who were entitled to rights were. However, the introduction of each new framework also agitated existing discursive assumptions and created the opportunity for these new frameworks to be reinterpreted in increasingly inclusively rooted ways. This happened both within the "development" framework (especially from "women in development" to "gender and development") and the "human rights" framework (from what could be seen as "the rights of man" to "women's rights as human rights"). The "security" framework has begun along the same trajectory, although it is still too early to tell if this pattern will be followed again in this case. As such, this analysis of evolving women's human rights discourse provides preliminary support for my conceptual model.

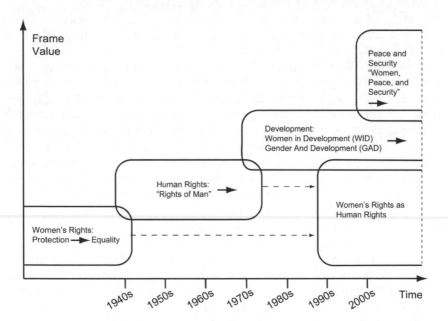

Figure 3.2 The evolution of women's rights discourse

Implications

This chapter has highlighted a conundrum for those who want to pursue more inclusive interests, whether in women's rights or in other fields. On one hand, it suggests that because dominant narratives rely on particular conceptions of *who those narratives are about* (the identity of the ingroup), utilizing abstract concepts—like "human" or "citizen"—tends to reinforce those frequently exclusive, hierarchical conceptions of ingroup narrative identity. This can problematically result in framing issues in ways which minimize or do not address important issues in the lives of many people. Furthermore, it often is particularly problematic for the experience of those who are not upper-class, white, Western men. For example, "security of person," which was affirmed by Article 3 of the Universal Declaration of Human Rights, was defined narrowly for a long time; only since the 1990s has it included rape as a violation of that security. The problem of defining things narrowly (e.g., based on elite male experience) is one which feminists have highlighted for some time.

On the other hand, however, recognizing ingroup complexity does not itself fully correct for this: increasing the inclusiveness of a group's borders or membership does not guarantee increasing the inclusiveness of its roots. In the area of women's human rights, this means that a strategy common today among activists lobbying the UN Committee on the Status of Women (CSW) of pushing to explicitly include lists of particular experience—such as gender, race, class, sexuality, development status, age, experience in armed conflict, marital status, etc.—is ultimately only a limited first step: It may raise consciousness to a limited extent, but does not guarantee equal valuing of difference. Particularly, tacking on "other" experiences (e.g., of non-elite women) in a "laundry list" fashion fails to equally prioritize or integrate those experiences within discourse. Consequently, this kind of approach frequently retains dominant (e.g., elite women's or men's) discursive perspective. In doing so, dominant concerns may be extended to other groups (increasing the inclusiveness of borders), but this is limited in its ability to deepen concerns based on diverse viewpoints (increasing the inclusiveness of roots). A more substantively inclusive alternative or second step would be to more extensively address particular issues from a broader range of perspectives; this would more meaningfully increase the inclusiveness of the roots of "women's interests." Feminist activist discourse which lobbies for "laundry lists" to raise consciousness would benefit from explicit recognition of the limits as well as benefits to this strategy, both to clarify feminist and broader inter-governmental discourse.[6]

The model which I have proposed suggests a broad principle for navigating this conundrum. First, it suggests that more *substantively* inclusive interests— with more inclusive roots, as well as borders—must rely on a narrative of group identity which *values* as well as recognizes complexity within its ingroup. Second, it also suggests that *claims* of inclusiveness—including "universal" rights—can be *evaluated* using the *standard* of "roots" and "borders": in particular, the inclusiveness of a discourse's roots can be evaluated by the extent to which the ingroup is recognized and valued in its membership complexity (reliance on an "old friend" model); and the inclusiveness of its borders can be evaluated by the extent to which the ingroup is recognized in its membership breadth (reliance on a "potential friend" or "bully" model).

In terms of social theory in general, this means that discussion of "the common good" must be held to explicit standards, since the "common good" is often less "common" than may at first appear: such "common good" should be evaluated relative to its roots and borders—How broadly based is the definition of "good"? (Who defines and interprets it?) And how broadly extended is the "good"? (Who benefits from it?) Because such a "greater good" tends to be defined by elites, the benefits of such good are frequently particularly interpreted and unequally distributed. Consequently, cloaking particular interests as the "common good" without evaluating who chose those particular goods as "the" good, and who benefits from them, can manipulatively rationalize unjust hierarchical systems with unequal distribution of goods, rather than promote goods which are more truly "common" for all.

This also means that certain costs or harms which are often rationalized for the pursuit of the "greater good" become much less acceptable: rationalization and normalization of hierarchy within and across issue areas supports narrow interests of elites over broader interests of others. Consequently, although it may seem counterintuitive to expend resources over more issue areas, focusing on any particular area (e.g., promoting either minority rights or women's rights) will ultimately be limited, because rationalization of hierarchical relations in one area support continuation of hierarchical relations both among and within other issue areas. This corresponds with some experience by women's rights activists, such as those who were successful in raising concerns against particular forms of Violence Against Women by recognizing all such violence as violations of women's human rights.

In terms of human rights in particular, this means that inclusiveness of the roots of rights can be evaluated by the extent to which "humans" are recognized and valued in membership complexity (who defines rights?) and the inclusiveness of the borders of rights can be evaluated by the extent to which "humans" are recognized as encompassing all people (who are rights extended to?). Furthermore, because more inclusive rights are possible under conditions of inclusive and egalitarian "friendship" than exclusive and hierarchal "bully" models, instances where rights appear to be in completion must be reevaluated in order to understand how assumptions of hierarchy or egalitarianism circumscribe opportunities for more just and inclusive definitions of rights for all.

Like Brooke Ackerly's "curb cut feminism," this approach similarly supports "destabilizing perspectives" to promote more inclusive interests under what I see as conditions of imperfect ideological hegemony. However, it also builds on Ackerly's work in two major ways. First, it suggests that because inclusive borders do not guarantee inclusive roots, it is not enough to rely on the skeptical scrutiny and guided deliberation of however diverse critics so "more of 'us' are visible" (Ackerly 2008b, 245). Instead diverse viewpoints must be valued (increasing inclusiveness of roots) as well as recognized (increasing inclusiveness of borders). Second, it provides a *standard* for evaluating inclusiveness claims, including "universal" rights claims: while Ackerly simply affirms contested rights as politically, rather than theoretically, disputed,[7] my approach can be used to evaluate how inclusiveness those claims are—whether restrictions are couched in political or theoretical language.

I will briefly reference one example in a "terrain of difficulty" particularly characterized by dispute, to illustrate without going into depth (see Ackerly 2008b, 241). In the case of sexuality rights, my approach suggests first that dominant human rights definitions have exclusive borders to the extent that they affirm the right to heterosexual identity but exclude the right to other kinds of sexual identity; and second that they have exclusive roots to the extent that they define human rights based on heterosexual human experience. Since, for example, the biological ability of two partners to conceive children together tends to be institutionally assumed and alternatives to this are not equally supported—and for LGBTIQ[8] individuals sometimes actively restricted—my approach suggests that both the roots and borders of rights in this area are limited in inclusiveness.

Although this is just one example, it illustrates how my approach complements Ackerly's by suggesting how a standard of inclusiveness which addresses limitations in existing "conversations" can be usefully applied. Future research which addresses pursuing more inclusive interests or rights would contribute usefully by developing these issues further as well as developing its applications and limitations. Useful questions to pursue include: What are the most effective ways to move from promoting more inclusive borders to more inclusive roots? How are such efforts made possible? Whose interests tend to remain excluded even from relatively "inclusively" oriented endeavors? Why? Research which begins to address these issues would increase the precision of the theoretical discussion and would provide valuable practical advice to practitioners in the process.

Conclusion

Like las Casas, women's rights advocates have gone through different journeys in pursuit of more inclusive human rights. In these journeys, advocates have pushed the discourse from exclusive and narrow "bully" relational models (similar to the Conquistador) to more inclusively bordered "potential friend" models (similar to the caring colonialist), to more inclusively rooted "old friend" models which value and recognize group diversity (similar to the other-respecting, anti-colonial, intercultural communicator). To pursue more inclusive women's human rights, or more inclusive interests of any kind, does not just require expanding the ingroup so that others like "us" can share rights or interests which "we" define (what I have called inclusive borders). It also requires increasingly recognizing the value and complexity within that ingroup so that there is a richer basis for articulating rights to begin with (inclusive roots). The most inclusively rooted rights also must be based on the principle of "all for one": where the interests of all can only be met when the interests of none are either exploited or exploitative. Although this may sound like an impossible ideal, this chapter has provided concrete strategies and standards which have been used and can continue to be used to progress in this direction.

Making the conceptual space of women's rights more inclusive is just one step in a broader struggle to make those rights meaningful to all people. Cheap talk is a serious problem, and big promises not backed up by action may be worse than none at all. Despite this, it is also evident that without bigger ideas, action is limited by the poverty of our imagination. As both feminists and Onufian constructivists recognize, relationships of power critically circumscribe such imagination. This chapter's focus was pursued with this in mind, and in the hopes that that this contribution to a "renewed conversation" between feminism and constructivist IR would help to create a richer basis for progressive and inclusive change.

Notes

1 For example, although human rights are supposedly indivisible and interrelated, civil-political ("first generation") rights supported by the West are frequently prioritized over socio-economic ("second generation") or group ("third generation") rights supported by developing and former Soviet bloc countries.

2 This is consistent with Hedley Bull's argument that: "to define the interests of mankind is to lay claim to a kind of authority that can only be conferred by a political process" (2002, 82).

3 Gramsci argued that the transformation of hegemony to overcome class-based political rule requires that "the relationship between teacher and pupil is active and reciprocal so that every teacher is always a pupil and every pupil a teacher" (Gramsci 1971, quoted in Rupert 2005, 491). While this approach has been interpreted economically for socialist, rather than capitalist, economies, it also more broadly supports a model of collaborative, rather than dominating, leadership.

4 "[W]hen the members' [of a cohesive ingroup's] strivings for unanimity override their motivation to realistically appraise alternative courses of action" (Janis 1972, 9).

5 My summary of the evolving human rights discourse relies on a Critical Discourse Analysis of women's rights discourse at the United Nations, 1948–2008, conducted in Ruane 2010. This focused on the following key events: the 1948 Universal Declaration of Human Rights; the 1979 Convention on the Elimination of All Forms of Discrimination Against Women, as well as its 1967 Declaration and 1999 Optional Protocol; the four UN Women's Conferences (1975, 1980, 1985, and 1995); and, to bridge analysis with discussion of important current events, UN Security Council Resolutions 1325 (2000) and 1820 (2008).

6 "Consciousness raising" as a term and method has been used in a broad and contested variety of ways, which makes it easy to blur different kinds of action together sometimes uncritically. This chapter suggests that the consciousness-raising process

(or "naming what's really going on" (Sarachild 1978)) can itself have inclusive roots and borders. Consequently, feminist activism for more inclusive rights can be evaluated using this chapter's proposed standard of inclusiveness. Furthermore, such activism *should* be evaluated if activists want to differentiate between more limitedly and more extensively inclusive steps taken, and avoid colonizing kinds of "inclusive" action.

7 Ackerly suggests that political, rather than theoretical reasons frequently underlie prevention of rights realizations for all but states that her approach "leaves no rights claims definitionally illegitimate" (2008b: 243, 269).

8 Lesbian Gay Bisexual Transgender Intersex and Queer.

Drawbridges, interests, and dialogue
An engagement with Abigail E. Ruane

Brent J. Steele

As a scholar trained as a constructivist but now dabbling in a variety of "schools" of thought including pragmatism, poststructuralism, and critical theory, I would like to begin by making the case that the prospects for dialogue between feminists and other IR scholars are better than many feminists or their critical scholar kin, might realize. If we choose to "cut" into theories and perspectives via the age-old "schools" way of thinking about IR theory, to organize our research questions based upon where they place us in terms of realism, constructivism, feminism, etc., then some of the explicit attempts at conversation and dialogue may indeed lead to the "awkward silences and miscommunication" noted by the editors in the Introduction. If, however, we instead approach our research questions in a second manner which is also intimated in the Introduction (citing Tickner 1997)—through the different questions that each *generation* of emerging critical scholars foreground in their work—then we might find much more intersectional ground. Indeed, I see in Abigail Ruane's essay a substantial amount of overlap with my own work, and find it a good starter (or "continuer") for a dialogue between feminist and other IR scholars

Feminist IR has had a nice rhythm of generations, and the current generation, while drawing on similar devices as previous feminist IR theorists, seem fully invested in their own set of unique research questions. Yet these questions are common to the current generation of other critical scholars. My own work in critical security studies, for instance, finds the themes explored by contemporary feminist security scholars such as Laura Sjoberg (2006) and Laura Shepherd (2005, 2008) quite instructive, for such work especially illuminates how different discourses create a variety of openings as well as exclusions for various global populations, and rearrange those subjects in "relation to each other" (see Shepherd 2005, 390). It is not a coincidence that many of the "cases" we engage and interrogate come from similar temporal (2000s) and spatial (U.S. security discourses) contexts. So it is in Abigail Ruane's essay, where we find an important set of devices—narrative, identity, security, and power—that both Onufian constructivists (I consider myself a qualified version of such), and more poststructural and critical feminist scholars utilize in their studies (Onuf 1989; Tickner and Sjoberg 2006).

Summary, overlap, and engagement

Abigail Ruane investigates how human rights via the notion of substantive interests might be both expanded and deepened to become more inclusive. Ruane's thesis rests on a fresh combination of Wendtian and Onufian constructivism, feminist theorizing (especially the work of Brooke Ackerly), and Gramscian notions of hegemony via "dominant narratives" to assemble a "feminist constructivist" model of inclusiveness regarding women and human rights. Looking back over this brief description, one can see just how ambitious this project is.

The model conceptualizes "interests" via Wendt as "beliefs about how to meet needs" (Wendt 1999, 130), where such interests are "informed by actors' narrations of their identities". Popular ideologies intervene, however, to "limit the creativity of the narratives of actors who draw on them." Onuf's intervention here is necessitated by his seminal observation that "rules yield rule," where relationships are in Ruane's characterization *asymmetrically patterned*. Yet these ideologies and the narratives that they manifest—drawing on the Gramscian notion of hegemony here—are like Machiavelli's centaur, both human and beast (Cox 1983, 164), resting on consent *and* force, and so they can be in Ruane's words *dominant* without necessarily becoming *dominating*.

This opens the door, then, to the possibility of inclusion. But, again, Ruane is cautious, taking nothing for granted about this oft-deployed concept. Her two-fold conceptualization rests on inclusive roots, those "diverse experiences from a broader range of group members, rather than ... elites," and inclusive borders, "big" (inclusive) versus "small" (exclusive) groups. She then illustrates this through a compact overview of such discourse—women's rights as human rights—in the United Nations.

While drawing on separate theoretical inspirations (McAdams/James for Ruane; Giddens and Foucault for me)—she and I can both be considered "Onufian constructivists" who centralize language and power in our studies. She, like I have in several studies (Steele 2007, 2008, 2010), focuses on the ability of narratives to constrain and enable different pathways for action. As she mentions, "high levels of ideological hegemony restrict creative reinterpretation of existing narratives." Language, to borrow the Giddensian frame (Giddens 1984, 1991), has a "duality." It enables action by simplifying the social world, ontologizing and organizing what is relevant from what is not "out there" and expressing the significance of the "who" of the subject towards this world. Yet language is also exclusive, identifying (in the context of rights), "who" deserves them, for what purposes and particular meanings.

But whereas certain docile forms of constructivism stop here, Ruane goes further, bringing forth the power in this, in two respects. First, power exists on the elite level with "those who construct meaning and create knowledge" (Tickner and Sjoberg 2006, 191). Such elites include those who embed meanings into these knowledge claims, who have the right to speak in the first place. Feminist analysis provides us a technique for how we might go about uncovering the implicit forms that power might take, and furthermore asks us to reflect upon how it operates even through our own "knowledge claims" (Ackerly and True 2008, 694). Power is also, in a second, more expansive notion, productive (Barnett and Duval 2005), manifesting through those subject to the ideological narratives who reproduce them (see also the Gramsci quote in her note 3). Such powerful narratives resist, in this level somewhat defiantly, a critical re-interpretation. In the "constraining" mode of discourse, low levels of ideological hegemony provide a different problem—they "limit the extent to which alternative experiences can be *understood and related to.*" What is the point of a simplifying narrative if it can be rearranged so easily? Such narratives are conservative to their core—speaking to (and for, and against) populations by standing the "test of time," excluding certain subjects over others.

Let's assess why Ruane's model is so important, so *vital*, for the topic at hand and the time we are in today. Primarily, it provides us an epistemological context, and medium, and diagnostic frame commonly ignored by liberals, liberal-constructivists, and liberal-feminists. It is rooted in a slow, nuanced, but sophisticated and *real* line of thinking that acknowledges the experiences of women in an expansion, and deepening, of human rights discourse. While liberal theorists like Michael Ignatieff might claim that the more such rights discourses are rooted in plural experiences, the more "watered-down" they become (2001), Ruane's model shows us the futility of such a "here are your rights, enjoy them" method of rights distribution. For unless they accommodate the context and dominant narratives that have to be "broken through," rights can have *no* meaning. There must be a dialectic that accommodates *interests*, in order for them to deepen, and to be more inclusive.

I only have two critical observations about Ruane's model. First, it is in between these two ideal-typical extremes that creativity finds its home, able to locate alternative and yet *intelligible* narratives (in periods of lesser dominance). Fair enough. But how do we "get" there—or, more properly, how do we move from one pole to the other? What "pushes" actors into a middle-ground of non-dominating but also intelligible, meaningful, narrative re-definition?

Ruane helpfully explicates the contours of the model itself, which on its own constitutes an ambitious-enough project, and she does indicate that "in between these two extremes, there is a broader variety of narratives available to be drawn on, and the *limiting factor is primarily the interpretation of existing narratives* as well as their number, value, accessibility and framing (e.g., the relative availability and perceived value of various relational models)" (my emphasis added). But to take it a bit further, let me suggest two ways in which this "narrative" understanding of action and identity can be manipulated to create the possibilities for what Ruane calls the broader inclusions of interests, ways which I and other collaborators have tried to outline in several other studies (Delehanty and Steele 2009; Steele 2010). To begin, if narratives depend upon some type of "internal feminine other" (and I think they do), then by the mere presence of this other, narratives can be rearranged—or at least reconfigured in ways that eventually "broaden" the field of inclusion. Further, what might push us towards a "deeper" understanding of rights, what forces us into this middle-ground of creative space—may be a traumatic experience— a "rupture" or "hole"—that demonstrates vividly what is "wrong" with par- ticularly exclusive narratives, a hole so substantial that it cannot be "talked around" or accommodated by the predominating narratives (see Debrix 2007). It must be altered, although this alteration itself is not free from poli- tics. Politics creates possibilities, exclusions, winners, and losers. The point is that these spaces (the "in-between" noted above), can be examined so that "it is possible to conceive of ways in which these objects and subjects could be *constructed differently*" (Shepherd 2005, 391).

A second observation is that, in an essay that I think diagnoses the "pro- blem" of discourse, power, identity, and human rights quite effectively, one might also consider how human rights and the language that invokes it/them, *is* a form of discipline (see Steele and Amoureux 2005). If the dominant but not dominating discourses in international politics are indeed masculinized (and I think they can be), a discourse which broadens and deepens still serves a multitude of interests, and it is a discourse that can come across as poly- valent—open to opposing interpretations, creating paradoxical relationships of conflict around the same discourses. An examination of the International Criminal Court, utilizing Ruane's model but also seeking out these relation- ships of conflict, would I think be fascinating, similar to the English School interpretation of the ICC by Jason Ralph (2005).

Future feminist-constructivist dialogues

While I am not in a position to comment on the past, present, and future of feminist IR research, I can, in the spirit of fostering a dialogue between fem- inist and constructivist research, suggest some opportune areas for intersec- tion and mutual engagement. My own recent work on aesthetics and power did engage—although in a much too limited fashion—the contributions of feminist work in uncovering and engaging the constructed notions of both power and beauty, and how these have implications for the security practices of global actors. My particular purpose in *Defacing Power* was to demon- strate how the bodies of global politics (my focus was on the U.S. "body") *practice* aesthetic branding, and that such a practice is itself part of a complex of *in*security. The insecurity, which is inevitably packaged in the hyper- masculinized ideologies like neoconservatism, comes from the inescapable attempt to attain an *ideal type* of (masculinized) aesthetic identity. I deter- mined that the highly emotionalized nature of aesthetic insecurity can be considered an almost anticlimactic by-product of a narrativized U.S. Self that centralizes "strength and will" against an internal feminine "Other" (see also Weldes 1999).

What I did not assert in that book, but should have, is that there is some- thing to be said for utilizing, before destroying or shattering, the dualisms or dichotomies that poststructural feminist IR has uncovered. Instead of dispensing with them, we might re-couple their appropriation—demonstrating how insecure, pressured, and cosmetically-focused modern U.S. and other Western security "practices" are, re-appropriating or inversing these dualisms/ dichotomies. This would entail a demonstration of how an "aesthetic identity" is itself a characteristic of the hyper-masculinized national/global "Self," but one that contains more "stock" for insecurity than any feminized identity or subject out there, carrying with it its own "beauty myth" (Wolf 2002). Like the famous exchange in the movie *Less than Zero*, it is not whether these "selves" of power are "happy" or even consistently secure, but whether they "look good." And in attempting to look good for an idealized masculine beauty that it can *never* fully attain, it has lost control of its own ontology, its own security.

A final point to consider in the conversations and dialogues over "rights", is the "voice" of the postcolonial feminist, namely how those rights are constructed and who gets to actually speak about these rights. A model like Ruane's should note how the notion that rights can be "extended and deepened" has to take care that it does not "repeat the pattern of subsuming non-western under western norms" (Hutchings 2008, 163). Yet this is indeed what her model begins to do, providing us with a good via media within which this conversation can continue. The expansion and deepening of rights discourses must be constructed amongst a *variety* of "alternative frameworks," but in doing so it is hardly a wild-eyed idealist articulation of cosmopolitan agreement over rights. Any expansion of borders or deepening of roots generates backlash—disruption, conflict, and even violence. Ruane's model is a welcome, cautious, and complex understanding of discourse, identity, and power. In other words, a perfect drawbridge upon which this generation of Onufian constructivists, critical scholars, and gendered theorists of IR and security, can continue to engage one another to avoid those awkward silences that have defined our various communities in the past.

4 Feminist problems with international norms

Gender mainstreaming in global governance

Jacqui True

Approaches to the study of international norms in IR have been informed primarily by constructivist frameworks. The rise of norms as a key concept in International Relations (IR) occurred at the same time constructivism emerged as a contending approach in IR in the early 1990s, part of the "reflectivist turn" in the field (Keohane 1989). The focus on "norms" emphasized the role of ideational factors in international politics that had been largely obscured by the field's predominantly materialist and rationalist ontologies. Since then, the topic of "norms" has become hugely successful, yielding an array of related concepts, such as socialization, normalization, diffusion, and the role of "norm entrepreneurs" in promoting the uptake of new norms (Finnemore 1996). But the process of norm creation and the power dynamics therein has largely escaped critical examination despite the constructivist focus on international norm-setting and diffusion as an alternative to the realist vision of the international system as competition among states for survival.

The assumption has been that international norms are "good things"; they are what bring states together to cooperate with one another beyond their narrowly conceived national interests, or, better still, as argued by Keck and Sikkink (1998) and others, they spread cooperative, liberal values throughout the international system, thereby socializing its actors into "better" behavior (see Finnemore and Sikkink 1998; Risse et al. 1999). "Gender" norms are among those thought to lead to better behavior. For instance, gender balance in state decision-making and women's presence as UN peacekeepers are emerging regulatory norms—justified on the basis of an embodied norm of gender difference—that are expected to promote more democratic, transparent, and less corrupt government and to civilize international peacekeeping thus bringing about greater peace and security.

Constructivists argue that ideas as much as material factors, such as a country's military strength and economic wealth, are major influences on international relations (Wendt 1999; Reus-Smit 2009). Purposive actors promote norms and over time these norms form structures which shape the interactions among states and non-state actors. Thus, norms engender both stability and change in world politics. As constructivist scholars have shown, new international norms often originate from the initiatives and activism of principled non-state actors, such as transnational advocacy networks, NGOs, global civil society, and/or social movements. Like constructivists, feminists are concerned with understanding normative change but they are equally concerned with bringing about normative change, removing old norms, such as patriarchal traditions and discriminatory bureaucratic rules, and creating new norms, for instance prohibiting violence against women globally, respecting women's rights as human rights, and promoting gender equality through gender mainstreaming and gender-balanced decision-making. By contrast as well with IR constructivist approaches, critical feminists seek to *trouble* old and new norms and uncover their possible biases, exclusions or silencing. The process of normalization, whereby certain ideas and relations are taken for granted, embodied and deployed to force conformity of subjects, is highly problematic from a feminist perspective. The key paradox explored in this chapter, is that even seemingly progressive international normative change involves a process of normalization wherein certain ideas and practices are taken for granted and thereby depoliticized. Feminists are advocates of norm change but not of change for its own sake that removes the debate and the argumentation behind the norm from explicit public consciousness. Normalising a certain idea, even the idea of gender equality, can render it static and unable to see new forms of violence and oppression. This process of normalization may effectively serve to undermine goals of gender equality. At the same time, what makes change so difficult from a feminist perspective is that efforts to bring about a new consciousness of gender equality which challenges traditional gendered hierarchies constantly run up against counter-norms and ambivalences, and consequently gender equality initiatives often fail to become institutionalized or widely practiced.

Given this major tension in grappling with norms and normalization, should IR scholars, including feminist IR scholars, promote norms, including those about gender equality or other new, gender behavioral practices? How could norm diffusion be a good thing from a feminist perspective given that those ideas and practices which claim to be normal or natural such as keeping women at home, in purdah, or protected as civilians or at work are often precisely the ideas and practices which have been known to harm women?

Having observed how norms of hegemonic masculinity and femininity have harmed so many women and men and have been so difficult to struggle against, feminists are hesitant to recommend the normalization of appropriate gender-specific behavior (Sylvester 1994b; Enloe 2004). The large-scale rape of women and girls in contemporary warscapes such as in Bosnia, East Timor, the Congo, and Darfur, for instance, provides disturbing illustrations of how embodied gender norms literally kill and provide a legitimate defense, drawing on traditional values, for femicide and other egregious violence against women. In order to answer "Why do soldiers rape?" Maria Eriksson Baaz and Maria Stern (2009) analyze the discourses soldiers use to explain the sexualized violence they commit. They show how the soldiers' explanations are "crafted out of statist norms around heterosexuality and masculinity produced within their society's military institutions and armed forces" (2009, 514). Moreover, they reveal how militarized masculinities in the Congo are constructed against femininity and use degrading images of women. In interviews with one of the authors, soldiers expressed their frustration at not being able to be a "real man" (able to provide for their wives and children and to receive in return the fulfillment of sexual and other needs) and discussed how this frustration "manifested in a negative and sexualized image of women" (2009, 507). For critical feminists, as with constructivists, there are no inherently good and bad women or men although constructed behaviors and norms are judged good and bad. However, feminists see gender socialization as a form of normalization and subject formation that is inextricable from a process of othering (Butler 1990, 1999). The creation of new subjects and citizens may aim to eradicate violence and hierarchy as in the cases of social movements against slavery in the nineteenth century and women's subordination in the twentieth century. But the "good" norms produced by these movements have in unintended ways also reproduced violence and oppression within the subject—for instance, as women and African-Americans have struggled to approximate white/male norms in order be considered equal citizens—and more generally—for instance, as the prohibition of (race-based) slavery and the legal achievement of women's equality have made it difficult to see and redress other forms of labor exploitation and violence against women in the private sphere.

The first part of the chapter discusses three major problems feminists have with the conceptualization of international norms by IR constructivists and provides an alternative conceptualization of norms from a feminist perspective. The second part of the chapter explores how two different types of norms—regulatory and embodied norms—interact in ways that serve to subvert good intentions and normative change in the fields of international development and security. Gender mainstreaming, an approach to integrating awareness of gender inequalities and differences in policymaking processes for the purpose of achieving greater gender equality and justice is taken as an example of a *regulatory* or *governmental norm* that is thought to lead to better behavior by states and non-state actors, conventional binary gender identities are taken as the example of an *embodied norm* that is often repressive to women and men. This part of the chapter argues that mainstreaming can reinforce "normal" gender relations despite the policy norm's transformative intent. Further, gender mainstreaming has been deployed instrumentally to further neoliberal forms of globalization and state security. Thus, processes of socialization that position international organizations as suppliers, teachers, and enforcers of norms may face various forms of resistance and are implicated in the production of power relations.

Problematising norms in International Relations

From a feminist perspective there are three main problems with constructivist approaches to international norms: (1) norms are not fixed rules, but are plural and dynamic in their content and in the degree to which they are internalized; (2) norms are not power-neutral—implementing them may create new patterns of domination and marginalization and feminists are skeptical that the process of internalizing norms will effectively bring about normative change and; (3) norms do not stand above power but result from global power relations and thus can reproduce them. Constructivist accounts of norms stress the power of ideas and are pitted against rationalist explanations of power as material—economic, military, and territorial. The power dynamics of norm creation and diffusion are seriously under-theorized in existing accounts. Each of these problems is discussed in turn.

Many constructivist scholars use the concept of "norms" to examine empirically and analytically aspects of international relations without explicitly addressing their content.[1] Constructivist approaches tend to treat discrete norms, for example the norm promoting international election-monitoring in new democracies, banning landmines or proscribing violence against women, as "things" that remain fairly stable in terms of their content (for a fuller argument see Krook and True forthcoming). Norms may take different forms, but while there is clear interest in norm creation, relatively little attention is paid to the power relations that give birth to—and continually shape and reshape—these norms.[2] For instance, we do not know enough about how the norm of human rights excluded and later came to include women's rights, how it was contested and expanded to take into account economic, social, and cultural rights as well as civil and political rights. Rather, in much of the constructivist literature the content of the norm is taken as given and "good," while scholars investigate an often one-way process in which norms emerge and are then diffused through international communication, advocacy and socialization (for example, on human rights see Risse et al. 1999).

In order to adequately comprehend processes of norm creation and contestation I distinguish two types of norms from a feminist perspective: embodied and regulatory/policy norms. *Embodied norms*, such as gender, race, and heterosexuality, are internalized in bodily practices and constitute the subject and his or her recognition by others. In this sense gender is not just a norm to be regulated but is itself part of the meta-normative structure that conditions what norms are possible (see Barnett and Duvall 2005, 20). Embodied gender norms determine how actors are allowed to define and pursue their interests and ideals. They define what legitimate knowledge is and what counts as a problem, and whose voices are represented, and whose are marginalized. Gender is not merely something to be added to IR research designs, like a new statistical method, let's say. Nor is gender equality to be studied as the diffusion of just another international norm, since gender together with race and other social categories are part of the discursive structure of all norms (see Prügl 1999; Hansen 2006).

The second type of norm is more familiar to IR literatures: *regulatory or governance norms* structure decision-making and policies at all levels. Examples include non-intervention, sovereign equality, rules determining citizenship and human rights as well as normative behavioral requirements such as accountability, transparency, and gender mainstreaming (Kardam 2002; True and Mintrom 2001; Krook 2009; Lombardo et al 2009; Wiener 2009). Regulatory norms such as gender equality may be adopted by states and NGOs in spite of the fact that they go against traditional gender norms precisely because they mean different things to different actors (Van Kersbergen and Verbeek 2007). The acceptance of a norm may initiate rather than resolve struggles over its content as it generates unexpected winners and losers (Sandholtz 2008). Given that such norms are constantly being negotiated in practice, they do not retain a single meaning, but develop many and shifting meanings in response to various interventions (Lombardo et al. 2009; Wiener 2009) and in different contexts. Gender norms are particularly elusive in this sense because they consist "of two parts, 'gender' and 'equality,' that are each highly contested" (Lombardo et al. 2009; Krook and True forthcoming). Due to variations in meanings across national contexts, the global gender equality regime has been "a story of debate, contestation and dissent in norm development" (Kardam 2004, 91). A telling indicator is the UN Convention on the Elimination of All Forms of Discrimination against Women (CEDAW), which is not only the most ratified human rights treaty by states but also the one with the most state reservations.

To summarize the argument thus far, norms can be distinguished by type and are often plural in their constitution and implementation. The failure of constructivist IR scholars who study norms to acknowledge and theorize this complexity has both impoverished our understanding of normative change and, from a feminist perspective, limited our ability to effect change. For instance, we may be more likely to succeed in bringing about global gender equality if we engage others in a debate about the meanings of gender equality normatively and empirically, knowing that these will be multiple and changing as they run up against socially-constructed, culturally-specific embodied norms, than if we assume there is a uniform, static benchmark of equality to achieve, and that we are the ultimate judges of success.

A second problem that goes largely unrecognized in the IR literature, but is illuminated by a feminist perspective, is that successful norm diffusion requires the displacement or silencing of competing and inconsistent norms. Meaning is made precisely by demarcating "other' subjects and practices which are "beyond the pale." It is a well–known insight in feminist, critical, and poststructuralist theories that meaning is made through difference and the production of otherness (Sylvester 1994b; Campbell 1996; Doty 1996). Subjects characterized as "other" in social and political relations experience both epistemic as well as direct forms of violence as a result (Jabri 2003). For example, in Peru, international development projects with mandates to promote gender equality often silence indigenous Andean women who may be in favor of a norm of gender "complementarity" with men rather than western versions of gender equality. This silencing has the unintended consequence of provoking everyday resistance, not only among men and women in indigenous communities, but among local NGOs who resist gender equity mandates (intended to address violence against women) imposed on them by Northern funders (Barrig 2006).

Marginalization, moreover, is part of the process of gendering—becoming a man or a woman—but also of the "degendering" that is required by some gender equality norms because they are seen as signifiers of (gender) oppression. Female genital cutting, wife-beating, and various forms of veiling are widely considered to be markers of women's subjugation and therefore inconsistent with gender equality norms associated with being a "modern", "western" or "civilized" citizen. France and Quebec, for example, have outlawed the practice of veiling in public legal and school systems while other western countries such as the United Kingdom have had controversial debates about the public presence of the veil. Gender equality norms ostensibly intended to empower women by expanding their freedom and autonomy often derive meaning from the cultural and political expressions they prohibit. But ironically these prohibited expressions, which, with the exception of veiling, are defined as forms of violence against women in international law, may be given political meaning and legitimacy by women precisely because they have been stigmatized by Western feminists (see Mohanty 1987; Merry 2006).

Given that an international norm may have different meanings and that this vagueness to the range of people who are required to change their behavior is precisely what facilitates consensus, determining what behavior constitutes a clear violation of the norm may be difficult. Yet it is crucial to identify the practices that violate the norm in order for a norm to function. Thus, in some cultural contexts, practices of veiling, wife-beating or genital cutting—*embodied gender norms*—provide the "negative" practices that must be eliminated which, along with the "good" behaviors to be encouraged, provide the content of *regulatory norms* of gender equality. These examples show why international norms, even gender equality norms, can be problematic from a feminist perspective. Regardless of their good intentions, norms universally applied frequently do not take account of power relations and cultural contexts nor do they anticipate the unintended consequences of adopting certain norms. Not only are norms such as gender equality vague, slippery, and incompletely adopted, they are substantially weakened by being both elitist—involving few stakeholders or voices—and subject to bureaucratic fads, so that other norms may continually compete with them.

Without participatory debate that allows women living under local customs to find a way to buy into new norms such as gender equality, they may be vulnerable to cooptation, attrition or even reversal as new norms emerge and take over the public space (cf. Crawford 2002). As feminist advocates of social change we cannot assume, for example, that gender equality, the meaning of which is always subject to contestation, has been achieved even in those contexts which have made seemingly impressive progress toward gender equality. The cost of making such an assumption that we have reached gender equality may conversely increase contestation of gender equality as a fundamental norm and lead to the ceding of legitimate political space for making arguments about gender inequality and injustice.

Feminists highlight a third problem with the constructivist view of international norms. Although feminist and constructivist approaches share social constructivist ontologies, constructivist scholars neglect power in analyzing norm creation and diffusion. They consider power to be external to norm creation, "treating it either as a material quantity or as located in institutions of the state" (Locher and Prügl 2001, 113). For example, Keck and Sikkink (1998) do not consider the international interests, agenda-setting and linkage politics that may lead some NGO and state actors to promote or adopt practices and laws against gender discrimination or violence while failing to adequately implement these laws at local and national levels (see Savery 2007). Feminists are deeply aware of how power shapes the very construction of identities or *embodied norms*, not just the *regulatory norms* that may be designed to change them. The power of the male gender or of whiteness, for example, is precisely in their normality, their invisibility and taken for granted status. Constructivist approaches focus on the international politics of norm creation and ignore the importance of embodied norms to subjectivity. Even when research on international norms does take account of gender or race or sexuality it tends to treat them in a nominal way, as independent causal variables or as case studies rather than something that is a core factor in how norms change and needs to be explained (see Carpenter 2006).

What are the implications of this feminist engagement with IR scholarship on international norms? Specifically, what are the implications of the discursive approach to gender as a traditional, embodied norm as well as a regulatory norm oriented toward changing behavior for understanding gender mainstreaming policies in global governance? What are the forms of power that the global diffusion of gender mainstreaming has produced, and what are its unintended consequences? Is gender mainstreaming better analyzed as a process of *normalization* rather than as a case of *norm diffusion,* and how do they differ? (cf. Krook and True forthcoming; True and Mintrom 2001). The next section considers some common feminist problems with the norms of gender mainstreaming as illustrated by the way gender mainstreaming works in international security and development policymaking.

Making gender a "normal" part of global governance

The United Nations, the international institution with the broadest global scope, defines mainstreaming as applying "a gender perspective in all policies and programmes so that, before decisions are taken, an analysis is made of the effects on women and men, respectively" (United Nations 1995, 116). Mainstreaming is based on the argument that gender equality cannot be achieved without considering the consequences of all policies on women as well as men, especially those that are disproportionately detrimental to women. The Beijing Platform for Action ratified by all state parties present at the 1995 Fourth UN World Conference on Women advocated mainstreaming as a new policy "norm" that involves working to "promote a gender perspective in all legislation and policies" (paragraph 207, section d). Mainstreaming is to be aided by the generation and dissemination of gender-disaggregated statistics, in order to "eliminate obstacles to the exercise of women's rights and eradicate all forms of discrimination against women" (paragraph 207, section c). Yet, the meaning of "gender" and "gender equality" are not well defined or discussed in the Platform for Action or in the UN Economic and Social Commission's definition of mainstreaming. Process is emphasized: a gender perspective is considered to be successfully mainstreamed "when it is so routine that it provokes neither conflict nor comment" (Bedford 2008, 95–96 quoting World Bank 2000, 2). Gender mainstreaming is clearly intended to change norms but the idea that a gender perspective will be made *routine*, and therefore *normalized* as opposed to reflective practice seems to run contrary to the very practices of gender analysis and feminist struggle in perennially making visible taken for granted power relations. Certainly advocates and analysts involved in gender mainstreaming should not be expected to continually justify their purpose and goals in the face of bureaucratic resistance but by the same token the arguments at the heart of the quest for gender equality need to be always refreshed rather than made routine and therefore ineffectual.

During the 1990s the mandate of many existing international and national agencies was expanded to include gender mainstreaming, replacing or supplementing their earlier focus on women's specific programs and women's development projects in response to changing political circumstances in global political economy and aid frameworks (see True 2003; Squires 2005; Jaquette and Summerfield 2006).[3]

A feminist approach to norms prompts us to ask what kind of social capacities, meanings, and knowledge does gender mainstreaming produce? Mainstreaming invokes demands to include perspectives on women's as well as men's lived realities to inform policymaking. The shift from women in development (WID) to gender and development (GAD) approaches brought men back in, and with that a concern to take culturally-sanctioned gender differences into account in the design, implementation and evaluation of policies in order to empower women in particular. Moreover, some current approaches to gender mainstreaming understand the subjects of policy as diverse with respect to gender, ethnicity, race, sexuality, class, etc. and incorporate this diversity in the policymaking process by addressing gender difference but displacing it as the sole axis of difference (Squires 2005; Verloo 2005).

In previous work I argued that the problems with gender mainstreaming had mainly to do with the diffuse way mainstreaming was implemented (Staudt 2003; True 2003; Barrig 2006; Hirschmann 2006). Here I am concerned with the concept of gender mainstreaming as well as its implementation. I use the critique developed above to analyze gender mainstreaming as it has been incorporated in peacekeeping and economic development policies carried out by UN agencies. The upshot is that in the many settings where it has been tried, mainstreaming has often failed to defend women's rights. As with most norms, the implementation of gender mainstreaming has provoked ambivalence and contradictory practice in local and global organizations, and among bureaucrats and citizens.

International development policy

Feminist development researchers agree that the adoption of mainstreaming norms in organizations like the World Bank is a successful outcome at the level of policy but has been less so at the level of practices (Jaquette and Summerfield 2006; True 2008; Prügl 2009). Jane Jaquette and Gale Summerfield (2006, 13) observe that in the 1990s in particular, "private investment greatly outpaced public capital flows reducing the reach of gender equity policies, which can shape bureaucratic but not market behavior." Constructivists have noted that the most contested norms are the least specific, while the least contested are the most specific, (i.e. those that are formulated as standardized, technical procedures, (Wiener 2009, 185)). Where gender mainstreaming has gone beyond rhetoric in development practices it has been implemented as an advanced technique requiring specific methodologies of policy analysis, impact assessment, monitoring, indicators and measurement of women's participation and gender equality. Gender is increasingly treated as a policy input rather than a normative ideal based on equality as well as recognition of difference. But ironically, as in the European Union, because development aid budgets have already been "gender mainstreamed" and therefore combined with the general foreign assistance budget, there is meager financial support to implement and monitor the strategy (Debusscher and True 2008).

"Gender equality is smart economics" according to the 2007–10 World Bank plan for addressing women's empowerment and gender equality in development. Even non-feminist IR scholars have begun to notice the Bank's take-up of gender mainstreaming as an illustration of international norm change. But what is most remarkable is the virtual failure of this analysis of World Bank gender mainstreaming to investigate either the origins of the mainstreaming policy norm at the Bank or its contested content (e.g., Hafner-Burton and Pollack 2002; Weaver 2010). Feminist analysis, by contrast, stresses the importance of looking at the very conception and origins of the norm as well as its contestation in, what constructivists call, "the external norm community" (i.e., those outside the institution, in this case, within feminist development movements) if you want to understand why it has failed to reach expectations, to produce "rule-consistent behavior."[4]

For instance, feminists analyze key weaknesses in the conception of the gender mainstreaming norm—that it focuses on acknowledging and addressing gender differences in policymaking while gender equality is often left relatively undefined—as well as its incomplete implementation. For example, Maruja Barrig (2006, 28–29) found that attempts to integrate gender in Andean development projects by international donor agencies ran up against the resistance of local (often male) practitioners who resented the imposition of so-called western gender norms. As a result, donor organizations came to understand hierarchical gender differences as cultural characteristics that should be respected by outside groups. Such political compromises perpetuate gender inequalities, including men's violence against women.

Making analysis of gender differences a core part of policymaking, however, does have the potential to destabilize gendered meanings and masculine hegemonies. As Elisabeth Prügl (2009) argues in her study of gender mainstreaming in German and European Union agricultural policy, well-administered gender mainstreaming may be able to recognize differences among women and the intersectionality of gender, ethnicity, indigeneity, class, sexuality and so on, including previously marginalized groups in policymaking. Compared with "equal rights discourses" which neglected women farmers, gender mainstreaming policy in EU rural development has allowed the recognition of new identities and agency for women as rural entrepreneurs. But this recognition also proscribes the possible meanings of women's difference through governmental practices, simultaneously producing empowerment and *normalization* of a particular version of rural femininity. This new norm of rural femininity is based on the observed binary difference of women's and men's entrepreneurship, wherein women's economic behavior is cooperative, sustainable, careful, modest, and contributing to rural development (as a state project) rather than any other goal (Prügl 2009, 187–88). Prügl concludes that gender mainstreaming is relatively successful in promoting the equal participation of women in current economic arrangements (2009, 194). The example of World Bank international development policy below further corroborates this finding.

Mainstreaming in the World Bank, the world's flagship development policymaking institution, has promoted international development policy and programming on men's role in the family and their equal responsibility with women for unpaid social reproduction activities (see Elias and Ferguson 2009). This policy focus has the potential to undermine men's hegemony in both public (labor market) and private (family/household) spheres by redefining gender roles. Kate Bedford (2008) shows how anti-poverty, gender equality policy in Ecuador promotes the model of dual earner/dual care family households. Bank gender policy seeks to expand women's labor market participation and "entrepreneurialism" while addressing their overburden of care responsibilities in the household. In order to achieve this goal, development projects are designed to help men acquire parenting and domestic skills and share responsibility for social reproduction activities with women. Bedford interprets these projects as normalizing heterosexual marriage as an anti-poverty strategy but they also promote women's economic independence and the possibility of cohabiting in families without marriage (also Bergeron 2003).

Nonetheless, as it is implemented, gender mainstreaming policy in the World Bank effectively privatizes (within the family) responsibility for development outcomes (Bedford 2008, 91–92). It does not address structural or institutional barriers to women and men's economic productivity including the lack of flexible work schedules and socialized childcare in many developing countries. Nor does the focus on redistributing the responsibility for social reproduction among women and men consider the gendered impacts of macro-economic restructuring and debt on people by suggesting institutional or structural changes to financing, investment, social-security or labor-market policies. Rather, Bank policy individualizes the problem and the solution as one of creating responsible citizens and appropriate gender relations ("gender sameness based on a male norm rather than difference") in the private sphere (see also Schild 1998, 2007). The dependence of national and global economies on informal household economies—and especially women's work—goes unquestioned. Embodied gender norms are redefined but also reinforced by the policy norm of gender mainstreaming.

Securitizing gender in international policymaking

As with international development policy, similar problems of cooptation and the normalizing of particular notions of gender identities and differences can be seen in efforts to connect mainstreaming to the remit of security policies within the UN system. Gender mainstreaming has made major inroads into UN peacekeeping and peacebuilding missions through the mandate of Resolution 1325 and, since 2009, UN Security Council Resolutions 1820 and 1888 (True 2009). Like earlier Women in Development (WID) language that has been accused of merely "adding" women to "development." Resolution 1325 proposes gender mainstreaming as a means to redress women's marginalization in peace negotiations, peacekeeping missions and peacebuilding processes (Cohn 2008). Resolution 1325 recognizes the need for greater gender expertise in planning peace and security operations, but focuses primarily on greater participation of women in peacekeeping roles, and much less so on the disproportionate impact of peacekeeping and peacebuilding operations. These impacts include the number of women who are internally displaced persons, the ongoing issues of violence against women, abuse by local and international peacekeepers, and sex trafficking. Women are expected to "civilize" peacekeeping missions and operations through their mere presence (New York Times 2010).[5] Claims have also been made that the presence of women has made an observable difference to peacebuilding outcomes in

Liberia where the first all-women UN peacekeeping troops have been stationed since 2008. The UN Secretariat has repeatedly emphasized the proven benefits of having more female peacekeepers, especially in regions where sexual violence has been or still is a serious problem.[6]

Here there is an assumption that uniformed female personnel will have more expertise and experience in addressing sexual violence, that they enhance confidence-building with the local community by presenting an organization that looks more like a civilian society than a military occupation force. Interestingly, as Jane Jaquette and Kathleen Staudt (2006, 31) argue, "mainstreaming might dismiss women-specific projects as too narrowly conceived but in the end" it needs to advocate for women-specific policies and programmes for practical reasons, for instance, because "women's leadership [or peacekeeping] is more readily nurtured in women-specific projects than in mixed groups". However, in so doing, mainstreaming essentializes women's difference from men rather than emphasizing women's equality with men— where equality is conceived as sameness of individuals as in the case of the World Bank programmatic focus on "reproductive sharing" above. Gender stereotypes are reinforced by the idea implicit in some gender mainstreaming that only the personal experience and gender identity of police or peacekeepers can increase responsiveness to protect and prevent sexual violence as opposed to a political mandate supported by leadership performance indicators and professional training of police and peacekeepers regardless of gender.[7]

Gender mainstreaming, as represented in UN Security Council Resolutions 1325 and 1820, is chiefly limited to the inclusion of women's issues, such as "women's role in peace-building," "the protection of women," and "women and girls affected by armed conflict." Conceptually, at least, women and girls remain passive victims protected by male soldiers, militarized states, or their male representatives on the UNSC. Such victimhood denies women the agency extended by Resolution 1325, perpetuating the stereotype of women as nonviolent peacemakers and men as violent aggressors. Resolution 1325 on women, peace, and security is also silent about the underlying gender roles that celebrate masculine aggression and condone violence against women, as well as the gendered socio-economic inequalities that make women more vulnerable during conflict and post-conflict situations.

The UN is a crucial actor in teasing out the contours and meanings of mainstreaming and gender equality norms, introducing opportunities but also possible limitations, such as reinforcing gender difference, in their effects. In countries like Congo, Liberia, Kosovo, and East Timor, local women's organizations have worked very closely with the UN Gender Advisor and Gender Affairs Units within UN peacekeeping missions to integrate gender perspectives in peacekeeping missions, transitional, and new governments. Together, they have promoted registration of female voters, and trained female candidates for campaigns and elections, coordinated gender mainstreaming across mission departments, and developed gender-sensitive programs and training for UN personnel and local police, including demobilization programs for security and military personnel (see True 2009). These initiatives in particular have tended to emphasize visions of gender equality that are not based on male as norm behavior or models but are sensitive to differences between women and men while not fixing or essentializing these differences.

Gender mainstreaming has been readily assimilated in these peacebuilding policy processes because it is presented as an organizing principle guiding policy that can be carried out with the use of technical tools. For instance, while consulting with women's organizations may be a key criterion on a gender mainstreaming checklist, mainstreaming does not necessarily mandate or monitor a gender quota for policy or decision makers.

A further critical problem with gender mainstreaming in international security as well as in development policy is that it has become closely aligned with neoliberal international norms seeking to incorporate women into western markets and individualism, even in conflict or post-conflict settings. In this context, where gender equality norms have been ostensibly "internalized" by western, developed states gender inequality and injustice are seen primarily as problems of developing countries. Yet the meanings of gender equality are always subject to contestation and to powerful interests affecting the implementation of gender mainstreaming in developed as well as developing countries. For example, the three UN Security Council Resolutions on women, peace, and security face serious implementation shortfalls.[8] In part, these shortfalls stem from the way these resolutions conceptualize the gender mainstreaming norm and international security as discussed above, but they also result from the power relations among states and UN agencies, bureaucratic delays, and deep organizational pathologies resistant to change—all of which undermine mainstreaming efforts in international security policy.

Gender mainstreaming in UNSC resolutions is based on a narrow, traditional vision of state security that, in the context of UN peace-building operations, privileges physical security and electoral machinery over social and economic security. This vision impairs the ability of women to procure basic housing, food, health, and education. For instance, after the withdrawal of Indonesian forces from Timor-Leste, the UN introduced a Transitional Administration (UNTAET) to govern the new nation from 2000 to 2002. Although immediately following the passage of Resolution 1325, UNTAET established formal legal and political institutions rather than addressing basic economic and social needs or human rights violations in the private sphere. The culture of impunity regarding violence against women was pervasive during the Indonesian occupation because women's lack of access to economic and social rights greatly increased their vulnerability to violence. Under UNTAET, domestic violence against women remained widespread and frequent across society (Hall and True 2009, 163–65). In the context of the newly formed state, "[v]iolence within the family became a way for men to reassert their domestic power" (Fitzsimmons 2007, 351–53). There are other post-conflict and reconstruction processes that mirror the situation in Timor-Leste.

Consequently, gender mainstreaming in UN peacekeeping missions has yet to bring about a real, substantive improvement in women's material lives following conflict.

Power relations among states and UN agencies have also limited implementation of gender mainstreaming in international peacekeeping and peacebuilding. Most member states have yet to adopt national action plans for the implementation of UNSC Resolution 1325, and the prospect of collective action remains bleak, since no conflict country will likely produce a national action plan unless other conflict countries do so as well. Some conflict countries actually perceive these national plans as tools of rich donor countries applying conditionality to their development assistance and with private investment interests, and in fact the majority of states that have already created national action plans for implementing 1325 in their foreign and security policies are Northern, developed nations.[9]

In the years since its official adoption at the 1995 UN women's conference in Beijing, mainstreaming has evolved into a highly-specialized approach within national and international politics increasingly emphasizing state security rather than equality or justice. We have seen extreme examples of instrumentalizing "women's rights" in security policy. Violations of women's rights have been used as an excuse to justify the invasion of Afghanistan (and the need to maintain troops there (Shepherd 2006)), and to legitimize the resistance of the Mexican and Australian governments to indigenous demands for autonomy (Speed 2007). But perhaps the most dramatic example is the way in which the goals of gender mainstreaming have been shrunk to fit in with the recent mandate to make protection from and prevention of sexual violence in international conflict a priority (e.g., in the UN mission in the DRC (MONUC)). Focusing on sexual violence in the context of state insecurity and conflict, while seemingly appropriate given its gravity, risks perpetuating the invisibility of various other forms of violence against women, including routine domestic violence in peacetime and within ethnic/national borders. Lacking any thoroughgoing analysis of the complex gendered social, political and economic inequalities that shape women's vulnerability to violence in whatever setting, UN mainstreaming of sexual violence tends to reinforce embodied gender norms that view women as inherently victims of violence—and thus, objects of protection—and men as the power holders.[10] A systemic, human security response involving the provision of social and health services and access to justice rather than merely a state security response is required to begin to address and alleviate the causes of egregious and endemic sexual violence in conflict and post-conflict settings.

In sum, gender mainstreaming is not so much an advance on previous global and state strategies for achieving gender equality than a deployment of different forms of power, privileging different kinds of subjects; female entrepreneurs more than undocumented women workers, female peacekeepers, and victims of sexual violence in armed conflict rather than domestic violence victims or male and female social workers. As gender has become more *de rigeur* in international security and economic development policymaking it has become increasingly diffuse and able to be assimilated within bureaucracies without challenging political or economic power structures (Hirschmann 2006; Jaquette and Staudt 2006). Yet, for new democracies or developing countries there is little practical UN, World Bank or EU guidance as to how to implement mainstreaming given limited public resources and the increasing reliance on private investment in meeting development and security objectives. As a result, the gender mainstreaming norm may mean very different things across diverse states. In a post-conflict peacekeeping operation, there is likely to be minimal state administration; in these instances officials may focus on one achievable goal, often that of increasing women's participation in decision-making processes. By contrast, developed states with existing bureaucracies have greater capacity for applying gender analysis to government policies. Thus, mainstreaming gender equality meanings and perspectives in ways that challenge and seek to change existing hierarchical and embodied gender norms requires strong states or international administrations not the lean, efficient states purported in recent neoliberal development and security thinking.

Conclusion

Feminists in IR are concerned both with identifying salient gender norms and with displacing them, to the extent that they fix the possible meanings of women, men, and gender equality, and constrain women's autonomy in particular. By contrast, IR constructivists have focused largely on documenting and examining the global diffusion of new international norms, paying less attention to their normative content and power dynamics. This constructivist predilection is due undoubtedly to its theoretical purpose of countering rationalist arguments about the primacy of material power over ideas and norms in international relations. Despite these differences in approach, both feminist and non-feminist IR scholars have noticed the currency of gender mainstreaming as an approach to achieving gender equality and as a case of international norm diffusion. However, only feminist perspectives subject gender mainstreaming to critical analysis, given feminist skepticism about theories of norms and international diffusion, and the normalization they imply.

A critical feminist perspective concludes that while gender mainstreaming has made small achievements toward changing organizational structures and policy rhetoric in global institutions, the spread of the policy norm has not yet made ending gender inequalities a sustained or central objective of state or international organizations. Rather, mainstreaming often strategically deploys and reinforces traditional embodied gender norms at the same time as it has made it easier to use women's rights, participation and productivity as a means to achieving international development and security goals that are often not directly connected to women's rights or empowerment. As teachers of norms, international institutions are not removed from power politics or the perpetuation of global injustice. Indeed, efforts by these institutions to mainstream and diffuse gender equality may end up entrenching—rather than transforming—dominant gender norms and international power relations as discussed here with respect to international development and security policy-making.

Notes

1 As well as taking issue with constructivism's self-avowed "non-normativity," critical theorists and feminist scholars observe the inconsistency between the social constructivist ontology informing constructivism as a theoretical approach and the rationalist or objectivist epistemology and methodology deployed in some constructivist research [Price and Reus-Smit 2001; Locher and Prügl 2001]. For feminist scholars contributing to the constructivist research programme, denying the scholar's own normative position and relationship to research subjects, and adopting rationalist methodology both contradicts feminist commitments to reflexivity in research and reinforces conventionally masculinist ways of knowing (see Ackerly and True 2010).
2 For important exceptions see critical-constructivist scholarship by Reus-Smit (2001; Carpenter (2007)).
3 Jaquette and Staudt (2006: 18) argue we should see WID and Gender and Development (GAD), later gender mainstreaming, models as successive efforts to respond to—and influence—the changing policy environment, that included the shift from a Keynesian to a neoliberal economic framework, rather than "competing truths" about how to approach women and development.
4 For a critical analysis of the evolution of women and gender in international development norms see Jaquette and Staudt (2006).
5 Doreen Carvajal, "The Female Approach to Peacekeeping." *New York Times*, March 5, 2010; see www.nytimes.com/2010/03/06/world/africa/06iht-ffpeace.html?ref=global-home.
6 "Women UN Peacekeepers more needed – an advantage." IRIN Global – Humanitarian News and Analysis – a project of the UN Office for Humanitarian Affairs, May 20, 2010.
7 For instance, it has been possible to train police in New Zealand to protect and prosecute domestic violence incidents, which represent over 50 percent of all police call-outs although more than 85 percent of police are male (notwithstanding efforts to promote gender integration within the New Zealand Police Force).
8 The examples in this section draw substantially from True 2009.
9 In the case of developed nations this includes the provision of aid to developing countries to develop and implement their own action plans.
10 In Resolutions 1325, 1820, and 1889 the UNSC has linked the scourge of sexual violence to international insecurity and stressed that it needs to be addressed in all conflict situations. In the most recent Resolution 1889, the UNSC has elevated ending sexual violence in conflict above other forms of violence against women and all other issues and objectives relating to women and gender equality in peace and security, including the importance of women's participation in conflict-resolution and peace-building (see True 2010).

Problems, norms, and global governance
An engagement with Jacqui True

Jane S. Jaquette

Whether "mainstreaming" is effective has been debated since it was introduced over 20 years ago. The arguments for mainstreaming, as an improvement over women-specific programs and projects carried out by bilateral and multilateral assistance programs, are well known. The arguments against it have largely focused on lack of implementation. Mainstreaming requires a high level of commitment on the part of the organization as a whole, which is rarely forthcoming. Mainstreaming is a norm that has not been "normalized." To this literature, which focuses largely on practices and bureaucratic obstacles, Jacqui True has added a theoretical dimension, bringing a critical feminist perspective to bear on the process of international norm creation itself.

In doing so, True raises several important points worth pursuing. The first is True's feminist critique of norms and normalization. True asserts that constructivists view norms as unproblematic, discrete, and stable "things" to be advocated, taught, and internalized in order to produce "better behavior" while ignoring the role that power plays in these processes. But, she argues, norms are not discrete givens, like laws, but rather performative and open to interpretation. As evidence, True cites Van Kersbergen and Verbeek's (2007) thesis that flexible, "regulatory" norms are the most likely to be adopted because "they mean different things to different actors" (6). In the UN context, for example, countries can agree to abide by gender equality norms, but both are contested terms, so the content is not clearly spelled out. To this I would add this touch of "realism": that countries may make commitments when they do not expect to be held to account. This makes a project like the Chilean-based Index of Commitments Fulfilled (ICC), which has been established in several Latin American countries to keep track of how well governments are doing on reaching the goals they committed themselves to in Beijing and Cairo, an important initiative (Valdés and Donoso 2009).[1]

Norms may be "slippery" but True also believes they have consequences. Drawing on Barnett and Duval (2005), she argues that gender is among those "normative structures and discourses" in the international arena that "generate differential social capacities for actors to pursue their interests and ideals" and that "constitute the possible, the natural, what counts as a problem, as legitimate knowledge, and whose voices are marginalized." This opens up two additional questions that go beyond implementation: who is empowered by gender mainstreaming, and who is marginalized by it?

Finally, True is concerned that feminist norms or prescriptions for change have been hijacked to serve other purposes. The treatment of women under the Taliban was used by the George W. Bush administration (with support from many feminist groups in the United States) to help justify invading Afghanistan. Women's need for cash incomes has been used to induct them into the globalized labor market. An earlier but still powerful example of instrumentalizing is the way maternal and child health programs were used to promote population control, an issue on which feminist criticism was much needed, but almost entirely lacking until the 1994 Population Conference in Cairo (see Jaquette and Staudt 1988).

As I grappled with what I considered some of the main problems with True's critique, I realized that what I considered flaws in her argument instead provide important windows into the increasing complexity of promoting gender equity on a global scale and pose challenges to contemporary feminist practice as well as theory.

Norms and normalization

True asks how norm diffusion could be a good thing given that ideas and practices, seen as normal, are often harmful to women (p. 74). But, I wondered, is it a good idea for feminist theory to "trouble" norms by being skeptical of processes of normalization? Isn't True ignoring the critical importance of norm change as a feminist strategy? I believe it was Shulamith Firestone who pointed out that feminists are not going to succeed by arming themselves and building a revolutionary base in the Adirondacks. Norm change is unquestionably women's most effective weapon and, given that norms have to change for laws and behavior to change, indeed, their only weapon. So the idea that feminists should be skeptical of norms *per se* seemed self-defeating, and that True's desire to use gender mainstreaming to attack constructivism seemed to say that feminist theory should cut the ground out from under virtually all feminist advocacy.

In addition, I thought True has missed an important distinction between *normalization*—the unexamined and unquestioned acceptance of rules that are internalized from habit or fear—and *norms*, in the constructivist and feminist mode, which involve a conscious process of rule creation precisely to challenge "normalized" behavior, with the gender lens (ideally) assuring that men, too, are involved in the process. In general, efforts to construct, disseminate, and teach (new) international norms can be defended as counterhegemonic, undermining existing practices that are deemed unfair and oppressive (or, in the case of the environment, practices that may be profitable and convenient in the short term but damaging and unsustainable over time).

These "new" norms deploy moral arguments against existing practices that have become "normalized" as natural, or self-interested, or both. That is what makes them "constructed" rather than given.

Although True distinguishes "embodied" from "regulatory" norms, she does not make a distinction that would be salient to realists: the difference between norms and laws. When there is wide international agreement, and states are willing to band together to use force to implement them, norms can meet Hobbes's criterion for laws, i.e. that rules can only be understood as laws when they are punishable by the sword (*Leviathan*, Chapter 15). Even a cursory look at the last half century of international relations suggests that there are many more examples of norm creation than of effective norm enforcement, so few norms are actually laws in Hobbes's sense. What makes norms effective is not the coercive power of a sovereign state, but *social control*. This is generally considered a good thing by constructivists, because social control appears to achieve order by "consensus" and without violence. Many constructivists also like the way that processes of norm creation and implementation blur the distinction between states and civil society, and involve many actors, not just the state.

As Michel Foucault has made us aware, however, social control is a coercive normalizing process that leads to the acceptance of rules, both old and new, that should be questioned on the grounds of whom they benefit and whom they may marginalize or exclude. It is not the unquestioned weight of patriarchal traditions that is worrisome, then, but the contemporary power of social control, "normalization" in real time. This makes True's questions of urgent concern. Who is the "we" that participates in the construction of contemporary norms? What are the power dynamics at play in gender mainstreaming? Who benefits? Who is marginalized?

Gender mainstreaming as a bureaucratic strategy: cui bono?

Gender mainstreaming is an international norm that arose from a debate between two models of doing development work "for" women. Gender and Development (GAD) emerged in the 1980s as a critique of WID (Women in Development), which had only gotten off the ground in the mid-1970s. I worked in the WID office of the United States Agency for International Development (USAID) in the late 1970s, when getting women on the international agenda and into the routinized practices of foreign assistance agencies was seen as a daunting challenge (cf. Goetz, 1997; Staudt 1997). I first heard of mainstreaming (before the term "gender" itself was in wide use) at a conference hosted by the Population Council in 1981, where Nadia Youssef (who had gone from the International Center for Women's Research in Washington to the United Nations Children's Fund (UNICEF)) argued forcefully that trying to reach women through projects focusing on women alone was too narrow an approach, and that having an office specializing policies and programs for women only "ghettoized" women's issues. Instead, UNICEF was giving up its equivalent of the WID office and "mainstreaming" attention to women throughout its programs.[2]

The debate over mainstreaming versus women's "units" eventually settled into an agreement that both are needed. Mainstreaming is necessary to expand the scope of impact and women's offices are needed to monitor, advocate, and innovate. By the end of the decade, mainstreaming as a practice (as distinguished from what was characterized as WID's "women only" approach) became a key component of the new gender and development (GAD) strategy as championed in an article by Caroline Moser in *World Development* (Moser 1989). Moser's outline of what GAD offered had several elements. GAD was egalitarian in its view that women should be trained in "male" skills, not just be trained to market the "female" skills they had in crafts or food production, as WID had done. GAD emphasized that women had rights to land and housing, and focused on women's need for child care (although some WID projects also promoted these objectives). GAD chided WID for failing to recognize that women already had serious constraints on their time, arguing that women's unpaid and undervalued work already meant they were "integrated" into development, but in very exploited ways.

Unlike WID, GAD would look not just at women but at men, at "gender relations," recognizing explicitly that the power relations between men and women would be relevant to the effective design and implementation of projects. And unlike WID, GAD was critical of the policies of the "Washington Consensus." Moser's critique was not directed solely at USAID, however, as she asked pointedly whether UNICEF's structural adjustment programs to establish a "safety net" for women disadvantaged by neoliberal cutbacks in state spending could possibly "increase the independence of women."[3]

On one level, GAD can be understood as a successful constructivist power play that constructivists would recognize as their own in that it involved redirecting policies by changing the normative structure in which women were included in foreign assistance programs. GAD displaced WID as the dominant paradigm. Part of its success was due to its bureaucratic appeal, as GAD offered agencies suffering from "WID fatigue" a fresh approach. And part of it was its value to the European and Canadian bilateral assistance programs as well as UN agencies in displacing USAID from its leadership role in the field and in associating USAID (which focused on microcredit and "entrepreneurship" during the Reagan administrations of the 1980s) with "neoliberalism." The turn to gender also had an internal bureaucratic dimension. Moser argued that, by bringing men back in, GAD could distance itself from the feminist shrillness associated with WID, which would create less resistance from men. Although it identified gender as an issue for development programming, GAD did not require that programs for women confront gender inequities. Moser adopts Maxine Molyneux's distinction between practical and strategic gender interests (with practical referring to women's survival needs, and strategic to gender power relations), but changes "interests" to "needs" to more closely conform to development discourse which recognizes "needs" but not the more political "interests." She then suggests that aid agencies do not need to frame their projects in "strategic" gender terms as Moser argued that not every program needed to raise "strategic" issues (which she relabeled "needs"), but suggested that "Third World women themselves could chose how to make their practical needs strategic" (quoted in Jaquette and Staudt 2006, 30–31).

Finally, it must be said that, although discussions of these issues were informed by project experience, including needs assessments, evaluations, and considerable soul-searching involving practitioners, policy-makers, and academics, the women "beneficiaries" of WID and GAD projects did not have a voice in these debates. As True notes, "[w]ithout participatory debate that allows women living under local customs to find a way to buy into new norms such as gender equality, they may be vulnerable to cooptation, attrition or even reversal as new norms emerge and take over the public space" (p. 78).

Gender mainstreaming, marginalization and social control

In applying the gender equality norm to an assessment of gender mainstreaming, True seems genuinely, even passionately, committed to two positions that seem contradictory. On the one hand, she questions whether the norms that underlie development projects intended to empower women are the right ones. Would Andean women prefer complementarity to equality as the appropriate norm for gender relations in their communities, she asks (p. 78), drawing on a study of NGO resistance to implementing gender equality criteria in development projects in Peru (Barrig 2006). Later, however, True faults the lack of full implementation of the gender equality norm as the problem when, citing the same article (Barrig 2006), she argues that when donor recognition by donor organizations recognize that "hierarchical gender differences" as [were] "cultural characteristics that should be respected by outside groups" this is a represented "compromise" that "legitimate[s] and perpetuate[s] gender inequalities, including forms of violence against women" (p. 82). Thus, although "Western" egalitarian views can "marginalize" indigenous women, the failure to address the patriarchal practices of indigenous cultures denies women's rights. And, as she notes, gender equality norms "ostensibly intended to empower women by expanding their freedom and autonomy often derive meaning from the cultural and political expressions they prohibit" but "ironically these prohibited expressions ... may be given political meaning and legitimacy by women precisely because they have been stigmatized by Western feminists."

True observes that "processes of socialisation that position international organizations as suppliers, teachers, and enforcers of norms may face various forms of resistance and are implicated in the production of power relations" (p. 75), while suggesting that it is one thing to talk about regulatory norms and quite another to engage in promoting social change in "embodied" norms, that shape an individual's identity and moral anchors. An example of the difficulties that arise here can be seen in her discussion of child care. At one point, True is quite critical of programs that simply assume that women will continue to perform their traditional gender roles, providing free caretaking labor, but at another she cites Kate Bedford's critique of a World Bank project in Ecuador (Bedford 2005), which promoted shared male responsibility for child care and household work, as "normaliz[ing] heterosexual marriage" (p. 83). As the study's author, Kate Bedford herself, writes:

> the Bank … reinforces a definition of good gender analysis as requiring sharing, balanced partnership, a profoundly privatizing conceptualization which leads to privatizing policy solutions fixated on micro-adjustments in loving partnerships. The conflicts likely to step from these adjustments are overlooked.
>
> (2005, 316)

Is Bedford's critique telling because it opposes "heteronormativity"? Because it suggests that trying to change "embodied norms" inevitably crosses a line of "intimacy"? Because the project was carried out to "privatize" development solutions, thus implementing the neoliberal model? Or all three? In the end, True recognizes a "compromise" of sorts. Although Bedford interprets these projects as normalizing heterosexual marriage as an anti-poverty strategy, True notes that they also "promote women's economic independence and the possibility of cohabiting in families without marriage" (p. 83).

After pondering what seemed to me inconsistencies, or perhaps "compromises" in True's argument, I finally concluded that they are in fact a reflection of the complexity involved in doing "women in" or "gender and" development. As more projects are tried, no matter what their rationale, the more difficult it becomes to develop projects around the norm of gender equality while at the same time respecting the norm of diversity. These conflicts may be negotiated over time, but doing so will require "compromises." Further, those compromises will inevitably blunt the power of the gender equity norm itself, which has had a significant impact globally, nationally, regionally and locally, as demonstrated by a plethora of UN conventions, regional institutions, and even declarations made by various indigenous groups.

This tension between gender equality and feminist diversity is clearly visible in Virginia Vargas's recent essay on the challenges and opportunities for feminists in the World Social Forum (CWSF). For example, although the right to abortion has been seen as an important goal of feminist movements in Latin America as well as in countries of the global North, as a measure of women's rights and therefore of gender equity, feminists in India see abortion as the means by which parents exercise their preference for male children by aborting female fetuses, a consequence abhorrent to feminists. Vargas remains optimistic: "In this process, struggles *against* material and symbolic exclusions and *for* redistributive justice and recognition create a new politics of the body.

Dialogue among diversities constitutes one of the ways feminist and women's movements are seeking to have an impact" (Vargas 2009, 150).

Yet Vargas also reports that at the WSF meeting in Nairobi in 2007, a Catholic leader, Fray Beto, whom she describes as "a well-known progressive theologian committed to social movements," gave a speech in which he declared that the feminist movement "rose and fell in the twentieth century" and that feminists should no longer be considered international actors or committed to the transformations called for by the struggle against neoliberalism" (Vargas 2009,154). There was a strong feminist response to this charge, but Fray Beto's dismissal of feminism as no longer relevant is a worrisome sign. Social movements follow an arc of rising and declining influence. Their most important impact is that they change social norms, and they are in trouble when their normative claims and commitments are not taken seriously and this in turn may affect the ways in which other groups in "international civil society" will choose to invest their moral and material resources, support feminists have been able to rely on, but feminist influence internationally may be waning.

Instrumentalizing the gender equality norm: the case of neoliberalism

Frey Beto's comment is unintentionally ironic given that academic and activist feminists, in North and South, have been virtually unanimous in their condemnation of "neoliberalism," and it is throwing down the gauntlet to expel them from the ranks of the loyally opposed. On one level, this confrontation at the WSF could be predicted given the growing hostility of the Catholic Church to feminist demands for reproductive rights and sexual choice. But Fray Beto could have reason to believe that he is riding a new normative wave. Rural indigenous groups in Latin America, for example, question whether feminism is a "western" imposition and in so doing try to exclude the demands of a movement they label as white/mestizo, urban, upper class and "foreign." In the turmoil of Andean ethnic identity politics, which has been structured in part around opposition to "neoliberalism," the norms of gender equality and "women's rights" have become political footballs. The constructivist view that norms would emerge, be "taught" and internalized, and thereby create a new, progressive and relatively stable world order, seems a bit naïve (Waltz 1959).

True cites several studies that argue that WID and GAD projects have become coopted into the neoliberal project. But I believe that the argument that women and/or gender and development are simply tools to further "neoliberalism" is becoming increasingly dated. Veronica Schild's (2000) critique that support for women's participation in democracy in Latin America is creating "neocitizens" is a strong assertion of that point of view. It is similar to assertions of those like Nancy Postero (2007) or Charles Hale (2002), who argue that the association of neoliberalism with multiculturalism in Bolivia and Guatemala is a cynical ploy to coopt the indigenous. But these analyses underestimate the agency of the indigenous and, I would argue, of women, which True recognizes when she speaks of the resistance to efforts to impose international norms. The contemporary anthropological literature, including Postero's own account, shows that the indigenous are resisting, appropriating, and negotiating with "hegemonic strategies of incorporation and exclusion" (Paulson 2006: 662, quoting Carmen Medeiros), which go well beyond market rationality to the daily oppression of racism and classism.

In Bolivia, as Postero and others document, the indigenous used the opening given them by multicultural policies to organize, successfully oppose the privatization of water in Cochabamba, and elect Evo Morales Bolivia's first indigenous president; in Ecuador, protests led by indigenous movements helped throw out two presidents. What women or the indigenous do with agency once they have the space to exercise it cannot be judged by what those from the "outside" expect or would like them to do.

The coherence and power of the neoliberal model has been overrated and the model itself has been displaced, at least in Latin America, by the election of leaders in several countries who campaigned and were elected on anti-neoliberal platforms, and who have moved to strengthen the state. Today Latin Americans are debating the meaning of the "turn to the left" in countries from Brazil to El Salvador, with Venezuela declaring itself the exemplar of "21st century socialism." Yet the problems of empowering women remain. It is not too soon to observe that the more radical of these "new" leftist governments actually seem less interested in promoting feminist agendas than their "neoliberal" predecessors, and that some are proving themselves quite capable of excluding feminist groups, along with other independent civil society organizations, from the political arena. Neoliberal governments are now a distinct minority in the region, and it will be necessary to begin assessing these governments on the basis of their policies and performance, not on rhetoric alone.

Conclusion

What originally struck me as problems with True's argument—that women should be skeptical of normalization despite their dependency on the constructive power of norms, and that gender equality norms can be construed as both inappropriate *and* inadequately implemented—turned out for me to be spurs to recognizing where "we" are in the arc of a social movement based on "Western" political theory as well as to acknowledging that doing "development" for/with women has become a more complex and therefore more challenging task. True's point that theory has not caught up to experience is well taken.

Feminism is compatible with liberalism (and through guilt by association with neoliberalism) in its insistence on making the individual, and individual choice, core values. When Victoria Schild says that neoliberalism condemns women to a form of citizenship based on "individual choice, personal responsibility, control over one's own fate, and self-development" (2002: 282), feminists can hardly say they reject those goals. What feminists can reject, as Schild also urges, is the idea that these qualities of citizenship make women individually responsible for the economic conditions under which they live, denying the responsibility of the state for investments in education, health, and other social services.

Perhaps the new leftist governments in Latin America will also try to "coopt" gender equality norms, but I fear that, like Fray Beto, they will decide they can simply ignore a movement whose time has passed. It is already clear that even the most anti-neoliberal of the new leftist governments are also committing the "neoliberal" errors of relying on women's unpaid labor and reinforcing essentialist and "heteronormative" models of gender relations, while failing to address (or reversing progress made on) women's strategic gender interests.

In this emerging international environment, where indigenous and populist attacks against feminism find common cause with those put forth by the Catholic Church and radical Islam, feminists should not strive to delegitimize norms. Instead they should seek to find ways that "compromise" and "dialogue" can strengthen the norm of gender equality rather than consign it to history. Feminists must stop looking in the rear-view mirror and recognize the need to distinguish their core principles from political alliances of the moment. Feminism is ultimately an Enlightenment project, concerned that women as well as men can claim moral autonomy and human rights, and can do so as participatory citizens in a healthy body politic. How to accomplish women/gender and development cannot be a discussion limited to a few, but must actively involve those who are affected by "development" programs, however these come to be defined, in decisions about strategies and practices. Social movements have arcs for good reason: they too can become elitist and exclusionary. It is important, indeed essential, to criticize how new norms are created, implemented and internalized. But it is important to remember that feminist change cannot occur without them.

Notes

1 ICCs are developed, country by country, using a participatory methodology to choose the indicators, under three general categories: participation and access to power; economic autonomy and poverty, and women's health and sexual and reproductive rights (Valdés and Donoso 2009).
2 This was made somewhat easier by the fact that UNICEF focused on children, and children have mothers, but it is not intuitively obvious, for example, what the impact on women would be of building a dam or setting up electricity co-ops.
3 For a more detailed discussion, see Jaquette and Staudt 2006.

5 Security as emancipation[1]

A feminist perspective

Soumita Basu

Feminist contributions are integral to the revisioning(s) of Security Studies in the discipline of International Relations (IR), which traditionally focused on national security or security of the state. Using the concept of gender, feminist scholars revealed the gendered foundations of the study and practices of international security that privilege perceived masculine values such as rationality and autonomy over perceived feminine values such as emotions and dependence. In contrast to the national security approach, feminists have defined security "broadly in multi-dimensional and multilevel terms—as the diminution of all forms of violence, including physical, structural and ecological" (Tickner 1997, 625) This was part of larger efforts to liberate the concept of security from the limits of a statist perspective, military dynamics and, to varying extents, the scientific objectivist understanding of world politics exemplified by a positivist approach to the study of IR. In this chapter, I focus on a particular approach to conceptualizing security, which I identify as the notion of security as emancipation (SAE). The association of security with emancipation is implicit in strands of feminist contributions on security (Tickner 1992, 1995, 2001; Reardon 1993; Blanchard 2003; Hudson 2005) and has been discussed explicitly in the writings of Ken Booth (1991a, 1991b, 1997a, 2005a, 2007) and Richard Wyn Jones (1999, 2005).

As a feminist scholar interested in SAE, I seek to make two contributions to the field of security studies. First, I highlight the significance of the concept of emancipation as a guiding light in the politics of security, including in relation to feminist approaches to security. Second, I demonstrate the relevance of gender in studying security as emancipation. The discussions below draw primarily on writings identified with feminist and critical approaches to security, specifically the work of scholars such as J. Ann Tickner and Ken Booth who have engaged closely with the normative aspects of theorizing security. It is important to note here that both sets of literature embrace theoretical diversity, and are not mutually exclusive. My interest is in those strands of the literatures that are able to speak to each other on emancipatory approaches to the study of security (see, for instance, Tickner 1995, 2001; McSweeney 1999; Booth 2005a, 2007). As such, this chapter explores the scope for deeper engagement between these feminist and critical approaches in order to propose pathways for further development of SAE (in this respect, see also Husanovic and Owens 2000; Hudson 2005; Pettman 2005; Lee-Koo 2007).

I take as my starting point the 1991 journal article "Security and Emancipation," in which Booth argues, "emancipation, not power or order [traditionally identified with security], produces true security. Emancipation, theoretically, is security" (1991a, 319). He identifies three key features of this conception of security: individuals—not states or any other form of human collective—are identified as the *ultimate referents* of security; security is conceived as emancipation; and, security is constructed as praxis wherein scholars have an explicit political role. This is not only radically different from traditional approaches to the study of security in IR that tend to focus on issues of national security but also distinct from those critical conceptions that are essentially concerned with threats and emergency measures (see also Walker 1990). Feminist scholars, whose critique has drawn significantly on women's experiences of subordination (manifesting also in the continuum of violence against women in the public and private realms), share the skepticism about the sovereignty-based understanding of security that dominates IR (Peterson 1992a; Tickner 1995, 192–93). Located at the cusp of theory and practice, the legacy of feminist re-envisioning(s) of security, is central to my development of SAE.

The chapter is divided into three sections. The first section is a critical examination of SAE, as developed primarily by Booth and Wyn Jones, and focuses on the normative aspect of theorizing security. Drawing on the concept of gender, I propose a relational understanding of SAE in the following section. In the final section, I put forward a five-part strategic framework towards realizing emancipatory security praxis. The chapter has a crucial underpinning, that it is directed to the *study* of security in IR. The threats and responses—or more broadly, relations of insecurity and scope for transformations—identified in the discipline cannot claim to represent the security concerns of all the individuals in the world. However, as discussed below, scholarly endeavors are inextricably linked to "real world" security practices and may contribute to emancipatory security politics.

Security as emancipation

It is no coincidence that most critical approaches to security emerged in the early 1990s. These "grew out of dissatisfaction with the intense narrowing of the field of security studies imposed by the military and nuclear obsessions of the Cold War" (Buzan et al. 1998, 2). The beginning of what was perceived to be a new world order—not defined by superpower rivalry—was conducive to the development of these approaches. This was further stimulated by the rise of international environmental and economic agendas, on the one hand, and concerns regarding identity conflicts, sometimes manifesting in "ethnic conflicts," on the other. Attempts to reformulate security came from a variety of quarters in IR. Among these was the formulation of security as emancipation, proposed and developed by Ken Booth (1991a, 1991b, 1997a, 2005a, 2007), Richard Wyn Jones (1999, 2005) and others. In this section, I first briefly discuss the emergence of this body of literature and then present the three key components of SAE identified earlier—individuals as ultimate referents of security, focus on emancipation and significance of praxis. This is followed by a detailed critique of the conceptualization of security as emancipation.

Scholars critical of the national security discourse, which dominated security studies during the Cold War, were particularly interested in the "politics of security." Drawing on a range of theoretical inspirations, they problematized the treatment of security in terms of threats and responses, divorced from its broader political underpinnings and implications (Booth 1991a, 1991b; Dillon 1996; Krause and Williams 1997a; Peterson 1992a; Tickner 1992; Huysmans 1998; Williams 1998; also see Booth 2007, 149–81; Smith 2000). In this respect, feminist scholarship revealed the gender dimension of international security practices both with respect to specific roles attributed to women and men (e.g., militaries tend to be a male bastion) as well as the gendered foundations upon which the study and practice of international security is constituted (e.g., violence inside homes is not taken into account) (Enloe 1990; Peterson 1992; Tickner 1992; Reardon 1993).

The separation of security from politics that the critics highlighted corresponds to the differentiation imposed by some scholars between international relations theory and political theory, wherein the former is deemed to be oriented towards "questions of survival" and the latter towards theorizing about the "good life" (Wight 1966 cited in Huysmans 1998, 226). However, investigations into questions of survival are undertaken in, and for, the same human society in which scholars of politics seek the conditions of the good life. Separating the two can provide only a partial understanding of the normative goals of theorizing security.

Further, the "survival" approach does not place sufficient emphasis on the ways in which such conceptualizations of security emerge from everyday political crises. The channels of resource mobilization into the responses against threats, and away from the daily needs of people, are also not made clear. At the level of practice, manifestations of such an approach to security often trap women and men into security practices not of their own making, which may not be conducive to the fuller enjoyment of their lives and may even reduce the chances of their survival.[2]

In SAE, first individuals are brought to the center of analysis in order to ensure that security is not defined by narrow interests of any specific form of community including the state, which is inherently based on inclusions and exclusions. The emphasis on national security in mainstream security studies is based on the assumption that the state (and only the state) ensures the security of its citizens. However, practices from across the world demonstrate that states are not only unable to secure their citizens but in many cases pose direct or indirect threats to the very citizens they are contractually obliged to protect as a sovereign (Grant 1991, 16; Peterson 1992, 51; Hoogensen and Rottem 2004, 156). Instead, drawing on the Kantian idea of emancipation, Booth writes that people should be treated as ends and not means; and states, by contrast, should be treated as means not ends (1991b, 539; also see Sheehan 2005, 162). This change in focus does lead to recognition of countless referents of security. However, treating individuals as *ultimate* referents need not fore-close the possibility of using communities including states as referents—as well as agents—of security. Identifying human collectives as referents may even be necessary for scholarly analysis (Alker 2005, 192); but the case for regarding individuals as ultimate referents is made to de-naturalize the link between security of individuals and the state or indeed any other community of which they may be part.

Second, Booth and Wyn Jones present emancipation as the normative fra-mework within which the politics of security should take place. Emancipation originates from the Latin word *emancipare* meaning "the action of setting free from slavery or tutelage" (Wyn Jones 2005, 215; also see Booth 2007, 111; Husanovic and Owens 2000, 432). Booth defines it as "a discourse of human self-creation and the politics of trying to bring it about" (2005c, 181). Eman-cipation signifies the removal of constraints that bind human beings in order to enable them to lead a "good life" and realize their full potential. The concept of security, as used in IR, also corresponds to political practices aimed at transforming a particular set of circumstances, identified as threa-tening. It is, as Krause and Williams note, a derivative concept and can only be understood in relation to a corresponding threat (1997b, ix). One of the central concerns of security studies is to identify threats to the referents, following which suitable responses aimed at removing these threats are developed. Thus, both security and emancipation signify a change in status.

The difference is that security, as it is traditionally understood and without a normative commitment, is oriented to return to the *status quo ante* or a position of relative strength in relation to "the enemy." The responses to security threats are rarely designed to address the political practices that gave rise to the threats in the first place. In the language of power, the practice of security implies exercising power to remove threats to survival and values. Emancipation appears to indicate moving from a position of powerlessness to one that is free from the conditions that created and sustained the status of deprivation. As such, it involves finding and strengthening the agency of referents whose security is governed—partly/sometimes by their consent or passivity—by those that exert power over them. The two journeys—towards security and towards emancipation—thus seem to take place in opposing directions. As Claudia Aradau argues, emancipation is a concept informed by a logic, which is opposed to the logic of security (2004, 401). Associating security with emancipation, however, brings the two journeys in *tandem*. This brings ethical efficacy to the idea of security, so that its progress and achievement are measured in terms of emancipatory ideals and not as the reaffirmation of a possibly disempowering *status quo* (see Booth 1991a, 319).

The aim is to enable referents of security to become agents of their own security.

While it would be naïve to presume that power can be equally distributed among all individuals in this world, the idea of emancipation is useful to security studies scholars interested in human referents in at least two ways. First, by focusing on the marginalized, it disrupts the tendency of security politics to be driven only by the powerful. Second, it ties the achievement of security to historical progress by envisaging a better, more secure world community. This discussion leads into the concept of praxis, which is the third pillar of SAE. Defined as the crucial link between theory and political practice, it specifically brings into focus the role of scholars in security practices. The term "praxis" originates in the work of Sardinian Marxist Antonio Gramsci and has been adapted into the study of IR, featuring particularly in the work of critical international theorists such as Robert Cox and Stephen Gill. It refers to the inescapable link between theory and practice, thought and action (Hoare and Smith in Gramsci 1971, xii; also see Wyn Jones 1999, 154). Wyn Jones (1999) and Booth (2005a) recognize this association between security scholarship and practices in the "real world", and point to the need for praxis to be guided by emancipatory ideals (see also Booth 2005c, 182).

Following this outline of SAE, the two criticisms of the approach that I examine relate to its conceptual effectiveness and hegemonic implications of the concept of emancipation. First, for scholars interested primarily in the mobilizing power of security and therefore its practical implications for questions of "power" and "order," the association with emancipation serves to make security about everything and therefore analytically useless. Drawing inspiration from broad emancipatory ideals and not being guided by a predetermined agenda of threats does leave the notion of security—understood as such—in danger of being unwieldy at the conceptual level. Security from this perspective appears to have no intellectual boundaries. Any referent or issue could be potentially included in security studies and this, as critics have argued, would make analysis impossible. However, critical interrogations of security politics demonstrate that practices governed by power and order are oriented to serve the interests of ruling elites, which may be exploitative of others (for feminist perspectives on this, see *inter alia* Enloe 1990; Tickner 1992; Reardon 1996). The association with emancipation opens up the concept of "security" to be defined by a wider section of society, in particular those subordinated in everyday political processes. In the realm of competing security discourses, proponents of SAE see an important role for scholars and civil society actors who may be closely associated with marginalized sections of human society (Pettman 2005, 174). However, related to this move are critics' comments about the lack of clear guidelines to assess when, and the extent to which, security has been achieved in any particular case.

In response, it is important to note that proponents of SAE do not see emancipation as a grand endpoint. Booth refers to Joseph Nye (1987) to differentiate between "process utopias" and "end-point utopias"; the former are described as "benign and reformist steps calculated to make a better world somewhat more probable for future generations" (1991b, 536; 2007, 251). Along similar lines, Wyn Jones also makes references to "concrete utopias" and "realizable utopias" (2005, 230). If developed sufficiently along with empirical analysis, this approach can have strong epistemological and methodological moorings to guide practice and academic analysis; I suggest a possible conceptualization of SAE in the following sections.

Second, in the development of SAE, as discussed above, emancipation— presented as "the theory of progress" in the writings of Booth and Wyn Jones—has been based primarily on Western Enlightenment ideals that underlie Frankfurt School Critical Theory. As such, this formulation of security has been criticized for being Western-centric under the guise of universalism (Ayoob 1997; Kennedy-Pipe 2004; Barkawi and Laffey 2006; see also Fierke 2007, 188–89). In historical terms, the concept tends to be identified with the rhetoric of liberalism and economic determinism symbolizing rationality and freedom, and Marxism with its totalizing class politics. Described in this way, emancipation becomes a context for the "metanarratives of modernity" as understood through capitalism and communism, and manifests in exploitative hierarchies. For poststructuralists, critical of these hierarchies, and feminists, who argue that these metanarratives are based solely on male experiences, emancipation—understood as above—is problematic (Huysmans 2006a; see also Tickner 1997, 621; Lee-Koo 2007, 241–43). However, as Wyn Jones (2005, 215) writes, the concept of emancipation "has [also] been associated with some of the great progressive struggles in modern history" (see also Sheehan 2005, 159). These include social movements against slavery, colonialism, women's subordination and exploitation of labor. While not without problems, the visions associated with these movements point to alternative, multiple ways in which emancipation can be framed.

I support the general orientation of Booth and Wyn Jones' development of SAE, as discussed above; and, in the remaining part of this chapter, I draw primarily on feminist insights to demonstrate the ways in which the "universalism" of the current SAE literature can be set up for interrogation without taking away the potential it holds for building a secure world community. In seeking to bridge the gap, I move the focus of SAE from the "insecure individual" to the "relations of insecurity" that make the individual insecure. Using the notion of gender as a relational, transformative category, I seek to develop an approach to SAE that can be sensitive to pluralism and dynamism in security politics.

Security through transformations: a gender approach

Commenting on feminist scholarship on security in the nineties, Jill Steans notes that feminist perspectives in IR are committed to the "reconstructive" projects linked to "rethinking" security (1998, 129; see also Tickner 1997, 625; Blanchard 2003, 1305). There are differences within the literature about how security practices should be reconstructed, which represent the diversity within feminist IR. Depending on their particular perspective, scholars locate themselves at one or more "sites of change" such as local/global and/or practical/discursive. My interest here is in employing gender as a conceptual tool to propose an alternative approach to SAE. Also, I illustrate my arguments with debates from within feminist IR, as it relates to gendered foundations of security studies and women as referents of security.

As with other fields of study, feminist interventions into the study of security in IR began with the question: "Where are the women?" (see Enloe 1990, 190). Pioneers of feminist approaches to security such as Jean Elshtain (1987), Rebecca Grant (1991, 1992), V. Spike Peterson (1992) and J. Ann Tickner (1992) trace their critique of the discipline to Greek philosophical assumptions about the nature of men and the conduct of politics that inform realist theories of IR and, consequently, the conceptualization of security therein. The public sphere, identified as the arena of politics and citizenship, was defined by masculine values such as autonomy, reason and pursuit of power, which were attributed to men. Women and feminine values such as dependence and emotions, which supposedly weaken the pursuit of power, were relegated to the private sphere and excluded from political discourse (Ruddick 1990, 23). But this separation and exclusion was not free from value judgments.

Instead, the masculine nature of the public arena where men strove for transcendence—"the highest good"—was valued over and above the "private realm of necessity" which was occupied by women, slaves and children. Characterized by "production and reproduction that was the precondition of public," "this private realm of necessity," Peterson writes, "could not be abolished, but 'necessity' could not be permitted to contaminate the activities and relationships of the superior association [i.e., the public realm of politics]" (1992, 36). Thus emerged the binary relationship between masculine and feminine values, which continues to define the mainstream study of IR and security. Like men in the public sphere, states are seen to be rational actors. They are primarily driven by self-interest and seek to maximize their relative power and secure their sovereignty in an anarchical international realm.[3]

Feminist approaches "introduced gender as a relevant empirical category and theoretical tool for analyzing global power relations as well as a normative standpoint from which to construct alternative world orders" (True 2001, 231). Gender is defined as a relational notion that is articulated, paraphrasing Tickner (1997, 614), in a set of variable but socially and culturally constructed characteristics—such as power/weakness, autonomy/dependence, rationality/ emotion and public/private—linked to masculinity/femininity. Feminists find these relations set up in binary oppositions in political practices, as discussed above. As such, the emphasis is on "the ways that they disqualify one another rather than their interdependencies" (Ferguson 1991, 326). Thus, it would appear that any strength attributed to masculinities derives from being juxtaposed against supposedly weaker feminine counterpoints. This corresponds to the kind of relations between referents of security that focus on victory and defeat.

The national security of a state, for instance, is measured in comparison to that of other states. Relationships between states, in realist IR, are perceived in zero-sum terms wherein more power for one state can only imply less for another. The concept of gender brings clarity to such relations and their implications.

As a relational concept, gender is infused with fluidity. Indeed, "gender is a *transformative* macro-political category, not because once we understand it at work, we can do away with it, but because once we understand it we can transform how it works at all levels of social and political life" (True 2001, 258; emphasis in original). It signifies hierarchical relations that are oppressive to one or both sides, pointing to the need for such relations to be transformed. This corresponds to the normative vision that Blanchard identifies in relation to "feminist security theory": "[it] entails revealing gendered hierarchies, eradicating patriarchal structural violence, and working towards the eventual achievement of common security" (Blanchard 2003, 1305; see also Hudson 2005, 156, 169). Indeed, feminist scholars conducting research with women as subjects were among the first in IR to adopt the idea of structural violence proposed by peace researcher Johan Galtung (1969), wherein the understanding of security is not limited to ensuring protection from physical violence but also addressing underlying political structures that give rise to it (Tickner 1992).

Security does not lie in victory or defeat but in the transformation of the oppressive social relations underlying structural violence. Feminists focus, in particular, on forces of patriarchy that govern the ways in which women and men lead their lives. Briefly, patriarchal forces constitute a society that privileges masculine values and generates systematic marginalization of women in all spheres of life including international relations. These forces are transmitted through practices of both men and women. Threats to women's security, thus, may be embodied and enacted by individuals, groups, and institutions. The pattern of insecurities for women corresponds to the image of a matrix in which individuals are located in the security–politics continuum that constructs their lives. Thus, women's experiences of (and responses to) armed conflict may not always be delineated by categories such as "us" and "them", and "inside" and "outside." As Sylvester (2007, 552) writes, "it [gendered identity] cannot be existentially threatened in the same way that one's national, religious, or racial identity supposedly can be" (see also Hansen 2000). Ultimately these threats need to be traced to the structural forces such as patriarchy from which they emerge and grow.

In approaches without an explicit normative agenda, such as positivist security analyses, the identification of threats is followed by the evaluation of possible responses to eliminate those threats. When placed within a more complex network of individuals with multiple identities as ultimate referents, as described above, this kind of problem-solving will ultimately find few victors. In the web of identities within which individuals locate themselves, severed threads not only affect the "losers" but also others who are tied to them on different planes. Writing in another context, Nancy Hartsock argues for the need to identify the structures of domination that are part of "the metaphors of web and net" used to depict social relations. Without such analysis, "we are all responsible, and so in a sense no one is responsible" (1989–90, 23). One way of attributing responsibility, in order to transform relations, is to then deconstruct these structures of domination and identify the agencies that perpetuate and benefit from oppressive hierarchies. This corresponds to the mainstream security models wherein autonomous threats are identified and then responded to. However, the structures of domination are insidious and would implicate many if not all of us. We are all caught within these structures.

The alternative, or perhaps a complementary, approach is to use scholarly research to explore resources for transformation in the society—both within agencies and structures—that can overcome the structures of domination (Tickner 1992, 65; Hudson 2005, 162). Thus, drawing on the discussions above, and in response to charges against the concept of emancipation for being "metanarratives of modernity" that are not cognizant of the plurality of human experiences, it is proposed here that the normative ideals of emancipation can best serve the politics of security if they are conceived of as "moments of emancipation." These correspond to suggestions of "process utopias," "concrete utopias," and "realizable utopias" in the SAE literature discussed earlier but, as noted below, lead to an alternative conceptualization of achievement—realization—of security.

In her discussion of feminist critical theory, Jill Steans writes that "feminist critical theorizing involves constructing 'knowledge' about the world, not in the interests of social and political control, but in the service of an emancipatory politics. Thus, feminist critical theorists claim that knowledge is a *moment* of emancipation" (1998, 173; emphasis in original). If developed along the same lines, security studies discourse is enriched by multiple voices and not merely by those that dominate and are loud. The achievement of security is measured in transformations, each defined through empirical analysis guided by emancipatory ideals. Security conceived of as "moments of emancipation" highlights the need for dynamism in security politics. Moments pass, actors and contexts change, and any security practice identified as such has to re-evaluate its vision for transformations accordingly, in the quest for emancipation. It may be an opportunity for actors guided by emancipatory ideals to use this in favor of a wider section of the society, for individuals on both sides of the "threat" fence.

Security is defined here as progressive transformations in relations that threaten the values and survival of an identified referent. These are the "moments of emancipation." It is the emphasis on relations that separates the conceptualization of "moments of emancipation" from the references to short-term utopias in the writings of Booth and Wyn Jones (see, for example, Booth 2007, 110). The latter are determined by "conditions" of insecurity and security. SAE literature, as it stands, does not offer concrete tools to assess any change in the identified "condition." In this context, the emphasis on relations here can offer new analytical resources. Defined in this way, security may not be a permanent state because the new practices may create new relations and conditions of insecurity. It is only when the achievement of security is tied to ideas of emancipation that successive moments of security will erode those norms of human existence that create and sustain oppressive politics, which are at the root of insecurities. There may well be competing security interests. In such cases, as Michael Sheehan writes, "it is necessary to have normative criteria that can provide a basis upon which to judge such ethical claims" (2005, 159). In this respect, a necessary condition will have to be that "moments of emancipation" are defined in ways that do not threaten other individuals or communities except when the raison d'être of the latter is based on uncompromising dichotomies that threaten others.

Many questions emerge from such a formulation. First, "moments of emancipation" need to be identified in concrete terms. As Booth writes on security, "if we cannot name it, can we ever hope to achieve it?" (1991a, 317). This is particularly relevant when the "litmus test for critical [emancipatory] security studies" lies in its ability to inform emancipatory practices (Bilgin 2001, 278). Thus, first, there needs to be more clarity about the ways in which the transition from politics to security politics occurs and the conditions that can facilitate the transformations for emancipation. Second, associating security with emancipation may imply that security can never be fully realized. It is difficult to ascertain precisely when the "moment of emancipation" takes place. Even if context-specific goals are reached, the possibility of new insecurities emerging from the new context (which can never fully erase the past) and relationships remains. Security studies scholars may well play a key role in this respect by directing their research towards envisaging transformation of those political contexts that make referents insecure and human relations fragile. Their work should be poised to remain vigilant to the creation of new oppressive hierarchies.

Enduring debates within feminist scholarship on the meanings of sex and gender, and the nature of transformations to be engendered, are evidence of a strong tradition of critique that has developed around a theoretical endeavor with roots in emancipatory politics. Certain strands of feminist thought (see Sjoberg's response in this volume) are critical of the notion of emancipation but these too have aspiration(s) for transformations, and normative visions associated with them. It cannot be otherwise because of the intimate relationship between feminist theorizing and practice. Feminist praxis requires identification of referents, practices, and resources for transformation, which inevitably involves the value-laden assessment of scholars across the theoretical spectrum. In light of this, SAE, as discussed in this chapter, can offer concrete pathways for securing individuals while taking account of the contingent nature of security politics. Conversely, the tradition of feminist critique and commitment to "reconstructive" projects may be considered illustrative of the dynamic approach to SAE proposed here. Further, the concept of gender is recognized as a crucial theoretical resource in conceptualizing security as emancipation in this chapter. Drawing further on feminist IR as well as the existing literature on SAE, I offer in the final section a strategic framework for emancipatory security praxis of the kind conceptualized above.

Emancipatory security praxis

The role of security scholars is an underlying thread running through this chapter. This is not to overstate the significance of scholarship in security practices. Clearly, there are limitations to the influence of scholars in policy-making and indeed social movements, and great diversity in the interests and aspirations of individual scholars. However, the politics of "security studies" is intimately connected to the larger politics of international security practices. In line with SAE discussed here, security studies scholars can lend support to transformatory practices in the larger society using empirical analysis on which this approach to security is contingent. Further, there should be an attempt to engage with the scholarly community itself (see Ackerly and True 2006, 258–60; Sylvester 2007).

In this section, I seek to identify a concrete methodological approach to engage with SAE for empirical research. Framed within broader normative commitments, such analysis should also identify the agency, and the opportunities and challenges in its employment, which mark the transformatory potential of any *security problematique*. The five analytical moves identified below are put forward as a strategic framework for emancipatory security praxis. Broadly, these correspond to what Ackerly and True (2006) have defined as a "feminist theoretical method for International Relations," and are also informed by research questions used in empirical contributions to the SAE literature (see, for instance, Booth and Vale 1997).

Listen to the narratives of the politically marginalized in setting up security problematique(s) and the vision for security

Identifying individuals as ultimate referents of security makes it possible to bring human lives to the center of security studies, and to envision transformations based on experiences of marginalization and subjugation. This resonates with the epistemological claim of feminist standpoint theories that the voices of the disempowered should be privileged in the struggles for political change. Critics would point out that this is problematic since the recognition of the marginalized is filtered through a prior notion of what disempowerment is, and that this normative assumption may well be flawed and biased against individuals and groups. In this context, it is important to note that while feminist theories emerged out of women's lived experiences of patriarchy, only certain strands of thinking have clung to a rigid notion of who are to be identified as the disempowered.

Further, I do not see the individual referents as independent entities whose security, and therefore emancipation, lies in the ability to exercise free will (see Booth 2005b). As such, my worldview is relational as understood in feminist politics (Peterson and Runyan 1993, 152). The ontological premise here is based on individuals in the human population whose security and well-being is constructed and reconstructed every moment by the multiple intersections of socializing forces such as class, ethnicity, gender, nationality, and race. In this respect, there are political implications of the collective naming of any group of individuals as referents—for instance, identifying women as referents of security—since they can never be a homogenous category (Fierke 2007, 204; see Stern 2006). Attempts to identify conditions for their security/emancipation run the risk of leaving out the narratives that could not be heard in this categorization. For many feminists, for example, the term "women" is itself a site for contestation (see Collins 1990; Sylvester 1994b; Zalewski 1994; Mohanty 2003).

Whilst it is important to challenge hierarchies, implicit even in the most benign political project, the critique should serve to indicate the complexities involved and not to deny the project in its entirety. Thus, in the case of identifying women as referents of security, the subjectivity of the subject should not become a case for the rejection of the subject itself. Instead, the category has to be (re)built on the basis of the multiplicities of concerns and interests that mark the lived experiences of women. Paraphrasing Cynthia Cockburn (2007, 7), the standpoints are not those of abstract, discrete individuals but generated collectively in local and global contexts (see also Hudson 2005, 169).

SAE draws prominently on the lived experiences of insecurity from hunger and physical violence, for instance, emanating from political, social, and economic contexts not of the individuals' choosing. Scholarly attention to these narratives can be what Pettman calls a "power corrective to more visible, elite, statist and militarized constructions of the identity-security nexus" (2005, 174; see Sjoberg 2010a, 5). From an emancipatory perspective, it is those who are least in control of these relations of power who can give a picture of the worst manifestations of the situation of insecurity. This is not to deny the agency of those who individually, or indeed communally, subvert or resist the circumstances in which they may find themselves; or, the limitations in capacity of those who dominate to transform the structuring powers. If "moments of emancipation" are to be envisioned, however, it is those that do not benefit from relations of insecurity whose voices and vision for security should be privileged.

Deconstruct the relationships of power that constitute the dentified situation

In political theories linked to emancipation—for instance, (standpoint) feminism—there is usually a shared understanding of who dominates and who is subjugated. As noted earlier, knowledge here emerges from listening to experiences of the subjugated and examining their position in oppressive structures of power. And, from the perspective of the subjugated, it becomes possible to see why change is necessary and what it might look like. But it is not enough to recognize this kind of power flow since change in the *status quo* may change who the dominant and the subjugated are but not necessarily the production of power—to dominate—in the relations. Transformation in relations of insecurity, the way in which I conceive of security in this chapter, is geared not only towards changing the direction of power flows but also towards changing the nature of power that is exercised. Security through transformations cannot, thus, be limited to disrupting or ending the power "over" and/or carried out through the distribution of existing power. Removal of immediate threats, which may be admittedly necessary in the short-term, would be less effective or sustainable if the processes that lead to the creation of these threats are not taken into account. Instead, progressive "moments of emancipation" are to be guided by the need to identify and strengthen mutually enabling "power to" be secure (see Tickner 1992, 65; Hudson 2005, 156).

The three kinds of power identified above draw on Amy Allen's (2008) categorization of the ways in which feminist scholars have understood power: as a resource that needs to be equally distributed amongst women and men; as domination, i.e., a "power-over" relation which is used to control or dominate the subjugated; and as empowerment, which signifies a "power-to" be able to transform oppressive politics (see also Peterson and Runyan 1993, 152–53). Michael Barnett and Raymond Duvall (2005, 10) offer a similar understanding of "power to" in the broader IR literature. Their emphasis, however, is on the "effect of social relations of constitutions on human capacity." Thus, the structural context give "power to" the actors to behave in particular ways. Allen (2008) suggests a more agency-based understanding and describes "power to" as the "reconceptualization of power as a capacity or ability, specifically, the capacity to empower or transform oneself and others." I would associate emancipatory security praxis with this understanding of power.

However, even as scholarly analyses should seek out and recognize the "power to" be secure for identified referents, there should be engagement with power that operates as a resource and is used to dominate. In the field of international relations, with multiple layers of representations, it is difficult to encapsulate the shifting power dynamics. Highlighting the existence of multiple hierarchies in the international system, Enloe (2004, 31) writes, "they relate to each other, sometimes in ways that subvert one another, sometimes in ways that provide each with its respective resiliency." Thus, while it is necessary to maintain a critique of the vertical flows of power between international actors and those they claim to represent, the horizontal "co-ordination" and contention between institutions and individuals is also crucial to grasp the transformative possibilities in the international realm.[4] The effects of these power dynamics and the scope for their transformations, however, would have to be assessed within particular local contexts.

Identify resources for transforming the relations of insecurity, and agencies that wield control over these

By privileging voices of the marginalized, it becomes possible to identify threats perceived by identified referents and the relations through which they are transmitted. If understood as a binary, the only two choices for transformation would be resistance, which may not be discernible, and revolution, which may replace one hegemon with another. Emancipatory security praxis would benefit from seeking resources for transformation on the spectrum of opportunities between, and including, resistance and revolution (see Husanovic and Owens 2000, 427). An examination of the practices through which relations of insecurity are produced and reproduced would suggest the potential "sites of change." Since emancipatory research must actively seek the resources for transformations, scholars cannot but also engage with the agents that are in a position to influence the relations of in/security at these sites.

Karin Fierke defines agency as being "about the potential for the individual or state [or any institution] to influence their environment as well as to be influenced by it" (2007, 61). This potential can be a key resource for transformations. As Neil Walker has pointed out also (albeit from a different theoretical standpoint), "agency is fundamental because trends in security and conflict resolution depend upon who does or does not get to decide upon or wield influence over problems of definition and resolutions, at what level and with what interests and values to the fore" (2006, 154). However, such prioritization of agency in the analysis of security practices is criticized by those who argue that neither agents nor structures are independent variables of analysis, and thus can be studied only by means of practices through which they are (re)constituted (Doty 1997; see also Shepherd 2008, 385). From the perspective of SAE, I would contend that even when agents and structures are considered to be mutually constitutive, it is necessary to identify the faultlines in the *status quo* that lend themselves to emancipatory politics/security practices.[5]

Moreover, I would argue that these lie in the agency of individuals and institutions that bind them together. As Booth writes on the agent–structure debate (whether agent determines the structure or vice versa), "structures cannot conceive new structures but human agents can, even if they cannot yet construct them" (2007, 217). This is a direct reference to the normative vision of human beings, and our ability to conceive of progressive futures (see also McSweeney 1999, 143). Agents are both constrained and enabled by structural factors, which Giddens (1984) describes as "rules and resources." While they may not be able to fully realize the imagined futures just "yet," their articulations/practices—through, for instance, discourse and resource mobilization—can contribute to the dynamics of politics/security. Discussions on security tend to take a limited view of human cognition, focusing on self-interest and survival and projecting this on to the state. This, as discussed earlier, feeds into the gendered construction of international security, which privileges specific masculine values in the study and practices of international politics. Instead, it is important to recognize that human society is also driven by feelings such as love, respect, and empathy. The challenge for emancipatory security praxis is then to project effectively this richer perception of human cognition on to the political realms that it examines.

Examine the areas of collaboration and contention between agencies in security practices, keeping in view the contingent factors that enable or limit the fulfillment of identified security goals

In my discussion on emancipatory security praxis, I privilege agency as the motor for progressive transformations and for the attainment of security. However, within the overarching material and discursive distribution of power in the international realm, actors—individuals and institutions—act in particular ways. In view of this, "the specifics of agency can only be analyzed in the situated practices of concrete manifestations of politics" (Jabri 2006, 151). Huysmans refers to such an analytical move in terms of "situated agency," which denotes both the relational nature of power as well as the context within which agency operates (2006b, 9–10). Thus, the agency of actors is evaluated in relation to that of the other actors embodying agency in an identified situation, taking into account the contingent factors that both enable and constrain their exercise of power. For instance, as Mark Duffield (2001) points out, international responses to the "new wars" in contemporary politics are governed by a "liberal peace" agenda. This constrains agency by imposing a particular understanding of economic development but it has also made possible the involvement of a range of actors through networks of "global liberal governance" (see Duffield 2001, 11, 44–45).

Further, since power can be articulated and its effects noted only through relations, it becomes imperative to examine the networks within which particular security issues are discussed, and resources mobilized in response. While the more diffused forms of power provide the broader context within which agency is employed, it is the ensemble of direct relations between the various actors that allows for particular responses to questions of security in the international realm. Strategies adopted by agencies—state/non-state, civil/military—to realize their goals have been studied extensively in the IR literature, for instance in strategic studies (Gray 1999), in international organizations and policymaking (Barnett and Finnemore 1999), and in agenda-setting by civil society actors (Keck and Sikkink 1998).

In this context, feminist scholars have highlighted the need to account for both global power relations and their local manifestations (Enloe 1990; Steans 1998, 175; True 2002, 15). It is political agency that can collaborate with, resist, or transform the employment of relations of in/security but it is important to have some understanding of the constitutive elements of any given site to comprehend the scope of the actors involved. Since emancipatory security praxis seeks to be driven by lived experiences of human populations, the manifestation of power relations has to be examined in particular contexts.

Reflect on the contingent nature of referents, issues, agencies, and security goals

Finally, the strategic framework includes an inherent critique of emancipatory security praxis. Engaging in this approach to studying security—for instance, privileging certain voices, or recognizing structural power within binaries—is fraught with dangers of marginalizing other voices or reinforcing the very binaries that sustain insecurities. I have discussed here the need to envisage the attainment of security through progressive transformations. It is important to conceptualize incremental change in concrete terms even as the aim is to transform the deeper relations—processes of power—that signify insecurity (see Ackerly and True 2006, 258). These concrete elements of the security *problematique* and the vision for security—in the short term—would need to be re-assessed on the basis of their manifestation in particular contexts. It is imperative then for scholars to reflect back on their own critique and terms of discourse in the light of any given context.

Conclusion

There is tendency to associate insecurity with weakness. An understanding of security that is based on the assumption of autonomous referents and threats necessarily implies that security comes with the attainment of power, and therefore superior strength. However, if security is associated with emancipation and is linked to addressing structural violence, as characterized in this chapter, it is valuable to untangle the conditions of insecurity from the referent who is made insecure and, possibly, even the perpetrator. This not only enables us to envisage the possibility of the referent being outside this condition of insecurity but also makes it possible to identify the potential for transformation that the referent may hold within herself/himself.

Thus, this focus on the relations—and not merely the symptoms—of insecurity is necessary to move beyond managing threats towards transforming the processes through with threats are produced. Using the notion of gender as a relational, transformative category, I identified the attainment of security as transformation in these relations of security. These were defined as "moments of emancipation," which are directed towards transforming these relations into being mutually enabling instead of being carriers of threats. Political agency, I have suggested here, is a key resource for the disruption of these relations, which are articulated in international security practices. Constitutive factors such as patriarchy, militarism, and liberal capitalism determine the scope of this disruption, and are not to be underestimated. However, it is through agency that it becomes possible to envision alternatives and mobilize discursive and material resources to realize transformations.

Individuals are not only the ultimate referents of security in SAE but it is human cognition—through which agency is operationalized—that presents these opportunities. Traditionally, it is a narrow understanding of the behavior of "man" (selfish and power-hungry) that has determined the behavior of states, generally recognized as the primary referents of international security (Waltz 1959). As has been pointed out in feminist scholarship, however, this emphasis on "power-over" is a masculine construction, and that it is also possible to envisage agency in terms of empowerment for oneself and others. Therefore, to obtain a fuller picture of the international realm than the one provided by mainstream security studies, it is valuable to consider the ways in which "power to" is mobilized in international politics, and to appreciate that security practices are not merely driven by aggression and self-interest but also by co-operation, collective interest and worldviews defined by peace and harmony. Finally, with the SAE emphasis on "real people in real places," it is crucial that human referents for whom security is envisaged are able to inter-rogate and contribute to its understanding and achievement. It is through such critique that universalist aspirations of common humanity and world security will be continually refined, with the realization of the potential for progressive "moments of emancipation" leading to more security for more sections of the human population.

Notes

1 I am grateful to Marie Breen-Smyth, Jenny Mathers, and João Reis Nunes for their engagement with early drafts of this paper. I also thank J. Ann Tickner, Laura Sjoberg, Maya Eichler, and other participants of the "Twenty Years of Feminist IR" conference held in April 2010 at the University of Southern California, for their comments on this version.
2 Individuals and communities may have accepted this as part of their citizenship contract; others may not have any say in the matter; or, indeed, may not be able to change the course of national and international security policies for both reasons.
3 Stereotypical masculine values such as rationality and autonomy, adopted as norms in the political sphere, however, draw upon a partial understanding of male behaviour. As R. W. Connell (1995) suggested, this partial understanding does not correspond to any generalizable behavior of men; it is a construct of an ideal dominant force that seeks to subordinate the mixed archetypes of masculinities and femininities that operate in society, including in international security practices.
4 Barnett and Duvall's (2005) conceptualization of power with reference to global governance is potentially useful for negotiating this terrain.
5 If structural forces determine all political life, immanent critique of any kind is ultimately pointless.

Emancipation and the feminist Security Studies project

An engagement with Soumita Basu

Laura Sjoberg

I appreciate Soumita Basu's well-thought out, well-argued, and well-written presentation of the case for an alliance between feminist security theorizing and the particular brand of critical security studies that focuses on security as emancipation (SAE). Particularly, Basu points out some important affinities between feminisms and SAE work that could prove to be common ground for the purposes of establishing a productive and enduring alliance. That said, I remain skeptical that SAE work has a value-added for feminist Security Studies specifically and for Security Studies more generally, less for the reasons traditionally expressed in feminist work in security (which Basu goes over and deals with very effectively) and more because I am concerned that there is an intellectual and political tension between the key tenets of SAE work and the key goals and ideas of feminism(s) in Security Studies as I see them.

In this conversation, it is important to recognize (as I have emphasized before) that there are a number of different epistemological and even ontological variants of feminist approaches to security specifically and international relations generally (Sjoberg 2006; 2008; 2009b; 2010; Tickner and Sjoberg 2006; 2010). As such, a partnership of feminist thinking and SAE is a part of the feminist Security Studies project writ large, even if there are other thinkers and scholars within that tradition (such as myself) who are skeptical of the ethical productivity of such a partnership.

In my comments, I will address the common ground between and potential utility of an alliance of feminist work in security and SAE work, particularly in light of Basu's resolution of some of the tensions traditionally identified by feminist scholars. I will then talk about some areas of remaining concern for me, particularly with SAE's focus on the individual as the ultimate referent of security praxis and with the epistemological, ontological, and political implications of relying on the idea of emancipation as a logic for changing the way that we (as people, as scholars, and as policy-makers) approach security.

There are a number of potential affinities between feminist security theorizing as I see it and SAE work as Basu explains it. I have articulated my vision of feminist work in Security Studies, seeing that feminists

> share a normative and empirical concern that the international system is
> gender-hierarchical. ... Whole gender hierarchy is a normative problem,

the failure to recognize it is an empirical problem for IR scholarship ... [which makes it] less descriptively accurate and predictively powerful for its omission of this major force in global politics ... gender is conceptually, empirically, and normatively essential to studying international security. ... [particularly] it is important for analyzing causes and predicting outcomes, and it is essential to thinking about solutions and promoting positive change in the security realm.

(Sjoberg 2009b, 185)

My articulations have emphasized a praxis element of feminist work in the theory and practice of security studies, and have emphasized the inclusion of gender analysis *all* scholarship (not just work that focuses on women or feminism explicitly).

As such, I am sympathetic with Basu's attraction to SAE work as it has explicitly discussed gender and feminist work in its articulations of what security studies is and should be. Particularly, I've read and have some interest in the utilization of feminist theorizing in Ken Booth's *Theory of World Security* (69–75). Booth introduces the section by talking about the invisibility but crucial relevance of women leading up to and in the U.S./British invasion of Iraq, and then discusses the central relevance of patriarchy in feminist theorizing, which he characterizes (citing a dictionary of feminist theorizing) as "the totality of oppressive and exploitative relations which affect women" (2007, 70) where the challenge (citing Beauvoir) is "to overcome being ... man's transcultural, transhistorical Other" (2007, 71). Booth tells us a few of the things that he finds to be crucially important from feminism:

> Power is complex. ... States, governments, and organizations are not neutral institutions; patriarchy and ideas about masculinity do a great deal of work in making the (social, political, and economic) world go around; ... the theorist is embedded and embodied; ... theorizing security is not an objective activity ...
>
> (Booth 2007, 75)

The most obvious connection here, and one that Basu draws out excellently, is the understanding of security theorizing as praxis (which I understand largely through the work of Marysia Zalewski). Marysia (1996) proposes two ideas that make this link: theory as critique and theory as practice. Theory as critique "collapses the subject-object distinction which indicates a clear break from the belief that events in the world are ontologically prior to our theories about them" (Zalewski 1996, 341). Theory as practice is theorizing that is both research in the traditional sense and a part of daily life *as politics*. This analysis is certainly something that provides fruitful grounding for a potential alliance between SAE theorists and feminist security theorists.

Another potential avenue of affinity, which Basu discusses at length, is the common interest in ending oppression and subordination between SAE theorists and feminist theorists, where SAE theorists are interested in human emancipation generally and feminist theorists interested, in Soumita's terms, in women's emancipation, or at least, the end to discrimination, subordination, and oppression based on and related to sex.

Finally, the approaches certainly share a critical/nuanced understanding of power—as Soumita notes, in fact, one that might be found in Amy Allen's feminist approach to the distinction between "power-over" and "power-to" where power-over is the ability to force, coerce, or cajole another actor into one's will, and power-to as the ability to transform power-over relationships transgressively.

All of that said, I think tensions remain between SAE and feminist security theorizing, and will discuss them below, organized by Booth's understandings of the tenets of SAE theorizing

Individuals are the ultimate referents

As feminists, we have written about the desire to widen and deepen security— expand what counts as security and who merits it, with, as Basu mentions, a particular eye towards those traditionally excluded from the power structures of global politics. Most of that work does not, and I argue, should not, and should not be read to, hold a liberal view of the individual, but would have to in order to find affinity with the SAE project as such. "Individuals are the ultimate referents" implies a discreet understanding of the individual as separable from other individuals, and of the individual's relationality as circumstantial rather than fundamental.

Feminist theorizing, though, has come a long way towards demonstrating that liberal individualism might not be how the world works. Instead, as Nancy Hirschmann argued, women, and indeed, people, are not discretely but relationally autonomous, and there is a "gender bias in an individualistic understanding of autonomy and obligation" (Hirschmann 1989, 1228). As Hirschmann explains, this has implications not only for the individual as the SAE referent but also for that individual's relationship with security-as-emancipation:

> If the conception of freedom as negative is premised on the struggle for recognition, particularly on the ability to be recognized without reciprocation; if non-recognition is a form of power and violence; freedom, too, must be at least in part an expression of that same power and violence.
> (Hirschmann 1989, 1238)

Instead, "feminist reformulations of consent show that even actors who behave as if they act independently hide relational elements of their decision-making" (Sjoberg 2006, 47; citing Sylvester, 1992) and their very essence. Relational autonomy preserves identity for "self" while recognizing the artificiality of self's radical independence and seeing the interdependence of self and other as ontologically foundational to humanity. Decisions can be made *within constraints* or *with* fellow constrainees but never without constraint.

Of course, those constraints govern humans omnipresently but unequally. Power-over is a liberal individualistic idea that one actor (however defined) can "beat" another actor (however defined), and power-to is the reactive idea that weaker actor(s) have hope against stronger actor(s), "the capacity of an agent to act in spite of or in response to power wielded over her by others" (Allen 1998, 34). I think, fundamentally, this concept, and the SAE concept of power, entrenches both liberal institutionalism and the agent/structure dichotomy in how we think about power (Sjoberg 2006, 69). While not directly excluding feminist work on consent that rejects liberal individualism in favor of actors-as-groups pooling themselves and their resources, such an approach does not embrace that understanding of human action as fundamentally relational either (e.g., Hirschmann 1989).

The individual as the ultimate referent for security politics in SAE obscures these nuances and important dynamics of feminist theory even when you, as Basu does, allow for the possibility that sometimes individual subordination and emancipation will play out at the group or state level. If the relational community is the ultimate referent of security (if there has to be one), then we can deal more effectively with relational autonomy in security politics, potential problems with security as a zero-sum game, and feminist politics of empathy as a path out of the conflictual nature of security politics. As such, collaborative politics of dialogue and emotional identification can be seen as the (missing) mechanism through which critical theorists can cooperate to achieve their security objectives, and care can be seen as the way through which human needs (in SAE, emancipation) are critically and comprehensively addressed.

Security as emancipation

This last point is a useful segue into my next concern about the proposed alliance between SAE and feminist theorizing about security, about the utility of (and even potential violences of) security as emancipation. If the individual is the ultimate referent of security, than the individual has to be discrete, categorizable, and detectable but at the same time a part of a human collective with essential characteristics. Both sides of that combination, I am worried, may be untenable.

The problematic nature of discrete identification of the individual comes in as one reads Basu's characterizations of women and feminisms. Basu describes feminisms as fundamentally interested in women's emancipation, and describes women in terms of their relation to men as a part of a sex dichotomy. While she notes that some feminists have a problem with the category of women, she does not note that this problem stems from a combination of socio-biological analysis (e.g., Fausto-Sterling 2005), queer theorizing about those people who are neither biological male nor female (e.g.,

Butler 2000), analysis of gender relations between masculinities (e.g., Connell 1995; Zalewski and Parpart 2008), and postcolonial critiques of universalistic assumptions about the nature and experience of gender oppression by women (e.g., Chowdhry and Nair 2002; Mohanty 2003). People are not strictly male *or* female, one identity *or* the other; identity is both relational and hybridized. Security *as emancipation* requires us to categorize individuals such that we can see what their identities demand they be emancipated from. Each of these critical approaches suggests categorization and distinction among and between individuals essential for "emancipation" (whether those categorizations be "male/female," "center/margin," "this race/that race") might have a potentially silencing impact not only on people but on groups' social welfare.

At the same time, a feminist SAE approach like the one that Basu suggests relies not only on categorizing individuals discretely but also on essentializing certain human characteristics. For the strategy that Basu proposes to be implemented, people must at once be gazed upon as members of groups *and also* be considered a part of a human collective with essential characteristics. The second is as problematic as the first. Feminist postcolonial theorizing has critiqued the assumption that an elite, Western and largely white group of feminists (or, here, critical theorists more generally) can decide what "emancipation" might be and what fundamental rights humans *as humans* are entitled to. This problematic tendency can be seen in Ken Booth's (2007) explanation of what he takes from feminist theorizing, which demonstrates universalistic tendencies:

> Jean Elshtain has warned against any essentializing of the difference between males and females on the basic ontological level, casting the one sex as corrupt and violent and the other sex as innocent and nurturing. In the same spirit, Brooke A. Ackerly envisioned feminism as *human*ism.
>
> (Booth 2007, 73, citing Elshtain 1981; Ackerly 2000)

The "we" see emancipation for "them" (however those categories are understood) could be characterized as inherently patriarchal, where there is a comfort in speaking for those who cannot speak for themselves, so long as we are under the impression we are doing so for the Other and in their interest, and especially when we fetishize oppression and emancipation at the margins of global politics.

The praxis implications of feminist SAE

There are also, I believe, problems with the praxis implications of a feminist-SAE alliance. Basu cites Jill Steans as an example of a project of feminist critical theorizing aligned with the emancipatory politics of SAE. This mention however begs the question—if a project of feminist critical theorizing exists, and has not aligned itself with SAE theorizing, why? Quoting more from Steans' discussion:

> *Feminist critical theorists* are trying to find a way forward which retains both gender as a category of analysis and the historical commitment to the emancipatory project in feminism, but which takes on board the postmodern and postcolonial critique of the exclusionary practices of Western feminism.
>
> (Steans 1998, 29)

It is the second part of that discussion that is crucial to think about when discussing a potential alliance between feminism and SAE work, where SAE work has neglected the postmodern and postcolonial critique of the potential essentialist and imperial implications of declaring the need for emancipation for Others and then actively pursuing it, often without their input or consent.

While, as I have argued before (Sjoberg 2009a, 201), "critical theories' failure to embrace feminism does not itself answer the question of what intellectual and practical differences there are between those approaches and feminist approaches," there remain crucial differences. One is the assumption both in critical theorizing work that listening is itself possible outside of the previously constructed power dynamics in and around global security politics. Quite the contrary, Gayatri Spivak suggests that there are times when the disempowered in global politics cannot speak even when they are being "listened to" as a result of the interlaced politics of race, class, and gender domination. Lene Hansen (2000) suggests, along similar lines that the endorsement of acts of listening and consciously pooling agency "presupposes the existence of a situation where speech is indeed possible" and neglects those who are "constrained in their ability to speak security and are therefore prevented from being subjects worthy of consideration and protection."

This critique has implications for the practice of security politics as such, and also for the practice of security theorizing, as Sarah Brown explains:

> The danger in attempts to reconcile international relations and feminism is twofold. Most immediately, the danger lies in uncritical acceptance by feminists of objects, methods, and concepts which presuppose the subordination of women. More abstrusely, it lies in the uncritical acceptance of the very possibility of gender equality.
>
> (Brown 1988, 470)

While Brown was talking about mainstream IR at the height of the neo-neo synthesis, and certainly not SAE theorists or other critical allies, I am concerned that a feminist SAE includes an uncritical acceptance of a concept which presupposes the subordination of women (a universalistic notion of human rights and entitlements) and an uncritical acceptance of not only the possibility of gender equality but also the idea that it can be achieved largely with an alliance with a theoretical approach which has often marginalized, oversimplified, and undervalued gender analysis.

There is, then, an important path to be navigated, which does not uncritically accept either the potential for gender equality (e.g., Zalewski 2007) or gender-subordinative concepts and understandings of security while at the same time finding ways to express complexity accessibly.

Ruminations

So, should there be a partnership between feminism and SAE approaches? At the minimum, it should be careful, and transformative to SAE. But perhaps the way to look at it is not to be happy that SAE work cites work *or* to start at SAE to see where feminism is compatible with it.

Instead, taking the feminist security project as itself intellectually and politically viable if diverse, I think the way to deal with the question of whether there should be an alliance between feminist work and SAE work is to ask what SAE adds to the feminist security project, and if what it adds counterbalances or outweighs what it takes away.

In my mind, then, what SAE adds to feminist security theorizing is numbers and allies, particularly outside of the feminist community. But in exchange for those numbers and allies, feminist security theorizing loses complex and contingent understandings of the subject of security, of voice in security politics, of what sex and gender are and how they operate in the world, and of what it means to be sensitive to voices that are not normally heard in global politics. Those costs may outweigh the benefits.

What might not, though, is another formulation of a potential partnership, led by a more nuanced understanding of critical theorizing and emancipation, such as that articulated in feminist IR and security work to this point. Particularly, instead of conceptualizing feminism as a standpoint approach that asks where the women are in global politics, a fruitful feminist–SAE alliance might follow the move in feminist theorizing from "where are the women" to "where is the gender" that this piece fundamentally does not adequately take account of.

Such a move would create space for a gender-inclusive critical theory of subordination politics, perhaps based on V. Spike Peterson's idea of feminization as devalorization, where to "*feminize* something or someone is to directly subordinate that person, political entitle, or idea, because values perceived as feminine are lower on the social hierarchy than values perceived as neutral or masculine" (Sjoberg 2006, 39, citing Peterson 1999). It is not only women who can be *feminized* in social and political life; feminization is something that can be done to people of any sex by people of any sex. It is only that we assume that the devalorization (see Peterson 2010b) and humiliation (see MacKinnon 1993) that comes with feminization is natural when it happens to women. In Peterson's words:

> Not only subjects (women and marginalized men), but also concepts, desires, tastes, styles, "ways of knowing" … can be feminized—with the

effect of reducing their legitimacy, status and value. Importantly, this devalorization is simultaneously ideological (discursive, cultural) *and* material (structural, economic). ... This devalorization normalizes—with the effect of "legitimating"—the marginalization, subordination, and exploitation of feminized practices and persons ... the "naturalness" of sex difference is generalized to the "naturalness" of masculine (not necessarily *male*) privilege, so that both aspects come to be taken-for-granted "givens" of social life.

(Peterson 2010b, 21)

Such an approach provides a way forward that neither requires radical individualism or essentialist notions of community, that understands the political existence and importance of silence, that provides room for varying interpretations of power, that takes explicit account of positionality, that doesn't need a woman's standpoint to emancipate or justify either women or feminism, and that might have the progressive potential Basu would like out of a feminist–SAE alliance while eschewing the discursive and actual violence inherent in the SAE understanding of people, their insecurities, their relations, and our re-presentations of them.

6 Russian veterans of the Chechen wars

A feminist analysis of militarized masculinities

Maya Eichler

Russia has waged two wars against the republic of Chechnya (1994–96, 1999–2009) since Chechnya's declaration of independence in November 1991. President Boris Yeltsin justified the first war with the need to restore constitutional order and disarm separatist forces in Chechnya. The war ended in a cease-fire agreement in August 1996, but a resolution of Chechnya's status was postponed. In Fall of 1999, federal armed forces were sent into Chechnya again, this time to wage a war against Chechen terrorism. The government declared an end to the counter-terrorist operation in April 2009, but violence continues to plague the North Caucasus.

The wars were not popular among Russians, except during the initial phase of the second war in 1999–2000 which coincided with the rise in popularity of Prime Minister Vladimir Putin and his election to the presidency. Not unlike the U.S. war in Vietnam, doubts about the wars expressed themselves in questions regarding the role of Russian troops in Chechnya. As Anna Politkovskaya (2004, 46) succinctly put it during the second Chechen war: "We all tried to make sense of these soldiers and officers who, every day, were murdering, robbing, torturing and raping in Chechnya. Were they thugs and war criminals? Or were they unflinching champions in a global war against international terrorism using all the weapons at their disposal, their noble aim justifying their means?" Dominant representations of the men who fought on the side of Russian federal forces in the Chechen wars (*chechentsy*) often diverged from the ideal of the heroic warrior. This chapter employs a gendered lens to ask how society and the state in post-Soviet Russia have regarded and treated the *chechentsy*, and also explores what these men think about their war and postwar experiences.

Doing feminist International Relations: militarized masculinities

My intellectual curiosity about veterans grows out of feminist International Relations (IR) scholarship on militarization and gender, which challenges assumptions about women's and men's *natural* roles in relation to peace and war. The association of women with pacifism and of men with militarism remains strong despite changes in the gender make-up of militaries during the twentieth century. Cynthia Enloe's work superbly illustrates that militarization relies on both men and women, and involves notions of masculinity and femininity] To assume that women are naturally peaceful overlooks the complexity of women's experiences (Enloe 2004, 151). [Women have been militarized both inside and outside of the military, as soldiers, military wives, prostitutes, nurses, rape victims, mothers, and feminist activists (Enloe 2000)]

[Neither can we assume men's militarism to be natural, as it relies on socialization, state policies such as conscription, and—increasingly—economic incentives.] The work by Enloe, Sandra Whitworth, and other feminist IR scholars sharpens our understanding of masculinity and militarism by examining both the *militarization* of men's identities and the *challenges* to their militarization. [First, feminist IR scholars use the concept of militarized masculinity to investigate how men's identities *become* militarized, how the meaning of manhood becomes linked to the military. They interrogate the policies and practices that militarize men's identities, such as conscription, basic training, hazing, and combat] (Altinay 2004; Enloe 2004; Whitworth 2004; Moon 2005). (Re)producing the link between masculinity and the military is important in order for the military to attract male soldiers, bolster morale, and engage in combat. [Two hegemonic representations of militarized masculinity emerge from feminist analyses of militarized masculinity: the citizen-soldier and the heroic warrior. Feminist IR scholars also investigate the violent consequences of militarizing men, which can be found in the sexual and other violence perpetrated by soldiers. This includes violent attacks against fellow soldiers and civilians during peace and war times, as well as during peacekeeping operations (Cockburn and Žarkov 2002; Whitworth 2004; Žarkov 2007). The second important contribution of feminist IR lies in uncovering the challenges and inherent contradictions to militarizing men's identities. Feminist scholars in IR expose the inherent fragility of militarized masculinity as it manifests itself in the post-traumatic stress disorder experienced by so many soldiers (Whitworth 2004, 2008). They also study draft evasion and war resistance as gendered processes through which demilitarization becomes possible (Enloe 1993, 53–54; Eichler 2006; Sharoni 2008).

This nuanced understanding of militarized masculinity developed by feminist IR scholars is particularly well suited to the study of veterans in post-Soviet Russia. It underscores the need to examine changes in militarized masculinity over time, and be attentive to the de- *and* re-militarization of men's identities. In the Soviet Union, a policy of universal male conscription reinforced the ties between the military, masculinity, and patriotism (Jones 1985). Veterans of the Great Patriotic War (World War II) were revered as heroes and exemplary citizens (Danilova 2007, paragraph 5). During the 1980s, however, the Soviet state began to encounter increasing difficulties with draft evasion and an overall loss of prestige for the military (Sapper 1994). In post-Soviet Russia, mass draft evasion and soldiers' mothers' activism indicate a full-fledged crisis of the citizen-soldier model.[2] In previous work I have explored how the crisis in militarized masculinity and patriotic motherhood has affected the Russian states' ability to wage war in Chechnya (Eichler

2006; see also Eichler 2008). In order to gain a more accurate picture of militarized masculinity in post-Soviet Russia, though, we also need to be curious about the men who *did* serve in the Chechen wars.

The chapter draws on a variety of sources, including fieldwork interviews conducted in Samara in 2006 as part of my dissertation research on militarized masculinity in post-Soviet Russia. Samara is the regional center of the Volga Federal District, located approximately 1,100 kilometers south-east of Moscow. I chose Samara for my fieldwork because I wanted to gain a better understanding of *regional* soldiers' mothers' groups, which had not yet received much scholarly attention compared with soldiers' mothers' groups in Moscow and St. Petersburg. Interviewees included soldiers' mothers' activists, draft evaders, veterans, and the chairs of veterans' organizations.[3] It should be noted that this chapter only examines Russian not Chechen, veterans, and also only explores male veterans of the Chechen wars.[4]

I focus on the representations of militarized masculinity in the stories of and about Russian veterans of the Chechen wars. I am interested in representations of Russian servicemen for what they tell us about gendered power relations.[5] One way to refine the question then, is to ask whether veterans serve as a model of masculinity in society. I argue that the ideal of the heroic warrior was challenged by three representations of the Russian serviceman: unwilling warrior, excessive warrior, and fragile warrior/marginalized citizen. I further argue that attempts to improve the image of the *chechentsy* have focused on representing them as patriotic heroes and male role models. Feminist analysis of veterans highlights the intimate relationship between gender inequality and militarism. It also acknowledges that gendered militarization is a complicated societal process: veterans may be celebrated and marginalized at the same time. Untangling these seemingly contradictory notions of militarized masculinity is key to improving our analysis of *how* militarization works. This I hope will contribute to the ongoing critique of militarism and militarized gender roles in feminist theory and practice.

Unwilling warriors

The Chechen wars exposed the diminished combat readiness of the armed forces in post-Soviet Russia. Military analysts linked the poor performance of Russian federal forces, especially in the first Chechen war to inadequate military preparation and soldiers' lack of training (Treenin and Malashenko with Lieven 2000, 109). Public opinion quickly turned against the war and media coverage was thorough in its depiction of both the plight of Russian soldiers and of civilians across the ethnic divide.[6] The first war became associated with an unheroic image of the conscript soldier as inadequately supplied, badly trained, and lacking morale.[7] Lieutenant General Aleksandr Lebed, one of the Kremlin's harshest critics on the war, famously disparaged the state of the Russian army by saying: "Russia no longer has an army—what it has is only military formations of boy-soldiers which are hardly capable of achieving anything" (quoted in Barylski 1998, 315). By referring to the troops as "boy-soldiers" he implicitly questioned their masculinity and ability to successfully wage war.

However, the first war also revealed that members of the military leadership did not embrace the role of heroic warrior. Over 500 officers, as well as a few prominent generals, resigned due to their opposition to the war (Goldstein 1997; Wagner 2000, 50). The officers and generals who remained did not necessarily support the war. General Lev Rokhlin, who commanded the northern group of forces in the Chechen operation and whose troops finally managed to take control of Grozny in January 1995, is a prominent example of this. Rokhlin was publicly skeptical of the official reasons given to justify the war. He considered the war to be politically motivated and thought it wrong for the military to be pulled into a "civil war." Rokhlin made a remarkable gesture when he refused all honors for his combat actions during the first Chechen war (Barylski 1998, 319).

To be a soldier means to be prepared to commit extreme physical violence on behalf of the state. Militaries are essentially about training men (and some women) to kill other human beings (Whitworth 2004, 151–52). When we look at the experiences of soldiers and officers fighting on the side of Russian federal forces in Chechnya, what emerges is a less-than straightforward relationship between masculinity and the ability to commit violence. In the interviews I conducted with veterans of the war during my fieldwork, I found stories of men who were morally opposed to the war or morally unprepared for war.

Mikhail R. served as a commanding officer in the first war but was troubled by the moral dilemmas of his participation. He commanded troops in the storming of Grozny on New Year's Eve 1994–95, during which his forces suffered huge losses with 62 men dead and 147 wounded. He described the night of December 31, 1994 as the worst day of his life and was especially distressed at having to hand over the bodies of dead soldiers to family members. Mikhail R. viewed the war as politically motivated and a result of the failure of the Russian and Chechen leadership to come to an agreement. He emphasized that he did not harbor negative feelings towards Chechens, who he considered to be "like us." In his opinion, the war was "unjust" in that "every people should decide its own fate." He therefore considered it "morally impossible" to fight a war against fellow citizens and regarded the casualties on both sides as a "senseless loss" (author Interview 2006).

The soldiers' lack of desire to fight was one of the main issues mentioned by Aleksei S. He served as a regiment commander during the first Chechen war, and focused on the insufficient "moral" preparation of soldiers when asked about his war experience. He described the soldiers under his command as fearful and overly concerned with the loss of human life, which undermined their ability to wage war. Aleksei S. acknowledged that experiencing fear is part and parcel of being a soldier and at times can be useful in war, but emphasized that overcoming fear was crucial to a soldier's ability to carry out his task, which is to "defeat the enemy." A well-trained soldier will be able to commit physical harm when ordered. According to Aleksei S., the Chechen wars signaled a change in the Russian soldier's ability to kill:

> Another important moral aspect is that a person who goes to war must be morally prepared for it. In which way? When he fires at a target, that is one thing. But when you have to fire at the enemy, at living people, that's a different matter. In Afghanistan our guys were prepared, but in Chechnya, unfortunately, they weren't.

> (Author Interview 2006)

The contrast with the Soviet–Afghan (1979–89) war is significant. It draws our attention not only to the superior combat capability of the Soviet army and its soldiers compared with the post-Soviet period, but also underlines the different ideological contexts within which the two wars were fought. The Soviet–Afghan war took place during the final years of the Soviet Union, which was still a time of ideological certainty compared to the ideological crisis of the post-communist years. As Dmitrii Pisarenko (1996, 13) points out, soldiers fighting in Afghanistan generally believed the official reasons given for the war. In the Chechen wars, societal uncertainty about the true reasons for the war translated into moral uncertainty for the soldiers fighting. The following quote from Arkady Babchenko's memoir of the wars nicely captures this feeling of uncertainty: "We don't know what we are fighting for. We have no goal, no morals or internal justification for what we do. We are sent off to kill and to meet our deaths but why we don't know" (Babchenko 2007, 161). The lack of certainty about the reasons for killing and dying makes evident the ideological (including gender) crisis surrounding these wars.

The two wars witnessed increased public debate and criticism of mandatory service, especially as conscripts, often poorly trained, were sent to the war zone. In a poll from January 2000, only 19 percent responded favorably to the idea of a close family member being conscripted. The most important reason for respondents' opposition to the drafting of a close family member was the "possibility of death/injury in Chechen-type conflicts" (48 percent) (Levada-Tsentr, "Armiia").[8] One of the draft evaders I interviewed, Nikolai mentioned the high casualty rates among conscripts during the first war as a reason for not heeding the draft: "It was a true 'meat-mincing machine' there, into which they threw untrained new conscripts. For many, that severely damaged their trust in the army. Nobody wanted to go to the army and die for no good reason" (author interview 2006). Distrust of the army significantly increased among Russians as a result of the first Chechen war (Caiazza 2002, 104–5).

During his presidential re-election campaign in 1996 Yeltsin pledged to abolish conscription by the year 2000 and to discontinue the practice of sending conscripts to conflict zones (unless they volunteered) (Barylski 1998, 373). Nevertheless, conscripts found themselves in Chechnya once again during the second war, and conscription continues to the time of writing.[9]

During the second war, the military switched its strategy from trying to reduce "collateral damage" to the massive use of force through air and artillery bombing to avoid federal troop casualties and, as one military analyst writes, to "compensate for the low quality of their fighting units in Chechnya" (Felgenhauer 2000). In early 2000, the Ministry of Defense promised that conscripts with less than six months of training would not be sent to the conflict zone (Sokirko 2000). In addition, President Putin declared that starting in 2005 federal forces in Chechnya would be composed entirely of contract soldiers (Tkachuk 2005). The state did increasingly use volunteers and professionals rather than conscripts to wage its war in Chechnya. While this reduced the conflict with society over the draft, it did not resolve the underlying problems of mismanagement and lack of morale which continued to plague the armed forces (Oushakine 2009, 134).

Excessive warriors

Running parallel to the unwilling warrior we find the representation of Russian servicemen as excessive warriors. International law and more specifically the Geneva Conventions outline the humanitarian treatment of prisoners and non-combatants, and set limits on the use of violence in war. The Chechen wars saw widespread violence against civilians, as documented by journalists and human rights activists (Human Rights Watch 2000; Politkovskaya 2001; also see Knight and Narozhna 2005). Though a majority of war crimes were never prosecuted, the representation of the excessive warrior potentially called into question the justness of the war and of the actions of Russian servicemen in Chechnya.

When soldiers and officers perpetrate violence against civilians rather than combatants, state and society may interpret their violent acts as excessive rather than heroic. Feminist scholars, however, argue that excessive violence perpetrated by soldiers is not incidental, but grows out of the very processes that help construct militarized masculinity. Sandra Whitworth (2004, 99) notes that military training "involves selecting for and reinforcing aggressive behaviour." Furthermore, the exaggerated ideals of manhood that are inculcated through military training often rely on the devaluation of (gendered, raced, and/or homosexual) "others." Excessive violence vis-à-vis the "other" is an outcome inherent to the making of soldiers (Whitworth 2004, Chapters 4 and 6). "The other" is central not only to the making but also to the reproduction of militarized masculinity. For example, a clear-cut picture of the "other" in war helps to justify more aggressive behavior toward the enemy. When soldiers start empathizing with the enemy, they lose their ability to commit physical violence.[10]

The close connection between excessive violence and the construction of the enemy was borne out in my interviews. Dmitrii, who served as a volunteer during the second war, is critical of the excessive force used by some servicemen in Chechnya. He stated in regards to the war: "It left an unforgettable imprint. But I don't feel hatred toward the Chechen people. I think that a soldier should not do everything in cold blood. If it is necessary, then he must fulfill his task, but without pouring out negative emotions" (Author Interview 2006). While Dmitrii rejected excessive violence, he considered a certain level of force necessary for a soldier to carry out the task he has been given.

In contrast, my interview with Anton illustrated a less restrained approach. A conscript during the first war, Anton was displeased with what he considered an inadequate execution of the war by his commanding officers. He favoured a more violent approach toward the Chechen fighters:

> Early on, I think it would have been necessary to do everything differently. It would have been necessary to be more tough, more brutal, simply to kill everyone, well, I don't mean to kill them all, but encircle the whole territory ... and announce, that whoever considers themselves a peaceful civilian should leave, we won't touch you ... and everyone who remains in the city, we'll consider a fighter.
>
> (Author Interview 2006)

Anton blames the military commanders for not permitting the soldiers to fight more brutally. Instead, he complains that the approach to the military operations in Chechnya was inconsistent. What bothered Anton most was the fact that federal forces lost the first war: "It hurts [*obidno*] that we weren't more brutal. War is war. People die" (Ibid.). Anton clearly was prepared to kill and commit the physical harm necessary to win the war. While Anton was careful to distinguish between Chechen fighters and civilians in the interview with me, a later conversation with him and his friends revealed that he held negative stereotypes towards Chechens, referring to them as "criminals" and "inferior beings."

Although Anton supported a more violent execution of the war, he was disappointed with the media portrayal of Russian federal forces as excessive warriors. In contrast to the many young men who have evaded the draft in post-Soviet Russia, Anton willingly embarked on his military service. He contrasted the voluntary nature of his service (despite being drafted) with the media's negative depiction of his service:

> I went voluntarily, I did everything I was told, I fulfilled all the tasks. My help was really needed there, I could tell, I spoke to the local population. I was really needed. ... And what did I receive in turn? What did they show on TV? That we are invaders. Especially NTV.[11] ... *That we were killing everyone* ... That we were unhappy fighters wandering about. The information flow was such ... *as if I was in the wrong. As if it hadn't been the country that sent us there, but we ourselves had decided to go.* That of course was not easy. ... The state wants to forget about the war as quickly as possible. It will all come out eventually
>
> (Ibid., emphasis added)

In Anton's view, the media betrayed the soldiers. It represented them as excessively violent, did not acknowledge their sacrifice, and blamed them rather than the state for the violence in Chechnya. The public depiction of the first Chechen war deeply affected Anton's sense of identity regarding his wartime role. As he stated above, he felt that the war was important and his role in it necessary, but he did not see this publicly recognized.

The themes of the "enemy" and of "betrayal" also appeared in the prominent case Colonel Iurii Budanov, the most prominent example of the excessive warrior in the Chechen wars. Budanov, commander of the 160th tank regiment in the second Chechen war, was arrested in March 2000 after strangling and killing a young Chechen woman, Elza Kungaeva. After an initial acquittal, Budanov was retried and sentenced in 2003 to ten years' imprisonment for the abduction and murder of Kungaeva. While there was strong evidence of Kungaeva's rape, this charge was dropped due to contradictory interpretations of whether the rape had taken place before or after her death (Sokolov undated, 1).

Budanov claimed to have arrested Kungaeva on evidence of her being a sniper and member of separatist forces. He explained that he had gone into a rage and killed her during the interrogation after apparently realizing that she was responsible for the recent death of some of his subordinates. Public criticism of Budanov was muted and there were few public calls for his conviction.[12] In general, more compassion was extended to Budanov than to Kungaeva, and this was achieved by falsely portraying the young Chechen woman as a combatant, despite the lack of evidence for her involvement with separatist forces (Regamey 2008).

Budanov's supporters emphasized his status as "military hero" and constructed an image of Budanov as the "victim" of the state and court system (Regamey 2008). Budanov received prominent support from Governor Vladimir Shamanov, a former general of the Chechen wars and previously Budanov's military superior. Shamanov interpreted Budanov's trial as "an ideological intervention of Western countries against Russia" and described him as "a true officer, commander, [and] the dignity of Russia" (quoted in "Sud dolzhen polnost'iu opravdat' polkovnika Budanova" 2001). Budanov also received support from the Committee of Soldiers' Mothers of Briansk and officers in Volgograd. The latter summed up the argument made by Budanov's supporters in the military: "in the person of Budanov they are judging the entire army for the fulfillment of its duty in Chechnya" (quoted in Sokolov undated, 2). For his supporters, Budanov become a symbol for the military's place in society and its role in the Chechen wars. If Budanov was on trial so was the army, and if his reputation was tarnished so would be the reputation of the army (Regamey 2008, paragraph 14).

This was one of the few legal cases that the Russian state has brought against armed forces personnel in Chechnya for crimes against civilians. The Putin administration and sections of the military leadership wanted to use the Budanov case to improve the reputation of the armed forces in Chechnya.

The chief of the Army's General Staff Anatolii Kvashnin, for example, commented after Budanov's arrest that "bastards like him have to be torn out of our Armed Forces by the roots" (quoted in Getmanenko 2000). Presidential aide Sergei Iastrzhembskii similarly reacted to Budanov's sentencing by stating: "The army is being cleansed of the people who have blackened its honor" (quoted in Andryukhin 2003). These prominent political and military figures were mostly concerned with the reputation of the armed forces and those who had served in the wars, arguing that Budanov just represented "a bad apple."

Representations of excessive warriors have the potential to de-stabilize militarism, as they highlight the violence and brutality of war and call into question its justness. Though the Chechen wars were generally not popular or considered just, they did not lead to a deeper public reflection on the excessive violence of militarized men. Instead, arguments about the enemy, betrayal, and a "few bad apples" sidelined the important issue of war crimes and sexual violence perpetrated by Russian servicemen in Chechnya.

Fragile warriors, marginalized citizens

The dominant representation of the Chechen war veteran is of a person who suffers from the "Chechen syndrome." The media, society, veterans' and soldiers' rights groups, and sometimes veterans themselves use the term to describe a cluster of problems associated with the transition from combat to civilian life of armed forces personnel who have served in Chechnya. As in other wars, many veterans experienced extreme levels of fear and stress during combat which led to post-traumatic stress disorder.[13] The Chechen syndrome entails psychological and medical problems such as depression, anxiety, and insomnia as well as alcohol and drug abuse (Russell 2007, 12).

Whitworth (2004) argues that there are inherent contradictions in militarized masculinity between the warrior image and men's actual identities that contribute to post-traumatic stress disorder (PTSD). The emotions some men experience in war such as anxiety, shame, and pain lay bare the contradictions and inherent fragility of militarized masculinity. Such emotions are usually associated with femininity and seen as contrary to the image of the tough military man (Whitworth 2004, 166–67). On the other hand, men who suffer from combat stress often deal with their condition by engaging in practices which Tracey Xavia Karner has called "toxic" masculinity: alcoholism, drug abuse, and aggressive behavior (Karner 1998, 231).

The tensions between the tough warrior image and combat-related stress were apparent in my interview with Anton, who served as a conscript during the first war. He began his recollection of returning home from combat like this: "I wouldn't say that I lost my mind … or that I saw some things. Nothing especially bad … but of course, it affected me" (Author Interview 2006). Anton emphasized that he did not suffer from combat-related stress. On the contrary, he argued that the war made him realize that he was well suited to deal with extreme situations. After making this assertion, he suddenly recalled:

"I can't at all watch war movies, not one. Before the army, I greatly enjoyed watching war movies. Now, as soon as the movie starts, I'm in tears, I'm crying" (ibid.). Though Anton viewed his own identity in terms of a tough version of militarized masculinity, it struck me that Anton had almost forgotten to mention the more "feminized" and emotional side of his postwar life.

Mikhail R., a commanding officer during the first war, described the effects of the war on his own life in terms of the Chechen syndrome. This is how he explained the Chechen syndrome:

> After a person has found himself in an extreme situation such as war he psychologically views life differently. Everything is divided into black and white, into true and false. The person develops a feeling of special justice and others no longer understand him. He turns inward and this process often involves the abuse of alcohol. This person now feels the need to speak the truth about anything he perceives as unjust, which creates conflict with others.
>
> (Ibid.)[14]

This quote speaks to the estrangement veterans experience when returning to civilian life, and the perceived incompatibility between military and civilian values. Veterans argue that civilian life is less sincere and truthful and that those who have not served in war can never truly understand them (Morgan 1994, 169; Pozhidaev 1999, 71; Babchenko 2007, 405).

The contradictions between the warrior ideal and men's lived experiences can continue into the postwar period, not just in terms of psychological difficulties, but also in respect to veterans' social marginalization. In the case of veterans of the Chechen wars, the Chechen syndrome and the lack of social and state recognition undermine their representation as heroic warriors. In addition, *chechentsy* have also experienced difficulty in living up to hegemonic representations of *civilian* masculinity, such as desirable husband or breadwinner.

Not unlike other veterans such as U.S. Vietnam veterans, Chechen war veterans describe their psychological difficulties as linked to the lack of understanding they encounter upon their return home. The ambiguous nature of the Chechen wars in Russian society may well have aggravated the Chechen syndrome. As Whitworth (2004, 168) notes, U.S. studies have found that "the incidence of PTSD appears to be higher among soldiers who participated in armed conflicts that resulted in an ambiguous military outcome, or in which they faced a less appreciative societal homecoming at the end of the hostilities." Writing towards the end of the first war, Pisarenko (1996) argued that the Chechen war would create a more serious "syndrome" compared with the Soviet–Afghan war. He linked this to the fact that for those fighting in Afghanistan "the sense of the war still held—propaganda still worked" (Pisarenko 1996). The author viewed societal opposition to the Chechen war as the main factor aggravating the Chechen syndrome. He asked how a young conscript would perceive his situation upon return: "Either he must consider himself wrong that he fought in Chechnya, or he must stand in opposition to society itself" (Pisarenko 1996). Opinion polls document that society has generally not supported the wars in Chechnya, except for the initial phase of the second war.[15] While only 5 to 7 percent of Afghan war veterans kept their service in Afghanistan a secret, this is apparently more common among Chechen war veterans according to the author. In addition, the Chechen syndrome is exacerbated by the fact that the soldier is "fighting on the territory of his own country" (Pisarenko 1996). And, finally, Pisarenko (1996) noted that soldiers are returning to a society undergoing post-communist transition and racked by instability itself, which "appears as a mini-model of a war situation." Afghan war veterans in contrast returned to a relatively stable and calm society which facilitated their transition to civilian life (Pisarenko 1996.).

The social conflicts which arise from combat-related stress are most intimately experienced by family members, especially wives (Shepeleva 2007, 110–16). On the other hand, unmarried veterans complain that it is difficult to find a woman who will put up with a Chechen veteran. As Vadim puts it in a documentary on the Chechen syndrome: "If you turn up in company, girls in particular are very wary. They think that people who have come back from Chechnya are really messed up, that we are grenades waiting to explode. But then, when they get to know us better they realized we are ... real men" (Sturdee 2007, part two). This quote points to the fact that Chechen war veterans are generally not seen as desirable men, although Vadim insinuates that he is more of a man than someone who has not fought in war.

Difficulty finding a job after returning from combat service is also a frequent complaint among veterans of the Chechen wars. Mikhail R. argued that veterans' strong sense of right and wrong makes it difficult for them to fit into a collective such as a workplace (author interview 2006).[16] However, most veterans describe the problem of one of potential employers' prejudice against them. This prejudice consists of labeling Chechen war veterans as being psychologically not in order (author interview 2006; also see Kay 2006, 51). As one veteran who was featured in a documentary film on the Chechen syndrome remarked: "When they find out you've served, they say you're not suitable. That happened to me. Because I was in combat in the North Caucasus, people say I'm psychologically disturbed" (Sturdee 2007, part one). In my conversations with soldiers' mothers activists in Samara, they complained that veterans were not treated fairly on the job market and were forced into criminal structures or the drug trade. Finding work for ex-soldiers was one of the areas of activity of the Samara soldiers' mothers group *Sodeistvie*. Maria, a member of the group, explained:

> After the first Chechen war guys had a hard time adapting. Nobody wanted to hire them: they had seen blood and had nightmares at night. It was considered that they are still at war and can't think of anything else ... Then societal organizations such as ours began to raise the issue

that veterans of armed conflicts need to be hired. Otherwise what happened is that such guys would "lose" themselves after returning from the army: there's no work, no money. They began to drink and take drugs ... We helped them find work. Some special security firms were created for them.

(Author Interview 2006)

In Russia's post-communist economy, militarized skills are in demand and the security sector seems to be one niche into which veterans can break. Ex-soldiers are most likely to find work in the private security industry as the state sector often rejects them (Oushakine 2009, 177). A survey conducted in 1996 among veterans of the first war found that more than 50 percent were intent on working in a private security firm or the state security structures (Pozhidaev 1999, 72).

The delay in state recognition further complicated the postwar status of Chechen war veterans. They fell between the cracks, as the law "On Veterans" (1995) only recognized veterans of the Great Patriotic War (World War II) and "participants in combat operations on the territory of other countries" such as veterans of the Soviet–Afghan war. In 2002, almost eight years after the start of the first Chechen war, the law "On Veterans" was finally amended to give Chechen war veterans the status of "veterans of combat operations," but not of veterans of *war*.[17] In line with the amendments, veterans of the Chechen campaigns are now entitled to a number of special benefits such as 50 percent discounts on social housing, free prescription drugs, free public transit, and more ("Sotsrochkoi na god: L'goty voevavshim v Chechne" 2003). The new law went into force in January 2004, but veterans report that it is hard to access the benefits. Members of both soldiers' mothers groups in Samara mentioned assistance to veterans in claiming benefits as an important part of their work (Author Interviews 2006).

There is a sense among Chechen war veterans that the state does not sufficiently acknowledge their service through social welfare provisions (Pozhidaev 1999, 72–73). All of my interviewees complained about the lack of adequate benefits for veterans, and framed their grievance in terms of a lack of dignity and respect. Anton who had served as a conscript in Chechnya remarked: "I wouldn't say that people relate negatively to those who served in the army. But I think that people who served are worthy of more attention, are *worthy of more respect* and I would like this to be reflected in a *concrete* way" (Author Interview 2006, emphasis added). Anton's observations make evident that for him the state's and society's recognition of servicemen should be reflected in concrete economic terms. A similar point was made by Dmitrii, a former contract soldier, who commented:

The state did not relate to my service entirely *worthily*. I am not only talking about myself, but also about many other people. People who choose service in the army for their whole life, go for many deprivations, and the state should relate to them with *respect*. The minimum should be the allocation of housing, and there are big problems with this. I'm not even speaking of vacations, sanatoriums, and other things.

(Ibid., emphasis added)

Both men argued that to show respect to ex-service people means to provide them with adequate social welfare (cf. Oushakine 2009, 164–65). The argument underscores the necessary material basis for a revival of militarized masculinity in post-Soviet Russia.

Veterans and their families have founded organizations to promote there interests vis-à-vis the state. For example, *Pamiat'* ("Memory") is a group in Samara made up of veterans of combat operations in Dagestan and Chechnya. With not much success, this group has tried to address the economic problems families face due to the loss of a breadwinner who has either been killed or is unable to work. Similarly, the Committee *Chechnya*, a Samara organization of widows and families of fallen soldiers, aims to secure housing and health benefits for families of fallen soldiers and education for the children. The group also works on legal reform to ensure that widows and family members of fallen *chechentsy* are entitled to benefits. Valentina, the chair of the Committee *Chechnya*, also ties the issue of benefits to the question of dignity: "The laws have not yet been brought to the level, at which families of the deceased can live with *dignity*. Why, for example, do widows get married for a second time? Because it is very difficult to raise kids by oneself" (ibid., emphasis added). As these examples show, the Russian state has not adequately addressed the difficulty of Chechen war veterans to play the role of breadwinner, or compensated for the lack of a breadwinner in families of fallen soldiers.

Representations of Chechen war veterans expose the inherent fragility of the warrior and the social marginalization of militarized men (and their families) in post-Soviet Russia. *Chechentsy* would have only been able to become a model of masculinity if they had received more adequate rehabilitation and welfare benefits to help them make the transition from military to civilian life, and if society had accepted the Chechen wars as necessary and just. However, the ideological and material conditions of post-communist transformation undermined this particular model of masculinity.

Chechen war veterans as patriotic heroes

During the second Chechen war, the political and military leadership as well as some veterans' groups attempted to improve the image of the *chechentsy* by portraying them as patriotic heroes and defenders of the motherland. This can be seen as part of President Putin's broader agenda to strengthen the state through a renewed emphasis on militarized patriotism. The political and military leadership formed a united front on the military operation, and rejected society's apparent betrayal of the military during the first war.

President Putin blamed defeat in the first Chechen war on society's lack of support for the soldiers:

> You would agree that Russia's defeat in the first Chechen war was due to a large extent due [sic] to the state of society's morale. Russians didn't understand what ideals our soldiers were fighting for. Those soldiers gave their lives and in return they were anathematized. They were dying for the interests of their country and they were publicly humiliated.
> (Putin with Gevorkyan, Timakova, and Kolesnikov 2000, 171)

Putin stressed the need to raise the prestige of the military and acknowledge the heroism of its service people.

The government's emphasis on militarized patriotism led to the reintroduction of patriotic education into Russian schools in 2000. The patriotic education program includes courses on Russian military history with a special emphasis on World War II, as well as participation in military-related clubs and events. The official aim of these educational programs is to instill loyalty to the motherland, and in young men a sense of obligation to serve in the military. The goal is thus to prepare children for military service and the defense of the country. Veterans are seen as an integral part of the state's patriotic education program, and are invited to give lectures and teach basic military skills (Sperling 2009, 230–41). The state has actively encouraged Chechen (and Afghan) war veterans to participate in the program, in order to replace the dwindling number of World War II veterans (Sieca-Kozlowski 2010, 77–78).

When veterans serve as a model of masculinity, there is usually not much room to question militarism or the myth of protection which posits men as the militarized protectors of women (Tickner 2001, 49–51). The celebration of male veterans as heroes reinforces militarized citizenship and its gendered assumptions. Through their involvement in patriotic education, Chechen (and Afghan) veterans serve as a model for the younger generations, just as veterans of the Great Patriotic War served as a model to their parents (Oblastnoi telekanal RIO 2008). A documentary on the Chechen syndrome features a Chechen war veteran, Vadim, who was not able to find work after his return from Chechnya but now leads the patriotic education program in a local school in Yaroslavl'. The gendered nature of this program becomes evident when the (female) principal of the school remarks on the positive influence Vadim has on the children, especially considering that many of them are brought up by single mothers and lack male role models (Sturdee 2007, part two). This remark recalls late Soviet debates which emphasized the importance of military service to male socialization in the context of the apparently growing "feminization" of Soviet society (Jones 1985, 103, 153). Elisabeth Sieca-Kozlowski (2010, 76) argues that the patriotic education program employs a pedagogy which "glorifies the soldier-hero and the feats of strong and courageous men, but also close friends and relatives, and fathers." The integration of Chechen war veterans into the patriotic education program helps both to rehabilitate the image of *chechentsy* and revive the link between masculinity, military service, and patriotism in society more generally. Sieca-Kozlowski argues that it can also be seen as a state tool to better control veterans, in particular in view of their involvement in violent and criminal acts upon their return from the war zone (Sieca-Kozlowski 2010).

During my fieldwork in Samara, I found that veterans' groups emphasized a representation of veterans as patriotic heroes and defenders of the motherland in order to further their goal of better material recognition. This entailed a focus on veterans' sacrifice and on memorializing fallen soldiers. For example, both the Committee *Chechnya* and *Pamiat'* were instrumental in having a town memorial erected that is dedicated to soldiers who died in local wars, including the Chechen wars.[18] Other local veterans' and soldiers' mothers groups were also involved in the process. The chair of *Pamiat'* named the construction of the memorial as his organization's main success, considering the lack of success it had in achieving improved economic and social conditions for veterans. However, veterans' groups use the politics of memorializing in their continued attempts to secure better material provisions for their members. They frame the issue in terms of a "social contract" between servicemen and the state: veterans fulfilled their duty vis-à-vis the state, and the state should acknowledge their sacrifice. The chair of the Committee *Chechnya* said about the soldiers who had served in Chechnya during the memorial celebrations of the fourteenth anniversary of the start of the first Chechen war: "They all worthily fulfilled their duty and we, their close ones, have nothing to be ashamed of in front of the state. We hope it too will not forget us" (quoted in Krainova 2008). Thus, the memorializing serves not only to integrate the memories of fallen soldiers into the memory of the nation, but functions as a basis for claims to the state.

Significantly, the memorializing of fallen soldiers and celebration of veterans relies on a reinterpretation of the wars, in which doubts about the war's necessity are replaced by a new certainty. Aleksandr Iaroslavets, commander of the 81st motor-rifle regiment during the first war, commented during the same memorial celebration:

> Much time has already passed since our regiment left Samara for Chechnya, but the pain of loss has not gone. Often I am asked: were these sacrifices necessary? In the beginning we ourselves did not know, whether we did the right thing to go there. But afterwards, when we saw the suffering of the civilian population, of children, all these horrors, our doubts disappeared. We were obliged to defend our citizens. Our memory will be eternal. Nobody will forget what was done.
>
> (quoted in Krainova 2008)

This constructed memory of the war is also one from which the war crimes committed by federal forces and the memories of those who refused service or served unwillingly are obliterated. It does not serve as a basis for anti-war activism, but rather works to re-militarize society. The possible disruption of militarized masculinity through the experiences of Chechen war veterans is negated when veterans participate in the reproduction of militarized patriotism (cf. Oushakine 2009, 185–90). Attempts to reinterpret the memory of the Chechen wars and reinvent Chechen veterans as role models may reshape how Russian society conceives of the wars and its veterans. However, they do not resolve the material challenges which continue to weaken militarized masculinity in post-Soviet Russia.

Conclusion

This chapter has analyzed notions of masculinity embedded in the stories of Chechen war veterans as well as in society's and the state's views of Chechen war veterans. The first war revealed not only many men's lack of willingness to serve, but the serious problems with morale among those fighting. At the same time, some federal servicemen in Chechnya represented excessive warriors who use undue violence and commit war crimes. Importantly, neither of these masculinities was ideologically useful to the waging of war and to increasing public support for the war. The representation of the unwilling warrior epitomized the diminished state of the armed forces in post-Soviet Russia compared to the Soviet Union. The representation of the excessive warrior cast doubts on the justness of the war and the military's actions in Chechnya. While the men who hesitated to kill often held a neutral or ambiguous view of Chechens, Budanov justified his killing of Kungaeva on the basis that he thought she was a sniper. Militarized masculinity and the legitimacy of the actions of militarized men are thus reinforced by a clear-cut definition of "the enemy." However, it has been precisely the ambiguity of Chechens as both the enemy and citizens of the Russian Federation which has made these wars so complicated both for society and armed forces service personnel.

The Chechen wars were not officially recognized as wars, and service personnel who fought in Chechnya were not legally recognized as veterans and thus not entitled to state benefits until 2002 (the law was implemented in 2004). Their ambiguous status and society's lukewarm support for the wars have made it difficult for these men to define their postwar identities. Many faced the negative psychological effects of combat experience, which further hinder their social and economic reintegration into society. Some veterans have attempted to shape public perceptions and state policy by promoting the symbolic recognition of veterans and fallen soldiers as heroes, which goes hand in hand with the state's renewed emphasis on militarized patriotism under Putin's presidencies (2000–2008). This leads to an uncritical view of the wars and its participants which silences the many contradictions of militarized masculinity that the Chechen wars revealed.

Many of the contradictions of militarized masculinity described here are not unique to the Russian-Chechen wars but linked to the very construction of the ideal soldier as tough and heroic warrior. Some men's hesitancy to kill, others' excessive use of violence, and soldiers' experience of post-traumatic stress are more common than states and militaries want to acknowledge, and can be found in many other contexts. What makes militarized masculinity such a salient issue in the Russian case is the context of post-communist transformation and crisis. Despite President Putin's emphasis on the image of the heroic Russian soldier fighting in Chechnya and other attempts to reshape the image of war veterans, the lack of ideological coherence regarding the wars and the lack of financial resources to support veterans undermined Chechen war veterans as a model of masculinity in post-Soviet Russia.

Notes

1 More recently, feminist research in IR has begun to examine women as perpetrators of violence across conflicts (Sjoberg and Gentry 2007; Sjoberg 2009b).
2 For most of the post-Soviet period, the Russian state was only successful in drafting about 10 percent of draft-age men. The rest either legally or illegally obtain an exemption or deferment, or simply fail to follow their draft summons (Golts 2004, 75). Soldiers' mothers' organizations such as the Moscow Union of Soldiers' Mothers' Committees of Russia and the Human Rights Organization Soldiers' Mothers of Saint Petersburg have been the most vocal supporters of draft evaders.
3 The names of the interviewees have been changed to protect their anonymity.
4 The number of female volunteers in the post-Soviet armed forces has increased, but not many women participated in the wars, and I was only able to interview one female veteran.
5 For the importance of linking the study of masculinity to an analysis of power, see, for example, Enloe (2007).
6 In December 1994 as well as in January 1995 only 30 percent of respondents supported "decisive measures to bring order to Chechnya," and between 60 and 70 percent rejected the use of force (Doktorov et al. 2002, 132).
7 For visual images of the unheroic conscript soldier, see the evocative photos by Heidi Bradner, available at www.heidibradner.com/galleries/lostboys/index.html#1.
8 The other most common reasons included "hazing" and "violence in the army" (34 percent) and "the difficult living conditions, poor food, and health hazards" (27 percent) (Levada-Tsentr, "Armiia").
9 There has, however, been an overhaul of the conscription system which led to a reduction of service from two years to one year as of 2008.
10 This process is evident in the stories of soldiers who become war resisters (e.g., Key and Hill 2007).
11 Anton is referring to the private network NTV's coverage of the first war which was highly critical of the official line on the war. For more on NTV's coverage, see Mickiewicz (1999, 242–63).
12 While public opinion was generally supportive of Budanov, Regamey (2008) points out that it is hard to distinguish public indifference from compassion for Budanov.
13 There is no available statistic on the overall number of Chechen war veterans suffering from the stress-related effects of combat, although the results of various medical studies indicate that as many as two-thirds of service personnel experienced combat-related psychological problems (Belinskii and Liamin 2000; Thomas and O'Hara, 2000).
14 This interview was not taped and the quote is based on detailed notes taken during the interview.

15 During the first war (1994–96), approximately one-third of the population supported the war (Doktorov et al. 2002, 132). The highest support for the second war (1999–2009) was recorded in February 2000, with 70 percent in favor, after which support began to decrease (Levada-Tsentr, "Chechnia").

16 Mikhail R.'s point was borne out in a survey among Chechen and Afghan veterans which found that a quarter of them had difficulty functioning in the work collective and half of them had repeatedly switched jobs. The survey was conducted in 1996 among 3,144 veterans of the Chechen and Afghan wars living in Riazan Oblast' (Pozhidaev 1999, 71).

17 While the state refuses to recognize the Chechen campaigns as wars, it is important to note that those who have fought on the side of federal forces refer to them as wars (Novikova 2007, 76).

18 By the end of 2008, 250 citizens of Samara Oblast' serving in the Chechen wars had been killed (Strelets 2008).

When feminists explore masculinities in IR

An engagement with Maya Eichler

Cynthia Enloe

I have learned so much from reading Maya Eichler's innovative analysis of the militarized politics of Russian ex-soldiers' masculinities. And, I think, what I've learned from Eichler has serious implications for all of us as we move forward now in our collective endeavor to employ feminist analyses to make better sense of the dense workings of international politics.

Let me try to spell out exactly what Maya Eichler's research and analysis have taught me. First, and particularly important at this moment in the evolution of international intellectual life, Eichler's work has reminded me to keep my *feminist* brain cells alert when anyone talks about masculinities. That is, as masculinities become the topic of more and more research, we all will need to avoid sliding into the practice of treating masculinities as singular, as static, or as de-contextualized.

That is, masculinities are as disparate as are femininities. And they are situated in specific times and places. Still, the growing evidence demonstrates, if any masculinity operates within a patriarchally organized society, it is likely (especially if it is deemed heterosexualized) to be placed hierarchically above most femininities. The socially constructed and valorized form of masculinity of a male nuclear weapons scientist and that of a bemedaled infantryman might be very different, yet both privileged in most contemporary patriarchal societies for being recognized as legitimate and socially valuable forms of militarized manhood. This is what the combined feminist scholarship of Carol Cohn (1987), Orna Sasson-Levy (2003), Sandra Whitworth (2004), Insook Kwon (2005), Sabine Frühstück (2007), Yasmin Husein Al-Jawaheri (2008), Ayse Gul Altinay (2009), as well as Jane Parpart and Marysia Zalewski (2008) and their contributor, Setsu Shigamatsu and Keith Camacho (2010) and their contributors, and Laura Sjoberg (2010b) and her contributors all together have persuasively revealed in their explorations of the politics of militarized masculinities. Maya Eichler is adding to the mounting evidence.

Simultaneously, we need to resist the creation of an investigatory model that licenses a new conceptual patriarchal model for dismissing women. While the social constructions and complex operations of diverse masculinities are indeed topics for international politics specialists, Maya Eichler confirms here what these same feminist scholars have exposed: that the militarized workings of, and the consequences of the constructions of diverse masculinities (a) are constantly contested both by men and by women, (b) are objects of statist militarizing manipulation, (c) are a cause for statist militarized anxieties, and (d) a basis on which male and female citizens create many of their own ideas about, and actions toward the state, security, the nation and the "Other." As Eichler and her feminist colleagues problematizing the militarization of masculinities demonstrate, the politics of masculinities are most reliably understood if they are explored using explicitly feminist concepts, feminist questions and feminist methodologies.

Second, Maya Eichler's careful study of the sometimes proud, often alienated, Russian men who served in the state's military during the two Chechnya campaigns has underscored for me the analytical value of feminist interviewing. That is, so much of the study of international relations—often out of necessity because of the cloak of secrecy and the power inequalities that characterize the international political arena—is done several handshakes removed from the actors that we can forget that individuals are diverse, complex, hard-to-fathom creatures. It takes feminist listening, therefore, to take on board interviewees' contradictions, confusions and anxieties. By feminist listening, I mean listening for not only what is said, but what is not said, listening for unspoken assumptions about achieving and holding on to respected forms of manhood, about fear of feminization, about ideals of relationships between men and between men and women. Feminist listening is not arrogant, however. That is it doesn't set the listener up as knowing more about what the speaker means than the speaker her/himself. Rather, it is a form of listening energized by a boundless curiosity about patriarchy's subtle ways of shaping our individual and collective lives.

It takes feminist reflexivity to prevent our carrying away from such puzzling interviews as Eichler conducted in Russia the dangerous conclusion that we as researchers are somehow more coherent, more logical, and less vulnerable than our interviewees.

That is, being consciously feminist in one's interviewing is a strong antidote to creating a power hierarchy between interviewer and interviewees. Yet, despite the difficulties of conducting interviews in a genuinely feminist manner, plunging into interviewing, as Eichler shows us, can expose surprising dynamics in international politics that we would otherwise miss. For instance, masculinized, militarized military veterans are not always likely to support their own masculinized, militarized state. This is one of the reasons almost all state elites worry about veterans—not necessarily worry in a way that produces valuable programs to support men (and the few women) once they've left military service. Rather, elites worry that precisely because in so many societies veterans, especially male veterans are held up as models citizens, as people who have sacrificed for the sake of the state and the nation, veterans speaking out against the state, or against a state's use of them, can seriously compromise the government's credibility. Many peace movement activists know this, of course, which is why they often deliberately seek to make alliances with disaffected military veterans, especially disaffected male veterans, since that enhances the masculinized credentials of often popularly feminized peace movements. Such alliances, are not without their risks, however. First, they may lure peace activists to privilege certain sorts of masculinity for the sake of gaining public approval. Second, disaffected veterans may nonetheless harbor distinctly patriarchal ideas and values that contradict those of many (not all) of the women who have invested their energies in peace activism.

A third lesson that Eichler has taught me: it is vital now more than ever to keep resisting the insidious tendency to universalize American experiences. Feminist work has led the way in internationalizing our sources of knowledge about global politics, and Eichler's essay is an excellent example. At a time when the US is the world's major weapons buyer and seller, when the US has more overseas bases and maneuvers than any other state, when English is the globally dominant language, and when the US government with seeming impunity refuses to join major international treaty regimes, it is sometimes difficult to resist focusing research gazes on the United States, and even more difficult to broaden students' conceptions of the important things to learn about the world. Especially when, inside the United States, American experiences of wars and of postwars, the American experiences of gendered militarization, the American experiences of gendered cultural story-telling, the American experiences of PTSD, and the American experiences of state manipulation and neglect attract the most media coverage, it is important to continue to study and teach about the lives of people who that coverage neglects. This is a role feminist work has played and can continue to play in the discipline and in global politics.

In her work, Maya Eichler has rowed against this Americanizing tide, and provided evidence that there are important sites of global politics all over the world. Eichler chose to study the Russian gendered experiences of militarized masculinities. She makes explicit the particular state contexts of the wars and postwar periods she investigates—the first, being when the Soviet Union was coming unraveled, the second being during the early stages of the post-Soviet Russian state's re-congealing. As I read this engaging chapter, I kept thinking of how little we know about Iraqi or Afghan male veterans' dynamic understandings of their manliness, about Chilean or Chinese men's thinking—and re-thinking—of how military service has enhanced or put dents in their own masculinized self-esteem. Thanks to the spread of feminist international political enquiries, we are starting to learn more about Turkish, Irish, Japanese, Fijian, British, Canadian, and South Korean militarized masculinities. But we are constantly on the verge of letting the American military, media, and economic global reach cast a shadow over other realities that we need to understand. In the last 15 years, especially, feminist researchers have taken deliberate steps to de-center American intellectual influence. If those steps continue, Maya Eichler shows us, we all will reap the intellectual rewards.

Fourth, and related, Eichler's delving into the intra-Russian processes of (a) individual gendered self-esteem and alienation, (b) cultural constructions and debates, and (c) domestic policymaking and official justification all together provides convincing evidence that the early feminist IR assertion remains valid: one cannot make reliable sense of international politics by treating any state as a monolithic actor. "The state" in reality is a bee hive of gendered, classed, raced, generational interactions. And those dense, historically situated, often behind-closed-doors interactions do not occur on a level playing field. Patriarchy, as feminists have shown, is one of the most potent "tilters" of the proverbial political playing field. What feminist analysts have done is to make the investigations of international politics a lot harder for the sake of making them a lot more realistic. They have shown that it is irresponsibly lazy for analysts to treat any state so simplistically. In fact, as Eichler's mind-opening study shows, not even "the state's military" can be reliably talked about as if it were one cohesive political actor. Any military's interactions with other sectors of the state, its fluctuating popular support over time, its internal cohesion or conflict, its operational capacity—each is determined in significant measure by the raced, ethnicized, and classed politics of masculinities.

Taking the lid off the state, revealing the gendered (usually patriarchal gendered) power dynamics that are at work every day to sustain the myth of the state-as-nation, the state-speaking-with-one-voice, was one of the most subversive intellectual actions of feminists. This move made it clear that the insights of "Comparative Politics," "Political Theory," and "International Relations" are all relevant to studying global politics, as are insights from anthropology, economics, history, literary and media studies, geography and sociology. While feminists are not the only scholars to have broken down the disciplinary barriers of political science or the subfield barriers within the discipline, feminists have uniquely leveraged those different perspectives to account for phenomena that traditional approaches to research in global politics cannot see, including but not limited to masculinities, femininities, patriarchy, and feminization from the centers of power to the very margins of global social and political life.

Finally, by comparing the quite different impacts of two postwar eras' assumptions about male veterans' self-esteem, Maya Eichler has reminded me that doing useful feminist analysis of international politics requires a long attention span. Eichler's research joins other feminists' new work on the genderings of politics of postwar eras. Eichler's questions and her findings remind me never to assume that any war is over when a peace agreement is signed, when soldiers are demobilized or news of armed conflict drops off the front pages.

Any war lasts as long as male veterans are proud of, or are resentful of, their military experiences. Any war lasts as long as women veterans suffer in silence. Any war lasts as long as state officials and cultural elites seek to shape male and female citizens' beliefs by constructing an image of heroic veterans of particular wars. Any war lasts as long as any woman in her role as a mother cares for a mentally or physically damaged military veteran. Any war lasts as long as a woman married to a male military veteran goes to his regiment's annual reunions, as long as she wonders what he won't tell her about his military experiences.

War and wars have attracted a stunning proportion of all IR's collective attention. That in itself may be problematic: has IR developed into a militarized discipline in so far as its scholars deem wars the most intellectually exciting international phenomenon to study? Yet feminist IR has valuably upset the study of wars by revealing that to explain and show the dynamics of and consequences of any war one has to train one's enlivened curiosity on the years before the war, on the lives of civilians, on the experiences and beliefs of women and men far from the centers of power, and on the prolonged aftermath of that war.

The feminist IR canvas is wider than the non-feminist IR canvas. The feminist palette holds a much wider range of colors and textures than the inadequate non-feminist palate, and the feminist paint brushes are far more numerous than those of the ill-equipped non-feminist painter. For the future, we may have to add even more space to our canvas, more colors to our palates and even more brushes to our kit. What I think is the hallmark of feminist IR is that we are not afraid of such a future.

7 The technoscience question in feminist International Relations

Unmanning the U.S. war on terror

Eric M. Blanchard

> Technoscience calls war into question (war will destroy the world) and simultaneously provides the rationales for continuing it (war can now be managed; war can be fought between bloodless machines).
>
> Chris Hables Gray (1997, 247)

> It's the changes in society that lead to the changes in the military. I do believe that to a considerable extent the nation makes war the way it makes wealth. What you're seeing is a restructuring of society with the information age.
>
> Arthur Cebrowski (in Der Derian 2009, 131)

During her visit to Pakistan in October 2009, United States Secretary of State Hillary Clinton received wide media coverage for her comments that she found "it hard to believe that nobody in [the Pakistani] government knows where they [al-Qaeda leaders] are and couldn't get them if they really wanted to" (Landler 2009). Receiving less attention was Clinton's encounter with the women of Pakistan during a town-hall style meeting in Islamabad on the final day of her trip. At this televised conference, Clinton took questions from a panel and audience made up of women activists, academics, lawyers, journalists, parliamentarians, and businesswomen from across Pakistan (Yusuf 2009). While the carefully staged meeting was meant to finish the trip on a high note, the female audience voiced dissatisfaction with the U.S. war on terror policy in Pakistan; as one journalist addressed Clinton, "You had one 9/11, and we are having daily 9/11s in Pakistan" (Rodriguez 2009). Another audience member asked Clinton whether the American use of "drones"—the unmanned aerial vehicles (UAVs) that have become a central component of the American war on terror—could be considered as an act of terrorism, comparable to the car bombing that killed 100 civilians in a crowded market in the city of Peshawar in the week just prior to Clinton's visit. Does terrorism include, the woman asked, "the killing of people in drone attacks?" (CBS News 2009). Clinton denied the linkage made by the woman, and declined to comment on "any particular tactic or technology" being used in the American effort.

Earlier that year, in July 2009, Code Pink brought their "Ground the Drones" campaign to Creech Air Force Base (AFB) in Indian Springs, Nevada, to call for an end to U.S. drone attacks in Afghanistan and Pakistan (Code Pink 2009). Code Pink is a grassroots peace and social justice movement, formed in 2002 by a group of American women in an attempt to stop the invasion of Iraq, whose name is a play on the Bush Administration's color-coded terror war alert system. This summer protest was modeled on action taken earlier in the spring of 2009, during which 14 members of social justice groups including Voices for Creative Nonviolence were arrested for nonviolent civil disobedience at Creech AFB. According to reports, Code Pink continued to stage their "Ground the Drones, Strike and Fast" campaign near Creech AFB throughout November and December of 2009 as part of a campaign aimed at "halting unmanned aircraft missile strikes controlled via satellite links from Creech and other bases" (Rogers 2009). The protesters targeted Creech AFB as the stage of their rallies and peace encampments because the base is a key site in the latest stage in the American war on terror, a distant node in the networks of technological violence the U.S. is depending on to wage that war.

The war on terror and information technology

The American military and intelligence campaigns in Afghanistan, Iraq, and Pakistan represent a new stage in the maturation of computer-aided global systems of military violence, and raise concerns about the continued reliance on technoscientific solutions to political problems. Once the stuff of fantasy, the use of roboticized warfare is increasing at a rapid pace; science fiction has been superseded by science fact. In Pakistan, where enemies of the U.S. are exploiting lightly governed regions as bases for their operations, the U.S. has turned to a targeted killing campaign run *covertly* by the Central Intelligence Agency (CIA) to attack militants. This campaign relies upon unmanned, tele-operated drone planes that, seen from the American government's perspective, offer a discriminating, humane, and less risky approach to the war on terror. Though initiated by the George W. Bush administration, the use of drone planes for the prosecution of the war on terror has become an integral part of the Obama administration's security strategy, particularly in Pakistan. This has resulted in silences concerning the human costs of this strategy. In part by making women visible in the war on terror, the vignettes above offer a starting point for attempts to locate gender in technological discourses that too often obscure such elements. They also demonstrate that, far from being passive victims of technologically advanced network-based warfare, women variously located at opposite ends of the drone war have been at the forefront of efforts to demand that the U.S. government account for these practices, and thus break this silence.

The information technology (IT) that imbues the virtual economic and security networks spread across military, social, economic, and political realms presents challenges to which academic International Relations (IR) has devoted relatively little attention. The revolution in IT has inspired optimism about technical solutions to security problems as well as more pessimistic efforts to secure information from "cyber-threat." But while analysts worried about an "electronic Pearl Harbor" crippling the United States, on 9/11 terrorists used cheap technologies to guide airplanes into their targets, after which they skillfully exploited global media to spread the impact of the resulting event. In the American response to these attacks, one facet of this technoscientific[1] revolution in networked warfare—the revolution in robotics—has rapidly become a key part of present (and future planning for) U.S. national security policy.

This chapter argues that feminist IR theory offers a rich tradition of insights and possibly the most appropriate set of tools to map out a future engagement with the problems of technowar and the silences it produces. In order to draw information technologies and their relationship to international politics within the scope of feminist IR, I first note efforts within IR to attend to the importance of IT for world politics and highlight some of the intellectual tools feminist theory offers the study of technology and IR. The second section then surveys the network and computer-enabled technological military revolution noting the difficulty of locating gender within its discourses. The final section of the chapter uses the lens of gender to look at a specific instantiation of the technological war on terror, the increasing American dependence on automated "drone" weapons technology in Pakistan.

The information technology revolution and war in International Relations

Eriksson and Giacomello (2006) point to the dearth of engagement on the part of IR theorists—realists, liberals, and constructivists alike—with the problems of the revolution in IT for international security. Mainstream IR, for its part, has moved slowly to incorporate new developments into its oeuvre. Some scholars have read the IT revolution back into the familiar statist framework of traditional IR (Keohane and Nye 1998). Others read the impact of the IT revolution in terms of the extent to which non-state forces are empowered and even threaten state security through particular threats to internal regime and external balance of power security, threats to the citizens of states, and threats to the state as a form of political authority (Herrera 2006).

In terms of the academic study of international politics, it has been mostly left to the critical traditions of IR scholarship to examine the consequences of IT for IR, and to try to make sense of the rapid and precipitous changes in warfare (see the essays in *Millennium*, 2003). For James Der Derian, "the central question considering information technology is how a revolution in networked forms of digital media has transformed the way advanced societies conduct war and make peace" (2003, 447). These traditions have emphasized the ethical importance of these transformations, warning that militarized information technologies will result in the compromising of relations with the "Other," that excluded grouping which differs from and is often subordinated to the self even while its existence constitutes the self. As Der Derian (1990, 298) notes, technologically enabled practices of simulation, surveillance, and speed generate a late-modern problematic: "the closer technology and scientific discourse bring us to the 'other'—that is, the more that the model is congruent with the reality, the image resembles the object, the medium becomes the message—the less we see of ourselves in the other."

Further critical scholarship points to more general concerns about the consequences of the shift to the information society. What are we to make of the fact that information networks—the same networks that enable and produce violence in the lives of distant Others—extend into every facet of our lives? While the potential of networks to at least evade if not challenge the control of the sovereign state is often recognized, of particular interest here is the relationship between lethal technological networks and the cultural norms of the Western societies in which they are largely enmeshed. Manuel Castells' (1997) explorations of the "network society" detailed the increasing reliance of modern societies on IT, stressing its consequences for nation-states and the emergence of alternative identities. Extending this, Levidow and Robins' (1989, 174) idea of the "military information society" is an attempt to capture the way in such a society, computer-based models of war promote military values, that is, the way "the war machine is shaping our sense of self, directly and indirectly." More recently, Deibert (2003) has directed attention to the ways the development of information warfare endangers the internet as a forum directed at global governance and civic communications. For Deibert, the militarization of cyberspace "operates on a new terrain, presenting many thorny legal and moral questions concerning the targeting of civilian infrastructures, and the boundaries between an armed assault, a probe, the collection of information, and the dissemination of propaganda" (2003, 518).

Just as the Pakistani women and Nevada protesters reveal blind spots in our view of the physical consequences of virtual reality, an understanding of the use of networked military violence in light of the "military information society" may help to remedy the general oversight in academic IR. War making cannot be seen without reference to its social and cultural context. Feminist theorists Carol Cohn and Sara Ruddick highlight the cultural "unboundedness" of war, arguing that, from an ethical feminist perspective, "culturally, war is understood as a creation and creator of the culture in which it thrives. War's violence is not understood as separate and apart from other social practices. There is a continuum of violence running from bedroom to boardroom, factory, stadium, classroom, and battlefield" (2004, 410). This amplifies a key theme in feminist IR work: the assumption of the separability of the public and private spheres constrains our understanding of security, marginalizing and obscuring actors and processes vital to the workings of international politics. But it also helps trace political violence as it moves between "feminized" domestic and "masculine" public realms.

Yet, even given the recognition of the ways in which information networks link the social and cultural practices of our daily lives with the military realm, questions remain as how best to build knowledge of and design research into these networks. Put differently, an ethical critique or "scientific" investigation of the networks that sustain this new form of militarized technological violence may be more difficult to construct unreflectively from within the privileged position of the Western scholar who is after all, enmeshed in significant ways in this military information society. As feminist philosopher of science Sandra Harding argues, "our cultures have agendas and make assumptions that we as individuals cannot easily detect," if cultural agendas have an unseen impact on our scientific knowledge process we must endeavor to make them explicit and subject to scrutiny (1991, 149). Objectivity in this understanding is about more than controlling the influence of values on scientific efforts; it can be strengthened by recognizing the distortions caused by privileging only the dominant perspectives of the privileged when conducting inquiry. Reflexive efforts to identify these "powerful background beliefs" as entailed by Harding's "strong objectivity" program can make us curious about what the widespread acceptance of technological mediation (seen in the rapid shifting of security, financial, social systems into the virtual domain) means for the types of warfare we come to see as natural.[2]

Feminist resources and tools for analysis

It is within the space opened by critical IR theory that we can begin to see the ways in which feminist approaches offer analytical leverage on the IT revolution and IR (IT/IR). Feminists working inside and outside of disciplinary IR have long been concerned with the components of IT/IR: science, technology, war, and security. Feminists have both offered a critique of the modern project of scientific mastery, and presented visions of science as an identity narrative with emancipatory possibilities. At a general level, Evelyn Fox Keller has noted the ways that natural scientific practices have both been produced "almost entirely by white middle class men" while representing a "particular ideal of masculinity" one that relied upon the language of gender while it sought to "bind Nature to man's service and make her his slave" (1985, 7). Feminists and feminist IR scholars have also voiced concerns regarding the masculine fascination with computer technology and masculine direction of the investigations of IT/IR. Reflecting on the discourse of IR, Charlotte Hooper worries that "dissident discussions on such topics as simulation, surveillance, and new technologies may unwittingly mark out the new agendas for hegemonic masculinities to colonize" (Hooper 1998, 46).

Other feminists see emancipatory potential in IT. Some highlight the radical potential of communications in cyberspace, focusing on how the Internet can provide a safe virtual space for the production of women's shared knowledges (Youngs 1999). Feminists have also engaged in efforts to rethink gender and technology "in the postmodern present where machines and bodies are indiscrete: that is, mutually implicated and cross-implicating" (Terry and Calvert 1997, 12). Donna Haraway in particular, has linked these renegotiations of organism and machine relations explicitly to practices of modern war, claiming "modern war is a cyborg orgy" (Haraway 1991, 150). Perhaps the best-known example of efforts to reshape these categories is Haraway's "Cyborg Manifesto," which imagines a post-gender ontological position that takes the "cyborg"—a cybernetic organism, "a hybrid of machine and organism"—as symbolic of a political project that draws upon socialist feminism to guide us through the present "movement from an organic, industrial society to a polymorphous, information system" (1991, 161). Jutta Weber discourages the "demonization" of technology and encourages the continued critical feminist questioning of technoscientific culture, writing: "On the one hand, relations of domination are becoming more complex and opaque. On the other hand, the reshaping of central categories through tech- noscientific practices opens up new options for refiguring gender, nature, and sociotechnical systems" (Weber 2006, 399).

In addition to identifying its perils and promise, feminists have highlighted the ways in which the informational and virtual worlds are dependent on productive and social relations being made invisible. Alison Adam shows the way technoscientific knowledge, such as artificial intelligence (AI) discourse depends on the displacement of certain historically female experiences, such as women's traditional labor in their care of children and the elderly (1998, 134). Judy Wajcman (2006) captures a feminist attitude towards the under- lying assumptions of digital triumphalism—the "widespread belief that pro- duction is no longer the organizing principle of contemporary society" and the privileging of "information, consumption, culture, and lifestyle" over production—when she reminds us that the social relations that support the existence of the post-industrial consumer-based society have not disappeared as much as they have been relocated to peripheral parts of the global econ- omy: "production has not disappeared, but is being carried out in strikingly novel forms on an increasingly global basis. Much low-skilled assembly-line work has moved offshore to the third world and is predominantly performed by women rather than men" (Wajcman 2006, 717–18).

These feminist interventions provide the basis for an inquiry into the kind of knowledge that is produced by IT-enabled networks of violence. A parti- cular kind of scientific knowledge is at the base of this approach to war, one that celebrates mastery and control, hallmarks of a very masculine project of modernity, and, feminists argue, is indicative of a masculine way of knowing. Such knowledge depends upon the complete mapping of the world's surface for military use, aided by global positioning satellites, and can be seen as the culmination of a segment of man's "obsessive quest for knowledge" or what Zoë Sofia would call "epistemophilia" (cited in Gray 1997, 104). For the U.S. military, "[m]astery of information and information processes leads naturally to increases in precision and lethality" because "what can be seen ... can be killed; with these new information technologies, nearly everything that is not hidden can be seen and is therefore vulnerable" (Henry and Peartree 1998, 114). The remote-controlled weapons patrolling the battle spaces of Afghanistan and Pakistan extend this logic, and robotics are thought to be tailored to the challenge of urban operations, for example those characterized by low-intensity warfare against insurgent movements blending into civilian population centers (Krishnan 2009, 29).

The network and computer-enabled technological military revolution

As Paul Edwards (1996) has demonstrated, the U.S. military was present at the creation, research, and development phases of the computer from the end of World War II to the early 1960s, serving as financing, "proving grounds" for embryonic ideas, a ready-made market, and an influential guiding force for the nascent computer industry. During the late World War II and immediate postwar era, military apparatus such as the War Department, Office of Naval Research, Communications Security Group and the Air Comptroller's Office funded and guided the development of computing technology initially in response to a World War II ballistics problem—the inability of ground-based antiaircraft gun operators to accurately keep up with the agility and speed of the rapidly advancing technologies of German warplanes (Edwards 1996, 43–45). Thus the rapid Western military and societal advances prompted by computer technology were militarized from the start.

While the history and development of computer technology has been intertwined with the military, women have been absent from the story despite being associated with the operation of computer technology from its earliest stages. The complex calculations needed to derive ballistics tables that would aid the functioning of guns were performed by young mathematicians known as "computers" during World War I (Edwards 1996, 45). During World War II, women were employed in the Army's Ballistics Research Laboratory by such founding fathers of cybernetics as Norbert Wiener and Oswald Veblen to "compute tables by hand using desk calculators" thus placing women among the first "computers" before the term was shifted to the machines we rely on today (Edwards 1996, 45). Computing was feminized; the occupation of computer operator was originally coded as women's work, due to its clerical nature (Light 1999). As Jennifer Light demonstrates, while women have been largely erased from the history of computer science and denied credit, the role of close to 200 civilian and military women in the development of the U.S. first electronic computer ENIAC renders problematic accepted narratives of women's wartime work.

Similarly, women and gender have been absent from the stories told about the technological revolution as it has related to the war system. To understand how military historians and scholars of international politics and security have approached the IT revolution, it is necessary to consider the conceptual development and practice of the Revolution in Military Affairs (RMA) discourse, with particular attention to its impetus in strategic,

societal, and economic realms. RMA discourse foregrounds the military consequences of technological innovation with transformative potential such as
the German *blitzkrieg,* the intercontinental ballistic missile (ICBM), the
machine gun, and the longbow (Hundley 1999, 12). According to American
strategist Andrew Marshall, whose writings catalyzed interest in RMA in the
West, an RMA is "a major change in the nature of warfare brought about by
the innovative application of new technologies which, combined with dramatic changes in military doctrine and operational and organizational
concepts, fundamentally alters the character and conduct of military operations" (quoted in Gongora and von Riekhoff 2000, 1). "Smart" weapons (or
precision-guided munitions, PGMs) may be the RMA's most recognizable
component, but RMA is made up of advances in organization, logistics, systems integration, simulation, training, satellite reconnaissance, electronic and
information warfare, and, by some accounts, includes the deployment
of nano-technology and space-based weapon systems. Technologically, the
origins of the IT-RMA are also to be found in the Cold War nuclear revolution, particularly American efforts to improve nuclear strategy. Lawrence
Freedman notes that many RMA technologies had emerged by the 1970s:
"precision guidance; remote guidance and control; munitions improvements;
target identification and acquisition; command, control and communications; and electronic warfare" (Freedman 1998, 21). According to Eliot
Cohen (1996), one of the major civilian developments that underwrote the
development of RMA was the society-wide advent of IT, with military applications such as computer-aided intelligent weapons, intelligence collection,
and control over information. Because it ideally promises to reduce loss of
American lives and avoid excess "collateral damage," RMA is commensurate
with post-Vietnam humanitarian era concerns increasingly voiced on the international stage. In strategic-economic terms, RMA was in some sense enabled
by a post-Cold War environment and, until September 11, 2001, the lack of a
clear threat to American military predominance. As John Arquilla writes,
it is likely that recent RMA was triggered "by the perceived need on the
part of the military both to stabilize defense spending in a time of fiscally
strained conditions and to demonstrate the continuing usefulness of various military tools in an environment seemingly devoid of serious threat"
(1997/8, 32).

As noted, the showcase for RMA came in Operation Desert Storm, as a
United States-led coalition decimated Iraqi forces numbering in the hundreds
of thousands, losing only 240 lives in the process, making the 1991 Gulf War
"a shaping event for defense planning in the 1990s in much the same way as
the painful defeat in Vietnam came to shape U.S. planning in the 1980s"
(Biddle, 1996, 142). Though many argued the relationship between RMA and
massive coalition success were overdrawn and misleading (for example,
pointing out that the use of traditional munitions outweighed the use of smart
weapons, the "smart" patriot missiles did not function well against the
"dumb" Scud missile, and collateral damage was not avoided as much as

promises of "surgical strikes" implied), the Gulf War became a point of reference for investigations of RMA (Freedman 1998, 31).

Throughout the post-Cold War era, the ideas of IT-RMA could be found in documents such as the Joint Chiefs of Staff's *Joint Vision 2010* (1996), *Joint Vision 2020* (2000), and the 2001 Quadrennial Defense Review (QDR), indicating their increasingly central role in the American strategic approach to warfare. These documents contained the conviction that the "key to military success in the future would not be military mass but information superiority. Overwhelming force would be less important than decisive force. Military operations would emphasize agility and speed, and occur concurrently rather than sequentially" (Goldman 2010). Promoted by military thinkers like Andrew Marshall, Vice Admiral Arthur Cebrowski ("network-centric warfare"), and Secretary of Defense Donald Rumsfeld (fewer troops and lighter forces), RMA found a home in the George W. Bush administration, which embraced RMA and put it at the center of efforts both to transform the military, and put the vision to use in response to 9/11 (Singer 2009b, 186–87). After 9/11, early results in Afghanistan seemed to validate Rumsfeld's elevation of network-centric warfare to a guiding principle.

Yet the difficulties the U.S. has faced in counterinsurgencies in Iraq and Afghanistan, along with its continuing encounter with the non-state, yet technologically adept al-Qaeda network, have again led to doubts as to whether the technological component of the RMA has been oversold. Discussions of RMA were muted when it became clear that the Bush Administration's declaration of "Mission Accomplished" was premature, and critics of technology-centered transformation concepts have been increasingly vocal. Analysts writing in military journals declared the IT-RMA informed American doctrine— aimed at "exploiting its strengths, such as information and knowledge of the battlespace, precision munitions, rapid mobility, and decision making"—a failure in the Afghan and Iraqi theaters; RMA was now supplanted by attempts to leverage cultural competence: "Designed for conventional battles, surgical invasion and withdrawal, and swift, overwhelming strikes, America's military was unprepared for the post invasion disorder in Iraq, and the intimacy of prolonged contact with a complex foreign society" (Porter 2007, 47). For other observers, the RMA, "rather than forcing the pace of the enemy's decision cycle," was derailed and reduced to reactive efforts when the U.S. faced insurgencies after early victory over Saddam Hussein and the Taliban (Schnaubelt 2007, 105). One historian drew the lesson that the setbacks in Iraq signaled an inability to deal with unconventional threats through an RMA approach, arguing that "the more evident the U.S. inability to deal with guerrilla or terrorist tactics, the more prevalent those tactics will become. There is a limit to how much 'smart' weapons can achieve against a shadowy foe" (Boot 2005, 104). In sum, the RMA model of military transformation through technoscience seemed at risk after the lessons of the Bush war on terror.

However, as the following discussion shows, IT-RMA endures in Department of Defense planning and in the prosecution of war in Iraq, Afghanistan, and the subject of the following case study, the covert CIA war in Pakistan. To be sure, traditional security analysts have pointed to significant weaknesses in the RMA model, for example in terms of its deterrent value (Morgan 2000, 149), or the challenges it poses to arms control strategies (Freedman 1998, 71). However, existing scholarship fails to give us a complete picture of the effects of the IT-RMA-enabled war on terror and its current manifestation on the (human) security of men and women.

Drone warfare and the war on terror: people among the predators

In the context of IT-RMA, the use of drones reflects several on-going historical military developments that, in turn, reflect the culture and values of American society (though these weapons have been deployed by other states, particularly Israel). The increasing reliance on precision weaponry (seen in Vietnam, Kosovo, Afghanistan, and Iraq) reflects both American technological idealism (in the pursuit of "decisive," technological fixes to the problem of war), and an effort to seize the moral high ground through more humane approaches capable of garnering public support (Gillespie 2006, 173). The evolution of UAVs from their important role as nodes in battlefield reconnaissance in 1990s RMA information networks to their current role is also part of a continuous trend towards the automation of weaponry (Krishnan 2009, 27–31). These increasingly automated weapon systems are, in turn, suited to the requirements of industrialized societies with reduced civilian pools to draw upon for military service, and those that face shrinking military budgets in the future (Krishnan 2009, 35–36).

Drones, or UAVs, are but one kind of unmanned vehicle currently operated to fight wars in air, ground, and maritime domains; in addition to unmanned aircraft systems (UAS), the use of unmanned ground vehicles (UGVs), and unmanned maritime vehicles (UMVs) are active components of current American military planning. An unmanned aerial vehicle is defined by the Department of Defense as a "powered, aerial vehicle that does not carry a human operator, uses aerodynamic forces to provide vehicle lift, can fly autonomously or be piloted remotely, can be expendable or recoverable, and can carry a lethal or nonlethal payload" (U.S. Department of Defense 2001).[3] The Air Force's remotely piloted aircraft, such as the MQ-1 "Predator" drone, its functions including "armed reconnaissance, airborne surveillance and target acquisition," and its larger and more powerful cousin, the MQ-9 "Reaper," are both operated out of Creech AFB (U.S. Airforce 2010).

In 2009, the U.S. Department of Defense released a document, *FY 2009–2034: Unmanned Systems Roadmap* (U.S. Department of Defense 2009) which indicates both the centrality of, and enthusiasm for, an unmanned revolution among American planners. The report prioritizes a relatively sanitized list of main objectives of unmanned crafts: reconnaissance, "target identification and designation," counter-Mine and Explosive Ordnance Disposal (maritime and land), and Chemical, Biological, Radiological, Nuclear

(CBRN) reconnaissance. But more importantly, it also indicates the DOD's level of investment (strategic and financial) in the future of unmanned systems, and speculates on "the types of missions that could be supported in the future by unmanned solutions" (xiv).[4]

The use of UAVs in Iraq and Afghanistan has been relatively well documented and relatively transparent. Reports released by the U.S. Air Force in 2010 indicate that Air Force flown "Predators" and "Reapers" used 31 missiles and bombs in 2010 (as of late February), 219 in 2009, 183 in Afghanistan in 2008, 74 in 2007 at suspected Taliban militants in Afghanistan (Drew 2010). For comparison, the same report noted that the "number of weapons fired in Iraq, where about 10 Predators still fly each day, dropped to 6 in 2009 from 77 in 2008 and 46 in 2007" (Drew 2010).

The use of UAVs on the Pakistani front of the war on terror has increased with the Obama Administration's attention to Pakistan's border with Afghanistan. Although authorized by the Bush Administration in 2008, plans to install a covert ground presence in Pakistan were derailed when Pakistani outrage in the early stages forced the U.S. to develop a new approach of relying on Predator strikes. Since the U.S. Army is not authorized to use Predators within Pakistani territory, the Central Intelligence Agency (CIA) is running the program, with the tacit approval of the Pakistani government, in a manner that is widely known despite its covert status. By December 2009, the Obama administration had authorized an expansion of the CIA's drone program to allow strikes in Pakistani tribal areas that are thought to be Taliban and al-Qaeda strongholds such as North Waziristan. In May 2009, the leak of a confidential report written by Army Gen. David H. Petraeus, then head of U.S. Central Command, revealed internal concerns about anti-American sentiments among Pakistanis over civilian casualties resulting from drone strikes (DeYoung 2009).

Despite this controversy, military support for the drone program remains strong. Among the motivations for the battlefield deployment of unmanned systems and intelligent robots are force multiplication, the expansion of battlespace, the extension of individual soldier capabilities, and the reduction of American casualties (Arkin 2009, xii). As a component of the war on terror, drone attacks appeal to military policy makers because their remote killing avoids U.S. casualties, and seems to have had an impact constraining and disrupting enemy operations and killing terrorist leadership (Kilcullen and Exum 2009).[5] The drone program has bipartisan support among U.S. politicians. Conservative voices in the public sphere have supported drone attacks, denying reports that these attacks produce destabilizing civilian casualties as a cost of business. As the *Wall Street Journal* editorialized, "When Pakistan's government can exercise sovereignty over all its territory, there will be no need for Predator strikes. In the meantime, unmanned bombs away" (2009, A11). Jane Mayer (2009) cites politicians and pundits across the political spectrum, from George Will to Joe Biden, as agreeing that the American focus should shift from the stabilizing of Afghanistan to the leveraging of technology through antiterrorist surgical strikes aimed at al-Qaeda leadership and the Pakistani front.

Meanwhile, domestic and international critics in media and intergovernmental circles have raised ethical and legal concerns over drone use. To be sure, the removal of human soldiers from the battlespace and reliance on robotic warriors gives rise to ethical questions with no easy answers. For instance, the use of robots could promote various ethical goals: the protection of human life, the minimization of the environmental impact of large armed forces, the limitation of troops exposure to risks beyond those that are necessary, and the honoring of humanitarian peacekeepers' moral entitlement to be kept out of danger (Krishnan 2009, 122). The Bush and Obama administration strategies of targeted killing with drones raise a host of ethical issues, such as the protection of innocents and the proportionality criteria of the laws of war (well summarized in Sharkey, 2009). Critics claim that decisions about the "trade-off between civilian deaths and target value" (Sharkey 2009, 18) are being made without transparency and little public oversight. These issues have prompted questions about whether covert CIA drone use for targeted killing constitutes a violation of the ban on such activity (in place since the Ford Administration) and critics have pressed the U.S. to clarify its doctrine on targeted killing (Cohen 2010).[6] While women represent a significant portion of these civilian populations, the public inquiries have yet to specifically inquire into the drone program's gendered impact.

Given the degree of commitment to this program the American government has demonstrated, and the secrecy in which large parts of the American effort are shrouded, how could feminists go about producing useful knowledge on the RMA and drone war in Pakistan? Sandra Harding's (1986) epistemological typology suggests that we organize this venture in terms that start from the standpoint of women and those who are marginalized in relation to these networks that have come to be seen as natural. Originally proposed as a way to justify feminist knowledge practices in the face of dismissal from philosophy of social science (as biased, etc.), Harding's division of feminist epistemologies into empiricist, standpoint, and postmodern provides a foundation for feminist research in IR and elsewhere and a touchstone for approaches to the social sciences that take gender seriously (see, for example, the interpretations of Sylvester 2002, 166–81; Weldon 2006).

Standpoint epistemologies suggest that the experiences of women and marginalized men provide different questions than the dominant framework (Weldon 2006). Modulated to avoid essentialist assumptions and recognize gendered hierarchies among women, the achievement of a feminist standpoint in the case of the Pakistani drone campaign might involve highlighting the voices of the group of Pakistani women that met with Clinton or the women peace protestors at Creech Air Force Base, recognizing variegated marginality for example, by noting that the Pakistani women's relatively elite status in Pakistani society (as officials, educators, media, etc.) would situate their positions differently than others affected by the drone campaigns. Attending to the perspectives of those located outside the scope of dominant "knowing agents" (such as American robotics scientists, military and political officials), feminists can locate voices that contest the effects of clean, technological warfare on populations—the weapon's terrorizing effects and the substantial loss of life they cause—that are not made available to us by official sources.

A feminist starting point also identifies and challenges the dominant discourses of technowar that sterilize warfare and promote goals such as servicing "high value" targets (al-Qaeda operatives for example) without disrupting populations. Conceptualizations of the robotics revolution in warfare that have wrestled with "the imminent disappearance of humans in the battlespace" (Krishnan 2009, 61) illustrate the dangers of accepting this "disappearance" at face value. Akin to the specialized language and metaphors used by male intellectuals that served to legitimate U.S. nuclear strategic practice during the Cold War, the discourse of technowar features tropes of information and intelligence; for example, "smart' weapons launched by artificially "intelligent" computers are indicative of a discourse that "can be used only to articulate the perspective of the users ... not that of the victims" (Cohn 1987, 686). That the victims, increasingly civilian men and women, do not enter into the discursive structure of technowar draws our attention to the "power of a system of representations which marginalizes the presence of the body in war, fetishizes machines, and personalizes international conflicts while depersonalizing the people who die in them" (Hugh Gusterson quoted in Gray 1997, 46).

There is growing evidence that drone warfare is neither humane, nor is it accepted by the affected populations. Reported rates of civilian death seem to undermine technowar's claims to humane and discriminate warfare. The statistics available from non-Western and unofficial sources are difficult to confirm, but suggestive. Citing Pakistani authorities, *The News International*, Pakistan's leading English newspaper, reported that out of 60 cross-border U.S. drone strikes in Pakistan between January 14, 2006 and April 8, 2009, "only 10 were able to hit their actual targets, killing 14 wanted al-Qaeda leaders" while killing "687 innocent Pakistani civilians" (Mir, 2009). Using public sources, in 2010 Peter Bergen and Katherine Tiedemann of the New America Foundation reported the results of a study of 114 drone strikes that killed over 1,000 people in northwestern Pakistan. They found that 32 percent of those individuals killed in northwestern Pakistan by U.S. drones over the past six years have been civilians (Bergen and Tiedemann, 2010). An Al Jazeera survey conducted in late July and released in August of 2009 by Gallup Pakistan, an affiliate of the Gallup International polling group, asked specific questions about drone use in Pakistan. The study, which surveyed more than 2,500 men and women across the rural and urban areas of all four provinces of Pakistan, found that a majority (67 percent) opposed U.S. drone use and, more significantly, found the United States was regarded as more of a threat (59 percent) than the Pakistani Taliban (11 percent) or India (18 percent) (*Al Jazeera*, 2009).

Women in combat and reconfigurations of masculinity

A feminist approach suggests two additional lines of analysis of the war on terror within IT/IR: the ways in which the "unmanning" of combat destabilizes already vexing discussions of women in combat, and its possible effects on hierarchies of militarized hegemonic masculinities. IR feminists have enriched our understandings of the events of September 11, 2001 and the war on terror by, for example, highlighting the ways in which a resurgence of masculinity found in the symbolism surrounding the events of September 11, 2001 denied women a chance to participate in the heroic confrontation with terrorism, analyzing the use of women's rights as justificatory strategy for the campaign in Afghanistan, and shedding light on the ways in which high-profile cases such as those of Jessica Lynch, Shoshana Johnson, Cindy Sheehan, and Lynndie England acted to gender representations of the war on terror (Tickner 2002; Sjoberg 2007; Steans 2008). Feminist analysis helps us understand how war on terror discourses rely upon gender stereotypes even as they offer problematic ideals of the women soldier, unsettle our expectations about female violence, and contribute to the evolution of constructions of militarized femininity.

Further, IR feminists have shown how narratives about (male) protector and (female) protected in the war on terror have been "central to boundary-drawing processes since they construct a clear division between the 'war front'—a masculinist domain in which masculinity if affirmed in the heroic actions performed on the battlefield—and the 'home front'—a feminised realm of domesticity and peace" (Steans 2008, 160). The unmanning of combat has complicated these boundary drawing practices greatly, troubling assumptions about women in combat (questions about women's capability in performing equal roles in combat), the nature of heroism, as well as problematizing the battlespace/domestic space dichotomy.

Ostensibly, advances in technology should favor women who want to participate in the armed services allowing them to bypass debates about the lack of upper-body strength that detractors often claim is a prime obstacle to their participation. The right to die in combat has historically been denied to women, and as Tickner observes, "giving one's life for one's country has been considered the highest form of patriotism, but it is an act from which women have been virtually excluded" (Tickner 1992, 28). Traditionally consigned to domestic nurturing roles, women have recently gained entry to the military ranks, only to find positions that may very well be automated in the near future. In the meantime, however, it is much more difficult to argue that women lack the inherent physical ability to operate the keyboards and joysticks that control UAVs or other unmanned weapons. However, the female tele-operators of unmanned technologies will likely have to guard against a similar devaluing of their work as took place during their prominence as computer programmers.

Similarly, the evolving norm of riskless warfare also raises questions for women. Stiehm (1983) argues that the state typically denies women the opportunity to be societal "protectors," assigning to them the role of "protected" despite the predatory threat often posed by their ostensible state guardians. If military service is tied to women's status as citizens and opportunities for political participation, then what effect will the "unmanning" of combat have on this dynamic? In other words, when soldiers are no longer asked to put their lives at risk for the state, what becomes of women's struggle to overcome second-class citizenship and solidify the gains seen in the hard-won privilege of military service? Also, the expansion of unmanned warfare further frustrates the development of what Judith Stiehm calls a "defender" society, one "composed of citizens equally liable to experience violence and equally responsible for exercising society's violence" (1983, 367), already limited by a masculinist state.

Drone warfare represents a new stage in what Jean Elshtain identified as the American military policy of "combatant immunity," the practice of "riskless warfare" which relies upon aerial bombing campaigns that punish foreign noncombatants (especially women and children) while prioritizing the avoidance of U.S. casualties (Elshtain 2000, 447). Aside from the ethical issues this practice raises, it is conceivable that the unmanning of combat will be interpreted as American cowardice thus prompting perhaps a revision of notions of heroism and an unsettling of certain American warrior masculinities. Peter Singer of the Brookings Institute wonders whether the message the American use of unmanned warfare is sending abroad may be counterproductive, recounting the Lebanese editor who referred to Israeli and American users of UAVs as "cowards because they send out machines to fight us. ... They don't want to fight us like real men. ... So we just have to kill a few of their soldiers to defeat them" (Singer 2009a).

Recognition of the interplay of masculinities with technology reveals further developments. As Lauren Wilcox has demonstrated in her study of offense–defense theory, technologies during World War I were interpreted, "not on their material contribution to offensive or defensive combat strategies but instead on their relationship to idealized images of soldiers' masculinity bound up in strength, bravery, and chivalry" (2009, 225). These images of warrior masculinity undergo a reconstitution when those prosecuting the war are tele-present, yet operate at a physical remove, suggesting new views of how gender works to bring meaning to warfare. These shifts can be placed in historical perspective, and the unmanning of warfare, both as an integral part of U.S. military strategy and as on-going practice in the current military campaign, raises important questions for hierarchies of masculinity within the armed forces. Steve Niva argues that the media coverage of the Gulf War of 1990–91 marks a shift in masculinity, whereby infantrymen "took a backseat in war coverage to computer programmers, missile technologists, battle-tank commanders, high-tech pilots, and those appropriately equipped and educated for new world order warfare" (Niva 1998, 119). For Niva, the feminization of American manhood caused by the Vietnam War was overcome by the emergence of a new hegemonic military masculinity suited to technowar

conditions, one that "accentuated the technological and civilizational superiority of the U.S. military and society" re-asserting the pre-eminence of the
Western type of man (1998, 119).

Reconfigurations of masculinity will undoubtedly intersect with questions
of honor and heroism. Feminist scholars have noted the dangers of abstractions enabled by the use of precision guided munitions, pointing out how they
can foster indifference to the targets and the illusion of safety, blinding the
soldier to the brutality of their actions (Cohn and Ruddick 2004, 414). The
potential for moral disengagement has long characterized modern warfare,
yet the increasing remove at which war is conducted would seem to have
consequences for some of the values that underwrite the meaning war has for
participants. For instance, the physical safety enjoyed by U.S. drone pilots
complicates honor claims. As one Afghanistan drone pilot comments: "It
sounds strange but being far away and safe is kind of a bummer. The other
guys are exposing themselves, and that to me is still quite an honorable thing
to do. So I feel like I'm cheating them. I'm relatively safe" (Pitzke 2010). The
meaning of heroism under conditions of remote warfare will likely be subject
to renegotiation. In an early indication of the direction of this transformation,
in 2007 Greg Harbin became the first UAV pilot to receive the Distinguished
Flying Cross for piloting one of the first Predators over Bosnia from his desk
in Hungary out of the path of a school yard of children (Garreau, 2007).
Soldiers engaged in the removal of improvised explosive devices in Iraq also
report forging emotional connections with masculinized, anthromorphized
robotic assistants, giving the robots names, battle commendations, and even
taking them fishing.[7] As Tickner, following Elshtain, has noted, a society's
war stories are key to galvanizing support for the war effort; these stories
depend on heroism, strength, and other qualities characterized as masculine
(2001, 56–57). What remains to be seen is in what ways tele-operated combat
can continue to be subject to heroic narrativization.

These configurations of masculinity may need to be negotiated amidst
widening notions of what constitutes "battlespace." Media reports of the
drone program have focused on the ways in which the frontlines of war have
seeped into the domestic space. Representations have highlighted the domestic
lives of Nevada UAV pilots, particularly the ways in which these remote
operators are susceptible to stress and psychological problems seen in
"normal" combat participants (Zucchino 2010). Adjustment to this encroach-
ment of the battlespace on the domestic space may increase the burdens on
(typically female) care-givers on the homefront, while adding the potential for
domestic violence. Further, the circulation of images of war over networks
arguably expands the space of war without prompting reflection on the ethical
effects of mediated proximity. The circulation of "war porn"—official (and
unsanctioned) battlefield videos taken from the Afghanistan and Iraq
conflicts from UAV cameras often accompanied by heavy metal music and
violent commentary—has become a troubling form of domestic entertainment. Critics argue these one-sided video representations "with a videogame

sensibility ... fetishize—and warp—the most brutal parts of these high-tech wars" (Ramirez 2010).

Conclusion

In the face of the possible dangers produced by the malign use of robotics, as well as nanotechnologies and genetic engineering, some have suggested "relinquishment" as a solution, that is, taking the lessons of the nuclear era (such as the possibility of total human extinction and the dangers of arms racing) to warrant limiting the scientific development of dangerous technologies and thus, the restriction of the pursuit of certain types of knowledge (Joy 2000). Others working in the robotics sphere have proposed instead that ethics be incorporated into the design of lethal robots. The stated goal of one such effort (funded in 2006 by the Army Research Office) is to produce "a new class of robots termed *Humane-oids*—robots that can potentially perform more ethically in the battlefield than humans are capable of doing" (Arkin 2009, xvi).

If relinquishment seems unrealistic in the face of the American investment in, and commitment to, its (relatively) cost-effective comparative advantage in technowar (not to mention the modern pursuit of scientific progress), and the prospect of humane-oid killers too terrifying to contemplate, the need for an "ethics of networks" seems clear. It is urgent that scholars continue to grapple with the ethics of networks and its symptom, "combatant immunity." Gender analysis has an important role to play in understanding the consequences of the willing transfer of the operations of wealth, sociality, and now political violence to these networks. A feminist approach suggests a different type of ethical intervention, one that asks questions about the ways the gender system maps onto, or overlaps with, the information society, and about the consequences of technowar for actually existing women and men. Claims to epistemic privilege are particularly dangerous in conditions of late modern military "epistemophilia," so further efforts at developing standpoints that reflect the knowledge of those directly affected in order to contest tele-operated violence are to be welcomed.

Feminist IR scholars, then, can add to the voices of Pakistani women and Code Pink activists by developing a better account of the militarization of virtual reality in multiple spheres of social and political life, not just the war on terror. For, while "[m]ilitarization relies on distinct notions about masculinity, notions that have staying power only if they are legitimized by women as well as men," the embedded effects of militarization outlast any particular war (Enloe 1993, 3), perhaps even the war on terror.

Notes

1 According to Jutta Weber, "The term 'technoscience' marks the merging of science, technology, industry, and the military, as well as the intensified amalgamation of

science and technology, of society fusing with the technological, and of a new effi-
ciency in industrial technologies which refigures the organic in a new and most
efficient way" (Weber 2006, 407).

2 Our very scientific (and social scientific) standards are biased, as illustrated by
Harding's point about replicating scientific observations within communities that
share cultures, values, etc. Harding asks, "if all observers share a particular such
cultural element, whether this arrives from the larger society or is developed in the
group of legitimated observers, how is the repetition of observations by these like-
minded people expected to reveal" androcentric, Eurocentric or other biases?
(1998, 135).

3 UAVs are distinguished from ballistic or semi-ballistic vehicles, cruise missiles, and
artillery projectiles, as well as from remotely piloted vehicles (RPV), an earlier
acronym discarded in the face of the growing autonomy (from piloting) of a
number of such vehicles. Weaponized UAVs are known as UCAVs (Unmanned
Combat Aerial Vehicles). For an excellent review of UCAV history, see Clark 2000.

4 The "Roadmap" report responds to the goals laid out by Congress in 2001 in the
Floyd D. Spence National Defense Authorization Act for FY2001 (Public Law
106–398) regarding the development of unmanned weapon systems: "First, that by
2010, one third of the aircraft in the operational deep strike force should be
unmanned, and second, that by 2015, one third of the Army's FCS operational
ground combat vehicles should be unmanned" (United States Department of
Defense 2009, 5). Congressional preference for unmanned systems acquisitions was
also expressed in the John Warner National Defense Authorization Act for
FY2007 (Public Law 109–364).

5 Jane Mayer (2009) lists the "high value" targets killed by Predators: Taliban leader
Baitullah Mehsud,'Nazimuddin Zalalov, a former lieutenant of Osama bin Laden;
Ilyas Kashmiri, Al Qaeda's chief of paramilitary operations in Pakistan; Saad bin
Laden, Osama's eldest son; Abu Sulayman al-Jazairi, an Algerian Al Qaeda plan-
ner who is believed to have helped train operatives for attacks in Europe and the
United States; and Osama al-Kini and Sheikh Ahmed Salim Swedan, Al Qaeda
operatives who are thought to have played central roles in the 1998 bombings of
American embassies in East Africa.'

6 In October 2009 United Nations human rights investigator Philip Alston, in a
report to the UN General Assembly's human rights committee and in public
comments, pressed the U.S. to articulate the international legal basis it sees for its
use of drone weapons to target individuals, and "to reveal more about the ways in
which it makes sure that arbitrary executions, extrajudicial executions, are not in
fact being carried out through the use of these weapons" (Lederer 2009). In March
2010, the American Civil Liberties Union filed a Freedom of Information Act
(FOIA) lawsuit asking that the U.S. government divulge the legal basis for the
drone program, and provide information as to the legality of targeted killing and
data about the number of civilians and non-civilians killed in the strikes (American
Civil Liberties Union 2010).

7 As Sgt. Michael Maxson of the 737th Ordnance Company commented on the
Company's robot "Sgt. Talon": "We always wanted him as our main robot. Every
time he was working, nothing bad ever happened. He always got the job done. He
took a couple of detonations in front of his face and didn't stop working" (Garreau
2007).

Gender, technoscience, and militarism

An engagement with Eric M. Blanchard

Sandra Harding

Eric Blanchard has provided an ambitious, rich, and provocative program for drawing "information, its technologies, and their relationship with international politics within the scope of feminist IR." I especially learned from his history of IT's role and its limitations in military practice and planning. I found illuminating his extensive set of proposals for examining gender issues about the new forms of warfare. Particularly intriguing is his identification of possible destabilizations of ideals of the warrior, the hero, and of the role of military service in citizenship. His call for an ethics for networks deserves attention. Of course I am honored by the uses of my work in his project.

Here I will comment on just two issues that his discussions brought to mind, and their implications for gender analyses. One is historians' argument that militarism has always been the single most powerful motor for the advance of scientific and technological knowledge in the modern West. A second is an implication of the powerful uses Blanchard makes of standpoint methodology.

Militarism as a motor of science, and vice versa

Blanchard notes that computer technology was militarized from the start. This should be entirely expectable; however, it is usually glossed over or treated as a benign phenomenon. Historians have indeed pointed out that from the origins of modern Western sciences through the present day, militarism has been the single most powerful motor for the advance of scientific and technological knowledge (e.g., Jacob 1988). Galileo worked in the Venice armory. A few centuries later, it was the development of the atomic bomb in the Manhattan Project that earned U.S. physicists membership in the international scientific community that had earlier been constituted almost entirely by Europeans. As Blanchard points out, it was the military that generated ENIAC in Washington D.C. in the 1940s. Indeed, historian Margaret Jacob (1988) reports that prior to the Vietnam War, virtually no participants in public debates in the West raised questions about putting science and engineering in the service of national security. Except for a couple of physicists who had qualms about using the atomic bomb on Japan, it was thought to be a patriotic duty to do so.

Yet many fewer historians have been willing to recognize that the causal relations also run in the opposite direction: scientific and technological advances have been powerful motors for the advance of militarism and the increasing militarism of many societies. That is, modern Western sciences and Western militarism have co-produced, or co-constituted, each other. Of course historians are not alone in a reluctance to countenance this kind of dark side to the "growth of scientific knowledge" itself, not just its uses. Even to bring up this topic is to challenge the triumphalism (as historians refer to it) that is not only the standard scholarly and popular attitude toward the history of modern Western sciences, but also deeply embedded in the sense of moral self of just about everyone who does scientific research. We do it because we think that more knowledge is in itself a good thing. How people use that knowledge can have bad effects, we say. But more knowledge in itself is a powerful constituent of social progress. We live in, and recruit innocent young people to, globally powerful institutions grounded in such assumptions.

States and their militaries have needed the knowledge and technologies sciences and engineering can produce. In turn, sciences and engineering have needed the moral and political support, financing, and access to far-flung parts of nature that states and their militaries provide. This mutually-dependent relation has resulted in militarisms and scientific institutions and cultures that co-produce, or co-constitute, each other. As indicated, societies and their sciences have always co-constituted each other. Military metaphors have long been called on to raise the moral and political stakes for investing in scientific projects. Thus we have scientists described in terms of chivalric virtues (e.g., as good knights) in fifteenth- and sixteenth-century Spanish, Portuguese, and British projects focused on the advancement of cosmography through the "voyages of discovery" (Canizares-Esguerra 2005). Recently, we have had the "war on cancer." And those sciences have in turn contributed to raising the moral value of militarized forms of social relations. Similarly, the very language of our national histories in the modern West routinely invokes science on behalf of imperial projects: we teach our young people about the "voyages of discovery."

This history is pertinent to Carol Cohn and Sara Ruddick's argument, cited by Blanchard, that "Culturally, war is understood as a creation and creator of the culture in which it thrives. War's violence is not understood as separate and apart from other social practices. There is a continuum of violence running from bedroom to boardroom, factory, stadium, classroom, and battlefield" (2004, 210). I suggest that to this continuum should be added the laboratory and field research sites. This is so even though scientists are expected to think that if they are ignorant of the uses to which their research will be put, or even if they are aware of such intended uses, what goes on in the lab is only pure science and basic research. They still are trained to think like Werner Von Braun in Tom Lehrer's Vietnam-era ditty. Von Braun sings that his task is only to get the rockets up; where they come down is someone else's job. Clearly the successes of science's and militarism's projects are dependent on each other's resources and achievements; each is a creation and creator of the cultures in which they thrive.

The masculinity studies on which Blanchard so effectively draws are indeed valuable for critical IR projects. Such approaches are especially useful for institutions from which women have been excluded from the design and management, such as militaries, science and engineering, and states. Thus women have been considered unsuitable for the most powerful positions in these institutions because the intellectual and moral worth of those institutions is itself defined against whatever counts as "the feminine" at any particular historical moment. Modern Western militaries, science and engineering, and states themselves have been haunted by the terrifying threat of feminization.[1] What would each look like were it guided by feminist values, interests, desires, and practices?

As I have been indicating, this history of co-productive relations between sciences and militaries is part of a larger phenomenon. An influential but now suspect historical and philosophic tradition has long argued that scientific research can and should be kept autonomous from society, and that that the highest achievements in the history of science demonstrate that this has been done. This view has structured theories of method and methods courses in the natural and social sciences for a very long time. It is not entirely wrong, either, since social values and interests that have permeated research projects but that differ between individuals or labs can easily be detected. Yet, as Blanchard points out, political, social, economic, and psychic concerns shared by all legitimate observers can be virtually impossible to identify.

This insight of standpoint theory (Harding 2004b), to which I shortly return, emerged in parallel with development of the field of science studies, which had been stimulated by the insights of Thomas Kuhn and other historians and sociologists of the 1960s and early 1970s (Biagioli 1999; Hackett 2007). By now science studies has demonstrated that the feat of producing "autonomous science" is impossible. Consequently, so is the absolute social neutrality regarded as the hallmark of objectivity (or, rather, "objectivism," as many observers have come to label it). Instead, societies and their sciences again and again can be seen to co-produce each other. They bring each other into existence as emerging social relations need and produce the kinds of knowledge and technologies that will improve their lives, and as new knowledge and technological possibilities enable changes in the existing social relations (Jasanoff 2004). One could substitute the word "science" for "war" in the first sentence of the Cohn and Ruddick quotation to characterize the framework of this field: "Culturally, science is understood as a creator and the creation of the culture in which it thrives" (2004, 410). So it is bad news, if not surprising, to learn that male supremacist societies, such as modern

Western ones, will tend to produce male-supremacist sciences and national security projects, and vice versa.

Co-production as an agent's project: standpoint theory

However, there is good news here too. When social orders are transformed by social justice projects such as feminist ones, so too will their sciences and national security projects be similarly transformed, and vice versa. (Sooner or later, of course!) This is probably too obvious to deserve attention, yet I want to dwell on this point briefly. In science studies "co-production" or "co-constitution" of sciences and their societies has been presented as a powerful analytic tool that enables us better to understand how it is that the knowledge systems of different cultures and different eras within a single culture tend to share so many central features. Yet it is also an agent's or actor's category, we can change how we produce knowledge as well as the kinds of social relations that are both necessary for and products of such transformed sciences.

This has always been an important aspect of the standpoint theory on which Blanchard draws. For researchers to start off their projects from what appear as issues, problems, puzzles, in the daily lives of oppressed groups, and to focus such research questions on the dominant institutions, their cultures and practices, (to "study up") is a powerful methodological and epistemological move. It is also a powerful political move, however, as critics of standpoint projects have always sensed.[2] Science and politics cannot be kept or pried apart in standpoint projects. Of course this also turned out to be the case for mainstream sciences and their political surrounds, contrary to the prevailing proclamations of the "autonomy of science from society."[3] Whatever appear as problems for one must also be resolved in the other. Women, their conditions and concerns, will not be treated as fully human in political life until they are also so treated in sciences and their philosophies, and vice versa.

Thus I was thrilled to see the innovative standpoint projects Blanchard identifies. While listening to women's voices is always a valuable research strategy, Blanchard is clear that the distinctive benefits of standpoint methodologies require moving beyond that familiar kind of research technique in order to bring the issues and questions that appear in women's daily lives to bear on the nooks, crannies, and lofty heights of national security policies practices that have only rarely been accessible to women or feminist researchers.[4] Building on the earlier work of feminist IR scholars, Blanchard asks important questions about how changing forms of warfare are affecting practices such as domestic life and seeking careers in politics offices that are seemingly far removed from the "front lines." My point here is that Blanchard's questions and analyses are not only illuminating in themselves and valuable guides for future research; they also participate in, are a central part of, a political transformation of dominant institutions, their assumptions and practices that of course must occur in IR research no less than in the larger global social relations in which IR plays such a vigorous role.

Conclusion

Questions such as those raised in feminist IR can only become increasingly important within research disciplines across the social sciences as we all try to figure out in just what respects we want to pull free of positivist legacies. Such legacies have vigorously shaped so much of prevailing research institutions, their cultures and practices as well as the social relations co-produced with them. Yet they have remained powerful long past the demise of the social worlds for which they were initially designed. The social and intellectual fears and anxieties that motivated the new philosophies of sciences in the first half of the twentieth century are no longer the ones that threaten sciences and their societies today. While there is certainly much to value and retain in these older conceptual worlds, it has become clear that they just do not have sufficient methodological and epistemological resources to engage effectively in our worlds, today. They are epistemologically underdeveloped. They require a new kind of modernization. It is exciting to get to see the new directions in feminist IR science-and-politics already being co-produced in Blanchard's analysis.

Notes

1 A question: the "nerd" already is a masculine figure. Will he be turned into a noble, heroic one in the context of the Revolution in Military Affairs (RMA)? Or in this era of skepticism about purported heroes, has he already become one of Carol Cohn's likeable guys, for whom it is the use of domestic and also dehumanizing language that makes it possible for him to enjoy designing and managing horrific projects?
2 See Harding 2004a for some of these debates.
3 This is not to deny the importance of attempting to identify the social interests and values that do co-produce scientific projects, or to attempt to eliminate from research those which work against desirable intellectual and political goals. Of course all the terms of this caveat are controversial and must be debated.
4 Carol Cohn's (1987) work, cited by Blanchard, is one of the small number of such powerful earlier feminist IR analyses.

8 Targeting civilians in war

Feminist contributions[1]

Laura Sjoberg and Jessica L. Peet

Civilians should not be killed in wars. The non-combatant immunity principle has been phrased in various ways with various "lines in the sand," but this is the gist: civilians should not be killed in wars. Despite the inherent simplicity of that principle, however, it remains that, despite the non-combatant immunity principle, whether or not they should be, civilians are frequently killed in wars. As Alex Downes (2006, 152; 2008) has pointed out, "war has always been hard on civilians," and it seems that twenty-first century war, if anything, shows that it is getting tougher, not easier, on civilians, as civilians become a larger percentage of war deaths (Eckhardt 1989, 91; Goldstein 2001, 399). Civilians "have constituted half of all war-related deaths. In the twentieth century alone, an estimated 50 million non-combatants perished from war-related causes, accounting for 60 percent of all deaths from warfare in the last 100 years" (Downes 2006, 153).

The question of how non-combatants are treated in war has been of interest to just war theorists for centuries (Elshtain 1982; Hartigan 1982; Chesterman 2001). Transnational advocacy networks like the International Committee of the Red Cross, Amnesty International, and Human Rights Watch have been interested in identifying and remedying civilian accidental and collateral injury and death in war (Carpenter 2005, 2007). States making wars are careful to claim their compliance with the non-combatant immunity principle.[2] Academic interest in the logic and effectiveness of civilian immunity has increased in recent years (Ghobarah et al., 2003; Carr, 2002). Debates about who "counts" as a "civilian" and what "immunity" those civilians merit have been intense, and have not fully been resolved (Walzer 1992; Yoder 1996; Sjoberg 2006b). Still, recent scholarly interest has focused on another puzzle concerning non-combatants: why the non-combatant immunity principle is *deliberately disobeyed* by belligerents (Pape 2003; Huth and Balch-Lindsay 2004; Downes 2006, 2008). As Alex Downes (2006, 152) relates, the "startling number of civilian casualties in wartime" seems paradoxical for two reasons:

> First, belligerents often target non-combatants despite the widespread belief that killing innocent civilians is morally wrong. ... Second, killing civilians

in war is widely believed to be bad strategy: it rarely helps perpetrators achieve their goals, and it can be counterproductive by strengthening an adversary's will to resist.

(Downes 2006, 152–53)

As a result, scholars have asked—if targeting civilians is both ethically problematic and strategically ineffective, why do belligerents do it? And why do they do it in almost a third of all conflicts where they have the military capacity? (Downes 2006, 152).

Several explanations for belligerents' (mainly states')[3] decisions to attack civilians are featured in this growing literature. Many explanations center around a state's form of government, but debate the way that forms of government influence the likelihood of civilian victimization. Particularly, some scholars argue that democracies are less likely to intentionally target civilians than authoritarian regimes, given democracies' accountability to their citizens for the war crimes that they commit (Rummel 1996; Merom 2003). Others argue that democracies are likely to see targeting non-combatants as a cheap and quick way to win wars and avoid democratic audience costs, and therefore democracies are more likely to target civilians (Reiter and Stam 2002). Other scholars see form of government as mattering less than states' self-identities and/or their perceptions of enemies. Particularly, these scholars argue that the laws of war are seen to apply to opponents that belligerents consider "civilized," but not to those that belligerents consider "barbaric," so perceived cultural inferiority dictates civilians' fates (Salter 2002; Kinsella 2005).

Downes (2006, 154) argues that all of these explanations are fundamentally inadequate, and "identifies two factors that cause states to target civilians regardless of regime type or how they perceive the enemy's identity." He explains:

First, civilian victimization results from desperation to win and to save lives on one's own side induced by costly, protracted wars of attrition. … Second, belligerents' appetite for territorial conquest leads to civilian victimization when the territory they seek to annex is inhabited by enemy non-combatants, which typically occurs in wars of territorial expansion or when hostilities break out between two intermingled ethnic groups that claim the same territory as their homeland.

(Downes 2006, 154)

We find this argument compelling, on the one hand, given that it is able to "explain" or predict more cases of civilian victimization in war than previous work in the area. On the other hand, we see this schema as still fundamentally lacking some key components. Specifically, why is it that desperation leads to a strategy of civilian victimization, particularly when civilian victimization is seen as strategically ineffective? What makes belligerents feel entitled to territorial conquest? Why do belligerents feel entitled to conquer others' territory? And why is *exterminating* civilians preferable to *expelling* them?

But, fundamentally, we are interested in what belligerents are *trying to accomplish* when they intentionally attack civilians. While Occam's razor says "they are trying to win wars," and correlative evidence supports that conjecture, we are concerned with the intervening "variables," or in the question of how belligerents think (either explicitly or in the collective consciousness) attacking civilians will get them closer to the goal of winning wars. In this chapter, we critically evaluate the civilian victimization debate through feminist lenses, asking how gender weighs into belligerents' decisions to intentionally target civilians. After exploring previous feminist contributions to the debate about the meaning and effectiveness of the non-combatant immunity principle, we introduce a theoretical approach to civilian victimization in war inspired by feminist thinking about the gendered nature of war and militarism. We argue that states use "civilian" as a proxy for "women" as a Clausewitzian center of gravity for state and nation, and therefore attack civilians *to attack women to attack the essence of the enemy*. We then offer empirical evidence in support of this theoretical interpretation in two forms: statistical work on the relationship between sex, gender, and other factors that the civilian victimization literature has identified as influential, and a case study about the British blockade of Germany in World War I. After evaluating the evidence, we argue that belligerents do not attack a gender-neutral category of "civilians" when they attack non-combatants. Instead, they attack women. Still, attacking women is not the whole story: belligerents attack women not *as women* but instrumentally as proxy for state and nation.

Feminist work on non-combatant immunity

Feminists have critiqued the gendered nature of just war theorizing generally and the non-combatant immunity principle specifically, asking "what assumptions about gender (and race, class, nationality, and sexuality) are necessary to make particular statements, policies, and actions meaningful."[4] In feminists' understandings, these gendered narratives within the just war tradition mask the ineffectiveness of the immunity principle and gender subordinations in its implementation (Sjoberg 2006b). In this understanding, gender cannot be operationalized as a "yes" or "no" (or "male" or "female" question), or as a matter of degree.[5] Instead, it is a complex map of hierarchical social forces. In feminist evaluations of the non-combatant immunity principle, "gender hierarchy is seen as a normative problem, which can be revealed and analyzed through scholarly evaluation" (Sjoberg 2009b, 203).

The gendered story around the non-combatant immunity principle classifies men as combatants and women as passive victims, and, in so doing, lends moral legitimacy to war-making. As such, "war as an institution depends on gendered images of combatants and non-combatants" (Sjoberg 2006b, 895). Jean Elshtain (1987, 1992) has argued that the immunity principle constitutes and is constituted by the idealized images of maleness and femaleness that are predominant in contemporary politics. These images depict men as "just

Christian warriors, fighters, and defenders of righteous causes" and women as "beautiful souls, ... frugal, self-sacrificing, and, at times delicate" who avoid political entanglement" (Elshtain 1992; see also Peach 1994, 152). As Judith Gardam explains, the immunity principle subordinates women and puts their lives at risk while appearing to protect them:

> Although in practice non-combatant immunity is the rule most relevant to the protection of women, it would be a mistake to assume that the origins of the rule and its theoretical underpinnings are consistent with feminist concerns. Non-combatant immunity is a means of containing or limiting violence. Although it can be regarded as based on principles of humanity, in reality it serves the purposes of the patriarchal State by keeping society stable and allowing the fighter to return to the hearth once the battle is finished. Its derivations are all gendered: from the chivalric tradition, based on the patronizing of women, to the canonical doctrine which primarily protected the Church's own to the exclusion of women.
>
> (Gardam 1993, 338)

Though most women have no say in most wars, men fight those wars (or claim to fight those wars) *for* women.

Just wars, then, valorize masculinity *and* men, who are heroes because they fulfill their roles as just warriors. On the other hand, men who fail to fulfill those gendered expectations are feminized. In this way, war-fighting capacity and skill is a measure of masculinity. As such, "the social construct of what it is to be male in our society is represented by the male warrior, the defender of the security of the state. Those who do not take up arms are equated with female" (Gardam 1993, 348). Feminists have explained this process in terms of feminization. To "*feminize* something or someone is to directly subordinate that person, political entity, or idea, because values perceived as feminine are lower on the social hierarchy than values perceived as neutral or masculine" (Sjoberg 2006a, 34).[6] V. Spike Peterson sees feminization *as* devalorization:

> Not only subjects (women and marginalized men), but also concepts, desires, tastes, styles, "ways of knowing" ... can be feminized—with the effect of reducing their legitimacy, status and value. Importantly, this devalorization is simultaneously ideological (discursive, cultural) *and* material (structural, economic). ... This devalorization normalizes—with the effect of "legitimating"—the marginalization, subordination, and exploitation of feminized practices and persons ... the "naturalness" of sex difference is generalized to the "naturalness" of masculine (not necessarily *male*) privilege, so that both aspects come to be taken-for-granted "givens" of social life.
>
> (Peterson 2010b, 19; see also Peterson and Runyan 2010)

In this understanding, masculinity depends on being framed in opposition to a subordinated femininity because "real men" cannot be heroes without "innocent women" to "save" and be heroes for. As such "the image of masculine heroism is not *culturally* irrelevant. Something has to glue the army together and keep the men in line, or at least enough in line for the organization to produce its violent effects" (Connell 1995, 214). Therefore, women's need for protection justifies wars generally and individuals fighting in them specifically. If women's need for protection justifies wars, it also justifies the social dominance of masculinity, which is required for and defined by war-fighting. In this way, masculinity constructs war which constructs masculinity.

The gendered just war narrative therefore provides legitimacy, justification, and sometimes even possibility for making war (Young 2003, 4). This is because innocent, defenseless women to fight for motivate men to fight, even when they have no other motivation, as Nancy Huston explains:

> But there always remains at least *one* good reason to make the supreme sacrifice, at least *one* transcendental value that justified rushing headlong into as insane an undertaking as war; very often it is Woman; the virtue she represents for the warrior, the love she bears him, the tears she will shed when he is slain.
>
> (Huston 1983, 279)

Therefore, men who "plan, prepare for, conduct, conclude, describe, and define war" do so motivated by women for whom wars are planned, conducted, and fought (Stiehm 1983, 245).

Far from being passive beneficiaries, however, women must react to, manage, and protect themselves from wars that are often most damaging to the very people they glean their legitimacy from protecting. While one would expect wars to routinely spare women as innocent and virtuous, the real impacts of war-fighting are very different. Women have always been and remain overrepresented in war's civilian casualties, victims of physical and sexual abuse, and sufferers of long-term health and economic hardships (Enloe 1993). Women are disproportionately negatively impacted by war even when the civilian immunity network *and* relevant belligerents emphasize the protection of women and children (Karam 2001; Ghobarah et al., 2003).

The protection of women in war is, therefore, an illusion created and reinforced by the gendered elements of just war narratives. Just warriors, who are categorized as righteous by default, "protect" women, who are categorized as helpless by default. Some see this as favoring women. For example, Charli Carpenter (2005) argues that "a discourse that [unrepresentatively] promotes the use of 'woman' as proxy for 'civilian' encourages belligerents to act contrary to the immunity norm itself."

Feminist work has argued that there is more to it than the use of women as a proxy for civilian. Instead, investigation into the gendered nature of warfare suggests that the gendered tropes in the immunity principle *harm women* rather than *favoring* them. This is because, in Lauren Wilcox's words, "not only does the protection racket legitimate war, it may be said to legitimate the state's constitution as the provider of security," which feminists have documented allows the state to pose a threat to its (particularly female) citizens (2009, 243). Wars are often couched in terms of their protection of women, even when that is not their primary purpose or primary goal.[7] What just warriors have defended, throughout history, is *their* women and children. Defining women as innocent and in need of protection, then, is not only productive of gender subordination but also of war itself. Feminists have argued that "wars are humanized by their function of protecting women, because Just Warriors make the world safe for their women and protect other women who are being abused" (Sjoberg 2006b).

Attacking civilians *as women* as strategy

While feminist analysis has investigated the complex gender hierarchy inherent in the non-combatant immunity principle's discursive successes and operational failures, it has not directly contributed to the discussion about why and how *intentional* civilian victimization is committed in war. Particularly, if just warriors fight to protect their beautiful souls, it *might* follow that beautiful souls are either protected effectively or incidental victims, but it is hard to understand them as intentional victims. At the same time, the very logic of flawed civilian protection that comes from gendered analysis suggests a logic of civilian victimization as well. If the *casus belli* for which just warriors fight is *their* women, it follows that one wins an absolute victory by exterminating women understood as "belonging" to *the opponent*. Feminist analysis of non-combatant immunity to this point has focused on domestic claims to protect civilians, the gendered hierarchy within those claims, and the resultant ineffectiveness. This chapter is interested in exploring what the gendered logic of the protection racket for *women inside the state* means for belligerents' reactions to their opponents' civilians. We initially read this through Clausewitz's idea of centers of gravity.

The Clausewitzian account of strategy focuses on belligerents' centers of gravity, an idea which combines materiality and the power of ideas. A center of gravity is "neither a strength nor a source of strength, per se, but rather a *focal point* where physical (and psychological) forces come together" (Echevarria 2002, 5). Clausewitz defined the "notion of the centre of gravity as the pivot against which decisive force should be applied, or in the case of our own centres, be resolutely defended" (Stephens and Baker 2006, 29). In other words, belligerents should try to destroy the symbolic centers of their opponents' societies, while protecting their own. This concept has become one of today's most popular military concepts. This approach recognizes that an attack that does not have a large effect on capacity can cause the enemy's moral surrender in addition to or instead of its physical surrender (Echevarria

2002, 12). Accordingly, "Clausewitz emphasized that we should look for CoGs [centers of gravity] only in wars designed to defeat the enemy completely" (Echevarria 2002, 15). In such wars, "in order to generate a strategic outcome, it is imperative that strategists define both their own and their enemy's centre/s of gravity" (Stephens and Baker 2006, 7) Still, as Stephens and Baker (2006, 7) note, it is sometimes difficult to find the enemy's center of gravity. They ask, "Is it the army? The leadership? The economy? Civilian morale? Does it vary between nations, cultures, and eras?"

We argue that states often see their own and other states' centers of gravity in the control, protection, and symbolic function of "their women." As Nancy Huston (1983, 273) explains, "the plot [of a war story] includes the 'good guy' or 'just warrior' fighting against the 'bad guys' for valorous reasons (often, even, for women) and ... winning the good fight." If "beautiful souls" are simultaneously a *causus belli* because they represent everything good that just warriors fight for and uninvolved in the fighting because violence would corrupt their purity, war is therefore necessary because the world would be unthinkable without innocent women. In this way, gender has not only been a legitimating force for war-making, but has promoted war-fighting (Wilcox 2009).

If the presence and protection of innocent women necessitates war, it follows that women are a "center of gravity" to be attacked in order to deprive the opposing belligerent of a reason to fight the war. If feminist just war theorizing provides a logic that suggests states might see women as Clausewitzian centers of gravity, then empirical evidence from states' foreign policy rhetorics, war-fighting tactics, and portrayals of patriotism and national pride suggests that these theoretical suppositions are operational in "real-world" war-fighting.

As Jill Steans notes, in many states, "the rhetoric of ethnonationalism is heavily sexualized and gendered" (Steans 1998). In gendered nationalism, women are "biological reproducers of group members needed for defense, signifiers of group identities, agents in political identity struggles, and members of sexist and heterosexist national groups" (Sjoberg 2006b, citing Peterson 1999). Anne McClintock (1993, 61) has argued that "all nations depend on powerful constructions of gender. Despite nationalisms' ideological investment in the ideal of popular *unity*, nations have historically amounted to the sanctioned institutionalization of gender *difference*." Gendered imagery constructs national identities as well as boundaries and inequalities between groups in a state (Wilcox 2009). As such, "nationalism is naturalized, or legitimated, through gender discourses that naturalized the domination of one group over another through the disparagement of the feminine, which draws on and reproduces discourses of naturalness of male dominance over women" (Wilcox 2009, citing Peterson 1999). This sexualized ethnonationalism is most evident in the perpetration of wartime rape, which "becomes a metaphor for national humiliation ... as well as a tactic of war used to symbolically prove the superiority of one's national group" (Wilcox 2009, 233).

Feminists have documented that gendered nationalism mirrors the idealized, or hegemonic, version of masculinity dominant in culture.[8] Characterization of national defense as "homeland" or "motherland" security relies on the image of women, mothers, and the homes they live in as beautiful, pure, and in need of protection. In this way, the protection of the feminine is a crucial cause of war and a crucial strategic consideration that states use when calculating their own or their opponent's strengths or weaknesses. States fight for "their women" as their centers of gravity, and attack their opponents' women, hoping to dislodge their very will to fight and the fabric of their societies. As Joshua Goldstein (2001) notes, "women in some sense embody the nation" in war rhetoric.

If women *are* the nation, men are to protect it. States then "use stereotypes of masculine heroism and protection to encourage men to fight, and to shame them when they are unwilling" (Goldstein 2001, 273). If it is a sense of masculinity that inspires men to fight and gives them pride in themselves and the cause that they are fighting for, it is essential to construct the enemy as something other than the masculine ideal that brings pride to the good men who fight wars. As such, belligerents seek to "*feminize* other masculinities in conflict, maintaining power and control" (Sjoberg 2007, 94). One way they do this is to render opponents' men incapable of performing their own masculinity by targeting, killing, and humiliating "their" women.

It follows, then, that states will always feminize their enemies if the valorization of their masculinity is key to their will to fight. Still, states' victimization of their enemies' women is not constant across wars. Goldstein implies that the feminization of enemies depends on the absence of actual women in the conflict, which "frees up the gender category to encode domination" (Goldstein 2001, 356). Others have suggested that the feminization of the enemy depends on the racial/cultural dynamics between self and other, with hyperfeminization being applied to those seen as culturally or racially inferior (Eisenstein 2004). Still others have suggested that the feminization of a state's enemy is based on its size and perceived virility in the international arena (Ehrenreich 2004). A last group of theorists have suggested that the degree of feminization of the enemy is related to the seriousness of the conflict and the willingness to permanently alienate the enemy, because a belligerent responds to extreme feminization extremely.

These theoretical suppositions suggest that when belligerents attack civilians, they are attacking women. Still, civilians are not always women.[9] Although many tactics within the strategy of civilian victimization either directly target or disproportionately victimize women,[10] some have little gender-differential impact and some are targeted towards civilian men.[11] We are not arguing that states exclusively kill women when they attack civilians. Instead, we are arguing that states are symbolically and actually aiming at the women they see as their opponent's center of gravity, while fighting to protect the women that are their own center of gravity. In the process, civilian men are killed and civilian men are protected, but secondarily, as the "civilians" who belligerent parties are interested in are gendered feminine.

Feminists have argued that, while others perceived that the concept of "women and children" is used as a proxy for civilian in civilian immunity discourses (Carpenter 2006; 2005), in reality the combatant/civilian dichotomy relies on the naturalization of the gendered roles of just warrior and beautiful soul. In other words, "it is not the advocacy groups' words that are responsible for the perpetration of gendered war-fighting, but the salience of gendered war-fighting that inspires advocacy groups' words" (Sjoberg 2006b, 891). It is possible, then, that in the case of civilian victimization, "civilian," is a proxy for women (which is itself a proxy for nation), not the other way around. This proxy at once "creates the illusion of protection while failing to provide it in reality, and serves to legitimate war-making" (Sjoberg 2006b, 900–901). But it does more than that.

The protection racket[12] places women at the center of gravity in a society's understanding of its purposes and motivations for war-fighting. A theoretical approach that sees women as belligerents' centers of gravity, and "civilians" as (actual or perceived) women allows us to envision an alternative causal mechanism which would produce the outcome found by Downes. States actually attack what they see as each other's center of gravity, their civilians (again, as a proxy for women) whose gendered roles are a linchpin in the moral framework that legitimates the making and fighting of wars. This seems especially true in the wars where Downes notes that civilians are most likely to be targets—those wars where the complete defeat of the enemy is seen as necessary. This is because, in such wars, the attacking state often sees its entire "way of life" threatened, another proxy for the need to protect its women in the face of an unreasonable attack.

Quantitative insights into gender and civilian victimization

The statistical evidence in this chapter is derived from the work of Alexander Downes in his book *Targeting Civilians in Wars*, where he tests various hypotheses about the causes of civilian victimization, including those concerning regime type, cultural difference, territorial annexation, and what Downes identifies as desperation. Downes' data are mapped as dyads, where civilian victimization between each relevant party in wars is evaluated separately, allowing for different regime types among allies and different choices about civilian victimization among enemies.

We keep Downes' operationalization of the dependent variable, civilian victimization, throughout our statistical (re)evaluations. Downes defines civilian victimization as "military strategy in which civilian are either targeted intentionally or force is used indiscriminately such that tens of thousands of civilians are killed ... bombardment of urban areas, starvation blockades, sieges, or sanctions, population concentration or relocation, massacres ... " (2008, 44). Downes codes this dichotomously. When it is operationalized this way, "fifty-three belligerents—16 percent of all interstate war participants, and 30 percent of those deemed capable of attacking targeting civilians—victimized noncombatants" (Downes 2008, 44).

As mentioned above, Downes addresses a number of potential causes for civilian victimization in war. The first independent variable in his analyses is regime type. He uses dummy variables from the Polity Dataset and from Michael Doyle's classifications of states as liberal or not to test various (often conflicting) hypotheses about whether democracies are more or less likely to target civilians. The second independent variable which Downes uses is civilizational or cultural difference, which is meant to be a stand-in for the hypothesis that Mark Salter and Helen Kinsella put forward that the non-combatant immunity principle is a norm only between states which perceive each other as civilized, and not for states which perceive themselves as civilized when fighting states they perceive as barbaric (Salter 2002; Kinsella 2006). Downes explains that, to get at this issue, he "coded whether states belonged to different civilizational blocs, such as Western European, Eastern Orthodox, Islamic, Hindu, Sinic, Japanese, African, or Latin American" (2008, 47).[13]

A third independent variable Downes uses is the one that he finds most theoretically interesting, and presents as the major original contribution of his work. This variable is desperation. Downes argues that states are more likely to attack civilians when they are desperate. For robustness' sake, he operationalizes desperation using a number of different indicators. As Downes (2008, 47) explains, "to test the desperation argument, I coded indicators of costly and protracted wars, such as battle deaths, war duration, rising or total war objectives, and whether the conflict was a war of attrition." The final independent variable of interest to Downes is the second half of his explanation for civilian victimization in war. Downes argues that belligerents attack civilians when they are desperate, *or* when they are looking to conquer territory that "enemy" civilians inhabit. So, to test this explanation, Downes (2008, 48) codes "whether a state intended to conquer and incorporate territory from another country into its own state."

In addition to these independent variables of interest, Downes controlled for several variables likely to be influential in determining civilian victimization, including the relative material capabilities of the states in the dyad, the ability of the opponent to attack a belligerent's civilians in retaliation (e.g., deterrence), whether a state's civilian population was first targeted by their adversary, and a dummy variable for post-World War II (with the assumption that civilian victimization in interstate war has decreased since World War II). Using Downes' data,[14] we were able to replicate his results.

Downes found that indicators of desperation and territorial annexation were both highly influential and significant in determining civilian victimization in war. Particularly, in different models (see Table 8.1), he found different indicators of desperation to be individually significant, including wars of attrition, battle deaths, war duration, and expansive war aims. Each indicator of desperation showed that increasing desperation increases the likelihood of targeting civilians. These variables were significant regardless of the significance of regime type, which varied with the use of different indicators of

Table 8.1 Replication of Alexander Downes' work in *Targeting Civilians in War*

	1	2	5	6	7
Democracy	1.52**	–	1.54***	1.27**	1.30**
(Polity dummy)	(.596)		(.539)	(.519)	(.519)
Democracy	–	0.718	–	–	–
(Doyle dummy)		(.537)			
Cultural difference	-0.38	-0.31	0.18	0.01	0.10
	(.532)	(.514)	(.482)	(.476)	(.489)
Wars of attrition	2.84***	2.72***	–	–	–
	(.576)	(.563)			
Battle deaths	–	–	0.52*	–	–
			(.196)		
War duration	–	–	–	0.89**	–
				(.336)	
Expansive war aims					1.30**
					(.492)
Territorial annexation	4.49***	4.44***	3.75***	4.00***	3.75***
	(.737)	(.723)	(.620)	(.623)	(.614)
Relative capabilities	2.38**	2.42**	1.80**	1.74**	1.33*
	(.900)	(.883)	(.744)	(.724)	(.751)
Deterrence	1.84***	2.20***	1.96***	2.16***	1.87***
	(.622)	(.595)	(.537)	(.531)	(.548)
State is a target of	1.44**	1.35**	1.75**	1.62**	1.93***
civilian victimization	(.575)	(.552)	(.533)	(.533)	(.547)
Post-1945	-1.16**	-1.23	-0.88	-1.18**	-1.22**
	(.629)	(.609)	(.561)	(.551)	(.556)
Constant	-5.58**	-5.54***	-6.56***	-6.42***	-4.54***
	(.849)	(.850)	(1.165)	(1.106)	(.641)
N	298	300	291	00	300
Log likelihood	-56.05	-58.64	-67.72	-68.05	-68.30
Wald Chi^2	54.21***	57.25***	77.66***	75.96**	81.74***
Pseudo-R^2	0.60	0.58	0.50	0.51	0.51

Notes:
Dependent variable is civilian victimization
*significant at the .1 level; **significant at the .05 level; ***significant at the .01 level

liberalness or democracy. As Downes also predicted, other indicators like relative capability, deterrence, and a belligerent's own civilians being victimized also increased the likelihood of civilian victimization. In most of the models, the dummy variable for post-1945 was significant in decreasing intentional civilian victimization.

After replicating Downes' results, we turn to evaluate the empirical evidence in terms of our theoretical logic, asking if feminist theories provide a competitive reinterpretation of the causes of civilian victimization. Our theoretical logic suggests that there should be a relationship between desperation, violence against women and femininity, and civilian victimization. If intentional civilian victimization is really a proxy for the victimization of women (as nation), then we should expect the form and demographic results of violence towards civilians to differ from cases of incidental or collateral civilian victimization. Particularly, we should expect that gender-specific forms of intentional violence will be a significant part of civilian victimization campaigns, where incidental or collateral civilian damage will not include systemic attacks *on women specifically.*

If states attack civilians as a proxy for women, then a form of civilian victimization *entirely left out of* previous work, wartime rape, can be both analytically useful and potentially explained alongside or along with the categories of civilian victimization traditionally seen in the field of Security Studies. Our argument is that level of wartime rape will be a strong predictor of attacking civilians *because civilians are a proxy for women.* It follows, then, that states *attempting to attack women* will attack "civilians generally" and *women specifically.* Also, the literature on wartime rape suggests that the symbolism that we see in attacking civilians is also in wartime rape—raping women as a metaphor for raping the nation. One way domination over the nation is achieved is through the domination of the enemy's women both physically and sexually through rape.

Wartime rape is an experience which is almost exclusively reserved for those persons biologically classifiable as female, and exclusively for those who are gendered female (and feminized) in political and social relations. Several feminist scholars have identified wartime rape as a key threat to women's security (e.g., Hansen 2001). Judith Gardam (1993, 359) explains that "it is difficult to find any support for the view that non-combatant immunity at any time in its development has included [effective] protection from rape." Gardam contends that this is a linchpin of gender subordination because "nowhere is women's marginalization more evident than in the attitude of the law of armed conflict to rape, an experience limited to women" (Gardam 1993, 358–59). She notes, therefore, "in one sense, rape is never truly individual, but an integral part of the system ensuring the maintenance of the subordination of women" serving the purpose of state and nation (Gardam 1993, 363–64).

In order to get at this for the purpose of interrogating and reformulating the work of Downes and others on civilian victimization, we added a variable called "level of sexual violence." This variable is coded on a scale of 0–10, with 0 being a code for there being no significant reported sexual abuse, and 10 being the highest levels of sexual abuse in conflicts (where more than 10 percent of the relevant female civilian population is victimized by systematic sexual violence).[15]

Our analysis also incorporates a second potential indicator about the influence of "women" as a Clausewitzian center of gravity and/or what states are really trying to attack when they go after "civilians." If states are trying to attack women, they will not, of course, only "get" women, but they are likely to "get" more women than if the civilian deaths in war are random. As such, we would expect the ratio of women's deaths to men's deaths in wars to be different in those wars where civilians are intentionally targeted. "Accidental" civilian deaths will include less women than intentional attacks on civilians-as-women. To test this supposition, we coded a variable we call "sex ratio" to see the population effects of civilians deaths in war. The "sex ratio" variable here is a dichotomous scale based on the gender-differential effects of wars on population growth curves in victim societies.[16]

We found both the level of sexual violence in war and the ratio of women as immediate civilian deaths robustly significant, even when added to Downes' models which already explained half of the variation in civilian victimization in war (see Tables 8.2 and 8.3).

Both indicators of a gender component to attacking civilians are highly significant across Downes' varying models. The strength of sexual violence as an indicator of civilian victimization renders insignificant a number of indicators that were found to be significant in Downes' model, including relative

Table 8.2 Level of sexual violence in war

	1	2	5	6	7
Democracy (Polity dummy)	2.23*** (.825)	–	2.092*** (.713)	1.975*** (.707)	2.191*** (.749)
Democracy (Doyle dummy)	–	1.546** (.725)	–	–	–
Cultural difference	-1.24 (.684)	-1.099 (.660)	-.962 (.643)	01.081 (.641)	-.878 (.661)
Wars of attrition	2.53*** (.711)	2.37*** (.682)	–	–	–
Sexual violence levels	**1.238*** (.244)**	**1.199*** (.230)**	**1.191*** (.211)**	**1.205*** (.211)**	**1.266*** (.226)**
Battle deaths	–	–	0.251 (.240)	–	–
War duration	–	–	–	0.386 (.381)	–
Expansive war aims	–	–	–	–	1.722*** (.657)
Territorial annexation	3.96*** (.844)	3.979*** (.833)	3.555*** (.799)	3.674*** (.795)	3.612*** (.808)
Relative capabilities	1.434 (1.084)	1.627 (1.092)	0.682 (0.971)	0.793 (.959)	0.286 (1.01)
Deterrence	-.528 (.834)	-.101 (.895)	0.074 (0.702)	0.178 (.689)	-0.197 (.741)
State is a target of civilian victimization	1.283 (.753)	1.196 (.726)	1.132 (.664)	1.077 .674	1.358 (.712)
Post-1945	1.024 (.812)	0.758 (.760)	.524 (.675)	.393 (.653)	0.478 (.681)
Constant	-8.46*** (1.44)	-8.395*** (1.411)	-8.052*** (1.551)	-7.982*** (1.456)	-7.836*** (1.230)
N	288	290	281	290	300
-2 Log likelihood	73.641	77.581	87.535	87.752	81.346
Wald Chi^2	95.921***	97.166***	94.71***	97.166**	97.166***
Pseudo-R^2	0.818	0.807	0.768	0.778	0.796

Dependent variable is civilian victimization
**significant at the .05 level ***significant at the .01 level

capabilities, deterrence, the state as a target of civilian victimization, and the post-1945 dummy variable. In statistical terms, odds ratio calculations show that sexual violence as an indicator doubles the explanatory value of Downes' models.[17] The sex ratio variable is also highly significant, even if it is marginally less influential in predicting civilian victimization. This may be because only wars in which civilian deaths are extreme show any significant movement in the ratio of derivatives of population growth functions. Still, the significance of both variables, even taking account of the other variables in the civilian victimization debate, shows that there is a gender element to civilian victimization, manifested both in the sex ratios of civilian dead and in sexual violence in wartime.

Table 8.3 Sex ratio

	1	2	5	6	7
Democracy (Polity dummy)	1.540** (.626)	–	1.228** (.608)	1.391** (.581)	1.429** (.592)
Democracy (Doyle dummy)	–	0.999 (.594)	–	–	–
Cultural difference	-0.612 (.583)	-0.572 (.565)	-0.317 (.569)	-0.291 (.543)	-0.224 (55.2)
Wars of attrition	2.024*** (.635)	1.88*** (.621)	–	–	–
Sex ratio	**1.320**** (.640)	**1.289**** (.626)	**2.151**** (.680)	**1.898**** (.672)	**1.609****
Battle deaths	–	–	-.103 (.242)	–	–
War duration	–	–	–	0.48 (.407)	–
Expansive war aims	–	–	–	–	.779 (.600)
Territorial annexation	4.649*** (.932)	4.719*** (.939)	4.257*** (.858)	4.304*** (.854)	4.266*** (.864)
Relative capabilities	3.215** (1.051)	3.349*** (1.052)	2.531*** (.902)	2.52*** (.908)	2.182** (.940)
Deterrence	1.329*** (.648)	1.625*** (.628)	1.752*** (.603)	1.784*** (.598)	1.641*** (.611)
State is a target of civilian victimization	1.704*** (.649)	1.589** (.628)	1.974*** (.643)	2.006*** (.659)	2.123*** (.649)
Post-1945	-0.968 (.667)	-1.100 (.657)	-1.214 (.633)	-1.122 (.623)	-1.121 (.625)
Constant	-5.272*** (.954)	-5.234*** (.964)	-4.138*** (1.273)	-4.745*** (1.132)	-4.699*** (.798)
N	222	224	213	222	222
-2 Log likelihood	93.133	96.910	102.599	104.178	102.506
Wald Chi^2	57.500***	58.767***	55.059***	57.500**	57.500***
Pseudo-R^2	0.731	0.719	0.681	0.691	0.697

Notes: Dependent variable is civilian victimization
**significant at the .05 level; ***significant at the .01 level

Starving women, emasculating nation: the British blockade in World War I

Less than a year into World War I, the British instituted a blockade on Germany, which has been referred to as a "starvation blockade" or a "war of starvation."[18] The British had entered World War I with limited aims, including the liberation of Belgium and the ejection of Germany from the Channel ports. This war, they expected, would be quick, and mostly economic and naval. British war aims expanded quickly, however, to include "the overthrow of the German government and its rebirth as a democracy" (Downes 2006, 178).

The short, low-cost war that the British envisioned did not happen, and the British experienced heavy casualties in the fall of 1914, totaling almost 100,000 (Downes 2006, 179). Britain then decided that it would "stop all German trade, imports and exports alike, without reference to its contraband character, including food" in pursuit of its war aims (Siney 1973, 67). Over the course of the blockade, it is estimated that between half a million and 900,000 German civilians starved to death (McDougall 2006; UK National Archives accessed 2008).

In reference to the British blockade in World War I, Downes explains that, "despite a concerted effort to conceal their true intentions after the war, there is little doubt that British leaders intended to starve the German people, hoping that the suffering inflicted would destroy their morale" (2006, 180). He recounts that:

> In response to a memorandum by Lord Crewe in June 1915 querying "whether we should lose anything material by ceasing to prohibit the import of all foodstuffs into Germany through neutral ports and by falling back, as far as foodstuffs are concerned, upon the ordinary rules that apply to conditional contraband," the British government in an internal memo frankly admitted its intention to starve German Civilians. "Although we cannot hope to starve Germany out this year," Hankey wrote, "the possibility that we may be able to do so next year cannot be dismissed."
>
> (Downes 2006, 180, citing Crewe 1915a; 1915b)

In fact, during the blockade, "Pope Benedict XV called for an end to the 'war of starvation' being waged by Britain's blockade ... the War Cabinet flatly refused the Pope's request, largely because the blockade was most effective in the area of food" (War Trade Information Department 1918; Osborne 2004, 160). The strategy of starving German civilians (which continued for eight months *after* the ceasefire that ended the fighting) worked, as, in signing the Treaty of Versailles, "the German delegation pointed out that the people of Germany were on the verge of starvation and that food supplies must be sent at the earliest possibility" (Osborne 2004, 183).

Though there are few gender disaggregations of the civilian deaths caused by the British blockade of Germany, it is largely agreed that the great majority of the casualties were civilians, and the great majority of civilians were women (Osborne 2004, 110). The coding of the World War I case in our "sex ratio" indicator supports this, as the slope of population growth function in Germany (when controlling for military deaths) is offset substantially more for women than it is for men.

Above and beyond the deaths of civilian women, the blockade forced a substantial change in household provisions. By 1917, Germans were left to eat only potatoes and turnips, having little access to meats and fats. Previously, these foods were seen as only suitable to feed animals; during the blockade, they were the only food available. Perhaps more importantly, there were not enough potatoes to go around to feed the German people, especially as the war dragged on. Women had limited access even to these resources, which were often reserved for men who could fight or work in war-supporting industries. Women also suffered disproportionately because, "one of the most disastrous consequences … is its effect on pregnant women, who are subject to intensified nutritional needs and whose heath is imperiled by food shortages" (Cannon 1972, 34). At the time, however, German women could not "get sufficient food for even normal health, let alone the demands of pregnancy" (Cannon 1972, 35).

While most of the writing about the British blockade is interested in its potential influence on the development of National Socialism in Germany, both this chapter and Downes' work are interested in the question of the British motivation for putting the blockade in place. Downes explains the British blockade of Germany during World War I as a case of desperation, where Great Britain's need to win the war quickly combined with expansive war aims and a war of attrition on the battlefield. While this explanation might help us understand why the blockade was in place *during the war*, it is difficult to understand the decision to keep it in place for eight months after the ceasefire in those terms.

C. Paul Vincent (1985) offers an explanation of the blockade as driven by a combination of enthusiasm for and glorification of war in Britain (and among belligerents more generally) and what he characterizes as a "rabid nationalism" across states fighting in World War I. A somewhat famous debate between Winston Churchill (Secretary of State for War and Air) and Herbert Hoover (head of the United States Food Administration) about lifting the blockade in 1919 erupted into profanity when Hoover accused Churchill of "fighting women and children" and Churchill allegedly called Hoover a "son of a bitch" for protesting on behalf of the German civilian population. Churchill once explained that the "British blockade … treated the whole of Germany as a beleaguered fortress, and avowedly sought to starve the whole population, which falls mainly on women and children, upon the weak and the poor" (Churchill 1929). Answering Churchill, Hoover argued:

Nations can take philosophically the hardships of war. But when they lay down their arms and surrender on assurances that they may have food for their women and children, and then find that this worst instrument of attack on them is maintained—then the hate never dies.

(In Tansill 1952, 24)

These quotations show that Churchill *knew* that the blockade mainly affected women and others at the margins of German social and political life, but do not provide any evidence that he and/or the other leaders of the British military or British state saw themselves as attacking civilians as a proxy for women as the symbolic and material center of gravity of the state. But if Churchill does not show awareness of this connection explicitly, Hoover does. Hoover argues that the sort of hatred that the Germans (here, referring to the male population of Germany) will have as a result of the starvation of "their women and children" will be more extreme than any other animosity about the war. Hoover's argument even reaches into the logic of masculinity as protection, arguing that the Germans surrendered to protect "their women and children" when they realized they would be unable to fight to do so, characterizing surrendering as an act of chivalry akin to fighting to protect.

In this understanding, the blockade during the war attacked women as a material (but more importantly ideational) center of gravity of Germany generally and the German war effort specifically. This attack was successful, and Germany surrendered to "protect" those women. Hoover predicts that denying "their women and children" the protection that Germans surrendered for (and therefore denying Germany the right to dignity of nation) would have substantial consequences in terms of animosity between the Allies and Germany. While Churchill's words do not evince an explicit understanding of this logic of attack and defense, there is evidence that it was well understood by both the British who made the blockade and the Germans who were the target, during the blockade and in its immediate aftermath (see, e.g., Hawkins, 2002). Such an understanding of the blockade provides the missing link in understanding both the implementation of the blockade (to defeat Germany by attacking its center of gravity) and the continuation of the blockade after the signing of the armistice (because defeat was about the center of gravity and not the shooting), as well as the use of specific propagandistic statements about the gendered impacts of the blockade by those seeking revenge on behalf of the German state and population (because attacking women *is* attacking the very center of and justification for state and nation).

Conclusion

We are not arguing that women and only women are killed in civilian victimization. Such an argument would be both inaccurate and oversimplified. We are instead arguing that "civilian victimization" is, sometimes consciously and sometimes unconsciously, strategically *an attack on women*, where "civilian" is a proxy for women. But this proxy is not a simple, one-to-one mapping where belligerents think "civilian" but mean "women" (as women), even to the extent that belligerents are willing to admit attacking civilians. What the proxy is instead is a complex indicator of state/nation validity and justification. Belligerents attack (women) civilians for the same reason they claim protection for their own—because the "protection racket" is an underlying justification for states, governments, and their wars. Insomuch as women are indicators, signifiers, and reproducers of state and nation, belligerents attack *women* to attack the essence of state and nation. Such an explanation provides both greater theoretical leverage towards understanding the problem of civilian victimization than others provided up until this point, and greater empirical explanatory power for the particulars of cases of civilian victimization in war.

Notes

1 An exploration of the feminist theory implications of this argument can be found in our article, 'A(nother) dark side of the protection racket' in the July 2011 issue of the *International Feminist Journal of Politics*.
2 E.g., George W. Bush's 2002 State of the Union Address condemning targeting civilians; see also other examples in Sjoberg (2006a).
3 This chapter addresses a literature about explaining the causes and tactics of war that is heavily statist; a position which feminist theorizing has correctly critiqued and moved beyond. We believe the argument in this chapter applies to non-state belligerents, perhaps even more comfortably than it applies to state belligerents. Our future research in this area will address those crucial facets of politics and conflict in the global arena. That said, we do think that there is some utility to analyzing the interstate data, both intellectually on its own merits and as engagement with Security Studies.
4 See Wilcox 2009. While this sentence might appear to be advocating an essentialist notion of gender, it is not intended as such. Instead, we see masculinities and femininities are detectable at every observable point in human history, but not as static, temporally, geographically, or culturally. Quite the opposite, the dominant "masculinity" or "femininity" is different at different times, and in different places and cultures. While "the exact content of genders with various and shifting socio-political contexts, … gender subordination (defined as the subordination of femininities to masculinities) remains a constant feature of social and political life across time and space" (see also Sjoberg and Gentry 2007).
5 Feminists have argued that Carpenter's approach to studying "gender from a non-feminist perspective" relies on failing to interrogate the naturalness of sex, making it fundamentally at odds with feminist approaches whose work is built on a critique of the assumed immutability of the male/female dichotomy. (Lauren Wilcox makes this argument most articulately in an unpublished manuscript, "What Difference Gender Makes: Ontologies of Gender and Dualism in IR").
6 Feminization is something that can happen to one or be performed on any person, state, or other entity; it is just that appears to be natural to do to/perform on women, and aberrant in other contexts.
7 In his 2002 State of the Union address, United States President George W. Bush defended the war in Afghanistan by arguing that "violence against women is

always and everywhere wrong" and pointing out the Afghan government's systematic pattern of encouraging or ignoring abuse of women (2002). The National Organization for Women (NOW), a women's rights organization in the United States, agreed. In international political discourse about the sanctions on Iraq in the 1990s, the United States government and the Iraqi government took turns blaming each other for the "suffering of Iraqi women and children." Americans justified broadening the war on terrorism by talking about the "American way of life" and "soccer moms' ability to drive their kids to soccer practice" (Sjoberg, 2002). In just war narratives, the legitimate reason for fighting a war is *defense*. The concept of defense, however, is less obvious than it may at first appear.

8 R. W. Connell explains the idea of a hegemonic masculinity and subordinated masculinities operating in political and social space. Jennifer Heeg Maruska (2010) argues that the policy-making realm of a state is dominated by the hegemonic masculinity in that place and time.

9 While most women are civilians and most civilians are women, there are many, many men who experience war as civilians. See Chesterman (2001).

10 Directly targeting, e.g., wartime rape, forced pregnancy, prostitution; disproportionate effect, e.g., infrastructural bombing, economic and health consequences of war.

11 E.g., Srebrenica, see Rohde (1998).

12 See Peterson (1977) for an in-depth discussion of this term.

13 We think this is a terrible way to measure perceived civilization and barbarism (which we see as almost impossible to measure, but there are certainly better approximations). We chose not to change Downes' operationalization, however, because the variable is, in this case, theoretically insignificant (or at least secondary), and in most cases, statistically insignificant.

14 Downes' data is publicly available at www.duke.edu/~downes/publications.htm.

15 In this schema, codes 1–2 mean reported sexual violence above "peacetime" levels of sexual violence; codes 3–5 indicate reports of systematic intentional uses of sexual violence as a weapon of war; code 6 means that the sexual violence was quantified, and represents up to 2 percent of the relevant female civilian population as victims; code 7 represents up to 5 percent of the relevant female civilian population as victims; code 8 represents up to 8 percent of the relevant female civilian population as victims; code 9 represents up to 10 percent of the relevant female civilian population as victims. This scale was developed looking at a scatter plot of the data for both interstate wars (in this chapter) and intrastate wars.

16 To code this indicator, we found the derivative of the change in the slope of the population growth function over the course of the war for male citizens of the victim society and compared it to the derivative of the change in the slope of the population growth function over the course of the war for female citizens of the victim society, controlling for the number of (male) military deaths during the war. Cases where there is a statistically insignificant difference between the change in population growth for men (controlling for military deaths) and the change in population growth for women are coded "0," as in no gender-differential effects. This could mean one of two things: either not enough people/civilians died in the war to change population trends, *or* civilian victimization or incidental deaths were gender neutral. Cases where the change in the population growth for women is statistically significantly larger than the change in the population growth curve for men are coded "1," as in gender-differential effects on the civilian population. Cases for which there is not enough data to determine the gender-disaggregated effects of the war on populations of victim states are coded as missing data points.

17 Contact authors for calculations if interested.

18 "[S]tarvation blockade" is in Downes (2006, 178); "war of starvation" was a term coined by the pope at the time.

War and feminist lenses

An engagement with Laura Sjoberg and Jessica L. Peet

J. Ann Tickner

Since, in times of war, the majority of women are civilians on account of their exclusion from combat roles in most militaries, Laura Sjoberg and Jessica Peet have taken on a central issue for feminist security studies. Civilian protection has generated quite a bit of debate both in feminist IR and also in the growing field of feminist international law.[1] While published critiques of feminist IR scholarship more generally have been few, those which have offered the most thoroughgoing critiques of feminist IR scholarship have focused quite heavily on the issue of civilian protection. Critics have emphasized what they see as feminists' undue focus on female civilian casualties and their consequent neglect of harm that is incurred by civilian men in times of combat.

Sjoberg and Peet's chapter provides an important answer to this criticism because it offers a *feminist* framework for understanding civilian protection (or lack thereof) as it applies to both women *and* men. In addition to answering these particular critiques, Sjoberg and Peet also engage with the broader IR literature on civilian protection and further the debate as to the relevance of regime type for predicting civilian casualties—a debate that has emerged from the prolific democratic peace literature. While much of feminist IR scholarship has generally avoided social scientific methodologies, Sjoberg and Peet make use of both social scientific quantitative methods and poststructural gender analysis to construct their argument. I shall take up each of these three contributions,—critical, substantive, and methodological—contributions that, I believe, advance the debate about the gendered consequences of civilian protection as well as giving us some insights as to how feminists might fruitfully make use of quantitative methodologies.

Gendered critiques of feminist readings of civilian protection

Just war theory, one of the foundations of which is the imperative to protect civilians and innocents in times of war, has a long history in religious and secular political theory. While it was discussed in the context of the use of nuclear weapons during the Cold War, it began to receive more attention in IR in the 1990s in the context of the various wars fought in the name of humanitarian intervention, such as those in the former Yugoslavia.[2] IR also began to pay some attention to redefining security as human security as opposed to the excessively focused state security of the Cold War period and to research on transnational networks concerned with protecting civilians.

Feminist IR research, which also began to proliferate during the 1990s, fits more comfortably into the human security framework. Since women have been absent from most militaries and, therefore, fall almost entirely into the category of "civilian," when feminist IR has focused on civilian casualties it has tended to focus either implicitly or explicitly on women. This has generated a significant literature, which uses gender as a variable but which has been quite critical of IR feminism more generally. Literature that treats gender as a variable asks how (presumed) differences between men and women impact global politics often without paying attention to the power dynamics involved in classifying and organizing genders (e.g., Jones 1996; Carpenter 2005; Hudson et al 2009), while most IR feminist literature analyzes the ways that gender hierarchies reflect and are reflected in global politics.

The literature that uses gender as a variable has received quite a bit of positive attention from mainstream IR; its positive reception has, I believe, been due, in part to its grounding in social scientific methodologies.[3] The substantive concern of these critiques is that feminists have focused exclusively on women and not attended to the high rate of civilian casualties that men incur.

In one of the earliest sustained critiques of feminist IR, Adam Jones claimed, in 1996, that IR feminism focused almost exclusively on the question, "where are the women in IR?" and that when feminists used what he called the "gender variable" they were using it synonymously with women. While his critique was aimed at feminist scholarship more broadly, he concluded the piece by highlighting the fact that civilian men incur public violence in greater numbers than women. While he admits that most public violence occurs at the hands of men, he argues that it is mostly directed at other men; he concludes, therefore, that civilian men suffer direct casualties in larger numbers in contemporary wars than women. As evidence, Jones cites the first Gulf War where Kuwaiti men suffered atrocities at the hands of Iraqi troops in far greater numbers than women (Jones 1996, 425). Jones continues this line of argument in the introduction to his edited volume *Gendercide and Genocide* in which he claimed that non-combatant men are the population group most targeted for mass killings and state-based oppression (Jones 2004).

In a similar vein, Charli Carpenter has echoed this criticism of undue focus on women as civilian victims of war. Although asking a somewhat different question, Carpenter, in an article in *International Studies Quarterly*, asks why NGOs, in their efforts to advocate for the protection of civilians in international society, focus on women and children as "innocent' and "vulnerable," to the exclusion of men (Carpenter, 2005, 296). She concludes that there is little systematic research on whether states and their citizens do respond to this gendered imagery of civilians any more than they would to gender-neutral appeals. Like Jones, she provides evidence to suggest that civilian men are more likely to be victims of direct violence. She expresses irritation at data that emphasize women's victimization, suggesting that it is often wrong and may affect the implementation of civilian protection in sub-optimal ways that actually enable and legitimate the targeting of civilian males (Carpenter, 2005, 296).

Feminists have responded both methodologically and substantively to these critiques. In a direct response to Carpenter's article, Laura Sjoberg, in a subsequent article in *International Studies Quarterly* in 2006,[4] signals her present argument by outlining more explicitly what scholars who are critical of feminist work on civilian protection, such as Jones and Carpenter, miss by analyzing gender from what she terms "a non-feminist standpoint." War, Sjoberg claims, is humanized and legitimated by its function of protecting innocent and helpless women for whom male "just warriors" fight and die. It is not through the reframing of protection to include civilian men that the issue of civilian protection will be solved; rather it is by understanding its role in legitimating war (Sjoberg 2006a, 895–98). Jones' and Carpenter's critique of what they see as feminism's undue focus on women civilians perpetuates the myth of women as helpless victims unable to protect themselves. It also perpetuates the gender-subordinating effects of war-fighting and the illusion that women are actually being protected.

Sjoberg's earlier work on this topic has brought her to the position of the present chapter, co-authored with Jessica Peet,—that we need feminist analysis to give us an adequate picture as to why *both* civilian women *and* civilian men are dying in very large numbers in contemporary wars. Their case study of the British blockade of Germany after the end of World War I stimulates us to think about how we define wartime civilian casualties. Violence against civilians is not just about direct violence, on which Jones is focused, but on the long-term consequences of material depravations more generally. Sjoberg and Peet's central claim—that women embody the nation and that attacking civilians in general is an attack on the nation—is a provocative claim, as is framing it within the context of a gendered reading of Clausewitz. While many feminists are likely to be convinced by an argument placed within the context of the protector myth and a gendered reading of nationalism, using an ideational framework and offering a gendered reading of Clausewitz is sure to be a greater challenge for security studies scholars.

Engaging the democratic peace literature

A second strand of literature with which Sjoberg and Peet engage is the long-standing and robust IR debate about whether regime types are an indicator of how states conduct themselves during war and which types of states are more likely to intentionally target civilians. The much-cited democratic peace theory, which has hypothesized that democracies are more peaceful in their behavior—at least toward other democracies—than other types of regimes, has generally been more focused on the causes, rather than the conduct, of wars.[5] Nevertheless it, along with the literature on humanitarian intervention of the 1990s, has spawned a debate as to the behavior of democracies during wars. The issue of relevance to this chapter is why states intentionally target civilians and whether or not democracies are less likely to do so. Given their claim that democracies are more likely to win wars in which they are engaged, Dan Reiter and Allan Stam (2002), with whom Sjoberg and Peet engage, challenge the popular image that democracies are peace-loving.[6] They attribute their disproportionate success in wars to their need for accountability and legitimacy; they also attribute the fact that soldiers in democracies fight better to this need for the consent and support of their populations. While accountability would seem to suggest a lower tolerance for civilian casualties, Reiter and Stam claim instead that it necessitates a swift end to war before popular support erodes. This being the case, democracies have engaged in genocidal tactics with as great a frequency as other types of regimes (Reiter and Stam, 2002, 198–99). It is interesting to place Sjoberg and Peet's use of the British blockade of Germany in World War I, even after the war was over, within this literature on the war-fighting behavior of democracies.

Claiming, therefore, that civilian protection is not tied to regime type, Sjoberg and Peet's principal engagement with this literature is with Alexander Downes's (2006) thesis that targeting civilians is not tied to any particular regime type. Building on his hypothesis that desperation invites the targeting of civilians, Sjoberg and Peet take this argument further with their central claim that states intentionally target civilians—both women and men—as proxy for destroying the essence or heart of the nation. Their supporting evidence for this is the high incidence of wartime rape in wars in which large numbers of civilians are killed. As I said earlier, this is a provocative claim that, hopefully, will lead to further discussion among security studies scholars as well as feminists.

Should IR feminists use quantitative analysis?

Sjoberg and Peet employ quantitative analysis to support their claims. As I mentioned earlier, quantitative analysis has been used by many of the critics of IR feminism, including Charli Carpenter and Adam Jones, and particularly in scholarship that deals with civilian protection, but rarely by IR feminists themselves. IR feminists have generally questioned the usefulness of social scientific methodologies to answer the kinds of questions they have asked—such as the constitutive effects of gendered and other unequal socially constructed relationships on women's (and men's) lives and safety. Sjoberg and Peet's use of Downes' model and his data for wars since 1812, to which they add two variables, "sex ratio of civilian deaths" and "level of sexual violence," certainly offers support for their claim that sexual violence is high when civilian victimization is high. However, Sjoberg and Peet are using quantitative indicators generally and sexual violence indicators specifically to support an ideational claim—that wartime violence against women is a symbolic attack on the heart of the nation. This is intriguing and merits further discussion. The same issue arises with respect to the case of World War I. Certainly, imposing a blockade after the war was over caused undue harm to civilians, particularly women and children, but would social scientists be convinced that this policy was conducted largely for symbolic reasons?

Sjoberg and Peet are to be commended for their attempt to use social scientific and quantitative methods with a feminist sensibility. As I mentioned earlier, the most contentious debates in feminist IR have taken place on this terrain. Perhaps now is the time to begin a more fruitful engagement across this divide. A recent series of articles in *Politics and Gender* takes up this controversial issue also. Clair Apodaca (2009), a feminist who self-identifies as a positivist and an author in the *Politics and Gender* issue, makes the controversial claim that there are benefits in using the dominant language of the patriarchal system and that using data and statistical analysis is no less feminist than other forms of research. Laura Parisi, another author in this issue, asserts that we should not reject all positivist models because they are positivist, but rather, those that do not draw on theoretical insights from feminist scholars about gender relations (Parisi 2009, 411). For Parisi, the biggest challenge is to overcome the feminist concern that sex disaggregated data places too much emphasis on material dimensions of power, to the exclusion of social and ideological power relations. She concludes by suggesting that quantitative tools can provide an entry point for deeper qualitative analysis. It seems to me that Sjoberg and Peet are attempting to do this—to use quantitative data to talk about ideational power relations. Whether this is convincing either to postpositivist IR feminists or to scholars who use quantitative methods will be interesting.

Another obstacle to using quantitative indicators has been the lack of sex-disaggregated data and data about violence against women. Apodeca addresses this problem; as she asserts data collection is a political act—states and international organizations decide which segments of the population are considered worthy of being counted and which are ignored—with women usually in the latter category. She concludes that we need more, not less, data (Apodaca 2009, 422). Most feminists would probably agree; however, how to analyze these data is a more controversial issue.

Sjoberg and Peet attempt to bridge this divide. I hope that it will lead to more fruitful discussions between security specialists, those who self-identify as feminists and use quantitative analysis, and those feminists who are skeptical of such methods. There is much convincing to be done on all sides. Security scholars are likely to remain skeptical about talking about symbolic acts in quantifiable terms; most IR feminists, myself included, remain skeptical about bridging deep epistemological divides between positivist and postpositivist methodological traditions that take us well beyond debates about methods and into issues of power and whose knowledge gets validated by whom. Although Sjoberg and Peet do not take on this debate directly, they are well aware of these issues and this chapter gives us an opening to address them in new and intriguing ways.

Notes

1 Civilian protection and just war theory have been an ongoing concern in Laura Sjoberg's research. See Sjoberg (2006a) and (2006b). Other work on this subject by IR feminists and international lawyers is cited in Sjoberg and Peet's chapter in this volume.
2 In response to the UN's failure to act to protect civilians in Rwanda and the intervention in Kosovo in the name of humanitarian intervention, UN Secretary-General Kofi Annan put forward the idea of the UN's Responsibility to Protect in his 2000 report to the UN General Assembly. In 2001, an expanded version of this idea was later published by the International Development Research Center, Ottawa, Canada under the title "Report of the International Commission on Intervention and State Sovereignty."
3 An article by Adam Jones (1996) on this subject won a prize from the British International Studies Association and Charli Carpenter's work has been published in *International Studies Quarterly, International Organization,* and *International Security Studies,* all prominent IR journals.
4 For a comprehensive critique of Jones' 1996 article, see Carver et al. (1998).
5 See, for example, Doyle (1983); Russett (1993); Rummel (1995). The popularity of this thesis had something to do with the end of the Cold War and the collapse of Soviet-style authoritarian regimes.
6 This reference to peace-loving democracies is seen frequently in statements about foreign policy by western policymakers. It is actually a misstatement of Russet's thesis that offered the more modest claim that democracies are more peaceful only in their behavior toward other democracies.

9 Beauty and the *quinceañera*

Reproductive, productive, and virtual dimensions in the global political economy of beauty

Angela McCracken

News accounts frequently report the global dispersion of beautification methods, skin lighteners, plastic surgery, and body ideals. For example, a pageant in Nigeria decided to apply "global" standards of beauty to select a (tall, thin) Nigerian contestant in Miss World; she became the first black African to win a global pageant title, and thinness became a local fashion (Onishi 2002). In social science scholarship, the global spread of beauty products, practices, and Anglo-American standards of beauty are frequently cited as examples of globalization.[1] The globalization of ideals and practices of beauty raises the question of how gendered and racialized norms of beauty are shaping and being shaped by globalization.

Contributing to scholarship on the construction of gendered and racialized hierarchies through beauty norms (e.g., Chapkis 1986; Bartky 1990; Bordo 1993), feminist scholars have begun to explore the politics of globalizing beauty industries. Feminist scholarship on labor in the fashion and apparel industries exposes how Northern women's increased fashion consumption contributes to demand for Southern women's labor in the apparel industry (Collins 2003; Enloe 2004). Shop-floor analyses explore how export-oriented fashion industries exploit existing and create new gender and racial hierarchies (Salzinger 2003; Elias 2004). Seager (2003) illustrates the concentration of fashion and cosmetics consumption in the North, even as it proliferates in less developed regions. True (2003a) argues that the spread of Western beauty media to Eastern Europe has had contradictory consequences, introducing both Western gendered notions of beauty consumption and feminist discourses of empowerment. Others have begun to explore how the changing context of globalization intersects with historical beauty ideals and practices, creating new ideals of beauty tied up with nationalism, cosmopolitan ideals, and gendered hierarchies (Cohen et al. 1996; Brydon and Niessen 1998, Adrian 2003). These feminist insights into the globalizing beauty industries reveal that beauty production and consumption are closely tied to intersections of global, national, local, gender, and other statuses.

This chapter bridges feminist literatures on the labor, consumption, and cultural politics of beauty, by asking how the globalization of beauty products, images, and ideas affects and is affected by Mexican youth's standards and practices of beautification. Employing an embodied examination of globalization, the chapter focuses on the production of beauty in the *fiesta de quince años*,[2] an adolescent ritual in Guadalajara, Mexico.[3] I argue that the production of gendered and racialized beauty in the *quince* is an illustration of a global political economy (GPE) of beauty. This GPE of beauty is the product of intersecting local and global norms in the reproductive, productive, and virtual economies (Peterson 2003). The GPE of beauty is therefore both transforming and transformed by beauty practices of individuals, households, markets, and media in the *quince*.

The significance of the role of globalization in the production of beauty ideals in Mexico is twofold. First, it illustrates how the gendering and racializing of bodies, particularly among youth, is an engine of the globalization of material, social, and ideational exchange. Second, the global political economy of beauty in the *quince* illustrates a diversifying of expressions of gender in Guadalajara at the same time that traditional unequal gender relations are being reinforced. It is at least partly *through* the gendering of the beautiful feminine body that globalization operates, reproducing existing gendered inequalities. At the same time, however, the intersection of globalization with youth's desires and youth's practices means that new expressions of femininity and masculinity are emerging within a conservatively gender-coded custom.

The *fiesta de quince años*

A *quince* is a religious service followed by a celebration of a girl's fifteenth birthday. The format for celebrating the *quince* is varied because it is a living tradition whose rituals and meanings are continually negotiated (Davalos 1996, Cantú 1999, Stewart 2004). A typical *quince* in Guadalajara begins with attendance by family and guests at a religious service dedicated to the *quinceañera*. The Mass dedication may simply be a mention of the *quinceañera* during Mass, but often it includes special flower decorations, musical accompaniment, a grand entrance down the aisle by the *quinceañera* accompanied by her parents or up to 14 *damas* (ladies-in-waiting) and/or up to 15 *chambelanes* (chamberlains). During a formal *quince* Mass, the *quinceañera* kneels in front of the altar on a special pillow as in a marriage Mass, but alone, receives a blessing, and lays her bouquet at the feet of a statue of the Virgin Mary. After Mass, the *quinceañera* takes photos with family and friends.

After the religious service, 100–300 guests gather for a meal and a party at a rented hall or a large estate. Once family and guests are seated, the *quinceañera* makes a grand entrance and dances a waltz, leads a toast, and dances a "surprise" dance. She might perform any number of rituals, such as changing her flat-soled shoes to high-heeled shoes or the presentation of her symbolic last doll. After the dances and during the party, the *quinceañera* takes pictures with guests at every table, dances with her friends and family, and receives gifts at her table of honor. The event, from Mass to the party's end in the morning, is videorecorded. The preparation and execution of a *quince* is fairly compared to a wedding Mass and reception, and three to six months of preparation is considered reasonable.

Normalization versus particularization

Standards of beauty and beautification are not universal in the *quince* because beautification involves a process of social identification and differentiation (Cannon 1998). On the one hand, the *quince* is considered a traditional affair, with standards of presentation that are widely assumed, especially by celebrants' parents. In addition, the social dimension to the event calls upon celebrants, participants, and attendees, to dress appropriately in order to maximize their social identification. On the other hand, the *quince* is organized around celebrating the youth and increasing agency of a fifteen-year-old (Stewart 2004). Fifteen-year-olds have different ideas from their parents about what is beautiful and appropriate, and the party is an invitation to them to start using make-up and hair products, wearing new fashions, and dating.

Furthermore, youth universally express their desires to be unique through their sartorial displays. Indeed, youth participants self-reported their participation in beautification as a practice in uniqueness. Some participants allow that others may be conformist to a popular ideal, but all expressed themselves as having unique tastes. For example, one youth, when asked whether she was a fan of RBD, probably the most popular musical group in 2006, responded with a forceful negative and proclaimed "one has to be original, and they are way over."[4] This young woman had previously been a fan of the group; she later revealed that she had copied RBD singer Dulce María's red hair. This desire to be unique is universal among youth, and beautification, such as hair dying, is considered a practical way to establish originality.

The former Dulce María fan illustrates how youth experiment and display their uniqueness: through changing tastes rapidly. Dulce María and her red hair were still popular at the time of the interview, but this participant had already moved on; another year later, she was almost unrecognizable. Another participant went from being a disaffected, video-game-playing populist, to a brand-name-only, club-going devout Catholic in the short time I knew him. The rapid pace at which teens adopt and drop tastes suggests that the search for fashion *and* originality, social identification *and* differentiation, as more important than any particular trend.

As a result of the tensions between generations and peers, the negotiation between tradition and originality facilitates an ever-changing standard of beauty in the *quince*. The *quinceañera* is therefore a prism through which to see the construction of gendered beauty, including the dynamics of generational contestation, normalization and personalization.

Gender, race and beautification in the *quince*

Beautification is important for youth in Guadalajara. As one informant explained, "A person should always look fixed up. ... The more fixed up you are, I feel like, the more you have. More people will like you." Being both a family event and a *fiesta*, the *quince* is considered one of the most important times for beautification. *Quince* beauty standards, therefore, both reflect and exaggerate society-wide standards of beauty and beautification.

Beautification in the *quince* is gendered in that young men's production of beauty produces a markedly masculine body, while young women's production of beauty produces a body that is recognizably feminine. Beautification for girls includes preoccupation with dress, cosmetics, hairstyle, body shaping, and comportment. For boys, beautification means dressing, hairstyling, some body shaping, and learning dances. The result of gendered beautification is a stronger, more athletic, seemingly un-produced, and less visible masculine body, and a more visible, as well as visibly altered, feminine body.

Beautification practices are further gendered by the sources of media and marketing to young people. Young women use more sources of information, and more frequently, to gather inspiration for their "looks." They frequently collect and share magazines, enter online chats on beauty, and share information with their friends. Young men cited two magazines and the Internet as sources within which they might find beauty information. Young women cited the Internet, clothing, shoe and make-up catalogs, television stations and specific shows, and eleven magazines.

Few youth explicitly expressed a preference for racialized beauty, although a majority defined typical beauty ideals *among their peers* in terms of "fine features," light eyes, light hair, thinness, hourglass curves for women, and broad shoulders and slim hips for men. Very few considered beauty to be a question of skin color, although to those for whom it was an issue, lighter skin was the preference. As with beauty in general, youth were disinclined to make judgmental comments about their peers and themselves based on racialized assumptions, but felt that their peers were so judgmental.

The reproductive, productive, and virtual economies and the *quince*

The production of gendered beauty in the *quince* is intimately shaped by increasingly global exchange of products, ideas, and images. Peterson's (2003) "RPV" framing of the global economy as "intertwining and inextricable" reproductive (care), productive (market), and virtual (symbolic) exchange is therefore useful to understanding how local beauty practices are simultaneously embedded in global markets, intersecting social norms, and the exchange of symbolic information. This RPV framing is also useful in bridging the insights of feminist political economy and feminist cultural critique that inform the literatures on beauty politics.

In the *quince*, the productive economy of beauty is defined by market exchange in beauty products and services. The reproductive economy of the *quince* is defined by socialization in beauty practices, consumption, and information. The virtual economy of beauty is defined by the commodification and exchange of quince "traditions" and beauty ideals through media, marketing, and advertising.

The productive economy of the *quince* is immense. Preparants purchase many products and services: catalogs and magazines; church services; party venues; lighting; dresses; makeovers; dance choreography and accompaniment; accessories; shoes; video and photography; music; invitations; decorations; transportation; food, drink, and cake; the "last doll"; jewelry; attire for the *chambelanes* and a growing list of "extras" marketed to make a celebration unique. There are zones in the downtown business district dedicated to dress vendors; fabric shops; stationery printing; accessories; dolls; and party decorations that specialize in *quinceañeras* or *quinceañeras* and *novias* (brides). Beauticians, dance teachers and choreographers, videographers, photographers, suit rentals, party venues, and caterers are geographically dispersed throughout the city.

The role of the reproductive economy in the *quince* is also considerable. The religious service reinforces the religious institution and hierarchy, even asking the participant to reaffirm her faith and commitment to the church. The social role is also important, as friends, extended family, and family-members' friends are customarily invited, reinforcing social bonds and social status. The use of *padrinos* or sponsors for the party establishes and reinforces social networks. Spending time with family and friends was most cited as the most important aspect of the ritual for *quinceañeras*. The preparation and execution of the event is organized by daughter and mother, and teaches skills such as networking, budgeting, priority-setting, and negotiation (Davalos 1996; Stewart 2004).

The virtual economy is also deeply tied to the *quince* through the images and ideas presented to celebrants in television, print media, street-level marketing, and through social networks. Television talk shows frequently incorporate *quince*-related content. An MTV show has replicated the success of *My Super Sweet Sixteen* with *Quiero Mis Quince*, a show that shadows celebrants in preparations and executions of their "dream" parties. Print media include weekly social column announcements, media directed at *quince* preparation, and popular magazines that young people use to get information about beauty and fashion. The local industry contributes substantial street-level marketing. And there are party seasons when a youth and their family will be invited to one or more *quinceañeras* per weekend for several months.

In three snapshots below, I highlight the aspects of *quince* preparation that are most tied to the feminine gendering of the body: the dress, the makeover, and dance, and argue that they are shaped by and shaping the global political economy through the intertwining reproductive, productive and virtual economies.

The dress

Planning or remembering their *quince*, almost all interviewees start with their dress. Imagining, designing, shopping for, ordering, and fitting the dress is one of the most central aspects to the *quince*, and is often the starting point for planning the event. The chance to dress up may be one of a *quinceañera's* main motivations in having the party. Even if a *quinceañera* doesn't want to dress up like a princess, family and peer pressure to do so is powerful. In this sense, the *quince* is sometimes used as a chance to intervene on a young girl's sense of style. One interviewee was sent to beauty school, against her initial wishes, as part of her transformation. Another, resistant to her mother's interventions, eventually submitted to professional hairstyling as appeasement for the dramatic liberties she was taking with her *quince*—no princess dress, no waltz, and no *damas* or *chambelanes*.

The dress, as it is marketed in *quince* magazines, the Expo Quince, marketing materials, and on television, is a ballgown with a strapless corseted bodice and a very ample skirt. Still, the most important aspect of dress selection is making sure it is unique, and uniquely suited to the *quinceañera's* taste. This paradox first struck me in an early interview when a *quinceañera* proudly reported to me that she was content with her *quince* because she had had an original dress. She explained that she had looked a long time for her dress because she wanted it to be different, and it wasn't like all the others, and she had not seen anyone else with this dress. "Still," she said, "to this day I haven't seen anyone with a dress like this." I left puzzled as to why the dress was unique, but I came to find that all *quinceañeras* had a similar understanding of their dress as uniquely theirs. Some were more different from others, they all looked very similar to me, but all the dresses were seen to be reflective of a girl's personal taste, personality, and style.

Perhaps the most important element of the dress is color. Color is a favored topic of *quinceañeras*, who frequently discuss their desire to set themselves apart from the pastel norm by using a red, wine, or daringly black dress. These colors are rarely used because adults frown on them, but dark and bright turquoises, oranges, and pinks are increasingly common.

The dress is important because it sets the theme for color-coordination. As one participant explained, "If you are going to wear pink clothing, it should all match, from the shoes to the accessories: pink. The makeup … yep, also. Since you are wearing pink, you should wear pink eye shadow. Everything should match, even the rubber bands in your hair … should be the same color pink." Color combination is nowhere more visually conspicuous than in a *quince*. The dress color not only matches the *quinceañera's* eye shadow, fingernail polish, hairpiece, earrings, necklace, bracelet, ring, shawl, purse, and shoes. The dress also matches in color and shade the bouquet(s), the cummerbunds, waistcoats, and neckties on the *chambelanes'* tuxedos, flower arrangements, bows on dining chairs, centerpieces, streamers, party favors, and other decorations.

Chambelanes wear either a plain black suit, or a rented tuxedo. Tuxedo rental shops offer ten to fifteen styles of suits that use simple tailoring to evoke period themes. One might be fashioned around a Mandarin collar with a frock-length coat, another based on a military coat with tails, double-breasted. A color accessory usually matches the *quinceañera's* dress, but color-coordination is much more exaggerated among girls than boys.

Strict color combination is especially true for the *fresa*, or strawberry girls. A *fresa* at school is considered the most popular with the boys, the best dressed, and the target of other girls' jealousy. To be a *fresa*, a teenager has to be dressed in color-combined clothing, preferably by brand-name makers. For example, one group of *fresas* has a rule that they wear a maximum of three colors at a time. Wearing more than three colors, they say, looks disorderly, unkempt, or gypsy-like.

The *fresa* is a term that refers to the privileged girls who "have everything." For example, a *fresa* has the money to color-coordinate all of her outfits so that her accessories, her shoes, and her make-up match a two- or three-color scheme every day. The *fresa* ideal also implies European beauty standards because the privileged classes are historically light-skinned descendants from the area's Spanish and French colonials.

The opposite of *fresa* is *naca(o)*. *Naca(o)* is a derogatory term used to mean many things, but generally refers to poor people with little education in the manners and tastes of high society. Miss-matching colors and patterns; loud and ostentatious colors, patterns, and accessories; and over-done hair and make-up are considered *naca(o)*. A comedic parody of *naca(o)* adolescents on a popular television show has the *nacas(os)* chewing gum loudly and wearing tight, bright, multi-patterned, multi-colored clothing with numerous glittery accessories and gelled-down hair. In different skits they are domestic servants, unemployed, and street vendors, and they exhibit their ignorance of grammar and good manners at every chance.

The insult that someone is *naca(o)* because they use mismatching colors and prints is an insult to social class more than race or ethnicity, but has racial and ethnic implications. There is an unmistakable correlation between being *naca*, being poor, and having darker skin, because indigenous and black people historically have held the least paid and least skilled jobs.

The many indigenous groups in the area who dress in a manner that identifies them as ethnically indigenous also use bright, multi-colored ensembles. The preference for contrasting colors and patterns is seen as outside of local social norms and derided by youth. Recent indigenous youth migrants to Guadalajara have been observed changing their clothing styles, haircuts, and cosmetics usage in order to avoid discrimination among their peers (Martinez Casas and de la Peña 2003: 241). Other prejudices against indigenous beauty can be seen in the prejudices against short stature for men, dark skin, large facial features, a curved nose bridge, and natural hair. The distaste for mismatching colors illustrates a similar disregard for the indigenous styles that employ color contrast.

In addition to color-combination, *quinceañeras'* dresses feature corset bodices that make them look thinner, enhance their bust, and emphasize an hourglass shape. *Quinceañeras* usually wear matching shawls while in church and reveal a strapless or sleeveless bodice at the party. By contrast, boys' suits exaggerate broad shoulders and cover up boys' bodies. Bare skin through lower collars, higher hemlines, shorter sleeves, and a more visible form through tighter clothes has been the trend for girls, in contrast to the little-changing suit for boys.

The dress industry is the most obvious aspect of the *quince* productive economy to a casual observer, as offerings are made in almost every business district, and there are well-known dress districts in the city center that attract customers from all parts of the city and from the countryside. While not all of the interviewees purchased their dress in the city center, nearly all went to the downtown district to try on the dresses. Two of the celebrants who did not travel downtown to look at the dresses defined their *quince* celebrations as nontraditional partly because they did not buy the typical princess dress.

Among those 14 celebrants who viewed their *quince* as a more traditional endeavor, 11 bought their dresses downtown, and three chose a style at a store or out of a magazine and chose a seamstress to reproduce their desired style at a lower cost. After much searching, one participant found a dress in a shop in Tonolá, one of the municipalities on the Eastern side of the Guadalajara metropolitan zone, and had it reproduced by a seamstress who was a friend of her mother's. Dress copying is so common that dress-shop managers will not allow photographs of their product and will not allow known seamstresses into their shops. One celebrant's aunt sewed her dress, and they went downtown to one of the big fabric stores to pick out the fabric and design. She chose her dress design based on a composite of an evening dress she had worn before as a model and a corset and, per her aunt's insistence, made it more modest.

The production of the *quinceañera* dress operates in close connection with the global reproductive, productive and virtual economies. They are produced as part of the informal, flexible, or factory-based, and always-feminized dressmaking industry, or by female relatives. Their design is closely tied to the global virtual economy of signs, and youth's search for social identification and differentiation through fashion signs.

The downtown district for *quince* dresses is divided roughly into two types of dress vendors: resellers of mass-production dresses and independent designers. The independent designers, more likely to be located in the upscale Chapultepec zone, offer personally designed dresses in the 5000+ peso ($500+) category. These high-end stores also sell name brand designer dresses imported from the U.S., Europe, or Mexico City. The personal creations will be designed with the girl and her designer and usually her mother to satisfy the youth's desire to have a unique dress that expresses her personal style. Asked whether she had seen changes in the industry in the last ten years, a personal designer responded:

Yes, yes, many changes. The girls have become very daring and they no longer want a pastel gown with a large puffy skirt, they want black, red, they want it short, they want it daring and baring lots of skin, they like lots of dark colors and lots of contrast, red and black, white and fuchsia, fuchsia and blue, things like that. They no longer come in and mom says, my daughter, put this on, wear this. Now, they come in and the daughter says: "No, I don't like it. I want it like this and like this" and they have ideas from the centers of fashion, Hollywood, many Hollywood stars, New York, Europe. They find pictures in magazines, on the internet, and they say: I want this.

The designer noted Penelope Cruz, Salma Hayek, Avril Lavigne, and the Cure as influences she had seen among her clients.

This designer will sit down with a client and her family and discuss photos from international fashion magazines such as *Hola* (Spain) or *quince* magazines from Mexico City or Guadalajara, or a picture of a dress worn by a celebrity and published in magazines or on the Internet. The designer will negotiate between the photos, a *quinceañera's* desires, parents' fashion requisites, budgets, the *quinceañera's* body type and coloring, and the designer's own sense of color, fit, and design. This designer tells a story of a client who wanted an Avril Lavigne outfit, with a red skirt, white corset, and a small black jacket. The black was unacceptable to the designer because the client had dark skin, and the parents disliked the entire outfit. In resolution, the designer used fabric with black and white windowpane (*cuadrada*) for the skirt, added tulle to make it puffy, used white fabric with black polka dots for the top, and dropped the black jacket. The designer had maintained the stylistic cues popular with Avril Lavigne fans, and satisfied the *quinceañera*, her parents, and herself. The designer may manufacture the dress, but designer dresses are often subcontracted to individual seamstresses or factories that sew for much less than the designer.

The main source for dresses is the dress shops that carry facsimiles of designer dresses. While their merchandise is jealously guarded from independent seamstresses who make copies in home workshops, these shops sell mass-produced dresses that replicate designer styles in *quince* magazines and the Expo Quinceañera. These copy dresses typically sell at between 2,000 and 4,000 Mexican pesos, and are sold in dozens of shops at the heart of downtown. Shops do not sell the exact same dresses, but generally share two main manufacturers outside of Guadalajara. These two manufacturers produce simplified copies of dresses that are featured in designer advertisements or magazines, and sell models to the downtown vendors. Vendors can also special-order models with variations and in different colors, making the dresses more customized.

The designer and the copy dresses have been produced through a feminized and globalized chain of production that includes the virtual exchange of signs through fashion magazines, Japanese cartoons, the Internet, Hollywood celebrities, and international music stars. The abundant offerings within this market is partially a response to youth's desires, but also a result of the shift in the Mexican economy toward specialization in garment manufacture since the 1960s (Fernandez-Kelly 1983) and the proliferation of small-to-medium size garment manufacturers and distributors in Jalisco (Cota Yáñez 2004). Part of the success of the shift toward garment manufacture, and the reason for the industry's feminization, is the low value given to women's reproductive labor in clothesmaking (Mies 1986; Enloe 2004).

The production of the dresses cannot, however, be separated from the market that they serve: a demanding, informed base of youth seeking social identification and differentiation. The desire for uniqueness is universal among interviewees, so exclusivity of design is the thrust of designers' sales pitches and copiers' offerings. The rush to originality also inspires many youth to look to mass media and marketing for ideas. *Quince* magazines, the Expo Quinceañera, fashion and celebrity magazines become important in the process of informing a youth's search for her unique style. Dress designers' clients bring with them images, literal and imaginary, of what they want, based on information they gather through media and marketing. She might even actively seek out a style that is unique from what is considered "Mexican." For example, one young woman has chosen her *quince* dress design from a drawing of a Japanese cartoon character that "isn't available here in Mexico." The result is that now, as youth's access to information informs their search for unique expressions of their identities, the global virtual economy of signs informs their dress design and production.

Makeovers

Whereas their mothers' generation did not use beauty services at all, and used products sparingly, the new generation of *quinceañeras* almost universally uses beauty services and products to receive a beauty makeover for their *quinces*. In addition, *quinceañeras* will often pursue body makeovers, through diet, exercise, and dress.

Only the *quinceañeras* who identified themselves as having a "nontraditional" party did not have their hair and make-up done by a professional. The rest received the professional services of a female relative or friend of the family, a beautician in their neighborhood, or a beautician recommended by a friend. All but the most exclusive neighborhoods have a handful of beauty service providers within a short walking distance. Beauticians my informants consulted were all women, except for one supposedly gay man, whose services were sought out because men are considered superior beauticians.

Quinceañeras gave many reasons for getting professional makeovers. Some did it "just because," others in order to feel special, because a family member or friend offered their services, and because they did not know how to apply cosmetics themselves. Most receive permission to wear cosmetics for the first time on their fifteenth birthday.

Typical cosmetic application for a *quinceañera* looks like stage or fashion make-up in Mexico. One sees this type of cosmetic application on the female protagonists of *telenovelas*. For a *quinceañera*, it includes bright eyeshadow colors, dark and thick eyeliner, eyebrow shaping, eyebrow color definition, and false eyelashes and/or mascara, to make the eye look bigger and more pronounced. Any cosmetician will use facial foundation to make the color of a *quinceañera's* skin more even and cheek blush to give a rosy color back to the face and to make the cheekbones more prominent. A more professional cosmetician will use shading powder to make cheeks look hollow, nose bridges straighter, chins thinner, foreheads less prominent, or to otherwise "fix imperfections" of the facial features. The cosmetician will also use lip liner, lip color, and a lip gloss to give the *quinceañera* a lasting, rosy, shiny, and sparkly pout. Finally, the *quinceañeras* almost universally apply fingernail extensions with rhinestones and color-coordinated drawings.

Cosmetics use among young men in Guadalajara is a highly rebellious, counter-culture undertaking; the norm is for women to have makeovers and for men not to. One mother expressed concern that her son was so concerned with looks that he was even talking about using cosmetics. Another mother feared that her son's use of black clothing was making him depressed, and that he might take up the use of black eyeliner. Male cosmetics were a disturbing idea to these mothers, and a sign of loss of order and tradition.

The norm for *quinceañera* hairstyles is fixed "up" in a *chongo*. *Chongos* are made by processing clean hair with some hair products and either a blow dryer, hair curler, or hair straightener to make the hair's shape uniform. During or after this process, all or most of the hair is gathered toward the crown of the head, making the hair look like mounds of curls or mounds of straight but stylistically separated locks of hair sprouting out of the crown, falling forward over the top of the head, and streaming down the *quinceañera's* neck and back. The new hair shapes are held in place with bobby pins, hair clips, gel, and hairspray. The key to hairstyling is to modify it to some degree from its natural state. As one informant explained, "since I have straight hair, I curl it or make it wavy." In addition to her up-do, a *quinceañera* will wear a crown or a hairpiece of flowers and glittery things.

Boys' hairstyles are shorter, and generally less styled. The standard for a boy is to have a short haircut and to comb his hair into a shape using hair gel while his hair is wet from a shower, and let it dry. As one informant said: "I think gel is my most important fashion accessory, because that is what I use to style my hair." This type of styling often has a "wet" look but is firmly put, so that no hair falls out of place and the locks are hard to the touch. Despite their simple styling procedure, boys' hairstyles can still be supernatural. Short spiky and smooth helmet hairdos are most common. One interviewee who was also an amateur performer reported styling his curly, longish, hair with a straightening iron, and I also saw this used on all of the male participants at an adolescent beauty pageant, and at local fashion shows. Still, in mainstream styles it is highly rarified that a boy will go beyond the use of gel and a comb for styling. I observed it among those boys who would be going on stage.[5]

Body shape is a final area for *quince* makeovers. *Quinceañeras* often discussed body ideals and how to achieve them. The most important body-shaping exercise for the *quinceañera* is the use of the corset. The corset, in combination with a puffy skirt, forces a girl's waist into a curve, exaggerates her breasts, and creates or accentuates an hourglass shape. As one interviewee recounted, even a chubby girl can feel beautiful in a corset. This birthday girl was very happy with her photos and her presentation on the day of her *quince* because of the thin waist that her dress gave her, although she could "hardly breathe" and it was difficult for her to move.

Thinness and hourglass proportions are important beauty ideals for *quinceañeras*. The conspicuously serious moments in interviews with adolescent girls came when we talked about weight and wanting to be thinner. As one interviewee told me as she choked up with anger, "your skin can be purple, but you have to be thin." Besides corsets, many participants reported using diet and exercise to get beautiful before their *quince*. Echoing the sentiments of many, one lamented that she would like to "lose some kilos, that is the only thing I would change." A small number put themselves on diets to lose weight, however most reported trying to eat a "balanced diet" and the use of exercise to improve body shape. "Balanced diet" has become a code for "diet" as fad diet foods announce that they are "part of a balanced diet" and girls deny any weight loss measures "except for a balanced diet." Body-part-specific exercises, such as leg lifts to "lift the butt" and abdominal exercises to slim the waist were popular, as were cardiovascular exercises to lose weight.

This preoccupation with weight is gendered. Boys expressed less concern for their body shape than girls, and did not report preoccupation with weight or body shape specifically in preparation for their roles as *chambelanes*, although they did occasionally express concern for their height and build in general. *Chambelanes'* disinterest in weight and body shape is partially a function of the fact that they are chosen because they have the preferred characteristics of height and athletic build. In addition, boys regularly reported hours of athletic activity every week, a prerequisite for the favored athletic build, although they did not consider this to be a process of beautification.

To the extent that these mainstream boys discussed their concern for looking good, their concerns revolved around looking wealthy and diminishing ethnic identifiers by looking whiter, bigger, stronger, and more fine-featured. The three young men who spoke freely about their interest and investment in style spoke about trying to stay out of the sun to keep their skin from darkening, using exercises to try to make them taller, and using a nasal prosthetic to make a nose with a down-turned bridge appear to be upturned. One boy assured me that his dark-skinned friend would not be able to accompany him to a fashionable nightclub because of the color of his skin. He considered the idea that his friend might be able to dress like a very wealthy person in order to gain access, but was not convinced this would work.

Boys' attempts to diminish their sense of ethnic and class disadvantage through bodily modification reveal the importance of ethnicity, race, class, and gender to ideals of beauty. To be attractive, these young men are convinced that they should be tall, broad-shouldered, and have upturned noses and fair skin. Indeed, these young men take up the task of improving their racialized bodies in order to produce their ideal of masculinity, much in the way young women take up their bodies as tasks to produce themselves as recognizably feminine. It appears to be through racial transformation that some young Mexican men seek to achieve a more powerful masculinity. This evidence suggests that, in a non-Western context, and in the context of globalization, body politics are as much about race as they are about gender.

The importance of productive, reproductive and virtual exchanges in makeovers illustrates how *quinceañera* beauty is being shaped by and shaping a gendered political economy of beauty. The heavy employment of women in the beauty industry is part of the global trend toward flexibilization and feminization of labor markets, a product of the inextricable productive and reproductive economies. As women enter into the labor market, they enter it based on gendered cultural expectations as well as gendered demands on their time. These factors make working in beauty services an attractive option because it uses skills that they have developed through learning about becoming a beautiful woman in their personal lives, it gives them added cultural cache as an expert in beautification (a highly prized expertise in Guadalajara), and it allows flexible work options that allow them to fulfill family obligations. Indeed, the most common type of beauty salon in Guadalajara is run out of a beautician's home.

Additionally, the majority of interviewees purchase at least some of their beauty products from friends and relatives selling as direct-sales distributors for Avon, Jafra, Fuller, and Mary Kay beauty products. Avon, the first direct-sales beauty company to enter the Mexican market, claimed to have reached two-thirds of Mexican households every week by the late 1980s, and the competition has only intensified. This increase in direct sales indicates a flexibilization of the health and beauty industries, that uses a gendered "functional flexibility" through which international companies take advantage of women's supposedly "free time" to sell products for commission or discount only. As with beauty services, gendered expectations lead women to become both distributors and consumers of direct-sales beauty products.

The growth in beauty services and direct cosmetics sales cannot, however, be understood without also referencing the virtual economy. The financial sector motivates and shapes the marketing of beauty products in emerging markets in the developing world and to youth markets in particular. The ideas about women that make beauty services or network-marketing a good, even a "natural" option for women are implicated in the global exchange of signs. Most clearly, the exponential growth in beautification techniques and products is propelled by global marketing and media, leading women to seek more and more expertise, their own or others,' in order to successfully achieve a feminine gendered body. Likewise, the exponential growth in beautification techniques and products propels women to seek more products, and the spending money to buy them or the discount associated with being a net-work-marketing distributor. In sum, the beauty services and products indus-tries are shaping and shaped by both globalization and the production of the gendered body.

Dancing

Historically, a *quinceañera* celebrated her new social status as a young woman by dancing a waltz with her father or with her escort, or both. This tradition has evolved into one of the most important parts of the production and the most anxiety-producing: the waltz and the surprise dance(s).

The first waltz is an unchoreographed partner dance with the *quinceañera's* father figure(s). The second waltz, with her *chambelan-de-honor*, or lead escort, is choreographed to include her court of *chambelanes* and *damas*. *Chambelanes* are frequently hired from dance schools or dance companies or *chambelan* agencies, but they are also often brothers, cousins, nephews, and the popular boys at school. Waltzes are choreographed for simplicity, visual impact, and theatricality. The courts will fill up the dance floor and, walking around to the slow beat, use simple turns, back-and-forth steps, and theater to emphasize the *quinceañera's* star quality and heterosexual courtship. The *quinceañera* and her court will then perform a choreography called the *brin-dis*, or toast, in which the *chambelan-de-honor* hands the *quinceañera* a champagne glass and the court leads the room in a ceremonial, non-verbal, toast while waltzing.

Following the waltz and toast, the *quinceañera* will change her costume for the surprise dance(s), a twenty-first century tradition. Usually danced in a highly sexualized manner, these dances offer a very different picture of the *quinceañera*. When she returns to the stage, the *quinceañera* wears either a shorter version of her ballgown or a costume based on the surprise dance theme. *Quinceañeras* dance tango, Hawaiian/Tahitian, Arabic, salsa, hip-hop, reggaeton, *Grease*, Disney fairytale, *The Mask*, *Phantom of the Opera*, and countless other themes for their "surprise" dance. She may play the solo star, or a member of a group of booty-shaking divas, or the lead dancer in a hip-hop dance troupe, or the protagonist in a salsa or tango. The costume may be a clingy black dress for tango, shiny dress for salsa, jean miniskirt and mid-riff-baring shirt for rock and hip hop, chiffon skirt and brassiere for belly dancing, or grass skirt and a coconut shell brassiere top for Hawaiian dancing.

This dance, of the *quinceañera's* choosing, is not a surprise anymore because it runs against the norm to not perform one. The dance showcases the *quinceañera's* dancing skills and interests, based on either classes that she takes or a choreographed dance that she learned for the event. In the surprise dances, *quinceañeras* have extensive experience, and boys are more timid when it comes to learning and dancing these varied rhythms. And so, accompaniment in the surprise dance is usually made by girlfriends, dance classmates, dance teachers, and professional *chambelanes*.

Dance choreography, lessons and practice is often the most time-consuming and engaging aspect of *quince* preparation, and the emergence of choreographed waltz and surprise dances has created a blossoming industry of dance professionals. Dance classes, private chorographers, professional dance accompaniment, stage and lighting technicians, videographers, photographers, costumers, and agencies all contribute to the waltz and surprise-dance market.

The waltz plays an important role in the reproductive work of the *quince* through its role in performing and reproducing ideals of familial, gender, and sexual relations. The dance reinforces familial hierarchy as she dances her last dance as a girl with her father and her father inducts her into womanhood by placing her in high heels, and in the arms of her *chambelan-de-honor*. The dance also plays a symbolic role in her induction into heterosexual coupling as she dances with her *chambelanes* (Cantú 1999).

The productive economy of dances is local because many teens already attend their local dance school. They often hire their dance teacher as a choreographer. Dance teachers hire former students and friends as *chambelanes*. Alternatively, professional *chambelan* agencies advertise at the Expo Quince, in *quince* magazines, or through word-of-mouth. Finally, celebrants may purchase special clothing or costumes for the surprise dances.

The political economy of dance is global, though, through its links to the reproductive and virtual economies. One surprisingly globalized aspect to the dances is the varied dance styles and their execution. Waltzes tend to be more conservative, reiterating themes of earlier phases of globalization: colonial Spain and France. Still, the urge to express originality in the *quince* is leading to a diversification of waltz styles. Some of the old standards for *quince* waltzes are *Sobre las Olas* (Juventino Rosas 1884), a traditional wedding waltz, *De Niña a Mujer* (Julio Iglesias 1981), and *Tiempo de Vals* (Chayanne 1990). Chayanne's classic is still heard every weekend at a *quince* in Guadalajara, but more and more youth are choosing unconventional music from popular culture to choreograph their waltzes. Disney, pirates, movie romances, and Arabian nights themes from film scores, and pop stars like Paris Hilton are popular. Even as the music score changes, the waltz still plays out a prince and princess theme and reinforces classical ideas about gender roles: a beautiful dance partner with a corseted waist, taking dainty, controlled steps; romantic gestures made by a suitor; permission to dance granted by a father-figure; and the princess following the prince's lead.

Surprise dances are a new phenomenon, identified as special and exciting because they reflect the "unique desires" of *quinceañeras* and are used to show off their personal style and skills. As one mother complained, during the season her daughter's friends were turning 15, they had to stop attending *quinces* because they would get bored seeing one surprise dance follow another, and the dance floor was sometimes not opened until after midnight. While the youth's claims to originality may be in question, the surprise dances are important to the girls as sources of personal expression. It is in these that one can see the global virtual economy of signs best. Here, dances imitate pop stars like Shakira and Beyoncé and groups like Vaselina, and achieve a striking similarity to the pop culture music video form. They also commonly celebrate classic Latin American dance forms like tango and salsa. And they often pick up on the belly-dance-inspired dances popularized by Shakira.

Conclusion

As we can see from these three aspects of *quince* preparation, how young women dress, modify, improve, and move their bodies is shaped by a global political economy of beauty that includes productive, reproductive, and virtual dimensions. Not necessarily every aspect of the beautification of the *quinceañera* is global, but through the linking of the reproductive, productive, and virtual economies, we see that personal beautification is indeed very closely linked to a global political economy. The dress shop downtown is local, but the Hollywood imaginary and the European monarchies that inspire its style are part of the global virtual economy of signs. Likewise the global gendered division of labor, the restructuring of state policies, and the reorientation of national economic strategies that encouraged the feminization of dress manufacturing, the production of cheap cloth and the brand piracy industry link the production of the dress to changes in the reproductive sphere.

The significance of the relationship between globalization and the bodily modifications and comportment of young girls and boys in Guadalajara is twofold. First, it is important because it illustrates a diversifying of expressions of gender in Guadalajara at the same time that traditional unequal gender relations are being reinforced.

The relationship of globalization to the gendering of the feminine body is complicated because it is at least partly *through* the gendering of the feminine body that globalization operates and reproduces existing inequalities. This can be seen through the operation of the reproductive, productive, and virtual economies in the *quince*. Through gendered bodies, the productive economy relies on and supplies the reproductive economy and meets gendered consumer demands. This very process cannot help but reproduce those gendered divisions. For example, we see the increasing popularity of the *quinceañera* that gives form to strict gendered ideas about women's relationship to the church, the family, their bodies, and sexuality. At the same time, however, the tradition is quickly evolving to incorporate new ways of "being new" for the girls. In their dances, this includes exaggerated sexuality, autonomy, and personal freedom. In their dresses, it means bright colors and black or red as increasingly common symbols of youthful femininity as opposed to white and pastels. In terms of beautification, their mothers' and fathers' ideals of a "natural feminine beauty" have given way to increasingly alienesque, unnatural, and supernatural styles and the extensive consumption of beauty products. In short, while reproducing strict archaic gender norms, globalization is also undermining them, making them less natural, and creating more diversity among the young women of Guadalajara.

Second, it illustrates how the feminine gendering of the body can be seen as an engine of globalization. Feminist IR scholarship has foregrounded the politics of the gendered body within international relations through scholarship on gendered aspects of the global political economy and international security. IR feminists have called attention to how feminized bodies are central to the workings of the global political economy through their gendered work in the labor market, in the reproductive sphere, and in the informal market. For example, the feminized and racialized body itself, compliant and with nimble fingers, has been crucial to the successful feminization of export-processing labor (Elson and Pearson 1981; Enloe 1989, 2004; Salzinger 2003). Likewise, the sexualized and racialized body is central to the operations of the international sex industry (Pettman 1996; Agathangelou 2004). The feminine gendered body is a key site for the construction and contestation of competing nationalisms (Grewal and Kaplan 1994; Tickner 1996; Yuval-Davis 1997; Enloe 2004). Women experience particular forms of corporal control and violence due to the gendered nature of militaries and war (Moon 1997; Tickner 2001). Contests over women's bodies are a consistent source of NGO and social movement interest (e.g., Keck and Sikkink 1998).

This feminist scholarship in IR illustrates how the feminine gendering of the body plays a significant role in how power operates globally. Crucial to understand is that the feminine gendered body, through its successful feminization and concomitant devaluation, facilitates the unequal effects of such global politics as globalization and securitization. At the same time, these processes help to reproduce that recognizably feminine, subordinate, body.

This research highlights and extends the feminist project of making the politics of gender and bodies visible by looking at the very gendering of the body and how that gendering is influenced by and influencing processes of globalization. Drawing on feminist perspectives on "beauty politics," this research takes the project of linking bodies to international relations further, by making explicit the relations between producing the gendered body and the working of the global political economy of beauty.

Furthermore, the important role of youth beautification in globalization contributes to the argument that globalization is an intimate, non-totalizing process of global restructuring (Marchand and Runyan 2000). As postcolonial and postmodern feminists have noted, totalizing accounts of globalization as corporate capitalism writ large, including feminist ones, underestimate the power and participation of non-hegemonic forces in globalization (Gibson-Graham 1996; Chang and Ling 2000; Freeman 2001; Bergeron 2001). Youth's desires for social identification and differentiation through fashion and their central role in gendered fashion globalization are an example of how globalization should not be conceived as a totalizing or all-encompassing power. Rather, it must be understood as deeply intimate, indeed feeding into and being generated by all of our bodies, especially youth. Following Enloe's paraphrase of a feminist adage, the personal is political, the personal is economic, and the personal is international (Enloe 1989). In addition, I hope to stress that in this case at least it appears to be producing diversity, albeit within a conformist imperative.

Notes

1 For example, McGrew 1992: 65, 67, quoted in Tomlinson 1999: 2, Altman 2002: 58–61; Enloe 2004 chapter 3; Hammond and Prahalad 2004; Gray et al. 2006: 295.
2 Following custom in Guadalajara, I use *quince* to refer to the mass and celebration and *quinceañera* to refer to 15-year-old girls.
3 Ethnographic fieldwork was conducted over 14 months between 2006–7, and included semi-structured interviews with 40 14–16-ycar-old youth and a subset of older adults in aspiring middle-class families, participant observation with youth and their families, and participant observation in beauty classes, dance classes, and fashion events. Data is also drawn from archival material concerning the *fiesta de quince años* and beautification available to and used by youth in Guadalajara.
4 Quotes are based on the author's translations of recorded interviews or detailed notes taken during or after conversations with informants.
5 At the end of my research period, the "emo" style was increasingly popularized. In March 2008, while I was visiting friends in Guadalajara, I had the opportunity to witness a street demonstration of emos asking to be treated with respect and protected from discrimination. During this month, fighting between emos and other subcultures reached a crescendo and filled the national news as emos were attacked, some physically, for having poor taste or for being unauthentic "posers." Emo boys do make use of the hair straightener in order to make their hair fall in their face. During 2008 and 2009, the emo style has become common and normalized.

Femininity: culture, ideology and political economy

An engagement with Angela McCracken

V. Spike Peterson

I am pleased to be commenting on Angela McCracken's very fine chapter. In what follows, I both reflect on her research and, as I did in my spoken remarks,[1] situate her work in a larger context of feminist inquiry and activism. In particular, I draw linkages between McCracken's account of the *fiesta de quince años* and Chrys Ingraham's account of "white weddings."[2] A key question I ponder is how the *quince* and wedding ceremonies, and the *romancing of femininity they constitute*, operate to secure consent to capitalist masculinist (heteronormative and patriarchal) social relations.

My starting point is that McCracken's work engages with and advances our understanding of two key quandaries in contemporary scholarship and activism. In McCracken's words:

> The significance of the role of globalization in the production of beauty ideals in Mexico is twofold. First, it illustrates how the gendering of the body ... is an engine of the globalization of material, social and ideational exchange. Second, the global political economy of beauty in the *quince* illustrates a diversifying of expressions of gender in Guadalajara at the same time that traditional unequal gender relations are being reinforced. It is at least partly through the gendering of the beautiful feminine body that globalization operates, reproducing existing gendered inequalities. At the same time, however, the intersection of globalization with youth's desires and youth's practices means that new expressions of femininity and masculinity ... are emerging within a conservatively gender-coded custom (p. 195).

In my words, the first quandary is how to construe the relationship—typically cast as oppositional—between economic (material) and cultural (symbolic) phenomena. How do we move beyond (positivist, modernist) hierarchical dichotomies that privilege structure, institutions, materiality and objectivity over culture, discourse, abstractions, and subjectivity? The second quandary is how to understand the relationship—which appears paradoxical—

between enduring continuities (traditions, normalizations) and undeniable changes (reforms, challenges).[3] Why are apparent challenges—particularizations in McCracken's account—limited in their disruption of structural inequalities and systemic (capitalist, heteropatriarchal) normalizations? My objective in this engagement is to explore how the quandaries are interrelated and how heteronormativity is an under-acknowledged and inadequately interrogated obstacle to achieving what I deem a feminist objective: not just minor changes but a *systemic transformation* of all structural hierarchies that rely on devalorization of "the feminine" to normalize subordination.[4]

With respect to the quandary of relating economy and culture, McCracken has honored my work by employing the "RPV" framing—of mutually constituted reproductive, productive, and virtual economies—to argue that the global political economy of beauty shapes, and is also shaped by, the process of youth beautification (p. 207). I developed the "RPV" framing in my 2003 book *A Critical Rewriting of Global Political Economy: Integrating Reproductive, Productive and Virtual Economies.*[5] The book had three primary objectives: to generate a methodologically plural, transdisciplinary account of globalization; to "rewrite" global political economy by demonstrating the interdependence of reproductive, productive, and virtual economies; and to advance critical theory by illuminating the intersection of race, gender, and economic inequalities (within and among states) as structural features of globalization. Underpinning and fueling these objectives was a larger issue that I wished to address: the relationship of "economy" and "culture" in contemporary social inquiry.

Decades of theoretical debate had exacerbated the historical divide between disciplinary fields of instruction. Poststructuralist and postmodernist critiques had been relatively welcomed and adopted by scholars in the humanities where culture, subjective processes, representational practices and textual productions are typically foregrounded. Scholars in social science disciplines—especially economics and IR—continued to emphasize material and structural processes and to favor formal, empirical-positivist and modernist epistemologies. With many others, I lamented how these disciplinary and epistemological divides both fragmented our knowledge of social relations and perpetuated problematic dichotomies.[6] I wanted my work to "bridge" the structure *versus* culture divide by undermining its oppositional, either–or construction. In one sense then, my book was an attempt to generate a systematic description and critical analysis of globalization understood as *economic* restructuring—especially in light of transformations due to ICTs and neoliberal restructuring. But in an additional and more provocative sense I hoped that the description and analysis themselves exposed the centrality of *cultural* and virtual phenomena to our understanding of global political economy.

It is gratifying therefore, that McCracken found my analytical framing of use in her own research linking economic and cultural phenomena in the context of celebrating the *quince* in Guadalajara. McCracken has, through ethnographic fieldwork and sophisticated analysis, produced a rich and detailed case study. The quality and value of the study are enhanced by her lengthy residency (14 months), many in-depth interviews, astute participant observation, and appropriate archival research. The product is also a delight to read, as we are drawn into the imaginaries, emotions, and lived realities of the *quinceañeras*.

McCracken's case study reveals how the ideals of beauty operating at the local level and manifested in celebrating the *quince* are inextricable from the global economy of advertising, marketing, and the production and consumption of goods and services. With respect to my RPV framing, the "reproductive economy" (RE) operates in part through repetition of traditions and rituals that sustain gendered norms, expectations and cultural ideals. The *quince* is simultaneously a religious ceremony, family event, and social occasion. Its processes involve a (re)affirmation of faith-based commitments, a particular moment in parent–child relations, and a reinforcement of social bonds and social status within community networks. In what parallels a wedding, mother and daughter assume time-honored roles: variously agreeing and disagreeing as the primary decision-makers in planning, preparation, and execution of the celebration. Citing other research as well, McCracken notes that these activities are additionally "reproductive" in the sense of passing on to the girls skills of "budgeting, priority-setting, and negotiation" (p. 198).

Also like a wedding, the *quince* is one of the most visible occasions of beautification and display for participants and attendees alike (p. 195). It reproduces expectations and materializations of gender-differentiated beauty, bodies, fashion and comportment for all involved. Most obviously, the celebrant strives in multiple ways to ensure that she is looking her "best"— understood here as "fixing oneself up" as the true measure of looking good (p. 203). For most *quinceañeras* this involves efforts to assume an hour-glass figure (through exercise, diet, and wearing a corset for the event) and to appear stylistically beautiful (through extensive cosmetics, dramatic hairstyles, color-coordinated fingernail extensions, and a stunning dress). While the celebration itself is not global, the beautification practices and display it generates are informed by cultural ideals circulating in advertisements, popular media, and marketing strategies that are more often transnational than local or national. And while the *quince* is not celebrated globally, many cultures mark life-cycle transitions of youth with festive occasions where traditions of feasting, spectacle, and the celebrant appearing "at their finest" are reproduced. In particular, the *quince* has many suggestive, indeed instructive, parallels with (heteronormative, patriarchal) weddings that continue to be celebrated globally.

These diverse processes associated with the RE are inextricable from the productive economy (PE) as a more familiar site of "economic" activities. In addition to market activities that link the local to the global, there is an under-calculated amount of work required for—and an under-counted number of workers engaged in—sustaining cultural ideologies, religious institutions, and household reproduction. McCracken describes the beauty salon, rental, photography, video, and catering services, as well as the advertising, production, supply, delivery, and consumption of "goods" for the celebration.

The feminized and informal features of these "market dimensions" are of particular interest in the context of contemporary GPE. Decades of neo-liberal restructuring have as one effect a global *feminization* of employment, understood as simultaneously an embodied transformation of work practices (more women engaged in formal and informal income generation), a conceptual characterization of devalorized labor conditions (more precarious and poorly paid jobs), and a reconfiguration of worker identities (more feminized management styles and more female breadwinners).[7] Preparations and purchases for the *quince* offer an illuminating glimpse of these highly gendered market processes, and especially the predominance of feminized and informal labor in the services involved. Especially problematic is how the *romanticized* femininity that the event commemorates is inextricable from the *devalorization* of the feminine that the event operationalizes—through the global economy's structurally cheapened (feminized) labor and services.

Consider how the *quince* celebration (again, much like the wedding celebration) marks a highpoint of singularly *feminized* desire and spectacle: the fantasy tale of a beautiful *quinceañera*, her "uniquely" designed dress and color-coordinated accessories, and an elegant—perhaps dazzling—gala event. As McCracken discerns, the industry that sustains this fantasy and those who enable its embodied "realization" are highly feminized. From beauticians to dress makers and food preparers, most of the *work* is done by women— including mothers and daughters who coordinate the event—who labor in production processes that are marked by informal arrangements and flexible practices, and in jobs that are typically *de*valorized with respect to status and/ or remuneration. As one example, McCracken observes that "network marketing is a further flexibilization of the health and beauty industries, and a new, gendered type of 'functional flexibility' through which international companies take advantage of women's supposedly 'free time' to sell products for commission only" (p. 206).

At the same time, market processes associated with beautifying the *quinceañera* and lavishly celebrating the *quince* are inextricable from the "virtual economy" (VE). The latter has grown in significance as information and communication technologies (ICTs) have compressed time–space, enabled the shift from material-intensive to knowledge-intensive industries, facilitated the expansion of services and the exchange of intangibles, and fueled tremendous growth in financial market transactions. In effect, the VE features the exchange of symbols: primarily money in the context of global financial markets; but also information in the context of a "post-industrial," "informational," or "service economy"; and "signs" in the context of postmodern aesthetics, consumption, meaning, and culture.[8]

McCracken situates the *quince* in relation to the virtual economy primarily in terms of the cultural industry: advertising as it relates to promoting ideals of beauty and fashion, as well as entertainment media generating *quince*-related content. She notes the international fashion and Mexican *quince* magazines, television shows, the Internet and pop culture music videos as sources of ideas for how to plan the quince, design one's dress and appearance, and/or perform the "surprise" dance. But in addition to the cultural industry's promotion of gendered bodies, McCracken describes the effect of global marketing on "women's work." In her words,

> the exponential growth in beautification techniques and products is propelled by global marketing and media, leading women to seek more and more expertise, their own or others', in order to successfully achieve a feminine gendered body. Likewise, the exponential growth in beautification techniques and products propels women to seek more products, and the spending money to buy them or the discount associated with being a network-marketing distributor.
>
> (p. 206–207)

Even more could be said about the financial dimensions of the VE, especially given the "one-time only" nature of celebrating the quince (or first weddings). In effect, the beautification and "extravagant occasion" industries link household investment strategies and particular expenditures with global economics. The singularity of these "special" occasions presumably spurs particularly lavish spending, which has short- and long-term economic implications. The scale of expenditures shapes not only the global economy of work, workers and financial investments, but also what alternative expenditures and/or investments these extravaganzas preclude (for example, in education or health care). Without specific data regarding *quince* celebrations, one can only speculate about the scale of resources expended and corollary effects.[9] But McCracken's research suggests the significance of the occasion in Mexico, and we know that weddings constitute a very considerable household expense and a sizeable global industry.

Ingraham reports that Wall Street refers to the wedding industry as "recession proof," presumably due to emotional investments in this celebration that deflect "return on investment" concerns. The scale of expenditures is stunning. In 2005 industry estimates of the total annual revenues of the *primary* wedding market (rings, apparel, ceremony, reception, photos, honeymoons, etc.) in the U.S. alone ranged from $50 to $125 billion per year.[10] Most of the production and services in support of these events take place outside of the U.S. and involve transnational networks: the production of gowns, accessories and jewelry, household equipment and other favored gift items, and services associated with honeymoon travel. Ingraham captures the global intersections of hierarchies in this summary:

The heterosexual imaginary circulating throughout the wedding-industrial complex masks the fact that global, racial, class and sexual hierarchies are secured. ... The wedding industry depends upon the availability of cheap labor from developing nations with majority populations made up of people of color. The wealth garnered by white transnational corporations both relies on racial hierarchies, exploiting people and resources of communities of color ... and perpetuates them in the marketing of the wedding industry.

(2008, 112–13)

I conclude by returning to the quandaries posed at the outset. McCracken's detailed field work and careful analysis enable us to see quite clearly how a coming-of-age ceremony entails numerous processes that are variously shaped by the interaction of reproductive, productive, and virtual economics. With respect to the *quince* in McCracken's account, and "white weddings" in Ingraham's account, the interdependence of culture and economy—and their global contextualization—are well documented. These research projects demonstrate the value, indeed the necessity, of recognizing the cultural component of economic phenomena and vice versa.

In the process of her research, McCracken observes and analyzes how traditional heteronormative, patriarchal and cultural traditions are both reproduced by the *quince* celebration *and* altered by the young women's agency in "particularizing" their hairstyles, dresses, and the "surprise" dance. Here we observe the second quandary: the young participants create "new expressions" of gender that challenge and change the traditional ceremony, yet these hardly disrupt the larger (capitalist, heteropatriarchal) systems within which they are embedded. In this sense, they afford little hope of *transforming* structural hierarchies, and this raises the question of what *is* needed to *systematically* advance critical analysis and activism. In responding to that question, I return to the relationship between highly romanticized femininity, which is central to these occasions and emotional investments in them, and the *devalorization* of the feminine, which these events operationalize.

Consider how the *quince* celebration and "white weddings" are quintessentially *feminized* displays and spectacles: both the *quinceañera* and the bride are presented as their most beautiful and desirable—"best"—embodiments, and both are the focal point of everyone's attention—for that day. Beautification and admiration are sought through make-up, figure, dress and accessories, and success is measured by approximating the fantasy ideal of a princess who enjoys everyone's favor. We might describe the celebrant as "princess for a day" in the *quince* event and the bride as "queen for a day" in the wedding event. The earlier ceremony marks the transition to female adulthood, even as the celebrant remains subject to her father's "rule"; the latter marks the transition to a new family status: the bride leaves her father's "rule" to (conventionally) become subject to the "rule" of her husband with the purpose (presumably) of producing the next generation, that is, the transition to motherhood. In both cases, the event marking the transition is highly romanticized and lavishly produced. It is culturally represented and personally internalized as a—for some, "the"—peak moment in the women's lives. While much more is going on as well, in both cases the fantasy and spectacle are represented as idealized celebrations of the key females—and specifically, their dramatized, exaggerated femininity. While there are important exceptions, there is little question that many and perhaps a global majority of females long dream about and mentally plan for these life-cycle events, hoping to make them live up to extraordinary expectations and to generate memories that "last a lifetime."

In short, there is an intensity of emotional investments in both celebrations, and this intensity justifies both the fantasized expectations and lavish expenditures. It is therefore worth pondering: whose interests are served by the cultural and economic celebration of these rituals, and what are the political implications of these emotional investments? The romanticized view is that these events promise a very special day, indeed a uniquely *personalized* celebration of the *quinceañera* and bride—as storybook beautiful, admired, honored, and cherished. It would be foolhardy to deny the emotional appeal of this tale and the pleasure it promises, especially in the context of masculinist systems that obstruct self-esteem for females. But the emotional seduction operating here is problematic. In effect, romanticizing the gender coding that is central to these events occludes how they operate to secure our consent to heteropatriarchal social relations, and how they perpetuate exploitative economic relations. To be clear: the point is decisively not to deny or disparage human expressions of fantasy, ritual, and celebration (which need replicate conventional gender codes). It is rather to reflect critically on how power operates within *particular* expressions, and with what personal, social and structural effects. I find Ingraham's critical analysis of white weddings particularly compelling, and contend that her observations apply equally to other celebrations that so explicitly romanticize femininity:

> The engine driving the wedding market has mostly to do with the romancing of heterosexuality in the interests of capitalism. The social relations at stake—love, community, commitment, and family—become alienated from the production of the wedding spectacle, while practices reinforcing a heterogendered and globalized racial division of labor, white supremacy, the private sphere as women's work, and women as property are reinforced.

(2008, 112)

What I conclude is that "queering" our analyses is a central and ultimately essential dimension of transforming—not merely tweaking, modifying, or particularizing—dominant structural hierarchies. My argument is that the heteronormative order producing and produced by the binary of empirical (male–female) sex categories and the dichotomy of analytical (heteronormative, masculine–feminine) gender codes is so deeply internalized and historically institutionalized that it constitutes a formidable obstacle to critical reflection and analysis (Peterson 2010a). Critique of this heteronormative order is rendered immensely difficult, not least because it appears "natural" and has been normalized as "foundational," but also because it has so pervasively secured our consent—in part through rituals that "celebrate" femininity and invite our complicity.[11]

The particulars of fantasizing, celebrating, dancing, dressing up, etc. need not be characterized in gendered terms. But when we actively exalt "femininity" per se we necessarily—though often not intentionally—invoke and reinscribe the governing code of gender as masculine–feminine *difference*, and that difference is coded as *hierarchical*. I believe therefore, that it is crucial for feminists and others seeking *systemic* transformations to deconstruct this dichotomy and its gender coding. As Cynthia Enloe reminded us at the conference,[12] while analyzing IR we should never underestimate the importance and power—that is, *politics*—of marriage. I would add—with trepidation but determination—that this entails deconstructing the ways in which "romancing femininity" disempowers females—and all who constitute feminized Others.

Notes

1 I refer to my comments in response to Angela's presentation of her paper "Twenty Years of Feminist International Relations," University of Southern California, April 5–6, 2010.

2 This is how Ingraham (2008) characterizes the confluence of heteronormative, class and ethnic/racialized dimensions of the global wedding culture and industry in her excellent book. For recent feminist reflections on the politics of marriage see Critical Perspectives section, *Politics & Gender* 2010.

3 Insofar as it relates theory to practice, the second quandary preoccupies all who seek better tactics and strategies in pursuit of systemic transformations. It features in recent critical studies where feminist objectives appear to have been realized (gender quotas, mainstreaming, etc.) yet global inequalities and their insecurities— shaped by but not exclusive to "gender"—continue to escalate. See, for example, Squires 2007; Tiesson 2007; Peterson and Runyan 2010.

4 Here and elsewhere I am *not* arguing that sexism is the "primary" oppression, but insisting that gender hierarchy is a historically contingent structural feature of social relations, that the subordination of women is not reducible to other structural oppressions (or vice versa), and that the dichotomy of gender underpins—as the *devalorization of the feminine* naturalizes—intersecting hierarchies of ethnicity/ race, class, gender, sexuality and geopolitical "difference" (e.g., Peterson 2003, 2009).

5 My three "economies" are understood not in conventional but in Foucauldian terms: as mutually constituted—therefore coexisting and interactive—*systemic* sites through and across which power operates. These sites involve familiar exchanges but also include socio-cultural processes of self-formation and cultural socialization that underpin identities and their political effects. The conceptual and cultural dimensions of these interactive sites are understood as inextricable from (mutually constituted by) material effects, social practices, and institutional structures.

6 With other feminists I have long argued that positivist, modernist epistemologies afford important feminist insights with respect to "adding women" and questioning

androcentric inquiry, while their ontological assumptions deflect attention away from power operating in language and knowledge claims in ways that limit critical and especially intersectional analyses (e.g., Peterson 1992, 1999, 2006).

7 On the "feminization" of economic restructuring see, for example, Standing 1999; Beneria 2003; Peterson 2003; Berik et al. 2009.

8 I introduced the VE in my book because the exchange of symbolic goods (abstractions, ideas, information) is relatively under-theorized in prevailing accounts of GPE. How this neglect impoverishes analyses of financial dynamics is demonstrated by the "surprise" some expressed as the current crisis unfolded. On masculinism in the financial sector see, for example, McDowell 1997; Aslanbeigui and Summerfield 2000; Hooper 2001; Peterson 2003; Barker and Kuiper 2006; Elson 2009; Berik et al. 2009. In a wedding twist, Ingraham (2008, 42) notes that even insurers have entered the wedding market, offering to cover the cost of expenditures if the ceremony fails to occur.

9 Ingraham is able to secure global data regarding wedding expenditures and generates a variety of insights regarding their effects. Prompted perhaps by the economic crisis, the popular media have chimed in about the debt issues and long-term opportunity costs of lavish wedding expenses, e.g., Arends 2010.

10 The average couple in the U.S. spends almost $28,000 per wedding (an increase of 38 percent in the past 15 years), and in Japan—where only 1.4 percent of the population are Christian—Christian-style ceremonies now account for 75 percent of weddings at an average cost of $62,000 (Ingraham 2008, 11, 37).

11 Recent feminist IR critiques of heteronormativity include Bedford 2009; Bergeron 2009; Lind 2010.

12 "Twenty Years of Feminist International Relations," University of Southern California, April 5–6, 2010.

10 Conclusion

Looking forward for feminist International Relations

J. Ann Tickner and Laura Sjoberg

What does it mean to do research with a feminist curiosity about global politics, and how comfortably (or uncomfortably) does that research fit into the discipline of International Relations? What are the complexities in attempting to define "sex" and "gender," and what nuances are needed to understand how they are both produced by, and productive of, social and political interactions? How can we add the insights of intersectional analysis and queer theory to strengthen feminist IR's ideas about gender and diversity? How do we understand phenomena in global politics that may sometimes be gender-oppressive and yet also provide women certain opportunities? Given the complexities that these questions raise, what can feminist perspectives on global politics tell us about how we should "act" in the activist and policy worlds? What are the norms that would encourage gender equality, and how could they be diffused? How are gender hierarchies linked to political economy, and how can we understand these links more clearly? In sum, what do we want feminist IR to be able to tell us about global politics when we revisit it 20 years from now? What work needs to be done to make those visions realizable?

The chapters in this book have attempted to reflect on, and provide some answers to, some of these questions both in the text and in the oral conversations at the conference. Drawing on these written and oral conversations, this conclusion will elaborate on some of these questions and suggest some useful directions that feminist IR might take in the future to help answer these questions; of course we realize that this book is only a small part of an ongoing conversation about a wide variety of rich feminist research programs. As we noted in the Introduction, looking forward to the future of feminist theorizing about global politics is both complex and exciting; it is taking place in multiple locations and disciplines. The complexity comes from combining elements of challenge and aspiration—challenge to deal with the "hard questions" for gender theorizing and aspiration to do so in a way that makes feminist IR the best it can be, theoretically and empirically.

Feminist curiosity about global politics and International Relations as a home

In the Introduction, we described some insights that feminist scholarship has contributed to IR, including understandings of the meaning and importance of sex, gender, and gender hierarchies and its readings of IR as gendered. Feminists have looked at IR "through gendered lenses" in ways that identify with, critique, and rebuild realist, liberal, constructivist, critical, poststructuralist, and postcolonial theories and research agendas. The chapters in this book have demonstrated the theoretical and empirical diversity of feminisms' engagements with IR: from realist approaches to strategy to critical approaches to Security as Emancipation (SAE), and from Mexican beauty parlors to the battlefields of Afghanistan.

In the past, IR feminists have generally asked what their scholarship could contribute to a field that has so often been blind to gender analysis. However, many of the contributions to this book, and the discussions they generated at the conference, suggest that it may be time for feminist IR to start asking a different question. What can IR contribute to feminism? In other words, how comfortable (or uncomfortable) a home is IR for the work we now identify as feminist?

Recent demographic survey research on the IR discipline shows that, at least in the U.S. and in certain places outside it, IR offers a "chilly climate" for women and the study of gender; even more than other subfields in political science (Sarkees and McGlen 1999; Malinak et al. 2008). Whereas mainstream IR sees a world of states seeking to pursue their own interests in an anarchical international system, feminists see a world of social relations, particularly hierarchical gender relations; while social science IR strives for objectivity and universality, feminist IR assumes contingency and subjectivity. As we have noted, much of feminist IR is explicitly normative and emancipatory; while it shares many of these ontological and epistemological sensitivities with other critical IR traditions, critical IR has generally not engaged with gender analysis any more than the mainstream. As J. Ann Tickner (1997, 614) noted, "all too often, [the mainstream's] claims of gender neutrality mask deeply embedded masculinist assumptions which can naturalize or hide gender differences and gender inequalities." Given this gender blindness certain feminists are beginning to question whether IR is the appropriate home for "feminist IR."

While many scholars have characterized IR as an "interdiscipline" and encouraged researchers to take advantage of the many different disciplinary resources available for the study of global politics, many others have argued that IR is, and should be, a subfield of political science adhering to its disciplinary epistemological and methodological norms (e.g., Keohane 1988). While feminist work on global politics may have a home in the "interdiscipline" of IR, it has found it difficult to fit into an IR that defines it as a subfield of political science. Drawing connections between knowledge, individual experience, and an emancipatory politics of ending gender oppression (Jaggar 1989; Scheman 1993), feminist research has tried to break the chains of (falsely) objective positive social science. Chapters in this book draw from a variety of disciplines—Confortini from peace research, Ruane from psychology's Social Identity Theory, McCracken from economics, Blanchard from philosophy of science and True from international law. Feminist scholars in IR also draw from anthropology, sociology, geography, biology, philosophy, and history (see Tickner 2005). Given these multiple disciplinary identities, we should ask whether feminist IR in the future will look anything like IR?

In the concluding session of the conference, J. Ann Tickner referred to a conversation with feminist Peggy McIntosh, the Associate Director of the Wellesley Center for Women and a co-organizer of the 1990 Wellesley conference to which we referred in the Introduction. After hearing a description of the field, McIntosh observed that, while it sounded like an interesting field, IR seemed to be neither International nor about relations. Feminist work on global politics is increasingly both. When the conference attendees were asked about the trends they saw in feminist IR, the first observation, made by Cynthia Enloe and echoed by other conference participants, was that it is increasingly international. Scholarship in the flagship feminist IR journal, the *International Feminist Journal of Politics*, is increasingly both authored by and about people outside of the traditional "hotspots" of IR—in the U.S., Western Europe, and Australia/New Zealand.

This expansion is not just about the inclusion of more voices in feminist scholarship on global politics, but also about the inclusion of more perspectives. Increasingly, feminist IR scholars are realizing that, while it is necessary to value sex, sexuality, race, national origin, linguistic, and religious differences both among scholars and in global politics, there is more to embracing diversity than representational practices. Feminist IR has come a long way from the conclusion (Spivak 1988) that the subaltern cannot speak. While still concerned with silences and translations (e.g., Hansen 2000), feminists have increasingly engaged with persons whose lives and voices are usually not heard in IR. In the concluding discussion, Abigail Ruane raised these issues in terms of her chapter's theoretical framework. She noted that the "borders" of feminist IR are expanding rapidly, but wondered if the "roots" were expanding also. If the subaltern could speak, would "we" (as a Eurocentric research program) like what "she" had to say? Ruane noted that it is important for future feminist research in global politics to get beyond the "universalism" versus "relativism" debate about social and cultural values. In response V. Spike Peterson noted that it is important for a feminist research ethic of global politics always to take account of diversity and always to be aware that none of our claims will be "innocent" of the hierarchies we see (and sometimes replicate) in global politics.

While feminist IR is increasingly international, that "international" is not the system-level, macro-political "international" familiar to traditional IR.[1] Rather, it is an international that is not only global but local in its globalism.

At several points in conversations and writings, the authors noted that feminist work deconstructs the boundaries between comparative politics and IR by looking at the international in domestic politics and the domestic (both in the political sense and in the household) in the international. While feminists are not the first to draw attention to the usefulness of dismantling these boundaries,[2] feminist views of the relationship between the international and the local (based on feminist critiques of the public/private divide) provide an innovative and creative way of looking at these questions. As Cynthia Enloe (1990, 195) has noted, feminists believe that "the personal is international, and the international is personal," a statement that some of the conference participants reread to mean that "the global is local and the local is global." Feminists see links between issues such as household economics and global capitalism, and between violence against women and global wars.[3]

If feminist scholarship on global politics is increasingly international, it is also increasingly focused on relations—both international ones and scholarly ones. Internationally, feminists are interested in the *how* of political interaction, policy prescription, and normative change. Feminist work on empathetic cooperation, the ethics of care, relational autonomy, and responsibility[4] increasingly recognizes the interdependence, interlinking, and inseparability of human social and political interactions. In scholarly terms, while some feminists see IR (particularly in the mainstream and particularly in the United States) as narrowing, feminists are increasingly broadening their scholarship in relational and reflexive terms (Biersteker 2009). In constructing both the University of Southern California conference that inspired this book and the book itself, we intentionally conceived of feminist IR as an ongoing conversation rather than a destination. Sandra Harding described these conversations as "building a family of the field" or creating a living discipline from living conversations.

As the chapters in this book suggest, "making feminist sense" of global politics or approaching global social and political relations with a feminist curiosity involves asking very different questions from the ones that IR typically asks and reexamining how it goes about answering them. While most feminist scholars see feminist research as having the potential to transform IR, many now wonder if IR is the right place for "a more radical rethinking of what properly constitutes I/international R/relations to begin with" (Squires and Weldes 2007, 189). Asking what feminism has to offer IR has led to many productive insights; it is a question that feminist scholars should continue to ask and hope IR scholars will recognize as important. At the same time, we anticipate that the reverse question—what does IR have to offer feminism—will be increasingly salient over the next two decades. To the extent that IR is an uncomfortable home for feminist work on global politics, should it be made more accommodating or abandoned? How might the relationship between IR and feminisms evolve?

Asking these questions (either at the conference or in this text) should not necessarily imply that IR does not have anything to offer feminism, and that feminism should leave IR. In addition to contributing to IR, much feminist work (in this book and otherwise) uses and borrows from the insights IR has had about global politics. For example, Abigail Ruane and Catia Confortini borrow from the insights of IR constructivism; Soumita Basu draws from IR critical theory; and Laura Sjoberg and Jessica Peet build on IR realism. While not rejecting IR, we do remain committed to the claim that one cannot think about IR without thinking about gender, and without recognizing the transformative potential of feminist IR for the discipline. We maintain this commitment for a number of political reasons (many of which are discussed in the remainder of this Conclusion). However, this commitment should not prevent us from also asking what constraints IR places on feminist research, how feminism can transform IR, and when and how it is appropriate to transcend IR's disciplinary boundaries and/or roots.

The nuances of sex, gender, and the production of political relations

Another (related) question that the conversations in this book bring up is revisiting the meanings of sex and gender, particularly as they are constituted by and constitutive of each other in twenty-first-century global politics. Twenty years ago, responding to IR's gender blindness, both in its own work and in global politics more generally, the authors in *Gendered States* (Peterson 1992), asked what difference it made that foreign and strategic policies were made mostly by men. Feminists also began looking for women (their bodies, their lives, and their experiences). Looking at men and women's differing experiences with respect to international politics provided a way of asking how gender (particularly gender hierarchy) influences both the identities and functions of states in global politics.

As feminist scholars have begun to look for women in global politics, they have been finding a number of nuances in understanding sex and gender. As we suggested in the Introduction, while "sex" refers to biology (which could be male, female, or other), "gender" refers to the social characteristics (masculinities and femininities) that we assume to be necessarily related to biological sex (maleness and femaleness). At any given time or place in history, there is not just one masculinity and femininity, but several masculinities and femininities competing for dominance along gendered social hierarchies, although femininities are usually, if not always, subordinated to masculinities. These dynamics have called feminist attention to the role of masculinities in global politics. Feminists in IR (Zalewski and Parpart 1998, 2008; Hooper 2001) have noted that a hegemonic ideal-typical masculinity in any given sociopolitical context often sets the standard to which all men (and women, who will necessarily fall short) should aspire. This hegemonic masculinity shapes the gendered social hierarchies beneath it, and has a profound impact on the lives of people for whom it serves as a rule as well as for world politics more generally.

These views of gender as a socially constructed hierarchy that subordinates not only women but femininity and honors (some) men associated with hegemonic masculinities were innovations that led IR feminists to rethink their understandings of a wide variety of concepts, from the role of the individual in global politics to international social rules and norms.[5] However, more recent feminist work has suggested a number of ways in which feminists could see more complexity and more nuance in these dynamics, producing further insights both for how to think about global politics generally and IR specifically. We will discuss three issues that we believe could be useful as we look forward into feminist IR's future: complicating the idea of what gender is, complicating how we understand both the role and production of genders (particularly masculinities) in global politics, and incorporating queer theory and intersectional analysis into how we read (gender and) IR.

What gender is

Twenty years ago, it was important for feminists (in IR and elsewhere) to establish a distinction between "sex" as biological and "gender" as socially constructed in order to rebut age-old assumptions about characteristics "women" naturally had by virtue of their biological composition (like maternal instinct, peacefulness, weakness, irrationality, etc.). This important move translated to a useful canon of high-quality research about the roles that gendered social expectations create for people understood as "men" or as "women." Given the frequency with which work in political science generally and IR specifically continues to use "gender" (by which scholars mean "sex") as a variable, assuming some "natural" difference between women and men, it may well be necessary to continue to work on the sex/gender distinction. At the same time, however, recent feminist work has begun to complicate the idea that the biological and the social are entirely independent, or that they (individually or together) constitute "gender." Anne Fausto-Sterling (2005) has argued that the biological and the social ("sex" and "gender") are not independent or pre-determined, but instead co-constituted, where social gender performances are derived from (perceived) biological sex but also impact the biology of sex. Relatedly, feminists like Judith Butler (1993, 2000) have argued that gender is neither constructed nor given, but performed; therefore, it should be read differently from the way biologists or norm-analyzing social scientists might read it. These complexities are evident now in feminist IR—in work that analyzes women's violence (Sjoberg and Gentry 2007; Sylvester and Parashar 2009), in work that looks at corporeality in the "body" politic (Marlin-Bennett et al. 2010; Wilcox 2010), and in work that increasingly pays attention to the gendered nature of illness, disability, and disfigurement in global politics.[6] They are also evident in this book—where Angela McCracken explores the role of physical beauty in constituting femaleness, Eric Blanchard explores the performance of militarized masculinities, Catia Confortini observes WILPF struggling to understand what "women" are in the advocacy platforms of the "women's international league for peace and freedom," Laura Sjoberg and Jessica Peet's analysis of the relationship between the performance of gendered nationalism and intentional civilian victimization, and Maya Eichler's analysis of various (performed and inherited) militarized masculinities in post-Soviet Russia.

The production of genders (particularly masculinities)

In addition to suggesting the importance of recent feminist work on the meaning and performance of gender, the chapters and conversations in this book and at the conference encourage feminists to think more often and in more nuanced ways about the meaning of masculinities in global politics and how they are produced and maintained. Some feminist scholars are critical of the intellectual attention others give to men and (their) masculinities, concerned that it detracts from feminism's primary interest in women's emancipation and may even entrench women's subordination by focusing on men.[7] However, this critique makes two assumptions that recent work in feminist IR, and the work in this book, demonstrate to be erroneous: first, that we understand men and masculinity well enough to know how to emancipate women and femininity from their dominance; and second, that masculinity is not gender-oppressive to men as well as to women.

For example, feminist discussions of masculinity have often assumed R. W. Connell's (1995) explanation that there is a hegemonic (Weberian ideal-typical) masculinity in every social and political context, which differs across contexts but always exists and to which all men and masculinities are expected to aspire. But Maya Eichler's study of militarized masculinities in post-Soviet Russia suggests that perhaps there is no hegemonic masculinity, but instead a number of competing subordinated masculinities. This claim generated substantial discussion at the conference. Jacqui True suggested that this might be because the political economy of post-Soviet Russia generally (and the Russian–Chechen conflict specifically) undermined support for the reproduction of a hegemonic, prideful militarized masculinity.

Two ways to read this were discussed. First, Patricia Owens suggested that this indicates a flaw in Connell's idea of how masculinity operates, because masculinity is never truly hegemonic—it will always need to be reproduced. Second, we can start seeing that gender hierarchies sometimes take forms other than strict patriarchies anchored by strong, hegemonic masculinities. Brooke Ackerly asked whether Eichler's work said something about the opportunity to redefine subordinate masculinities in the absence of a hegemonic one. Certainly, these questions have implications not only for Eichler's case, but also for the nature of gender hierarchies in global social and political life more generally.

While we know that both masculinities and femininities are (plural and) varied in any given social and political context, it will be important for feminist IR looking forward to ask how particular masculinities and femininities are constituted, and how they come to be organized along gender hierarchies. What *is* a gender hierarchy, and how are relative positions along it determined? What content of particular gender tropes dictates superior or inferior positions along those gender hierarchies, and how does that content come to be? How are masculinities and femininities contested? Relatedly, who shapes those masculinities and femininities that are the subject of contestation and ranked hierarchically? In response to Angela McCracken's presentation, Jane Jaquette asked about the crucial role that young Mexican women's *fiestas de quince años* play in shaping both idealized masculine and idealized feminine identities, a question other feminist scholars have asked about militarized masculinities (e.g., Goldstein 2001) and chivalric ideal-types (e.g., Elshtain 1983).

The questions about what gender hierarchies are and who and what make men relate to another set of inquiries about how gender hierarchy (and therefore gender subordination) operates in global politics. In Laura Sjoberg and Jessica Peet's contribution, the civilian immunity norm appears to protect women from war (more so than men), but ultimately provides a logic, not only for neglecting women, but also for intentionally attacking them in sex-specific ways. In Angela McCracken's contribution and V. Spike Peterson's engagement, the quince celebration (and, relatedly, weddings) implicates and reproduces a number of gendered expectations about women's behavior and women's roles (like norms of physical beauty, women's need to announce their marriagability, the requirement that women play domestic roles in family structures, and various virtues of being feminine and/or lady-like). It also relies on many processes feminists have identified as gender-subordinating (such as global capitalism, the fashion industry, and cultural globalization). At the same time, these rituals provide opportunities for women, who sell cosmetics to support themselves and their families, appropriate their festivals as a means of self-expression, and redefine male–female relations in their own festivals in ways that are consonant with how they see their social positions. Jacqui True's chapter demonstrates that the diffusion of gender equality norms does not automatically produce gender equality or benefits for the status of women; but neither is it wholly counterproductive to the cause.

These examples share with other developing research programs a rising concern with how to understand incomplete, hybrid, or subtle gender oppression in a world where conscious and overt gender discrimination (both in the field and in global politics) is decreasing if not disappearing, and is often (if not always) met with normative disapproval. At the same time, however, feminist scholarship suggests that while some gender oppressions are being redressed, others are just "going underground," where they become less visible and more difficult to recognize and redress. For example, restrictive boundaries around the idea of femininity are easy to see when they are expressed in laws forbidding women to own property, or giving husbands different divorce rights from their wives. However, it is harder to see the operation of these boundaries in characterizations of women terrorists as depraved, vengeful mothers, or erotomaniacs (denying them agency in their violence) (Sjoberg and Gentry 2007; Alison 2008). Nevertheless, as long as there are things we see men as capable of and women as incapable of (even if they are bad things) women's capabilities and femininity are subject to constraint. The passage of United Nations Security Council Resolution 1325 has resulted in a dramatic spike in the number of women included at peace negotiations in conflict-ridden societies, yet the women included do not walk into a gender-equal negotiation room where their opinions are automatically valued as much as men's (Enloe 2004). Instead, women are "added" to political structures built by and for men and where masculinity is still the norm that even women are held to, and women's burden to prove that masculinity may well be greater than men's. These cases, as well as some of those referred to in this book, show that feminist politics is more complicated than recognizing and redressing gender-oppression through the reversal of gender-subordinating policies and the diffusion of gender equality norms. Instead, gender subordination is often partial, subtle, and hybrid, both in its performance and in its results. Future feminist IR will need to look more closely at, and develop new tools to consider, this nuance in what gender hierarchy is, how it is inscribed and performed, and its internal contradictions in theory and practice.

Pushing the boundaries of (feminist) International Relations: queer theory and intersectionality

Looking forward, one of the tools feminist work might use to complicate and reveal dimensions of the operations of sex, gender, and genderings in global politics is the insights of intersectional analysis and queer theory. While some work in feminist IR was initially hostile to or silent about diversity among women and diversity among feminisms, recent feminist research has gone a long way towards not only taking account of these differences but also developing important theoretical insights from them. For example, certain scholars (Mohanty 1987; Chowdhry and Nair 2002) have argued that even feminists, when situated in different political, economic, and cultural contexts, have different ideas about women's needs, women's rights, and women's advocacy. Relatedly, feminists have recognized that even feminist politics and scholarship have racial, class, religious, and cultural dynamics; in V. Spike Peterson's words mentioned above, no work we do will be "innocent" of the hierarchies both in our discipline and in the world. Still, by reading and taking account of the diversity among feminisms and the men and women they study, feminists have started to see the value of two gender-related concepts for analyzing people's experiences of the global sociopolitical arena: feminization and intersectionality.

Feminization is subordinating people, political entities, or ideas by associating them with values perceived as feminine (Peterson 2010b; see also Peterson and Runyan 2010). Feminization has been described at various points in this book as devalorization, as the naturalization and/or expansion of traditional(ized) gender roles and as a tool for projecting (devalued) femininity even onto traditionally masculine subjects and objects.

It is not only appropriate to look for gender in global politics in obvious places like the existence of wartime rape, the gendered division of labor in households or markets, and sex-differential requirements for state citizenship; interactions which do not appear to include "sex" at all can often be *gendered,* where masculinist behavior (which selects for masculinity to the social exclusion of femininity) on the part of people, states, and/or non-state actors, *feminizes* a devalued other. Feminist work has shown the importance of the existence of a feminized other in many of IR's power-politics relationships (e.g., Moon 1997; Enloe 2010).

At the same time, feminists are increasingly showing an understanding that gender dynamics do not operate in global politics in isolation—that gender dynamics are not only mapped onto but interact with racial, class, ethnic, religious, and cultural dynamics in a world of complex, interacting, *intersectional* dynamics. While feminists often stated the initial purpose of feminist IR as intersectional; to look at global politics at the margins (Tickner 1988) or for "the identification and explanation of social stratifications and of inequality as structured at every level of global relations" (Brown 1988, 461), what intersectionality means for feminist IR continues to evolve.

Some implications of this evolving concern are already evident. The first is that people (women and men) live multiple identities simultaneously, and therefore, that genders vary over time, place, culture, and context. Differences in descriptor-words ("white woman," "Asian woman," "trans- woman") are not only differences in wording but substantive both in terms of meaning and in terms of experience. Second, "these identity markers ... are not just additive, merely descriptive, or politically and socially neutral," instead, they interact (Peterson and Runyan 2010, 24–25). To oversimplify, but illustrate the point: we cannot find the experience of being an African-American woman by "adding" the experience of being a white woman and an African-American man. Lived experiences are more than (and different from) a sum of their parts. The "parts" of our identities are not weighted equally, and their weights (in personal and political terms) are different at different times. Though we read the kinds of masculinities and femininities people are expected to have through their race, class, religion, national origin, or sexuality, feminists have observed that these assumptions are sometimes at odds with people's lived experiences. Feminists have begun to read, think, research, and write intersectionally to avoid "essentialism" (assuming essential characteristics based on one part of a person's identity) and to gain deeper insight into what is happening in global politics. Still, in the coming decades, it appears clear that feminists will become more deeply involved in trying to understand and analyze difference in global politics than they currently are.

One way forward is evident in these chapters and conversations: thinking seriously about sexuality and recognizing heterosexism and cissexism[8] in addition to patriarchy in the many gender tropes that feminists routinely analyze. In this book, we see questions of heteronormativity in the structure and media portrayals of Russian soldiers' lives, in quinces, in advocacy communities' ideas of women's rights and (sexual) freedoms, and in the protection racket between soldiers and civilians. Yet many feminist scholars (and many of us) do not call attention to heterosexism (and even cissexism) where it exists in IR. While there is a thriving literature in queer theory more generally (e.g., Eng et al. 2005), little of it has been imported into feminist IR.[9] So far, feminist IR has used queer concepts like "performativity" or "crossing" to think about how the international arena works without explicitly acknowledging either the queer roots or queer functions of these concepts (Weber, forthcoming). Feminists in the future might integrate the way that sexuality and queerness bear on questions of interest to scholars of (gender and) global politics.

V. Spike Peterson (1999) has argued that the normalization of exclusively heterosexual desire serves the functions of maintaining the biological and social reproduction of nations, such that "in the context of systemic violence (within and between groups), heterosexism may be the historically constructed 'difference' we most need to see—and to deconstruct" (1999, 56). Perspectives like Peterson's suggest that, not only is queer theorizing relevant to IR, it provides a unique perspective unattainable without thinking not only about gender but also about sex and sexuality as markers of identification and difference in global politics. Asking these questions might make feminist IR richer, both empirically and theoretically.

Doing feminist global politics: puzzles and potential paths forward

In the policy world, gender is on the political agenda of most state governments, as well as the United Nations Security Council, the World Bank, the World Health Organization, the World Trade Organization, and a number of other multinational governmental bodies. As feminist IR enters its third decade, it has never been clearer that gender matters in global politics; yet how to impact both the policy world and the discipline of IR remain challenging questions. Feminist theorists have insisted that "gendered lenses" do not just criticize or add to IR, they fundamentally change what IR thinks about its subject matter. Looking at global politics through gender lenses asks for more than "gender mainstreaming;" rather, it calls for a fundamental critique and reconstruction of the masculinist model of global politics that forms the basis for interstate and international interactions in our contemporary world.

The contributions in this book argue, individually and collectively, that gender is necessary, conceptually, for understanding global politics, empirically, for discovering causes and effects of global political phenomena, and normatively, for finding solutions to the world's most serious problems. Seeing gender as a fundamentally transformative force is a logical extension of these arguments. Instead of thinking of feminism as a critique of (D'Anieri 2009), or paradigmatic approach to, IR (Goldstein and Pevehouse 2010), the authors in this book and conversants at our conference asked what IR would look like if feminism were to transform it. Instead of seeing women at the margins of global politics (Baylis et al. 2005) or increasingly at its centers (Sjoberg 2009b), our conversations suggested a third path, focusing on what the world would look like if we "selected for" values and persons associated with femininities rather than (only or mainly) values and persons associated with masculinities. Two missions emerge: to rewrite IR, and to provide advice, guidance, reformulation, and restructuring in the policy arena.

The mission of rewriting IR is one that feminist scholars have the tools to embark on. A variety of feminist work has argued that gender is a pervasive power structure in global politics, guiding divisions of power, violence, labor, and resources and playing a key role in the preservation of racial, class, sexual, and national divisions. Feminist scholars have articulated not only an intellectual vision for identifying what is wrong with the (gendered power structures of) the global political arena, but also a political vision for changing the world to make it more just, especially for those people who have been disempowered by existing structures of global social and political life. Feminists have looked to achieve the second, explicitly political, part of this vision through theoretical reformulations; arguing that global politics should be seen differently when one takes account of the existence and importance of gender and gender hierarchy. It seems appropriate that feminist IR in the coming decades not only critique IR and reformulate pieces of it, but rewrite IR theorizing—not critiquing IR through gender lenses, but theorizing gender internationally and IR as if gender matters, across IR theories, state borders, methodological interpretations, and different feminisms. Instead of thinking about "feminist IR" and "IR," such a project would think of "feminist IR," not as critique and reconstruction, but as transformation.

If rewriting, retheorizing, or transforming IR is a difficult and demanding task, its challenges pale in comparison to the challenges of providing advice, guidance, reformulation, and restructuring in the policy arena. There are a number of barriers to integrating gender emancipation into the existing structures of power in global politics. The first is doing policy-relevant work within the constraints of the structures and ideas of global politics, as they are currently constituted. While some feminists approximate this, working on security sector reform, gender and microloans, and other relevant issues,[10] many others focus their work theoretically, or on issues that the policy world at large has yet to recognize as important. The second obstacle, then, is convincing the policy world that gender issues are important, a painstaking process that often must be done by arguing that gender analysis will make policymakers and bureaucrats better able to perform a wide range of policy tasks, rather than arguing that gender analysis is valuable independently, in and of itself. Third, feminists must work to make their work both intellectually accessible and normatively compelling. Finally, feminists need to understand more about how the policy world (both in its formal and informal structures) works in order to be able to communicate with and transform that world.

There was a great deal of discussion at the conference about what a norm of gender equality for global politics is (or would look like), how we would know that it existed, and what the complexities of its implementation have been and would continue to be. Many of the conversations in this book address these issues. Catia Confortini provides an example of how feminist activism functions and how it can influence global politics, and Brooke Ackerly explores some of the contingencies of feminist social activism. Abigail Ruane looks at how and why the policy world produces particular frames for women's rights discourses at particular times, and suggests strategies for making both membership and influence in the global political arena more inclusive, and Brent Steele suggests that such approaches are key to thinking about rights-based social activism in the twenty-first century. Angela McCracken and V. Spike Peterson show that norm diffusion takes place in non-traditional places like beauty parlors (see also Enloe 2010). Jacqui True looks critically at some of the benefits and the drawbacks of the "diffusion" of the gender equality norm, which some conference participants saw as robust and building, and others saw as symbolic and even empty.

Looking forward with these authors, we can ask what gender equality (or ending gender subordination) in global politics would really look like, and how it might be achieved. This would involve understanding not only gender, gender hierarchies, and gender equality norms more fully, but also how norms diffuse, how to encourage norm diffusion in a culturally sensitive way, how to make sure diffusing norms of gender equality are substantive, not just symbolic, and how different norms interact at different levels of policy processes to produce different results.

Political economies of gender and global politics

Feminist analysis of the global political economy (GPE) has led to a number of important observations. For example, while there are enormous differences in the socioeconomic status of women depending on their race, class, nationality, and geographic location, women share a certain commonality since they are disproportionately located at the bottom of the socioeconomic scale in all societies, earning three-quarters of what men do, and constituting almost 70 percent of the people in the world who live in poverty. Feminist perspectives on political economy investigate how (globalized) capitalism and (capitalist) globalization impact women even when gender is invisible in the concepts used for analysis, the questions that are asked, and the policies that are made. Feminists have looked to understand the causes of women's various economic insecurities and the gendered divisions of labor that can be found across the global political economy. They have looked at ways in which the discourses and practices of development are gendered, seeing development as a double-edged sword, where poverty disproportionately affecting women exacerbates inequality, and gender inequality inhibits development and sometimes makes development processes harmful to women. Feminists have also argued that ignoring gender comes at great costs, not only to women, but also to men, to development, and to the flow of trade internationally. Feminists have also looked in new places to study the global political economy, looking not just at states and international organizations, but also at individual households, the flows of human migration and trafficking, and the sex trade. Feminists have worked on revealing gendered divisions of production and the importance of reproductive labor for the social and economic maintenance of people, states, and the global trading system.

Even with all of these insights, feminist political economy analyses and feminist analyses of norms, social movements, peace negotiations, wars and conflicts, and women's human rights are often somewhat insulated. Some of feminist IR has become somewhat subject-focused, like a subfield that has come to be known as Feminist Security Studies (FSS). Like the division between "sex" and "gender," some of these focused subfields have served a purpose for feminist IR, making it easier for feminist work to communicate with work in the mainstream of IR on those subjects. In other words, with more or less success, feminist work on security finds a home in Security Studies, feminist work on peace finds a home in Peace Studies, feminist work on human rights finds a home with other work on human rights, feminist work on terrorism finds a home in Terrorism Studies, feminist work in political economy finds a home in International Political Economy, and the like. While this field integration is important, it has sometimes led the various subfields of feminist IR to be more insulated than perhaps they should be and/or feminist IR's "founding mothers" intended for them to be. Our discussions suggest that this subfield insularity is problematic particularly because it obscures the breadth and depth of the influence of political economy across IR, which is particularly visible through gendered lenses.

Early feminist work in IR linked the meaning of security to the idea that insecurity can be caused by poverty as easily as by war and conflict.[11] While some of those links have been maintained (like in Katherine Moon's work linking the Korean War and the political economy of camptown prostitution), often, work that is not explicitly about political economy does not address economic issues and economic analysis. During the discussions at the conference participants who did not consider political economy a primary area for their research consistently heard questions from the political economists about the political economy dimensions of militaries, of norm framing, of technology, of movement organization, and of wars. It became evident that perhaps the subfields of feminist IR, particularly in the study of security, have been somewhat isolated from the broad, interlinked, multidisciplinary analysis that gender lenses inspire in feminisms.

While some of the more radical suggestions at the conference talked about walking away not only from IR but also from the concept of security as corrective to the narrowness of security analyses, others discussed what feminist

IR would look like if it started taking more systematic account of the political economy dimensions of gender hierarchies, the gender dimensions of political economy, and the pervasive impact of economic factors in social, political, and military lives. As some of the work in this book shows, political economies are not only salient in the obvious places like trade and development, but also in the gender dynamics of Russian society's treatment of veterans of the Chechen wars. Political economic dimensions of global politics such as the factors motivating and structuring marriages, the beauty industry, and the production of gender identities are as important for understanding global politics as is the World Trade Organization. It is important to see that these various dimensions are intellectually important and practically influential, but it is also important to see that they are interlinked. Economies of production and reproduction produce and are reproduced by gender hierarchies not only in trade and development, but also on battlefields and in brothels. The chapters of this book have the potential for understanding deeper dimensions of (gendered) political economies in (gendered) global politics. Angela McCracken's chapter and V. Spike Peterson's discussion of it show that global political economies operate at local household levels. Our conversations suggest that there are political economy aspects not only to those things which fall clearly in the realm of trade and consumerism, but also to the techno-strategic choices in Eric Blanchard's chapter, the targeting of civilians in Sjoberg and Peet's chapter, the advocacy strategies of WILPF in Confortini's chapter, and across the empirical concerns of feminist IR. We hope that these links are looked at with increasing scrutiny and increasing depth in the future.

Hopes for the future

In the concluding session of our conference, we asked participants what they saw as the important dimensions of, and developments for, feminist IR, looking forward. What do we want feminist IR to be when we revisit it 20 years from now? What work needs to be done to make those visions realizable? What conversations would we want to have with the next generation of feminist scholars in IR?

Participants envisioned feminist IR expanding and transforming IR while at the same time not being constrained by its ontological, epistemological, and methodological assumptions and blind spots. They saw feminists thinking in even more complicated ways about the nuanced, hybrid, and interlinked dimensions of sex, gender, genders, and gender hierarchies, especially as they evolve in a twenty-first century where some political events redress subordination, others reify gender hierarchy, others keep gender subordination alive but send it "underground," and others have bidirectional effects, both subordinating and providing opportunities for women. They saw feminist scholars thinking in increasingly sophisticated intersectional ways—thinking not just about men and women, but about sexes and genders; thinking not just about genders but also about race, class, ethnicity, religion, and other axes of power differentials in global politics; and thinking not just with the traditional tools of feminist theorizing and political science but also with the tools of queer theory, geography, sociology, philosophy, philosophy of science, psychology, and conflict resolution. They envisioned a feminist IR that tackled important questions both about how to rewrite IR and how to make policy prescriptions with increasing vigor and precision. They saw a feminist IR that was increasingly sophisticated in making links between different ideas about gender and different parts of IR, but at the same time increasingly accessible to, and communicative with, the wider discipline.

Some of the discussants expressed concern about the narrowing of the field that might make it even more inhospitable to feminism and gender analysis in the future. While these challenges certainly exist, others pointed out that, 20 years ago, feminist IR was a field almost small enough to fit in one conference and one edited volume. Now, the 16 contributors to this book are less than 5 percent of the membership of the Feminist Theory and Gender Studies Section of the International Studies Association, which is not representative of all of the scholars in the field. While it has been a struggle for feminists to relate to, with, and in IR, feminist IR has exploded, both in terms of its membership (its borders) and its research (its roots). Perhaps the optimistic sentiment was best expressed by Sandra Harding, that feminist IR is "on the right side of history" and effecting change in both the scholarly and the policy worlds. We can only hope, and feel fortunate, to see, experience, and participate in these changes, developments, and growths in the field, in the discipline, and in the world.

Notes

1 E.g., Waltz (1979); Keohane (1986); Wendt (1999). The "international" in those terms refers (almost exclusively) to interstate politics.
2 E.g., Keohane and Milner (1996) and Finnemore and Sikkink (2001).
3 See, e.g., Pettman (1996); Prügl (1999); Enloe (2010).
4 On empathetic cooperation, see Sylvester (1992, 1994b, 2002); on ethics of care, see Tronto (1987) and Robinson (1999); on responsibility, see Lennie (1999) and Sjoberg (2006b).
5 About the role of the individual in politics, see, e.g., Moon (1997); Enloe (1993); Sjoberg and Gentry (2007); about international rules and norms, see Prügl (1999); True (2001); Locher and Prügl (2001).
6 See, e.g., Stienstra (1999); Walby (2005).
7 We had a discussion like this at a workshop on "Security Studies: Feminist Contributions" at the 2007 Annual Meeting of the International Studies Association in Chicago, IL.
8 Cissexism is the naturalization of preference for those whose "biological sex" match their "assigned sex" and "perceived gender," that is, bias against those who are intersex or transgender.
9 See exceptions: Enloe (1993); Peterson (1999); Weber (1999); Cohler (2010); Rao (2010).
10 E.g., Meyer and Prügl (1999); Luciak (2001); True and Mintrom (2001).
11 See, e.g., Tickner (1988); Whitworth (1989); Peterson (1992).

References

Ackerly, Brooke. 2000. *Political Theory and Feminist Social Criticism.* Cambridge: Cambridge University Press.

——. 2008a. Feminist Methodological Reflection. In *Qualitative Methods in International Relations: A Pluralist Guide,* edited by A. Klotz and D. Prakash. New York: Palgrave Macmillan.

——. 2008b. *Human Rights in a World of Difference.* Cambridge: Cambridge University Press.

——. 2009. Why a Feminist Theorist Studies Methods. *Politics & Gender* 5 (3): 431–6.

Ackerly, Brooke and Katy Attanasi. 2009. Global Feminisms: Theory and Ethics for Studying Gendered Injustice. *New Political Science* 31 (4): 543–5.

Ackerly, Brooke and Jacqui True. 2006. Studying the Struggles and Wishes of the Age: Feminist Theoretical Methodology and Feminist Theoretical Methods. In *Feminist Methodologies for International Relations,* edited by B. Ackerly, M. Stern, and J. True. Cambridge: Cambridge University Press.

——. 2008. Reflexivity in Practice: Power an Ethics in Feminist Research on International Relations. *International Studies Review* 10 (4): 693–707.

——. 2010. *Doing Feminist Research in Political and Social Science.* Basingstoke: Palgrave Macmillan.

Ackerly, Brooke, Maria Stern, and Jacqui True. 2006. Feminist Methodologies for International Relations. In *Feminist Methodologies for International Relations,* edited by B. Ackerly, M. Stern, and J. True. Cambridge: Cambridge University Press.

Adam, Allison. 1998. *Artificial Knowing: Gender and the Thinking Machine.* New York: Routledge.

Adkins, Lisa. 2003. Reflexivity: Freedom or Habit of Gender. *Theory, Society, and Culture* 20 (6): 21–42.

Adrian, Bonnie. 2003. *Framing the Bridge: Globalizing Beauty and Romance in Taiwan's Bridal Industry.* Berkeley: University of California Press.

Agathangelou, Anna M. 2004. *The Global Political Economy of Sex: Desire, Violence, and Insecurity in Mediterranean Nation States.* New York: Palgrave Macmillan.

Agathangelou, Anna M. and L. H. M. Ling. 2009. *Transforming World Politics: From Empire to Multiple Worlds.* New York: Routledge.

Akersten, S. Ingvar. 1987. The Strategic Computing Program. In *Arms and Artificial Intelligence: Weapon and Arms Control Applications of Advanced Computing,* edited by A. M. Din. New York: Oxford University Press.

Al-Jawaheri, Yasmin Husein. 2008. *Women in Iraq: The Gender Impact of International Sanctions.* Boulder, CO: Lynne Rienner.

Al-Jazeera. 2009. Pakistan: State of the Natioon. *Al-Jazeera.net*, August 13, http:// english.aljazeera.net/focus/2009/08/2009888238994769.html.

Alcoff, Linda Martin. 2003. Rethinking Maternal Thinking. *APA Newsletter on Feminism and Philosophy* 3 (1): 85–89.

Alison, Miranda. 2008. *Women and Political Violence: Female Combatants in Ethnonational Conflict*. London: Routledge.

Alker, Hayward. 1996. *Rediscoveries and Reformulations: Humanistic Methodologies for International Studies*. Cambridge: Cambridge University Press.

——. 2005. Emancipation in the Critical Security Studies Project. In *Critical Security Studies and World Politics*, edited by K. Booth. London: Lynne Rienner.

Allen, Amy. 1998. Rethinking Power. *Hypatia*. 13 (1): 21–40.

——. 2008. Feminist Perspectives on Power. In *The Stanford Encyclopedia of Philosophy*, edited by E. N. Zalta. Palo Alto, CA: Center for the Study of Language and Information, Stanford University.

Altinay, Ayse Gul. 2004. *The Myth of the Military Nation: Militarism, Gender, and Education in Turkey*. New York: Palgrave Macmillan.

——. 2009. Refusing to Identify as Obedient Wives, Sacrificing Mothers and Proud Warriors. In *Conscientious Objection: Resisting Militarized Society*, edited by O. H. Cinar and S. Usterci. London: Zed Books.

Altman, Dennis. 2002. *Global Sex*. Chicago, IL: University of Chicago Press.

Alvarez, Julia. 2007. *Once upon a Quinceañera: Coming of Age in the USA*. New York: Viking Press.

American Civil Liberties Union. 2010. "ACLU Seeks Information On Predator Drone Program," (Press Release) March 16, available at www.aclu.org/national-security/ aclu-seeks-information-predator-drone-program.

An-Na'im, Abdullahi Ahmed, ed. 1995. *Human Rights in Cross-Cultural Perspective: A Quest for Consensus*. Philadelphia: University of Pennsylvania Press.

Andryukhin, Aleksandr. 2003. Officer's Last Word. *The Current Digest of Post-Soviet Press* 55 (30): 10–11.

Anthias, Floya. 2002. Beyond Feminism and Multiculturalism: Locating Difference and the Politics of Location. *Women's Studies International Forum* 25 (3): 275–86.

Apodaca, Clair. 2009. Overcoming Obstacles in Quantitative Feminist Research. *Politics and Gender* 5 (3): 419–26.

Aradau, Claudia. 2004. Security and the Democratic Scene: Desecuritization and Emancipation. *Journal of International Relations and Development* 7 (4): 388–413.

Arends, Brett. 2010. A Lavish Wedding Costs More than You Think. *Wall Street Journal*, February 20.

Arkin, Ronald C. 2009. *Governing Lethal Behavior in Autonomous Robots*. Boca Raton, FL: Chapman and Hall/CRC.

Arquilla, John. 1997/8. The "Velvet" Revolution in Military Affairs. *World Policy Journal* 14 (4): 32–48.

Aslanbeigui, Nahid and Gale Summerfield. 2000. The Asian Crisis, Gender, and the International Financial Architecture. *Feminist Economics* 6 (3): 81–104.

Athanasiou, Tom. 1987. Artificial Intelligence and Military Technology. In *Computers in Battle – Will They Work?* edited by D. Bellin and G. Chapman. New York: Harcourt Brace Jovanovic.

Ayoob, Mohammed. 1997. Defining Security: A Subaltern Realist Perspective. In *Critical Security Studies: Concepts and Cases*, edited by K. Krause and M. C. Williams. Minneapolis: University of Minnesota Press.

Baaz, Eriksson and Maria Stern. 2009. Why do Soldiers Rape? Masculinity, Violence and Sexuality in the Armed Forces in the Congo. *International Studies Quaterly* 53: 495–518.

Babchenko, Arkady. 2007. *One Soldier's War in Chechnya*. London: Portobello Books.

Baer, Gertrude. (1968). Confidential Evaluation Requested on Oct. 28/66, 1966, p. 1, box 92, folder 17, Circular Letters/Reports re: WILPF and UN 1949/1961-69, WILPF Second Accession, UCBA.

Ballantyne, Edith. 1975. League's Aims: As Valid Today as When Founded. *Pax et Libertas, Box 162, Folder 2 WILPF Second Accession, UCBA.*

Barkawi, Tarak and Mark Laffey. 2006. The Postcolonial Moment in Security Studies. *Review of International Studies* 32 (2): 329–52.

Barker, Drucilla and Edith Kuiper, eds. 2006. *Feminist Economics and the World Bank: History, Theory and Policy*. New York: Routledge.

Barnett, Michael and Raymond Duvall. 2004. Power in International Politics. *International Organization* 59(1): 39–75.

Barnett, Michael and Raymond Duvall. 2005. Power in Global Governance. In *Power in Global Governance, edited by* M. Barnett and R. Duvall. Cambridge: Cambridge University Press.

Barnett, Michael and Martha Finnemore. 1999. The Politics, Power and Pathologies of International Organizations. *International Organization* 53 (4): 699–732.

Barrig, Maruja. 2006. What is Justice? Indigenous Women in Andean Development Projects. In *Women and Gender Equity in Development Theory and Practice: Institutions, Resources and Mobilization*, edited by J. S. Jaquette and G. Summerfield. Durham, NC: Duke University Press.

Bartky, Sandra L.1990. *Femininity and Domination: Studies in the Phenomenology of Oppression*. New York Routledge.

Barylski, Robert V. 1998. *The Soldier in Russian Politics: Duty, Dictatorship, and Democracy under Gorbachev and Yeltsin*. New Brunswick, NJ: Transaction Publishers.

Baylis, John, Steve Smith, and Patricia Owens. 2005. *The Globalization of World Politics: An Introduction to International Relations*. Oxford: Oxford University Press.

Bedford, Kate. 2005. Loving to Straighten Out Development Sexuality and 'Ethnodevelopment' in the World Bank's Ecuadorian Lending. *Feminist Legal Studies* 13: 295–322.

——. 2008. Governing Intimacy in the World Bank. In *Global Governance: Feminist Perspectives*, edited by S. M. Rai and G. Waylen. Basingstoke: Palgrave Macmillan.

——. 2009. *Developing Partnerships: Gender, Sexuality and the Reformed World Bank*. Minneapolis, MN: University of Minnesota Press.

Belinskii, A. B. and M. V. Liamin. 2000. Mediko-psikhologicheskaia reabilitatsiia uchastnikov boevikh deistvii v mnogoprofil'nom gospitale. *Voenno-meditsinskii zhurnal* 321 (1): 62–66.

Beneria, Lourdes. 2003. *Gender, Development and Globalization: Economics as if All People Mattered*. New York: Routledge.

Benhabib, Selya. 2004. *The Rights of Others: Aliens, Residents and Citizens*. Cambridge: Cambridge University Press.

Bergen, Peter, and Katherine Tiedmann. 2010. *The Year of the Drone: An Analysis of U.S. Drone Strikes in Pakistan 2004–2010*. Washington, DC: New America Foundation, Counterterrorism Strategy Initiative Policy Paper.

Bergeron, Suzanne. 2001. Political Economy Discourses of Globalization and Feminist Politics. *Signs: Journal of Women in Culture and Society* 26 (4): 985–1006.

——. 2003. The Post-Washington Consensus and Economic Representations of Women in Development at the World Bank. *International Feminist Journal of Politics* 5 (3): 397–419.

——. 2009. An Interpretive Analytics to Move Caring Labor Off the Straight Path. *Frontiers* 30 (1): 55–64.

Berik, Günseli, Yana van der Meulen Rodgers, and Stephanie Seguino. 2009. Feminist Economics of Inequality, Development, and Growth. *Feminist Economics* 15 (3): 1–33.

Besson, Samantha, and Jose Luis Marti. 2006. *Deliberative Democracy and its Discontents*. Aldershot: Ashgate.

Biagioli, Mario. 1999. *The Science Studies Reader*. London and New York: Routledge.

Biddle, Stephen. 1996. Victory Misunderstood: What the Gulf War Tells US about the Future of Conflict. *International Security* 21 (2): 139–79.

Biersteker, Thomas. The Parochialism of Hegemony: Challenges for "American'" International Relations. In Arlene Tickner and Ole Waever, eds. *International Relations Scholarship around the World*. New York and London: Routledge.

Bilgin, Pinar. 2001. Theory/Practice in Critical Approaches to Security. *International Politics* 38 (2): 273–82.

Blackwell, Joyce. 2004. *No Peace without Freedom: Race and the Women's International League for Peace and Freedom, 1915–1975*. Carbondale, IL: Southern Illinois University.

Blanchard, Eric. 2003. Gender, International Relations, and the Development of Feminist Security Theory. *Signs: Journal of Women in Culture and Society* 28 (4): 1289–313.

Boot, Max. 2005. The Struggle to Transform the Military. *Foreign Affairs* 84 (2): 103–18.

Booth, Ken. 1991a. Security and Emancipation. *Review of International Studies* 17: 313–26.

——. 1991b. Security in Anarchy: Utopian Realism in Theory and Practice. *International Affairs* 67 (3): 527–45.

——. 1997. Security and Self: Reflections of a Fallen Realist. In *Critical Security Studies: Concepts and Cases*, edited by K. Krause and M. C. Williams. Minneapolis: University of Minnesota Press.

——. 2005a. Introduction to Part 2. In *Critical Security Studies and World Politics*, edited by K. Booth. London: Lynne Rienner.

——. 2005b. Introduction to Part 3. In *Critical Security Studies and World Politics*, edited by K. Booth. London: Lynne Rienner.

——, ed. 2005c. *Critical Security Studies and World Politics*. London: Lynne Rienner.

——. 2007. *Theory of World Security*. Cambridge: Cambridge University Press.

Booth, Ken and Peter Vale. 1997. Critical Security Studies and Regional Insecurity: The Case of Southern Africa. In Keith Krause and Michael C. Williams, eds. *Critical Security Studies: Concepts and Cases*. Minneapolis: University of Minnesota Press.

Bordo, Susan. 1993. *Unbearable Weight: Feminism, Western Culture, and the Body*. Berkeley: University of California Press.

Boulding, Elise. 1968. From Rhetoric to Reality. *Box 45, folder 3. Pax et Libertas*: WILPF SCPC Accession. UCBA.

Brown, Sarah. 1988. Feminism, International Theory, and the International Relations of Gender Inequality. *Millennium: Journal of International Studies* 17 (3): 461–75.

Brydon, Anne and S. A. Niessen. 1998. *Consuming Fashion: Adorning the Transnational Body*. New York: Berg.

Bull, Hedley. 2002. *The Anarchical Society: A Study of Order in World Politics (3rd Edition)*. Edited by A. Hurell and S. Hoffman. New York: Columbia University Press.

Bussey, Gertrude. 1980. *Pioneers for Peace: Women's International League for Peace and Freedom 1915–1965*. Edited by M. Tims. London: Women's International League for Peace and Freedom British Section.

Butler, Judith. 1990. *Gender Trouble: Feminism and the Subversion of Identity*. New York: Routledge.

——. 1992. Contingent Foundations: Feminism and the Question of Postmodernism. In *Feminists Theorize the Political*, edited by J. Butler and J. W. Scott. London: Routledge.

——. 1993. *Bodies that Matter: On the Discursive Limits of "Sex"*. New York: Routledge.

——. 1999a. Performativity's Social Magic. In *Bordieu: A Critical Reader*, edited by R. Schusterman. Oxford: Blackwell.

——. 1999b. *Subjects of Desire: Hegelian Reflections in Twentieth-Century France*. New York: Columbia University Press.

——. 2000. *Antigone's claim: Kinship Between Life and Death*. New York: Columbia University Press.

Buzan, Barry, Ole Wæver, and Jaap de Wilde. 1998. *Security: A New Framework for Analysis*. Boulder, CO: Lynne Rienner.

Cahill, Ann J. 2003. Feminist Pleasure and Feminine Beautification. *Hypatia* 18 (4): 42–64.

Caiazza, Amy. 2002. *Mothers and Soldiers: Gender, Citizenship, and Civil Society in Contemporary Russia*. New York: Routledge.

Canizares-Esguerra, Jorge. 2005. Iberian Colonial Science. *Isis* 96: 64–70.

Cannon, Aubrey. 1998. The Cultural and Historical Contexts of Fashion. In *Consuming Fasion: Adorning the Transnational Body*, edited by S. Siessen and A. Brydon. Oxford: Berg.

Cannon, Paul R. 1972. Food and the War. In *Medicine and the War*, edited by W. H. Taliaferro. London: Ayer.

Cantú, Norma E. 1999. La Quinceañera: Towards an Ethnographic Analysis of a Life-Cycle Ritual. *Southern Folklore* 56 (1): 73–101.

Caprioli, Mary, and Mark Boyer. 2001. Gender, Violence, and International Crisis. *Journal of Conflict Resoultion* 45 (4): 503–18.

Carlesnaes, Walter. 1992. The Agency-Structure Problem in Foreign Policy Analysis. *International Studies Quarterly* 36 (3): 1992.

Carpenter, R. Charli. 2005. "Women, Children, and Other Vulnerable Groups": Gender, Strategic Frames, and the Protection of Civilians as a Transnational Issue. *International Studies Quarterly* 49 (2): 295–335.

——. 2006a. *Innocent Women And Children: Gender, Norms and the Protection of Civilians*. Aldershot: Ashgate Publishing, Ltd.

——. 2006b. Women and Children First: Gender, Norms, and Humanitarian Evacuation in the Balkans, 1991–95. *International Organization* 57 (4): 428–77.

——. 2007. Studying Issue (Non)-Adoption in Transnational Networks. *International Organization*. 61 (3): 643–67.

Carr, Caleb. 2002. *The Lessons of Terror: A History of Warfare Against Civilians*. New York: Random House.

Carver, Terrell, Molly Cochran, and Judith Squires. 1998. Gendering Jones: Feminisms, IRs, and Masculinities. *Review of International Studies* 24: 283–97.

Castells, Manuel. 1997. *The Power of Identity*. Cambridge, MA: Blackwell Publishers.

CBSNews.com. 2009. Clinton Takes Heat for Drone Attacks. *CBS News*, October 30, www.cbsnews.com/stories/2009/10/30/world/main5458871.shtml.

Chan-Tiberghien, Jennifer. 2004. *Gender and Human Rights Politics in Japan: Global Norms and Domestic Networks*. Stanford, CA: Stanford University Press.

Chang, Kimberly, and L. H. M. Ling. 2000. Globalization and its Intimate Other: Filipina Domestic Workers in Hong Kong. In *Gender and Global Restructuring*, edited by M. Marchand and A. S. Runyan. New York: Routledge.

Chapkis, Wendy. 1986. *Beauty Secrets: Women and the Politics of Appearance*. Boston: South End Press.

Charlesworth, Hilary. 1994. Transforming the United Men's Club: Feminist Futures for the United Nations. *Transnational Law and Contemporary Problems* 4: 421–65.

Charlesworth, Hilary, Christine Chinkin, and Shelley Wright. 1991. Feminist Approaches to International Law. *American Journal of International Law* 85 (4): 613–45.

Checkel, Jeffrey T. 1998. Review: The Constructivist Turn in International Relations Theory. *World Politics* 50 (2): 324–48.

——. 2006. Tracing Causal Mechanisms. *International Studies Review* 8 (2): 362–70.

Chesterman, Simon. 2001. *Civilians at War*. Boulder, CO: Lynne Rienner.

Chin, Christine. 1998. *In Service and Servitude: Foreign Female Domestic Workers and the Malaysian Modernity Project*. New York: Columbia University Press.

Chowdhry, Geeta. 2007. Edward Said and Contrapuntal Reading: Implications for Critical Interventions in International Relations. *Millennium, Journal of International Studies* 36 (1): 101–16.

Chowdhry, Geeta and Sheila Nair. 2002. *Power, Postcolonialism, and International Relations: Reading Race, Gender, and Class*. New York: Routledge.

Churchill, Winston. 1929. *The World Crisis: 1911–1918*. New York: Simon and Schuster.

Cigar, Norman. 1992. Iraq's Strategic Mindset and the Gulf War: Blueprint for Defeat. *Journal of Strategic Studies* 15 (1): 1–29.

Clark, Richard M. 2000. *Uninhabited Combat Aerial Vehicles: Airpower by the People, For the People, But Not with the People*. USAF CADRE Paper No. 8. Maxwell Air Force Base, AL: Air University Press.

Coates, Jennifer. 1997. Women's Friendships, Women's Talk. In *Gender and Discourse*, edited by Ruth W. Wodak. London: SAGE.

Cockburn, Cynthia. 2007. *From Where We Stand: War, Women's Activism and Feminist Analysis*. London: Zed Books.

——. 2008. Feminist Antimilitarism and WILPF. www.wilpfinternational.org/events/2008IB/seminar_agenda.html.

Cockburn, Cynthia and Dubravka Zarkov, eds. 2002. *The Postwar Moment: Militaries, Masculinities and International Peacekeeping: Bosnia and the Netherlands*. London: Lawrence & Wishart.

Code Pink. 2009. "Peace activists to Rally Monday Outside Creech Air Force Base: Will call for End to U.S. Drone attacks in Afghanistan, Pakistan," (Press Release) July 10, available at www.codepinkalert.org/article.php?id=4987.

Cohen, Colleen Ballerino, Richard Wilk, and Beverly Stoeltje, eds. 1996. *Beauty Queens on the Global Stage: Gender, Contests, and Power*. New York: Routledge.

Cohen, Eliot A. 1996. A Revolution in Warfare. *Foreign Affairs* 75 (2): 37–54.

Cohen, Roger. 2010. An Eye for an Eye. *New York Times*, February 25, www.nytimes.com/2010/02/26/opinion/26iht-edcohen.html.

Cohler, Deborah. 2010. Fireman Fetishes and *Drag Queen Dreams*: Queer Responses to 9/11. In *Gender, War, and Militarism, Feminist Perspectives*, edited by L. Sjoberg and S. Via. Santa Barbara, CA: Praeger Security International.

Cohn, Carol. 1987. Sex and Death in the World of Rational Defense Intellectuals. *Signs: Journal of Women in Culture and Society* 12 (4): 687–718.

———. 2008. Mainstreaming Gender in UN Security Policy. In *Global Governance: Feminist Perspectives*, edited by S. M. Rai and G. Waylen. Basingstoke: Palgrave Macmillan.

Cohn, Carol and Sara Ruddick. 2004. A Feminist Ethical Perspective on Weapons of Mass Destruction. In Sohail H. Hashmi and Steven P. Lee, eds. *Ethics and Weapons of Mass Destruction: Religious and Secular Perspectives*. Cambridge: Cambridge University Press.

Cohn, Carol, Felicity Hill, and Sara Ruddick. 2005. *The Relevance of Gender for Eliminating Weapons of Mass Destruction*. Stockholm: Weapons of Mass Destruction Commission.

Collins, Jane L.2003. *Threads: Gender, Labor and Power in the Global Apparel Industry*, Chicago, IL: University of Chicago Press,

Collins, Patricia Hill. 1989. The Social Construction of Black Feminist Thought. *Signs: Journal of Women in Culture and Society* 14 (4): 745–73.

———. 1990. *Black Feminist Thought: Knowledge, Consciousness and the Politics of Empowerment*. Boston, MA: Unwin Hyman.

Confortini, Catia C. (2009) Imaginative Identification: Feminist Critical Methodology in the Women's International League for Peace and Freedom, 1945–1975, International Relations, University of Southern California unpublished Ph.D. thesis.

Connell, R. W. 1995. *Masculinities*. Berkeley: University of California Press.

Connolly, William. 1991. *Identity/Difference: Democratic Negotiations of Political Paradox*. Minneapolis: University of Minnesota Press.

Cortright, David. 1993. *Peace Works: The Citizen's Role in Ending the Cold War*. Boulder, CO: Westview Press.

———. 2008. *Peace: A History of Movements and Ideas*. Cambridge: Cambridge University Press.

Cota Yáñez, María del Rosario. 2004. Estructura Organizaciónal de las Empresas de la Confección de Zapotlanejo, Jalisco. *Problemas del Desarollo* 35 (138): 155–76.

Cox, Robert W. 1981. Social Forces, States and World Orders: Beyond International Relations Theory. *Millennium, Journal of International Studies* 10 (2): 126–55.

———. 1983. Gramsci, Hegemony, and International Relations: An Essay in Method. *Millennium: Journal of International Studies* 12(2): 162–75.

———. 1986. Social Forces, States, and World Orders: Beyond International Relations Theory. In *Neorealism and its Critics*, edited by R. O. Keohane. New York: Columbia University Press.

Crawford, Neta. 2002. *Arguments for Change: Ethics, Decolonization and Humanitarian Intervention*. Cambridge: Cambridge University Press.

Crenshaw, Kimberle. 1991. Mapping the Margins: Intersectionality, Identity Politics, and Violence against Women of Color. *Stanford Law Review* 43 (6): 1241–99.

Crewe, Lord. 1915a. 'Memorandum by Lord Crewe'. July 18, CAB 37/130/15.

———. 1915b. 'Notes on Lord Crewe's Memorandum'. June 23, 1915, CAB 37/130/25.

D'Anieri, Paul. 2009. *International Politics: Power and Purpose in Global Affairs*. Washington, DC: Wadsworth Publishing Company.

Danilova, Natalia. 2007. Veterans' Policy in Russia: A Puzzle of Creation. *The Journal of Power Institutions in Post-Soviet Societies* (6/7): www.pipss.org/index873.html.

Davalos, Karen Mary. 1996. La Quinceanera: Making Gender and Ethnic Identities. *Frontiers* 16 (2/3): 101–27.

de Sousa Santos, Boaventura. 2002. Toward a Multicultural Conception of Human Rights. In *Moral Imperialism: A Critical Anthology*, edited by B. Hernándes-Truyol New York: New York University Press.

Debrix, Francois. 2007. *Tabloid Terror: War, Culture, and Geopolitics.* London: Routledge.

Debusscher, Petra and Jacqui True. 2008. 'Lobbying the EU for gender-equal development.' In *The European Union and the Social Dimension of Globalisation*, edited by Jan Orbie and Lisa Tortell. New York: Routledge. 186–206.

Deibert, Ronald J. 2003. Black Code: Censorship, Surveillance, and the Militarization of Cyberspace. *Millennium: Journal of International Studies* 32 (3): 501–30.

Delehanty, Will K. and Brent J. Steele. 2009. Engaging the Narrative in Ontological (In)Security Theory: Insights from Feminist IR. *Cambridge Review of International Affairs* 22 (3): 523–40.

Der Derian, James. 1990. The (S)pace of International Relations: Simulation, Surveillance, and Speed. *International Studies Quarterly* 34 (3): 295–301.

———. 2003. The Question of Information Technology in International Relations. *Millennium, Journal of International Studies* 32 (3): 441–56.

———. 2009. *Virtuous War: Mapping the Military-Industrial-Media-Entertainment Network*, 2nd edition New York: Routledge.

Dessler, David. 1989. What's at Stake in the Agent-Structure Debate. *International Organization* 43 (3): 441–73.

DeYoung, Karen. 2009. Al-Qaeda Seen as Shaken in Pakistan U.S. Officials Cite Drones, Offensive. *Washington Post*, June 1, http://www.washingtonpost.com/wp-dyn/content/article/2009/05/31/AR2009053102172.html?hpid=topnews.

Di Stefano, Christine. 1991. *Configurations of Masculinity: A Feminist Perspective on Modern Political Theory.* Ithaca, NY: Cornell University Press.

Dillon, Michael. 1996. *Politics of Security: Towards a Political Philosophy of Continental Thought.* New York: Routledge.

Doktorov, B. Z., A. A. Oslon, and Petrenko E. S. 2002. *Epokha El'tsina: Mneniia rossiian. Sotsiologicheskie ocherki.* Moscow: Institut Fonda "Obshchestvennoe mnenie."

Donnelly, Jack. 1982. Human Rights and Human Dignity: An Analytic Critique of Non-Western Conceptions of Human Rights in Africa. *American Political Science Review* 76 (2): 303–16.

———. 2007. The Relative Universality of Human Rights. *Human Rights Quarterly* 29 (2): 281–306.

Doty, Roxanne Lynn. 1996. *Imperial Encounters: The Politics of Representation in North-South Relations.* Minneapolis: University of Minnesota Press.

———. 1997. Aporia: A Critical Exploration of the Agent-Structure Problematique in International Relations Theory. *European Journal of International Relations* 3 (3): 365–92.

Downes, Alexander B. 2006. Desperate Times, Desperate Measures: The Causes of Civilian Victimization in War. *International Security* 30 (4): 152–95.

———. 2008. *Targeting Civilians in War.* Ithaca, NY: Cornell University Press.

Doyle, Michael. 1983. Kant, Liberal Legacies, and Foreign Affairs. *Philosophy and Public Affairs* 12: 205–35.

Drew, Christopher. 2010. Drones Are Playing a Growing Role in Afghanistan. *New York Times*, February 19, www.nytimes.com/2010/02/20/world/asia/20drones.html?fta=y.

Duffield, Mark. 2001. *Global Governance and the New Wars: The Merging of Development and Security.* London: Zed Books.

Echevarria, Arturo J. 2002. *Clausewitz's Center of Gravity: Changing Our Warfighting Doctrine – Again.* Washington, DC: Strategic Studies Institute.

Eckhardt, William. 1989. Civilian Deaths in Wartime. *Bulletin of Peace Proposals* 20 (1): 89–98.

Edwards, Paul N. 1996. *The Closed World: Computers and the Politics of Discourse in Cold War America.* Cambridge, MA: MIT Press.

Edwards, Rosalind. 1997. *Feminist Dilemmas in Qualitative Research: Public Knowledge and Private Lives.* Thousand Oaks, CA: SAGE Publications.

Ehrenreich, Nancy. 2004. Prison Abuse: Feminism's Assumptions Upended, *Los Angeles Times*, May 16, www.barbaraehrenreich.com/prisonabuse.htm.

——. 2005. Disguising Empire: Racialized Masculinity and the "Civilizing" of Iraq. *Cleveland State Law Review* 52.

Eichler, Maya. 2006. Russia's Post-Communist Transformation: A Gendered Analysis of the Chechen Wars. *International Feminist Journal of Politics* 8 (4): 486–511.

——. 2008. Gender and Nation in the Soviet/Russian Transformation. In *Gendering the Nation-State: Canadian and Comparative Perspectives*, edited by Y. Abu-Laban. Vancouver: University of British Columbia Press.

Eider, Riane. 1987. *The Chalice and the Blade: Our History, Our Future.* San Francisco, CA: Harper & Row.

Eisenstein, Zillah. 2004. *Against Empire.* London: Zed Books.

Elias, Juanita. 2004. *Fashioning Inequality.* Aldershot: Ashgate.

Elias, Juanita and Lucy Ferguson. 2009. The Gender Dimensions of New Labour's International Development Policy. In Claire Annesley, Francesca Gains and Kirstein Rummery, eds. *Women and New Labour.* Bristol: Policy Press.

Elshtain, Jean Bethke. 1981. *Public Man, Private Woman: Women in Social and Political Thought.* Princeton, NJ: Princeton University Press.

——. 1983. On Beautiful Souls, Just Warriors, and Feminist Consciousness. In *Women and Men's Wars*, edited by J. Stiehm. Oxford: Pergamon Press.

——. 1987. *Women and War.* New York: Basic Books.

——. 1992a. Just War as Politics: What the Gulf War Told Us About Contemporary American Life. In *But Was It Just? Reflections on the Morality of the Persian Gulf War*, edited by D. E. Decosse. New York: Doubleday.

——. 1992b. Sovereignty, Identity, and Sacrifice. In *Gendered States: Feminist (Re) Visions of International Relations Theory*, edited by V. S. Peterson. Boulder, CO: Lynne Rienner.

——. 2000. "Shooting" at the Wrong Target: A Response to Van Crevald. *Millennium, Journal of International Studies* 29 (2): 429–42.

Elson, Diane. 2009. Gender Equality and Economic Growth in the World Bank *World Development Report 2006*. *Feminist Economics* 15 (3): 35–59.

Elson, Diane and Ruth Pearson. 1981. Nimble Fingers Make Cheap Workers: An Analysis of Women's Employment in Third World Export Manufacturing. *Feminist Review* 8: 87–107.

Eng, D. L., J. Halberstam and J. E. Munoz. 2005. *What's Queer about Queer Studies Now?* Durham, NC: Duke University Press.

Enloe, Cynthia. 1989. *Bananas, Beaches, and Bases: Making Feminist Sense of International Politics.* Berkeley: University of California Press.

——. 1990. *Bananas, Beaches, and Bases: Making Feminist Sense of International Politics.* Berkeley: University of California Press.

——. 1993. *The Morning After: Sexual Politics at the End of the Cold War*. Berkeley: University of California Press.

——. 1996. Margins, Silences, and Bottom Rungs: How to Overcome the Under-estimation of Power in the Study of International Relations. In *International Relations: Positivism and Beyond*, edited by S. Smith, K. Booth and M. Zalewski. London: Routledge.

——. 2000. *Maneuvers: The International Politics of Militarizing Women's Lives*. Berkeley: University of California Press.

——. 2004. *The Curious Feminist: Searching for Women in a New Age of Empire*. Berkeley: University of California Press.

——. 2007. *Globalization and Militarism: Feminists Make the Link*. New York: Rowman & Littlefield.

——. 2010. *Nemo's War, Emma's War: Making Feminist Sense of the Iraq War*. Berkeley: University of California Press.

Epstein, Charlotte. 2008. *The Power of Words in International Relations*. Cambridge, MA: MIT Press.

Eriksson Boaz, Maria and Maria Stern. 2009. Why Do Soldiers Rape? Masculinity, Violence and sexuality in the Armed Forces in the Congo (DRC). *International Studies Quarterly* 53 (4): 495–518.

Eriksson, Johan and Giampiero Giacommello. 2006. The Information Revolution, Security, and International Relations: (IR)relevant Theory. *International Political Science Review* 27 (3): 221–44.

Eschle, Catherine. 2001. *Global Democracy, Social Movements, and Feminism*. Boulder, CO: Westview Press.

Eschle, Catherine and Bice Maiguascha. 2007. Rethinking Globalised Resistance: Feminist Activism and Critical Theorising in International Relations. *British Journal of Politics and International Relations* 9 (2): 284–301.

Fausto-Sterling, Anne. 2005. Bare Bones of Sex: Part I, Sex and Gender. *Signs: Journal of Women in Culture and Society* 30 (2): 345–70.

Feldman, Leonard C. 2004. *Citizens without Shelter: Homelessness, Democracy, and Political Exclusion*. Ithaca, NY: Cornell University Press.

Felgenhauer, Pavel. 2000. Russia's Forces Unreconstructed. *Institute for the Study of Conflict, Ideology, and Policy's Perspective* 10 (4): www.bu.edu/iscip/vol10/Felgenhauer. html.

Ferguson, Kathy E. 1991. Interpretation and Genealogy in Feminism. *Signs Journal of Women in Culture and Society* 16 (2): 322–39.

Fernandez-Kelly, Maria Patricia. 1983. *For We are Sold, I and My People: Women and Industry in Mexico's Frontier*. Albany, NY: SUNY Press.

Fierke, Karin M. 2007. *Critical Approaches to International Security*. Cambridge: Polity Press.

Finnemore, Martha. 1996. Norms, Culture, and World Politics. *International Organization* 50 (2): 325–47.

Finnemore, Martha and Kathryn Sikkink. 1998. International Norm Dynamics and Political Change. *International Organization* 52 (4): 887–917.

——. 2001. Taking Stock: The Constructivist Research Program in International Relations and Comparative Politics. *Annual Review of Political Science* 4 (1): 391–416.

Fisher, Roger, Willian Ury, and Bruce Patton, eds. 1991. *Getting to Yes: Negotiating Agreement Without Giving In* (Second Edition). New York: Penguin.

Fitzsimmons, Tracy. 2007. Engendering Justice and Security after War. In *Constructing Justice and Security After War*, edited by C. V. Call. Washington, DC: United States Institute of Peace.

Fonow, Mary Margaret and Judith A. Cook, eds. 1991. *Beyond Methodology: Feminist Scholarship as Lived Research*. Indianapolis: Indiana University Press.

Foster, Catherine. 1989. *Women for all Seasons: The Story of the Women's International League for Peace and Freedom*. Athens: University of Georgia Press.

Frank, Libby. 1975. WILPF Middle East Mission, April–May: Report, 1975, p. 10, box 2, folder 10, IEC Meeting Germany October 1975, WILPF SCPC Accession, UCBA.

Freedman, Lawrence. 1998. *The Revolution in Strategic Affairs*. New York: Oxford University Press.

Freeman, Carla. 2000. *High Tech and High Heels in the Global Economy: Women, Work, and Pink-Collar Identities in the Caribbean*. Durham, NC: Duke University Press.

——. 2001. Is Local: Global as Feminine: Masculine? Rethinking the Gender of Globalization. *Signs: Journal of Women in Culture and Society* 26 (4): 1007–37.

Friedman, P. Kerim. 2005. Learning "Local" Languages. Passive Revolution, Language Markets, and Aborigine Education in Taiwan, Political Science, Temple University, unpublished Ph.D. thesis.

Frühstück, Sabine. 2007. *Uneasy Warriors: Gender, Memory, and Popular Culture in the Japanese Army*. Berkeley: University of California Press.

Galtung, Johan. 1969. Violence, Peace, and Peace Research. *Journal of Peace Research* 6 (3): 167–91.

Gardam, Judith G. 1993. Gender and Non-Combatant Immunity. *Transnational Law and Contemporary Problems* 3: 345–70.

Garreau, Joel. 2007. Bots on The Ground: In the Field of Battle (Or Even Above It), Robots Are a Soldier's Best Friend. *Washington Post*, May 6, www.washingtonpost.com/wp-dyn/content/article/2007/05/05/ AR2007050501009_pf.html.

Germino, Dante L. 1990. *Antonio Gramsci: Architect of a New Politics*. Baton Rouge: Louisiana State University Press.

Getmanenko, Oleg. 2000. What War Can Do to A Man. *The Current Digest of the Post-Soviet Press* 52 (13): 9.

Ghobarah, Hazem A., Paul Huth, and Bruce Russett. 2003. Civil Wars Kill and Maim People—Long After the Shooting Stops. *American Political Science Review* 97 (2): 189–202.

Gibson-Graham, J. K. 1996. *The End of Capitalism (As We Knew It): A Feminist Critique of Political Economy*. Oxford: Blackwell.

Giddens, Anthony. 1984. *The Constitution of society: Outline of the Theory of Structuration*. Berkeley: University of California Press.

——. 1991. *Modernity and Self-Identity*. Stanford, CA: Stanford University Press.

Gillespie, Paul G. 2006. *Weapons of Choice: The Development of Precision Guided Munitions*. Tuscaloosa: University of Alabama Press.

Glover, Jenna Ann. 2009. 'The Interpersonal Lives of Young Adult Women: A Study of Passionate Friendship', Psychology, Utah State University, unpublished Ph.D. thesis.

Goetz, Anne-Marie, ed. 1997. *Getting Institutions Right for Women in Development*. London: Zed Books.

Goetz, Anne-Marie, Robert O'Brien, Jan Aart Scholte, and Mark Williams. 2000. *Contesting Global Governance: Multilateral Economic Institutions and Global Social Movements*. Cambridge: Cambridge University Press.

Goldman, Emily O. 2010. Revolutions in Warfare. In *International Studies Encyclopedia*, edited by R. A. Denemark. London: Wiley-Blackwell, www.isacompendium.com/subscriber/tocnode id = g9781444336597_chunk_g978144433659717_ss1–13.

Goldstein, Joshua. 2001. *War and Gender: How Gender Shapes the War System and Vice Versa*. Cambridge: Cambridge University Press.

Goldstein, Joshua and Jon Pevehouse. 2010. *International Relations*. New York: Pearson Education.

Goldstein, Lyle J. 1997. Russian Civil–Military Relations in the Chechen War, December 1994–February 1995. *Journal of Slavic Military Studies* 10 (1): 109–27.

Golts, Aleksandr. 2004. The Social and Political Condition of the Russian Military. In *The Russian Military: Power and Policy* edited by S. E. Miller and D. Trenin. Cambridge, MA: MIT Press.

Gongora, Thierry, and Harald von Riekoff, eds. 2000. *Toward a Revolution In Military Affairs? Defense and Security at the Dawn of the Twenty-First Century*. Westport, CT: Greenwood Press.

Grabham, Emily. 2008. *Intersectionality and Beyond: Law, Power and the Politics of Location*. New York: Routledge-Cavendish.

Gramsci, Antonio. 1971. *Selections from the Prison Notebooks*. London: Lawrence & Wishart.

——. 1985. *Selections from Cultural Writings*. Cambridge, MA: Harvard University Press.

Grant, Rebecca. 1991. The Sources of Gender Bias in International Relations Theory. In *Gender and International Relations*, edited by R. Grant and K. Newland. Bloomington: Indiana University Press.

——. 1992. The Quagmire of Gender and International Security. In *Gendered States: Feminist (Re)Visions of International Relations Theory*, edited by V. S. Peterson. Boulder, CO: Lynne Rienner.

Gray, Chris Hables. 1997. *Postmodern War: The New Politics of Conflict*. New York: Guilford Press.

Gray, Colin. 1999. Clausewitz Rules, OK? The Future is the Past – with GPS. *Review of International Studies* 25: 161–82.

Gray, Mark M., Miki Caul Kittilson, and Wayne Sandholtz. 2006. Women and Globalization: A Study of 180 Countries, 1975 – 2000. *International Organization* 60 (2): 293–333.

Grewal, Inderpal, and Caren Kaplan, eds. 1994. *Scattered Hegemonies: Postcolonial and Transnational Feminist Practices*. Minneapolis: University of Minnesota Press.

Guttman, Matthew C. 2007. *The Meaning of Being Macho: Being a Man in Mexico City*. Berkeley: University of California Press.

Hackett, Edward. 2007. *The Handbook of Science and Technology Studies*, 3rd edition. Cambridge, MA: MIT Press.

Hafner-Burton, Emilie, and Mark Pollack. 2002. Mainstreaming Gender in Global Governance. *European Journal of International Relations* 8 (3): 339–73.

Hale, Charles. 2002. Does Multiculturalism Menace? Governance, Cultural Rights, and the Politics of Identity in Guatemala. *Journal of Latin American Studies* 34: 485–524.

Hall, Nina, and Jacqui True. 2009. Gender Mainstreaming in a Post-Conflict State. In *Gender and Global Politics in Asia-Pacific*, edited by K. Lee-Koo and B. D'Costa. Basingstoke: Palgrave.

Hammond, Allen L. and C. K Prahalad. 2004. Selling to the Poor. *Foreign Policy* May/June: 30–37.

Hansen, Lene. 2000. The Little Mermaid's Silent Security Dilemma and the Absence of Gender in the Copenhagen School. *Millennium: Journal of International Studies* 29 (2): 285–306.

——. 2001. Gender, Nation, Rape: Bosnia and the Construction of Security. *International Feminist Journal of Politics* 3 (1): 55–75.

——. 2006. *Security as Practice: Discourse Analysis and the Bosnian War.* New York: Routledge.

Haraway, Donna Jeanne. 1989. *Primate Visions: Gender, Race, and Nature in the World of Modern Science.* New York: Routledge.

——. 1991. A Cyborg Manifesto: Science, Technology, and Socialist-Feminism in the Late Twentieth Century. In *Simians, Cyborgs, and Women: The Reinvention of Nature*, edited by D. J. Haraway. New York: Routledge.

Harding, Sandra. 1986. *The Science Question in Feminism.* Ithaca, NY: Cornell University Press.

——. 1991. *Whose Science? Whose Knowledge? Thinking from Women's Lives.* Ithaca, NY: Cornell University Press.

——. 1993. Rethinking Feminist Standpoint Epistemology: What is "Strong Objectivity"? In *Feminist Epistemologies*, edited by L. M. Alcoff and E. Potter. New York: Routledge.

——. 1998. *Is Science Multicultural? Postcolonialisms, Feminisms, and Epistemologies.* Bloomington: Indiana University Press.

——. 2004a. Rethinking Standpoint Epistemology: What is "Strong Objectivity." In *The Feminist Standpoint Theory Reader: Intellectual and Political Controversies*, edited by S. Harding. New York: Routledge.

——. 2004b. *The Feminist Standpoint Theory Reader: Intellectual and Political Controversies.* New York: Routledge.

Hartigan, Richard Shelley. 1982. *The Forgotten Victim: The History of the Civilian.* Chicago, IL: Precedent Publishing.

Hartsock, Nancy. 1983. *Money, Sex, and Power: Toward a Feminist Historical Materialism.* New York: Longman.

——. 1989–90. Postmodernism and Political Change: Issues for Feminist Theory. *Cultural Critique* 14: 15–34.

Hawkins, Nigel. 2002. *The Starvation Blockades.* Washington, DC: Naval Institute Press.

Heeg Maruska, Jennifer. 2010. When Are States Hypermasculine? The War on Terror in Historical Perspective. In *Gender and International Security: Feminist Perspectives*, edited by L. Sjoberg. New York: Routledge.

Held, David, Anthony McGrew, David Goldblatt, and Jonathan Perraton. 1999. *Global Transformations: Politics, Economics and Culture.* Palo Alto, CA: Stanford University Press.

Henry, Ryan, and C. Edward Peartree. 1998. Military Theory and Information Warfare. In *The Information Revolution on International Socity*, edited by R. Henry and C. E. Peartree. Washingtom, DC: Center for Strategic and International Studies Press.

Herrera, Geoffrey. 2006. New Media for a New World? Information Technology and Threats to National Security. In *Globalization and National Security*, edited by J. Kirschner. New York: Routledge.

Hewstone, Miles, Mark Rubin, and Hazel Willis. 2002. Intergroup Bias. *Annual Review of Psychology* 53: 575–604.

Hirschmann, David. 2006. From "Home Economics" to "Microfinance" Gender Rhetoric and Bureaucratic Resistance. In *Women and Gender Equity in Development*

Theory and Practice: Institutions, Resources and Mobilization, edited by J. S. Jaquette and G. Summerfield. Durham, NC: Duke University Press.

Hirschmann, Nancy J. 1989. Freedom, Recognition, and Obligation: A Feminist Approach to Political Theory. *American Political Science Review* 83 (4): 1227–44.

——. 2003. *The Subject of Liberty: Toward a Feminist Theory of Freedom*. Princeton, NJ: Princeton University Press.

Hobbes, Thomas. 1982 (1651). *Leviathan*. London: Penguin.

Hoffman, John. 2001. *Gender and Sovereignty: Feminism, the State, and International Relations*. New York: Palgrave.

Hollis, Martin, and Steve Smith. 1990. *Explaining and Universtanding International Relations*. New York: Clarendon Press.

——. 1992. Structure and Action: Further Comment. *Review of International Studies* 18 (2): 187–88.

——. 1994. Two Stories about Structure and Agency. *Review of International Studies* 20 (3): 241–51.

——. 1996. A Response: Why Epistemology Matters in International Theory. *Review of International Studies* 22 (1): 111–16.

Hoogenson, Gunhild, and Svein Vigeland Rottem. 2004. Gender Identity and the Subject of Security. *Security Dialogue* 35 (2): 155–71.

Hooper, Charlotte. 1998. Masculinist Practices and Gender Politics: The Operation of Multiple Masculinities in International Relations. In *The "Man" Question in International Relations*, edited by M. Zalewski and J. Parpart. Boulder, CO: Westview Press.

——. 2001 *Manly States: Masculinities, International Relations, and Gender Politics*. New York: Columbia University Press.

Hopf, Ted. 1998. The Promise of Constructivism in International Relations Theory. *International Security* 23 (1): 171–200.

Hudson, Heidi. 2005. 'Doing' Security As Though Humans Matter: A Feminist Perspective on Gender and the Politics of Human Security. *Security Dialogue* 36 (2): 155–74.

Human, Rights Watch. 2000. *Welcome to Hell: Arbitrary Detention, Torture, and Extortion in Chechnya*. New York: Human Rights Watch.

Hundley, Richard O. 1999. *Past Revolutions, Future Transformations*. Santa Monica, CA: RAND.

Husanovic, Jasmina, and Patricia Owens. 2000. Emancipation: A 'Shrieking in Keeping'? An Email Conversation on Feminism, Emancipation and Security between Jasmina Husanovic and Patricia Owens. *International Feminist Journal of Politics* 2 (3): 424–34.

Huston, Nancy. 1983. Tales of War and Tears of Women. In *Women and Men's Wars*, edited by J. Stiehm. Oxford: Pergamon Press.

Hutchings, Kimberly. 1992. The Possibility of Judgment: Moralizing and Theorizing in International Relations. *Review of International Studies* 18 (1): 51–62.

——. 1999. Feminism, Universalism, and the Ethics of International Politics. In *Women, Culture, and International Relations*, edited by V. Jabri and E. O'Gorman. Boulder, CO: Lynne Rienner Publishers.

——. 2001. The Nature of Critique in Critical International Theory. In *Critical Theory and World Politics*, edited by R. Wyn Jones. Boulder, CO: Lynne Rienner.

——. 2008. *Time and World Politics: Thinking the Present*. Manchester: Manchester University Press.

Hutchinson, Dorothy. 1966. Most Dangerous Moment in U.S. History. *Pax et Libertas Box 45, folder 3* WILPF SCPC Accession. UCBA.

——. 1967. Chairman's Report to International Executive Committee, p. 1, box 2, folder 4, IEC Meeting 1967, WILPF SCPC Accession, UCBA.

——. 1968. Chairman's Keynote Address: The Right to be Human, p. 7, box 25, 16th International Congress Report 1966 and 17th International Congress Report 1968, WILPF SCPC Accession, University of Colorado at Boulder Archives.

Huysmans, Jef. 1998. Security! What Do You Mean? From Concept to Thick Signifier. *European Journal of International Relations* 4 (2): 226–55.

——. 2006a. Agency and the Politics of Protection: Implications for Security Studies. In *The Politics of Protection: Sites of Insecurity and Political Agency*, edited by J. Huysmans, A. Dobson and R. Prokhovnik. London: Routledge.

——. 2006b. *The Politics of Insecurity: Fear, Migration and Asylum in the EU.* London: Routledge.

Ignatieff, Michael. 2001. *Human Rights as Politics and Idolatry.* Princeton, NJ: Princeton University Press.

Ingraham, Chrys. 2008. *White Weddings: Romancing Heterosexuality in Popular Culture.* New York: Routledge.

Ives, Peter. 2002. The Grammar of Hegemony. In *Antonio Gramsci: Critical Assessments of Leading Political Philosophers*, edited by J. Martin. New York: Routledge.

Jabri, Vivenne. 2003. Explorations of Difference in Normative International Relations. In *Women, Culture, and International Relations*, edited by V. Jabri and E. O'Gorman. Basingstoke: Palgrave Macmillian.

——. 2004. Feminist Ethics and Hegemonic Global Politics. *Alternatives: Global, Local, Political* 29 (3): 265–85.

——. 2006. The Limits of Agency in Times of Emergency. In *The Politics of Protection: Sites of Insecurity and Political Agency*, edited by J. Huysmans, A. Dobson and R. Prokhovnik. London: Routledge.

Jacob, Margaret. 1988. *The Cultural Meanings of the Scientific Revolution.* New York: Knopf.

Jaggar, Alison M. 1989. Love and Knowledge: Emotion in Feminist Epistemology. *Inquiry* 32 (2): 151–76.

James, Christine A. 1997. Feminism and Masculinity: Reconceptualizing the Dichotomy of Reason and Emotion. *International Journal of Sociology and Social Policy* 17 (1/2): 129–52.

James, William. 1963. *Psychology.* Greenwich, CT: Fawcett.

Janack, Marianne. 1997. Standpoint Epistemology without the "Standpoint"? An Examination of Epistemic Privilege and Epistemic Authority. *Hypatia* 12 (2): 125–39.

Janis, Irving. 1972. *Victims of Groupthink: A Psychological Study of Foreign Policy.* Boston: Houghton Mifflin.

Jaquette, Jane S. and Kathleen Staudt. 1988. Gender and Politics in U. S. Population Policy. In *The Political Interests of Gender*, edited by K. Jones and A. Joansdottir. London: Dage.

——. 2006. Women, Gender, and Development. In *Women and Gender Equity in Development Theory and Practice: Institutions, Resources and Mobilization*, edited by J. S. Jaquette and E. O'Gorman. Durham, NC: Duke University Press.

Jaquette, Jane and Gale Summerfield, eds. 1996. *Women and Gender Equity in Development Practice: Institutions, Resources, and Mobilization.* Durham, NC: Duke University Press.

Jasanoff, Shiela, ed. 2004. *States of Knowledge: The Co-Production of Science and Social Order.* New York: Routledge.

Jauhola, Marjaana. 2010. Building Back Better: Negotiating Normative Boundaries of Gender Mainstreaming and Post-Tsunami Reconstruction in Nanggroe Aceh Darussalam, Indonesia. *Review of International Studies* 36 (1): 29–50.

Jones, Adam. 1996. Does 'Gender' Make the World Go Around? Feminist Critiques of International Relations. *Review of International Studies* 22: 405–29.

——. 2000. Gendercide and Genocide. *Journal of Genocide Research* 2 (2): 185–202.

Jones, Ellen. 1985. *Red Army and Society: A Sociology of the Soviet Military.* Boston: Allen & Unwin.

Jones, Adam, ed. 2004. *Gendercide and Genocide.* Nashville, TN: Vanderbilt University Press.

Joy, Bill. 2000. Why the Future Doesn't Need Us. *Wired*, April, www.wired.com/wired/archive/8.04/joy.html.

Karam, Azza. 2001. Women in War and Peacebuilding: The Roads Traversed, the Challenges Ahead. *International Feminist Journal of Politics* 3 (1): 2–25.

Kardam, Nuket. 2002. The Emergence of a Global Gender Equality Regime. *International Journal* 57 (3): 411–38.

——. 2004. The Emerging Global Gender Equality Regime. *International Feminist Journal of Politics* 6 (1): 85–109.

Karner, Tracy Xavia. 1998. Engendering Violent Men: Oral Histories of Military Masculinity. In *Masculinities and Violence* edited by L. H. Bowker. Thousand Oaks, CA: SAGE Publications.

Kay, Rebecca. 2006. *Men in Contemporary Russia: The Fallen Heroes of Post-Soviet Change.* Aldershot: Ashgate.

Keck, Margaret, and Kathryn Sikkink. 1998. *Activists Beyond Borders: Advocacy Networks in International Politics.* Ithaca, NY: Cornell University Press.

Keller, Evelyn Fox. 1982. Feminism and Science. *Signs: Journal of Women in Culture and Society* 7 (3): 589–602.

——. 1985. *Reflection on Gender and Science.* New Haven, CT: Yale University Press.

Keller, Evelyn Fox and Helen E Longino. 1996. *Feminism and Science.* New York: Oxford University Press.

Kennedy-Pipe, Caroline. 2004. Whose Security? State-building and the "Emancipation" of Women in Central Asia. *International Relations* 18 (1): 91–107.

Keohane, Robert O. 1986. *Neorealism and its Critics.* New York: Columbia University Press.

——. 1988. International Institutions: Two Approaches. *International Studies Quarterly* 32 (4): 379–96.

——. 1989a. International Institutions and State Power. *International Studies Quarterly* 41 (1): 1–25.

——. 1989b. International Relations Theory: Contributions of a Feminist Standpoint. *Millennium, Journal of International Studies* 18 (2): 245–53.

Keohane, Robert O. and Helen Milner. 1996. *Internationalization and Domestic Politics.* Cambridge: Cambridge University Press.

Keohane, Robert O. and Joseph Nye. 1998. Power and Independence in the Information Age. *Foreign Affairs* 77 (5): 81–95.

Key, Joshua, and Lawrence Hill. 2007. *The Deserter's Tale: The Story of an Ordinary Soldier Who Walked Away from the War in Iraq.* Toronto: House of Anasi.

Kilcullen, David, and Andrew McDonald Exum. 2009. Death From Above, Outrage Down Below. *New York Times*, May 16, www.nytimes.com/2009/05/17/opinion/17exum.html.

Kinsella, Helen. 2005. Securing the Civilian: Sex and Gender in the Laws of War. In *Power and Global Governance*, edited by M. Barnett and R. Duvall. Cambridge: Cambridge University Press.

——. 2006. Gendering Grotius: Sex Difference and the Laws of War. *Political Theory* 32 (4): 61–91.

Klotz, Audie, and Cecelia Lynch. 2007. Strategies for Research in Constructivist International Relations. In *International Relations in a Constructed World*, edited by V. Kublakova, N. Onuf and P. Kowert. Armonk, NY: M. E. Sharpe.

Knight, W. Andy, and Tanya Narozhna. 2005. Rape and Other War Crimes in Chechnya: Is There a Role for the International Criminal Court? *SpacesofIdentity* 5 (1): 92–93.

Krainova, Natalia. 2008. "Vechnaia pamiat." RIA "Samara," December 12, Available at www.riasamara.ru/rus/news/region/society/article36605.shtml (accessed April 15, 2009).

Krause, Keith, and Michael C. Williams. 1997a. Preface. In *Critical Security Studies: Concepts and Cases*, edited by K. Krause and M. C. Williams. Minneapolis: University of Minnesota Press.

——, eds. 1997b. *Critical Security Studies: Concepts and Cases*. Minneapolis: University of Minnesota Press.

Krishnan, Armin. 2009. *Killer Robots: Legality and Ethicality of Autonomous Weapons*. Burlington, VT: Ashgate.

Krook, Mona Lena. 2009. *Quotas for Women in Politics: Gender and Candidate Selection Reform Worldwide*. New York: Oxford University Press.

Krook, Mona Lena, and Jacqui True. Forthcoming. Rethinking the Life Cycles of International Norms: The United Nations and the Global Promotion of Gender Equality. *European Journal of International Relations*.

Kuhn, Thomas. 1970. *The Structure of Scientific Revolutions, Second Edition*. Chicago, IL: University of Chicago Press.

Kwon, Insook. 2005. How Identities and Movement Cultures Became Deeply Saturated with Militarism: Lessons from the Pro-democracy Movement in South Korea. *Asian Journal of Women's Studies* 11 (2): 7–40.

Landler, Mark. 2009. Clinton Challenges Pakistanis on Al Qaeda. *New York Times*, October 29, www.nytimes.com/2009/10/30/world/asia/30clinton.html.

Lapid, Yosef. 1989. The Third Debate: On the Prospects of International Theory in a Post-Postivist Era. *International Studies Quarterly* 33 (3): 235–54.

Latham, Robert. 1997. *The Liberal Moment : Modernity, Security, and the Making of Postwar International Order*. New York: Columbia University Press.

Lax, David A., and James K. Sebeneius. 1986. *The Manager as Negotiator: Bargaining for Cooperation and Competitive Gain*. New York: Free Press.

Lederer, Edith M. 2009. UN Investigator Warns US on Use of Drones: UN investigator Warns US that Use of Drones May Violate International Law. *ABC News*, October 27, http://abcnews.go.com/US/wireStory?id=8931296.

Lee-Koo, Katrina. 2007. Security as Enslavement, Security as Emancipation: Gendered Legacies and Feminist Futures in the Asia-Pacific. In *Critical Security in the Asia-Pacific*, edited by A. Burke and M. McDonald. Manchester: Manchester University Press.

Leeds-Craig, Maxine. 2002. *Ain't I a Beauty Queen? Black Women, Beauty, and the Politics of Race*. New York: Oxford University Press.

Lennie, June. 1999. Deconstructing Gendered Power Relations in Participatory Planning: Towards an Empowering Feminist Framework of Participation and Action. *Women's Studies International Forum* 22 (1): 97–112.

Levada-Tsentr. 2008a. Armiia. www.levada.ru/army.

——. 2008b. Chechnia. www.levada.ru/chechnya.html.

Levidow, Les and Kevin Robins. 1989. *Cyborg Worlds: The Military Information Society*. New York: Free Association Press.

Light, Jennifer. 1999. When Computers Were Women. *Technology and Culture* 40 (3): 455–83.

Lind, Amy, ed. 2010. *Development, Sexual Rights and Global Governance*. New York: Routledge.

Ling, L. H. M. 2002a. *Postcolonial International Relations: Conquest and Desire between Asia and hte West*. New York: Palgrave.

——. 2002b. The Fish and the Turtle. In *Millennial Reflections on International Studies*, edited by M. Brecher and F. P. Harvey. Ann Arbor: University of Michigan Press.

Lipschutz, Ronnie D. and Mary A. Tetreault. 2009. *Global Politics as if People Mattered*. Lanham, MD: Rowman and Littlefield.

Locher, Birgit, and Elisabeth Prügl. 2001. Feminism and Constructivism: Worlds Apart or Sharing the Middle Ground? *International Studies Quarterly* 45: 123–35.

Lombardo, E., P. Meier, and Verloom M., eds. 2009. *The Discursive Politics of Gender Equality*. New York: Routledge.

Luciak, Ilja. 2000. Democracy and its Discontents: Life in Post-conflict Central America. *Development* 43 (3): 43–49.

Lugones, Maria. 1987. Playfulness, "World-Travelling," and Loving Perception. *Hypatia* 2 (2): 3–19.

——. 1990. Playfulness, "World"-Travelling, and Loving Perception. In *Making Face, Making Soul = Haciendo Caras: Creative and Critical Perspectives by Feminists of Color*, edited by G. Anzaldua. San Francisco, CA: Aunt Luce Foundation Books.

MacKinnon, Catherine. 1993. *Only Words*. Cambridge, MA: Harvard University Press.

Malinak, Daniel, Amy Oakes, Susan Peterson, and Michael J. Tierney. 2008. Women in International Relations. *Politics and Gender* 4 (1): 122–44.

Marchand, Marianne H. and Anne Sisson Runyan, eds. 2000. *Gender and Global Restructuring: Sightings, Sites, and Resistances*. London: Routledge.

Marlin-Bennett, Renee, M. Wilson, and J. Walton. 2010. Commodified Cadavers and the Political Economy of the Spectacle. *International Political Sociology* 4 (2): 159–77.

Martínez Casas, Regina and Guillermo de la Peña. 2003. Migrantes y Comunidades Morales: Resignificación, Etnicidad y Redes Sociales en Guadalajara (Méjico), http://revistas.ucm.es/cps/1131558x/articulos/RASO0404110217A.PDF.

Mayer, Jane. 2009. The Predator War: What Are the Risks of the C.I.A.'s Covert Drone Program? *The New Yorker*, October 26, www.newyorker.com/reporting/2009/10/26/091026fa_fact_mayer.

Mazzetti, Mark, and Jane Perlez. 2010. C.I.A. and Pakistan Work Together, Warily. *New York Times*, February 24, www.nytimes.com/2010/02/25/world/asia/25intel.html?ft=y.

McAdams, Dan P. 1993. *The Stories We Live By: Personal Myths and the Making of the Self*. New York: William Morrow.

McCall, Leslie. 2005. The Complexity of Intersectionality. *Signs: Journal of Women in Culture and Society* 30 (3): 1771–1800.

McClintock, Anne. 1993. Family Feuds: Gender, Nationalism, and the Family. *Feminist Review* 44: 6154.

McDougall, Alan J. 2006. Dirty Hands: the Atrocities of World War I, channel4.com/ history. historylearningsite.co.uk/wei1.htm.

McDowell, L. 1997. Women/Gender/Feminisms: Doing Feminist Geography. *Journal of Geography in Higher Education* 21 (3): 381–400.

McSweeney, Bill. 1999. *Security, Identity and Interests: A Sociology of International Relations.* Cambridge: Cambridge University Press.

Merom, Gil. 2003. *How Democracies Lose Small Wars.* Cambridge: Cambridge University Press.

Merry, Sally Engel. 2006. *Human Rights and Gender Violence: Translating International Law into Local Justice.* Chicago, IL: University of Chicago Press.

Meyer, Mary and Elisabeth Prugl. 1999. *Gender Politics in Global Governance.* Lanham, MD: Rowman & Littlefield.

Mickiewicz, Ellen. 1999. *Changing Channels: Television and the Struggle for Power in Russia.* Durham, NC. Duke University Press.

Mies, Maria. 1985. *Patriarchy and Accumulation on a World Scale.* London: Zed Books.

——. 1986. Indian Women in Subsistence and Agricultural Labour. 12, http://agris. fao.org/agris-search/search/display.do?f=1987/XF/XF87011.xml;XF8660483.

Mir, Amir. 2009. 60 Drone Hits Kill 14 al-Qaeda men, 687 Civilians. *The News International,* April 10, www.thenews.com.pk/top_story_detail.asp?Id=21440.

Mobius, Markus M. and Tanya S. Rosenblat. 2006. Why Beauty Matters. *The American Economy Review* 96 (1): 222–35.

Mohanty, Chandra. 1987. Under Western Eyes: Feminist Scholarship and Colonial Discourses. In *Third World Women and the Politics of Feminism*, edited by C. Mohanty. London: University Press.

——. 2003. *Feminism without Boders: Decolonizing Theory, Practicing Solidarity.* Durham, NC: Duke University Press.

Mohanty, Chandra, Ann Russo, and Lourdes Torres, eds. 1991. *Third World Women and the Politics of Feminism.* Indianapolis: Indiana University Press.

Montero Recoder, Cyntia. 2008. Vieja a los treinta años': El proceso de envejecimineto ségun algunas revistas mexicanas de fines de siglo XIX. In *Enjaular Los Cuerpos: Normativas Decimónicas y Femininidad en México*, edited by J. Tunon. Mexico City: El Colegio de Mexico.

Moon, Katharine. 1997. *Sex Among Allies: Militarized Prostitution in US-South Korea Relations.* New York: Columbia University Press.

Moon, Seungsook. 2005. Trouble with Conscription, Entertaining Soldiers: Popular Culture and the Politics of Militarized Masculinity in South Korea. *Men and Masculinities* 8 (1): 64–92.

Morgan, David H. J. 1994. Theater of War: Combat, the Military, and Masculinities. In *Theorizing Masculinities*, edited by H. Brod and M. Kaufman. London: Sage.

Morgan, Patrick M. 2000. The Impact of the Revolution in Military Affairs. *Journal of Strategic Studies* 23 (1): 132–62.

Moser, Caroline. 1989. Gender Planning in the Third World: Meeting Strategic and Practical Gender Needs. *World Development* 17 (11): 1799–1825.

Mouffe, Chantal. 2000. *The Democratic Paradox.* New York: Verso.

Murray, Williamson, and MacGregor Knox. 2001. Thinking about Revolutions in Warfare. In *The Dynamics of Military Revolution 1300–2050*, edited by W. Murray and M. Knox. Cambridge: Cambridge University Press.

Nash, June, and Maria Patricia Fernandez-Kelly, eds. 1983. *Women, Men, and the International Division of Labor.* Albany: State University of New York Press.

Niessen, Sandra, and Anne Brydon, eds. 1983. *Consuming Fashion: Adorning the Transnational Body.* Oxford: Berg.

Niva, Steve 1998. Tough and Tender: New World Order Masculinity and the Gulf War. In *The "Man" Question in International Relations*, edited by M. Zalewski and J. Parpart. Boulder, CO: Westview Press.

Novikova, Asmik. 2007. Reabilitatsia veteranov Chechni. In *Militsiia mezhdu Rossiei i Chechnei: Veterany konflikta v rossiiskom obshchestve*, edited by O. G. Shepeleva. Moscow: Demos.

Okin, Susan Moeller. 1979. *Women in Western Political Thought.* Princeton, NJ: Princeton University Press.

——. 1999. *Is Multiculturalism Bad for Women?* Princeton, NJ: Princeton University Press.

Oblastnoi telekanal RIO "Vspominaia pogibshikh", December 12, 2008. Available at www.rio-tv.ru/index.php?link=news&action=show&id=1232 (accessed March 15, 2009).

Okin, Susan Moeller, and Brooke Ackerly. 1999. Feminist Social Criticism and the International Movement for Women's Human Rights as Human Rights. In *Democracy's Edges*, edited by I. Shapiro and C. Hacker-Cordon. Cambridge: Cambridge University Press.

Olson, Kevin. 2006. *Reflexive Democracy: Political Equality and the Welfare State.* Cambridge, MA: MIT Press.

——. 2008. Constructing Citizens. *Journal of Poitics* 70 (1): 40–53.

Onishi, Norimitsu. 2002. Globalization of Beauty Makes Slimness Trendy. *New York Times*, October 3.

Onuf, Nicholas. 1989. *World of Our Making: Rules and Rule in Social Theory and International Relations.* Charleston: University of South Carolina Press.

——. 1998. Constructivism: A User's Manual. In *International Relations in a Constructed World*, edited by V. Kublakova, N. Onuf and P. Kowert. Armonk, NY: M. E. Sharpe.

Osborne, Eric. 2004. *Britain's Economic Blockade of Germany, 1914–1919.* New York Routledge.

Ossman, Susan. 2002. *Three Faces of Beauty: Casablanca, Paris, Cairo.* Durham, NC: Duke University Press.

Otten, Sabine. 2002. I Am Positive and So Are We: The Self as Determinant of Favortism toward Novel Ingroups. In *The Social Self: Cognitive, Interpersonal, and Intergroup Perspectives*, edited by Joseph P. Forgas and Kippling D. Williams. New York: Psychology Press.

——. 2003. "Me and Us" or "Us and Them"? The Self as a Heuristic for Defining Minimal Ingroups. *European Review of Social Psychology* 13 (1): 1–33.

Oushakine, Serguei. 2009. *The Patriotism of Despair: Nation, War, and Loss in Russia.* Ithaca, NY: Cornell University Press.

Pannikar, Raimundo. 1982. Is the Notion of Human Rights a Western Concept. *Diogenes* 120: 75–102.

Pape, Robert A.2003. The Strategic Logic of Suicide Terrorism. *American Political Science Review* 97 (3): 343–61.

Parisi, Laura. 2009. The Numbers Do(n't) Always Add Up: Dilemmas in Using Quantitative Research Methods in Feminist IR Scholarship. *Politics and Gender* 5 (3): 410–19.

Parpart, Jane L., and Marysia Zalewski, eds. 2008. *Rethinking the Man Question: Sex, Gender, and Violence in International Relations.* London: Zed Books.

Pateman, Carole. 1970. *Participation and Democratic Theory.* Cambridge: Cambridge University Press.
——. 1988. *The Sexual Contract.* Palo Alto, CA: Stanford University Press.
Paulson, Susan. 2005. Body, Nation, and Consubstantiation in Bolivian Ritual Meals. *American Ethnologist* 33 (4): 650–64.
Pax et Libertas. Viet Nam. April–June, 1970. Box 45, folder 3. 'Pax et Libertas 1966–68'. WILPF SCPC Accession. UCBA.
Peach, Lucinda J. 1994. An Alternative to Pacifism? Feminism and Just-War Theory. *Hypatia* 9 (2): 151–72.
Peterson, Susan Rae. 1977. Coercion and Rape: The State as a Male Protection Racket. In *Feminism and Philosophy*, edited by M. Vetterling-Braggin, F. A. Elliston and J. English. Totowa, NJ: Littlefield, Adams & Company.
Peterson, V. Spike. 1989. Clarification and Contestation: Exploring the Integration of Feminist and International Relations Theory. Paper read at Women, the State, and War, at Los Angeles, California.
——. 1992a. Introduction. In *Gendered States: Feminist (Re)Visions of International Relations Theory*, edited by V. S. Peterson. Boulder, CO: Lynne Rienner.
——. 1992b. Security and Sovereign States: What is at Stake in Taking Feminism Seriously? In *Gendered States: Feminist (Re)visions of International Relations Theory*, edited by V. S. Peterson. Boulder, CO: Lynne Rienner.
——. 1992c. Transgressing Boundaries: Theories of Knowledge, Gender, and International Relations. *Millennium: Journal of International Studies* 21 (2): 183–206.
——. 1999. Sexing Political Identities/Nationalism as Heterosexism. *International Feminist Journal of Politics* 1 (1): 34–65.
——. 2003. *A Critical Rewriting of Global Political Economy: Integrating Reproductive, Productive, and Virtual Economies.* New York: Routledge.
——. 2006. Getting Real: The Necessity of Poststructuralism in Global Political Economy. In *International Political Economy and Poststructural Politics*, edited by M. de Goede. London: Palgrave.
——. 2009. Interactive and Intersectional Analytics of Globalization. *Frontiers* 30 (1): 31–40.
——. 2010a. A Long View of Globalization and Crisis. *Globalizations* 7 (1): 179–93.
——. 2010b. Gendered Identities, Ideologies, and Practices in the Context of War and Militarism. In *Gender, War, and Militarism: Feminist Perspectives*, edited by L. Sjoberg and S. Via. Santa Barbara, CA: Praeger Security International.
Peterson, V. Spike and Anne Sisson Runyan. 1993. *Global Gender Issues.* Boulder, CO: Westview Press.
——. 2010. *Global Gender Issues in the New Millennium.* Boulder, CO: Westview Press.
Pettman, Jan Jindy. 1993. Gendering International Relations. *Australian Journal of International Affairs* 47: 47–62.
——. 1996. *Worlding Women: A Feminist International Politics.* London: Routledge.
——. 2005. Questions of Identity: Australia and Asia. In *Critical Security Studies and World Politics*, edited by K. Booth. London: Lynne Rienner.
Pisarenko, Dmitrii. 1996. Rany voiny: Chechenskii sindrom. *Argumenty i fakty*, August 21, 13.
Pitzke, Marc. 2010. It is Not a Video Game: Interview with a Drone Pilot. *Spiegel International Online*, March 12, www.spiegel.de/international/world/0,1518,682842,00.html.
Politkovskaya, Anna. 2001. *A Dirty War: A Russian Reported in Chechnya.* London: Harvill Press.

——. 2004. *Putin's Russia*. London: Harvill Press.

Porter, Patrick. 2007. Good Anthropology, Bad History: The Cultural Turn in Studying War. *Parameters* 37 (2): 45–58.

Postero, Nancy Grey. 2007. *Now We are Citizens: Indigenous Politics in Post-multicultural Bolivia*. Palo Alto, CA: Stanford University Press.

Pozhidaev, D. D. 1999. Ot boevykh deistvii – k grazhdanskoi zhizni. *Sotsiologicheskie issledovaniia* (1): 70–74.

Predators and Civilians: An Intelligence Report Shows How Effective Drone Attacks Are. 2009. *Wall Street Journal*, July 14, http://online.wsj.com/article/SB124743959026229517.html.

Price, Richard and Christian Reus-Smit. 1998. Dangerous Liaisons? Critical International Theory and Constructivism. *European Journal of International Relations* 4 (3): 250–94.

Prügl, Elisabeth. 1998. Feminist Struggle as Social Construction: Changing the Gendered Rules of Home-Based Work. In *International Relations in a Constructed World*, edited by V. Kublakova, N. Onuf and P. Kowert. Armonk, NY: M. E. Sharpe.

——. 1999. *The Global Construction of Gender: Home-Based Work in the Political Economy of the 20th Century*. New York: Columbia University Press.

——. 2009. Does Gender Mainstreaming Work? Feminist Engagements with the German Agricultural State. *International Feminist Journal of Politics* 11 (2): 174–95.

Prügl, Elisabeth and Birgit Locher. 2001. Feminism: Constructivism's Other Pedigree. In *Constructing International Relations: The Next Generation*, edited by K. M. Fierke and K. E. Jorgenson. Armonk, NY: M. E. Sharpe.

Prügl, Elisabeth and Audrey Lustgarten. 2006. The Institutional Road Towards Equality: Mainstreaming Gender in International Organisations. In *Women and Gender Equity in Development Theory and Practice: Institutions, Resources, and Mobilization*, edited by J. S. Jaquette and G. Summerfield. Durham, NC: Duke University Press.

Prügl, Elisabeth and Mary Meyer, eds. 1999. *Gender and Global Governance*. Boston, MA: Rowman & Littlefield.

Putin, Vladimir, Nataliya Gevorkyan, Natalya Timakova, and Andrei Kolesnikov. 2000. *First Person: An Astonishingly Frank Self-Portrait by Russia's President Vladimir Putin*. London: Hutchinson.

Ralph, Jason C. 2005. International Society, the International Criminal Court, and American Foreign Policy. *Review of International Studies* 31(1): 27–44.

Ramirez, Jessica. 2010. Carnage.com: Videos Depicting the Gruesome Deaths of Enemy Soldiers—and Civilians—Have Taken the Internet by Storm. *Newsweek*, April 30, www.newsweek.com/id/237182.

Rao, R. 2010. *Third World Protest: Between Home and the World*. Oxford: Oxford University Press.

Rawls, John. 1958. Justice as Fairness. *The Philosophical Review* 67 (2): 164–94.

Reardon, Betty A. 1993. *Women and Peace: Feminist Visions of Global Security*. Albany, NY: State University of New York Press.

——. 1996. Women's Visions of Peace: Images of Global Security. In *The Gendered New World Order: Militarism, Development, and the Environment*, edited by J. Turpin and L. A. Lorentzen. London: Routledge.

Regamey, Amadime. 2008. L'Opinion Public Russe et l'Affair Boudanov. *The Journal of Power Institutions in Post-Soviet Societies* 8: www.pipss.org/document1493.html (accessed April 1, 2009).

Reiter, Dan and Allan C. Stam. 2002. *Democracies at War*. Princeton, NJ: Princeton University Press.

Renteln, Alison Dundes. 1988. Relativism and the Search for Human Rights. *American Anthropologist* 91 (1): 56–72.

Reus-Smit, Christian. 2001. Human Rights and the Social Construction of Sovereignty. *Review of International Studies* 27 (1): 19–38.

——. 2009. Constructivism. In *Theories of International Politics 4th Edition*. New York: Palgrave.

Richardson, J. L. 2001. *Contending Liberalisms in World Politics: Ideology and Power*. Boulder, CO: Lynne Rienner.

Richmond, Oliver P. 2008. *Peace in International Studies*. New York: Routledge.

Risse, Thomas. 2000. Let's Argue: Communicative Action in World Politics. *International Organization* 54 (1): 1–39.

Risse, Thomas, Stephen C. Ropp, and Kathryn Sikkink, eds. 1999. *The Power of Human Rights*. Cambridge: Cambridge University Press.

Robinson, Fiona. 1999. *Globalizing Care: Ethics, Feminist Theory, and International Relations*. Boulder, CO: Westview Press.

——. 2006. Methods of Feminist Normative Theory: A Political Ethic of Care for International Relations. In *Feminist Methodologies for International Relations*, edited by B. Ackerly, M. Stern and J. True. Cambridge: Cambridge University Press.

Rodriguez, Alex. 2009. Clinton's Pakistan Visit Reveals Widespread Distrust of U.S. *Los Angeles Times*, November 1, http://articles.latimes.com/2009/nov/01/world/fg-clinton-pakistan1.

Roger, Keith. 2009. War Protest Comes to Creech: Group Demonstrates Against Base's Unmanned Spy Planes. *Las Vegas Review-Journal*, November 29, www.lvrj.com/news/war-protest-comes-to-creech-73391637.html.

——. 2009. War Protest Comes to Creech. *Las Vegas Review-Journal*, November 25, www.lvrj.com/news/war-protest-comes-to-creech-73391637.html.

Rohde, David. 1998. *Endgame: The Betrayal and Fall of Srebrenica, Europe's Worst Massacre Since World War II*. Boulder, CO: Westview Press.

Roof, Judith, and Robyn Weigman. 1995. *Who Can Speak? Authority and Critical Identity*. Urbana: University of Illinois Press.

Rousseva, Valentina. 2004. Rape and Sexual Assault in Chechnya. *Culture, Society & Praxis* 3 (1): http://culturesocietypraxis.org/index.php/csp/article/viewFile/46/43 (accessed March 15, 2009).

Rowlands, Jo. 1997. *Questioning Empowerment: Working with Women in Honduras*. Oxford: Oxfam Publishing.

Ruane, Abigail E. 2010. 'Pursuing Inclusive Interests, Both Deep and Wide: Women's Human Rights and the United Nations', International Relations, University of Southern California, unpublished Ph.D. thesis.

Ruddick, Sara. 1989. *Maternal Thinking: Towards a Politics of Peace*. New York: Houghton-Mifflin.

——. 1990. The Rationality of Care. In *Women, Militarism, and War*, edited by J. B. Elshtain and S. Tobias. Savage, MD: Rowman & Littlefield.

——. 1992. From Maternal Thinking to Peace Politcs. In *Explorations in Feminist Ethics: Theory and Practice*, edited by E. Browning and S. M. Coultrap-McQuin. Bloomington: Indiana University Press.

——. 1993. Notes Towards a Feminist Peace Politics. In *Gendering War Talk*, edited by M. Cooke and A. Woollacott. Princeton, NJ: Princeton University Press.

Rumelili, Bahar. 2002. 'Producing Collective Identity and Interacting with Difference: The Security Implications of Community-Building in Europe and Southeast Asia', Political Science, University of Minnesota, unpublished Ph.D. thesis.

——. 2004. Constructing Identity and Relating to Difference: Understanding the EU's Mode of Differentiation. *Review of International Studies* 30 (1): 27–47.

Rummel, R. J. 1995. Democracies ARE Less Warlike than Other Regimes. *European Journal of International Relations* 1 (4): 457–79.

——. 1996. Democracy, Power, Genocide, and Mass Murder. *Journal of Conflict Resolution* 39 (1): 3–26.

Rupert, M. 2005. Reading Gramsci in an Era of Globalizing Capitalism. *Critical Review of International Social and Political Philosophy* 8 (4): 483–97.

Russell, John. 2007. *Chechnya – Russia's War on Terror*. London: Routledge.

Russett, Bruce M. 1993. *Grasping the Democratic Peace: Principles for a Post-Cold War World*. Princeton, NJ: Princeton University Press.

Safa, Helen. 1981. Runaway Shops and Female Employment: The Search for Cheap Labor. *Signs: Journal of Women in Culture and Society* 7 (2): 418–33.

Said, Edward W. 1993. *Culture and Imperialism*. New York: Knopf.

——. 2006. A Method for Thinking about Just Peace. In *What is a Just Peace?* edited by P. Allan and A. Keller. New York: Oxford University Press.

Salter, Mark. 2002. *Barbarians and Civilization in International Relations*. London: Pluto.

Salzinger, Leslie. 2003. *Genders in Production: Making Workers in Mexico's Global Factories*. Berkeley: University of California Press.

Sandholtz, Wayne. 2008. Dynamics of Norm Change. *European Journal of International Relations* 14 (1): 101–31.

Sapper, Manfred. 1994. *Auswirkungen des Afghanistan-Krieges auf die Sowjetgesellschaft: Eine Studie zum Legitimitätsverlust des Militärischen in der Perestroijka*. Munster: LIT.

Sarachild, Kathie. 1978. *The Feminist Revolution*. New York: Random House.

Sarkees, M. R. and N. E. McGlen. 1999. Misdirected Backlash: The Evolving Nature of Academia and the Status of Women in Political Science. *PS: Political Science and Politics* 32 (1): 100–108.

Sasson-Levy, Orna. 2003. How Identities and Movement Cultures Became Deeply Saturated with Militarism: Lessons from the Pro-democracy Movement in South Korea. *Sociological Inquiry* 73 (3): 440–65.

Savery, Lynn. 2007. *Engendering the State: The Internatinal Diffusion of Women's Human Rights*. New York: Routledge.

Scheman, Naomi. 1993. *Engenderings: Constructions of Knowledge, Authority, and Privilege*. New York: Routledge.

Schild, Veronica. 1998. Market Citizenship and the "New Democracies": Ambiguous Legacies of Chilean Women's Movements. *Social Politics. International Studies in State, Gender, and Society* 5 (2): 232–49.

——. 2000. Neoliberalism's New Gendered Market Citizens: The "Civilizing" Dimension of Social Programs in Chile. *Citizenship Studies* 4 (3): 275–305.

——. 2002. Engendering the New Social Citizenship in Chile: NGOs and Social Provisioning under Neo-liberalism. In Shahra Razavi and Maxine Molyneux, eds. *Gender Justice, Development and Rights. Substantiating Rights in a Disabling Environment*. Oxford: Oxford University Press.

——. 2007. Empowering Consumer Citizens or Governing Poor Female Subjects? The Institutionalization of "Self-Development" in the Chilean Social Policy Field. *Journal of Consumer Culture* 7 (2): 179–203.

Schnaubelt, Christopher M. 2007. Whither the RMA. *Parameters* 37 (3): 95–107.

Scott, Joan W. 1986. *Gender and the Politics of History*. New York: Columbia University Press.

Seager, Joni. 2003. *The Penguin Atlas of Women in the World*. New York: Penguin.

Sée, Yvonne. 1972. "On WILPF Aims and Purposes," p. 1, box 2, folder 8, IEC Meeting Switzerland August 1972, WILPF SCPC Accession, UCBA.

Sen, Amartya. 1997. Human Rights and Asian Values. *The New Republic* July 14–21.

Shah, Pir Zubair, Sabrina Taverise, and Mark Mazzetti. 2009. Taliban Leader in Pakistan Is Reportedly Killed. *New York Times*, August 8, www.nytimes.com/2009/08/08/world/asia/08pstan.html.

Sharkey, Noel. 2009. Death Strikes from the Sky: the Calculus of Proportionality. *IEEE Technology and Society Magazine*, Spring, 16–19.

Sharoni, Simona. 2008. De-Militarizing Masculinities in the Age of Empire. *Austrian Journal of Political Science* 37 (2): 147–64.

Sheehan, Michael. 2005. *International Security: An Analytical Survey*. Boulder, CO: Lynne Rienner.

Shepeleva, Ol'ga. 2007. Sem'i veteranov: Do i posle konflikta. In *Militsiia mezhdu Rossiei i Chechnei: Veterany konflikta v rossiiskom obshchestve*, edited by O. G. Shepeleva. Moscow: Demons.

Shepherd, Laura. 2005. Loud Voices behind the Wall: Gender Violence and the Violent Reproduction of the International. *Millennium: Journal of International Studies* 34(2): 377–400.

——. 2008a. *Gender, Violence, and Security: Discourse as Practice*. London: Zed Books.

——. 2008b. Power and Authority in the Production of United Nations Security Council Resolution 1325. *International Studies Quarterly* 52 (2): 383–404.

——. 2008c. Veiled References: Constructions of Gender in the Bush Administration Discourse on the Attacks on Afghanistan Post-9/11. *International Feminist Journal of Politics* 8 (1): 19–41.

Shigematsu, Setsu and Keith Camacho, eds. 2010. *Militarized Currents: Toward a Decolonized Future in Asia and the Pacific*. Minneapolis: University of Minnesota Press.

Shue, Henry. 1980. Second edition 1996. *Basic Rights: Subsistence, Affluence, and U.S. Foreign Policy, 2nd Edition*. Princeton, NJ: Princeton University Press.

Sieca-Kozlowski, Elisabeth. 2010. Russian Military Patriotic Education: A Control Tool Against the Arbitrariness of Veterans. *Nationalities Papers* 38 (1): 73–85.

Simma, Bruno and Phillip Alston. 1992. Sources of Human Rights Law: Custom, Jus Cogens, and General Principles. *Australian Year Book of International Law* 12: 82–108.

Simmons, Beth. 2009. *Mobilizing for Human Rights: International Law in Domestic Politics*. Cambridge: Cambridge University Press.

Siney, Marion. 1973. *The Allied Blockade of Germany, 1914–1916*. Westport, CT: Greenwood Press.

Singer, Peter W. 2009a. Wired for War: American Killing Machines. *Los Angeles Times*, January 30.

——. 2009b. *Wired for War: The Robotics Revolution and Conflict in the 21st Century*. New York: Penguin.

Sjoberg, Laura. 2002. Women's Lives as a Call to Arms. Unpublished paper, University of Southern California.

——. 2006a. Gendered Realities of the Immunity Principle: Why Gender Analysis Needs Feminism. *International Studies Quarterly* 50: 889.

——. 2006b. *Gender, Justice, and the Wars in Iraq.* Lanham, MD: Rowman & Littlefield.

——. 2007. Agency, Militarized Femininity and Enemy Others: Observations From The War In Iraq. *International Feminist Journal of Politics* 9 (1): 82–101.

——. 2008. The Norm of Tradition: Gender Subordination and Women's Exclusion in International Relations. *Politics and Gender* 4 (1): 73–80.

——. 2009a. Feminist Approaches to Political Leadership. In *The Ashgate Research Companion to Political Leadership*, edited by J. Masciulli, M. A. Molchanov and W. A. Knight. Aldershot: Ashgate Publishing.

——. 2009b. Introduction to Security Studies: Feminist Contributions. *Security Studies* 18 (2): 1–18.

——. 2010a. Introduction. In *Gender and International Security: Feminist Perspectives*, edited by L. Sjoberg. New York: Routledge.

——, ed. 2010b. *Gender and International Security: Feminist Perspectives.* New York: Routledge.

Sjoberg, Laura and Caron Gentry. 2007. *Mothers, Monsters, Whores: Women's Violence in Global Politics.* London: Zed Books.

Smith, Brett and Andrew C. Sparkes. 2006. Narrative Inquiry in Psychology: Exploring the Tensions Within *Qualitative Research in Psychology* 3: 169–92.

Smith, Steve. 2000. The Increasing Insecurity of Security Studies: Conceptualizing Security in the Last Twenty Years. In *Critical Reflections on Security and Change*, edited by S. Croft and T. Terriff. London: Frank Cass.

Sokirko, Viktor. 2000. U rodiny – nastoichivyi prizyv. *Moskovskii komsomolets* January 4.

Sokolov, Mikhail. "Predely primeneniia doktriny prav choloveka v sovremennoi rossiiskoi kul'ture: Sud nad polkovnikov Budnovym i ego protivniki." Undated manuscript. Available at www.iie.ru/ifp/Alumni/Sokolov/Downloads/art2.doc (accessed April 10, 2009).

Sotsrochkoi na god: L'goty voevavshim v Chechne. 2003. *Trud*, April 2, 30.

Special Issue: IR in the Digital Age. 2003. *Millennium, Journal of International Studies* 32 (3).

Speed, Shannon. 2007. *Rights in Rebellion; Indigenous Struggle and Human Rights in Chiapas.* Stanford, CA: Stanford University Press.

Sperling, Valerie. 2009. Making the Public Patriotic: Militarism and Anti-Militarism in Russia. In *Russian Nationalism and the National Reassertion of Russia*, edited by M. Laruelle. New York Routledge.

Spivak, Gayatri. 1988. Can the Subaltern Speak? In *Marxism and the Interpretation of Culture*, edited by C. Nelson and L. Grossberg. Urbana: University of Illinois Press.

——. 1998. Gender and International Studies. *Millennium, Journal of International Studies* 27 (4): 809–31.

Squires, Judith A. 2005. Is Mainstreaming Transformative? Theorizing Mainstreaming in the Context of Diversity and Deliberation. *Social Politics, International Studies in State, Gender, and Society* 12 (3): 366–88.

——. 2007. *The New Politics of Gender Equality.* New York: Palgrave Macmillan.

Squires, Judith and Jutta Weldes. 2007. Beyond Being Marginal: Gender and International Relations in Britain. *British Journal of Politics and Internaitonal Relations* 9 (2): 185–203.

Standing, Guy. 1999. Global Feminization through Flexible Labor: A Theme Revisited. *World Development* 27 (3): 583–602.

Staudt, Kathleen. ed. 1997. *Women, International Politics, and Development: The Bureaucratic Mire.* Philadelphia, PA: Temple University Press.

Staudt, Kathleen. 2003. Gender Mainstream: A Conceptual Framework. In *Mainstreaming Gender, Democratizing the State? National Machineries for the Advancement of Women*, edited by S. M. Rai. Manchester: Manchester University Press.

Steans, Jill. 1998. *Gender and International Relations: An Introduction.* Brunswick, NJ: Rutgers University Press.

——. 2003. Engaging from the Margins: Feminist Encounters with the 'Mainstream' of International Relations. *British Journal of Politics and International Relations* 5 (3): 428–54.

Steele, Brent. 2007. Making Words Matter: The Asian Tsunami, Darfur, and "Reflexive" Discourse in International Politics. *International Studies Quarterly* 51(4): 901–25.

——. 2008. *Ontological Security in International Relations.* London: Routledge.

——. 2010. *Defacing Power: The Aesthetics of Insecurity in Global Politics.* Ann Arbor: University of Michigan Press.

Steele, Brent and Jack L. Amoureux. 2005. Monitoring Genocide: The Benefits and Limits of Panopticism. *Millennium: Journal of International Studies* 34(2): 401–32.

Steffens, Dorothy. 1968. New Ways of Working in Africa, pp. 2–3, box 118, folder 13, Reports on Africa 1968–70/1994, WILPF Second Accession, UCBA.

Stephens, Alan and Nicola Baker. 2006. *Making Sense of War: Strategy for the 21st Century.* Cambridge: Cambridge University Press.

Stern, Maria. 2006. Racism, Sexism, Classism and Much More: Reading Security-Identity in Marginalized Sites. In *Feminist Methodologies for International Relations*, edited by B. Ackerly, M. Stern, and J. True. Cambridge: Cambridge University Press.

Stewart, Heather. 2004. 'Senoritas and Princesses: The Quinceñeara as a Context for Female Development'. Unpublished dissertation.

Stiehm, Judith. 1982. The Protected, the Protector, and the Defender. *Women's Studies International Forum* 5 (3/4): 367–76.

——, ed. 1983. *Women and Men's Wars.* Oxford: Pergamon Press.

Stienstra, D. 1999. Of Roots, Leaves, and Trees: Gender, Social Movements, and Global Governance. In *Gender Politics in Global Governance*, edited by M. Meyer and E. Prugl. New York: Routledge.

Strelets, Iurii. 2008. Vechnaia pamiat' pavshim. *Samarskie izvestiia*, December 13.

Sturdee, Nick. 2007. Chechen syndrome. Aljazeera documentary. Available at http://english.aljazeera.net/programmes/witness/2007/04/200852518464052803.html (accessed March 16, 2009).

Sud dolzhen polnost'iu opravdat' polkovnika Budanova. 2001. *Na Boevom Postu*, July 3, 2.

Swerdlow, Amy. 1993. *Women Strike for Peace: Traditional Motherhood and Radical Politics in the 1960s.* Chicago: University of Chicago Press.

Sylvester, Christine. 1992. Feminists and Realists on Autonomy and Obligation in International Relations. In *Gendered States: Feminist (Re)Visions of International Relations Theory*, edited by V. S. Peterson. Boulder, CO: Lynne Rienner.

——. 1994a. Empathetic Cooperation: A Feminist Method for International Relations. *Millennium: Journal of International Studies* 23 (2): 315–34.

——. 1994b. *Feminist Theory and International Relations in a Postmodern Era.* Cambridge: Cambridge University Press.

——. 2002. *Feminist International Relations: An Unfinished Journey.* Cambridge: Cambridge University Press.

——. 2007. The Anatomy of a Footnote. *Security Dialogue* 38 (4): 547–58.

Sylvester, Christine and Sylvester Parashar. 2009. The Contemporary Mahabharata and the Many Draupadis: Bringing Gender to Critical Terrorism Studies. In *Critical Terrorism Studies: A New Research Agenda*, edited by R. Jackson, M. Breen-Smyth and J. Gunning. London: Routledge.

Tansill, Charles Callan. 1952. *Back Door to the War: The Roosevelt Foreign Policy, 1933–1941*. New York: Greenwood.

Taylor, Verta. 1989. Social Movement Continuity: The Women's Movement in Abeyance. *American Sociological Review* 54 (5): 761–75.

Terry, Jennifer, and Melody Calvert, eds. 1997. *Processed Lives: Gender and Technology in Everyday Life*. New York: Routledge.

Thomas, Timothy L., and Charles P. O'Hara. 2000. The Equal Opportunity Disorder. *U.S. Army Medical Department Journal* (January–March 2000): http://fmso.leavenworth.army.mil/documents/stress.htm.

Tickner, Ann. 2002. Feminist Perspectives on 9/11. *International Studies Perspectives* 3 (4): 333–50.

Tickner, J. Ann. 1988. Hans Morgenthau's Principles of Political Realism: A Feminist Reformulation. *Millennium, Journal of International Studies* 17 (3): 429–40.

——. 1992. *Gender in International Relations: Feminist Perspectives on Achieving Global Security*. New York Columbia University Press.

——. 1995. Re-visioning Security. In *International Relations Theory*, edited by K. Booth and B. Smith. University Park, PA: Pennsylvania State University Press.

——. 1996. Identity in International Relations Theory: Feminist Perspectives. In *The Reture of Culture and Identity in IR Theory*, edited by Y. Lapid and F. Kratochwil. Boulder, CO: Lynne Rienner.

——. 1997. You Just Don't Understand: Troubled Engagements Between Feminisms and IR Theorists. *International Studies Quarterly* 41 (4): 611–32.

——. 2001. *Gendering World Politics*. New York: Columbia University Press.

——. 2002. Feminist Perspectives on International Relations. In *Handbook of International Relations*, edited by W. Carlesnaes, T. Risse, and B. Simmons. London: Sage.

——. 2005. What Is Your Research Program? Some Feminist Answers to International Relations Methodological Questions. *International Studies Quarterly* 49 (1): 1–22.

——. 2006. Feminism Meets International Relations: Some Methodological Issues. In *Feminist Methodologies for International Relations*, edited by B. Ackerly, M. Stern, and J. True. Cambridge: Cambridge University Press.

Tickner, J. Ann and Laura Sjoberg. 2006. Feminism. In *International Relations Theories: Discipline and Diversity*, edited by T. Dunne, S. Smith, and M. Kurki. Oxford: Oxford University Press.

——. 2010. Feminism. In *International Relations Theories: Discipline and Diversity*, 2nd edition, edited by T. Dunne, S. Smith, and M. Kurki. Oxford: Oxford University Press.

Tiessen, Rebecca. 2007. *Everywhere/Nowhere: Gender Mainstreaming in Development Agency*. Bloomfield, CT: Kumarian Press.

Tkachuk, Sergei. 2005. The President Will Want to Have a Pliable Successor. *Current Digest of the Post-Soviet Press* 57 (6): 13.

Todorov, Tzvetan. 1992. *Conquest of America: The Question of the Other*. Norman: University of Oklahoma Press.

Tomlinson, John. 1999. *Globalization and Culture*. Chicago, IL: University of Chicago Press.

Treenin, Dmitriv V., Aleksei Malashenko, and Anatol Lieven. 2000. *Russia's Restless Frontier: The Chechnya Factor in Post-Soviet Russia*. Washington, DC: Carnegie Endowment.

Trinh, T. Minh-Ha. 1989. *Woman, Native, Other: Writing Postcoloniality and Feminism*. Bloomington: Indiana University Press.

Tronto, Joan. 1987. Beyond Gender Difference to a Theory of Care. *Signs: Journal of Women in Culture and Society*. 12 (4): 644–63.

True, Jacqui. 2001. Feminism. In *Theories of International Relations*, 2nd edition, edited by S. Burchill, R. Devetak, A. Linklater, M. Paterson, C. Reus-Smit, and J. True. Basingstoke: Palgrave.

——. 2002. 'Engendering International Relations: What Difference Does Second-Generation Feminism Make.' Working Paper 2002/1. Canberra, Australia National University, RSPAS.

——. 2003a. *Gender, Globalization, and Postsocialism: The Czech Republic After Communism*. New York: Columbia University Press.

——. 2003b. Gender Mainstreaming in Global Public Policy. *International Feminist Journal of Politics* 5 (3): 368–96.

——. 2008. Gender Mainstreaming and Trade Governance in the Asia-Pacific Economic Cooperation Forum (APEC). In *Global Governance: Feminist Perspectives*, edited by S. M. Rai and G. Waylen. New York: Palgrave Macmillan.

——. 2009. The Unfulfilled Mandate: Gender Mainstreaming and UN Peace Operations. *Georgetown Journal of International Affairs* 10 (2): 41–50.

——. 2010. The Political Economy of Violence Against Women. *The Australian Feminist Law Journal* 32 (June): 39–59.

True, Jacqui, and Michael Mintrom. 2001. Transnational Networks and Policy Diffusion: The Case of Gender Mainstreaming. *International Studies Quarterly* 45: 27–57.

Twiss, Summer B. 1998. History, Human Rights, and Globalization. *Journal of Religious Ethics* 32 (1): 39–70.

UK National Archives. 2008. Spotlight on History: The Blockade of Germany, www.nationalarchives.gov.uk/pathways/firstworldwar/spotlights/blockade.htm (accessed June 3, 2008).

United Nations. 1995. *Beijing Declaration and Platform for Action*. New York: United Nations.

United States Air Force. 2010. *Factsheet: UAS*. Washington, DC: United States Air Force, http://www.af.mil/information/factsheets/index.asp.

United States Department of Defense. 2001. *DoD Dictionary of Military and Associated Terms*. Washington, DC: United States Department of Defense, www.dtic.mil/doctrine/dod_dictionary/

——. 2009. *FY 2009–34: Unmanned Systems Roadmap*. Washington, DC: United States Department of Defense.

Valdés, Theresa, and Alina Donoso. 2009. Social Accountability and Citizen Participation: Are Latin American Governments Meeting Their Commitments to Gender Equity? In *Feminist Agendas and Democracy in Latin America*, edited by J. S. Jaquette. Durham, NC: Duke University Press.

Valentino, Benjamin, Paul Huth, and Dylan Balch-Lindsay. 2004. "Draining the Sea": Mass Killing and Guerrilla Warfare. *International Organization* 58 (2): 375–407.

Van Kersbergen, K. and B. Verbeek. 2007. The Politics of International Norms. *European Journal of International Relations* 13 (2): 217–38.

Vargas, Virginia. 2009. International Feminisms: The World Social Forum. In *Feminist Agendas and Democracy in Latin America*, edited by J. S. Jaquette. Durham, NC: Duke University Press.

Vellacott, Jo. 1988. Women, Peace and Internationalism, 1914–20: Finding New Words and Creating New Method. In *Peace Movements and Political Cultures*, edited by C. Chatfield and P. Van den Dungen. Knoxville: University of Tennessee Press.

———. 1993. A Place for Pacifism and Transnationalism in Feminist Theory: The Early Work of the Women's International League for Peace and Freedom. *Women's History Review* 2 (1): 23–56.

Verloo, Mike. 2005. Displacement and Empowerment: Reflections on the Concept and Practice of the Council of Europe Approach to Gender Mainstreaming and Gender Equality. *Social Politics, International Studies in State, Gender, and Society* 12 (1): 344–65.

Wagner, Claudia. 2000. *Rußlands Kriege in Tschetschenien: Politische Transformation und militärische Gewalt*. Munster: LIT.

Wajcman, Judy. 2006. The Gender Politics of Technology. In *The Oxford Handbook of Contextual Political Analysis* edited by R. E. Goodin and C. Tilly. Oxford: Oxford University Press.

Walby, Sylvia, ed. 2005. Special Issue: Comparative Gender Mainstreaming in a Global Era. *International Feminist Journal of Politics*.

Walker, Neil. 2006. Sovereignty, International Security and the Regulation of Armed Conflict: The Possibilities of Political Agency. In *The Politics of Protection: Sites of Insecurity and Political Agency*, edited by J. Huysmans, A. Dobson, and R. Prokhovnik. London: Routledge.

Walker, R. B. J. 1990. Security, Sovereignty, and the Challenge of World Politics. *Alternatives: Global, Local, Political* 15 (1): 3–27.

Waltz, Kenneth N. 1959. *Man, the State, and War: A Theoretical Analysis*. New York: Columbia University Press.

———. 1979. *Theory of International Politics*. New York: Random House.

Walzer, Michael. 1992. *Just and Unjust Wars: A Moral Argument with Historical Illustrations*. 2nd edition. New York: Basic Books.

War, Trade Information Department. 1918. Summary of Blockade Information, 31st May – 4th, edited by U. K. War Trade Information Department: CAB 24/53 (PRO), GT Series.

Ware, Vron. 1992. *Beyond the Pale: White Women, Racism, and History*. London: Verso.

Weaver, Catherine. 2010. The Strategic Social Construction of the World Bank's Gender and Development Policy Norm. In *Owning Development: Creating Global Policy Norms in the IMF and the World Bank*, edited by S. Park and A. Vetterlein. Cambridge: Cambridge University Press.

Weber, Cynthia. 1994. Good Girls, Little Girls, and Bad Girls: Male Paranoia in Robert Keohane's Critique of Feminist International Relations. *Millennium: Journal of International Studies* 23(4) (337–49).

———. 1999. *Faking It: U.S. Hegemony in a 'Post-Phallic' Era*. Minneapolis: University of Minnesota Press.

———. Forthcoming. *Queer International Relations*. Oxford: Oxford University Press.

Weber, Jutta. 2006. From Science and Technology to Feminist Technoscience. In *Handbook of Gender and Women's Studies*, edited by K. Davis, M. Evans, and J. Lorber. London: Sage.

Weinhold, Barry K. 2000. Uncovering the Hidden Causes of Bullying and School Violence. *Counseling and Human Development* 32 (6): 1–18.

Weldes, Jutta and Judith A. Squires. 2007. Beyond Being Marginal: Gender and International Relations in Britain. *British Journal of Politics and International Relations* 9 (2): 185–203.

Weldes, Jutta. 1999. The Cultural Production of Crises: U.S. Identity and Missiles in Cuba. In *Cultures of Insecurity*, edited by Jutta Weldes, Mark Laffey, Hugh Guterson, and Raymond Duvall. Minneapolis: University of Minnesota Press.

Weldon, S. Laurel. 2006. Inclusion and Understanding: A Collective Methodology for Feminist International Relations. In *Feminist Methodologies for International Relations*, edited by B. Ackerly, M. Stern, and J. True. Cambridge: Cambridge University Press.

Welsh, Ian. 2000. *Mobilizing Modernity: The Nuclear Moment*. New York: Routledge.

Wendt, Alexander. 1987. The Agent-Structure Problem in International Relations Theory. *International Organization* 41 (3): 335–70.

——. 1991. Bridging the Theory/Meta Theory Gap in International Relations. *Review of International Studies* 17 (4): 383–92.

——. 1992. Anarchy is What States Make of it: The Social Construction of Power Politics. *International Organization* 41 (2): 335–70.

——. 1992. Levels of Analysis vs. Agents and Structures, Part II. *Review of International Studies* 18 (2): 181–85.

——. 1994. Collective Identity Formation and the International State. *American Political Science Review* 88: 384–96.

——. 1995. Constructing International Politics. *International Security* 20 (1): 71–81.

——. 1996. Identity and Structural Change in International Politics. In *The Return of Culture and Identity in IR Theory*, edited by Yosef Lapid and Friedrich Kratochwil, Boulder, CO: Lynne Rienner.

——. 1999. *Social Theory of International Politics*. Cambridge: Cambridge University Press.

Whatever Happened to Feminist Critiques of Marriage? 2010. Critical Perspectives Section of *Politics & Gender* 6 (1): 119–53.

Whitworth, Sandra 1989. Gender in the Inter-Paradigm Debate. *Millennium: Journal of International Studies* 18 (2): 265–72.

——. 1994. *Feminism and International Relations: Towards a Political Economy of Gender in Interstate and Non-Governmental Institutions*. London: Macmillan.

——. 1994. Gender, International Relations, and the Case of the ILO. *Review of International Studies* 20 (4): 389–405.

——. 2004. *Men, Militarism, and UN Peacekeeping: A Gendered Analysis*. Boulder, CO: Lynne Rienner.

——. 2008. Militarized Masculinity and Post-Traumatic Stress Disorder. In *Rethinking the Man Question: Sex, Gender, and Violence in International Relations*, edited by J. L. Parpart and M. Zalewski. London: Zed Books.

Wiener, Antje. 2009. Enacting Meaning-in-Use: Qualitative Research on Norms and International Relations. *Review of International Studies* 35 (1): 175–93.

Wight, Colin. 1999. They Shoot Dead Horses, Don't They? Locating Agency in the Agent-Structure Problematique. *European Journal of International Relations* 5 (1): 109–42.

——. 2000. Interpretation all the Way Down? A Reply to Roxanne Lynn Doty. *European Journal of International Relations* 6 (3): 423–30.

——. 2006. *Agents, Structures, and International Relations: Politics as Ontology*. Cambridge: Cambridge University Press.

Wilcox, Lauren. 2009. Gendering the Cult of the Offensive. *Security Studies* 18 (2): 214–40.
——. 2010. Gendering the Cult of the Offensive. In *Gender and International Security: Feminist Perspectives*, edited by L. Sjoberg. New York: Routledge.
Williams, Michael C. 1998. Identity and the Politics of Security. *European Journal of International Relations* 4 (2): 204–25.
WILPF. 1959. International Congress Resolutions, box 26, folder 8, Circular Letters January 1958–November 1959 and 1969[-}70, 1.
WILPF IEC, 1959, box 5, folder 10, IEC Meeting Minutes 1955–59, 8, WILPF SCPC Accession, UCBA.
WILPF International Office. n.d. Reports of the International Congresses, 1926–53. Microfilm reel 141.2, SCPC.
WILPF International Office. n.d. Reports of the International Congresses, 1956–86. Microfilm reel 141.3, SCPC.
WILPF SCPC Accession. n.d. 'no title' UCBA.
WILPF Second Accession. n.d. 'no title' UCBA.
WILPF. n.d. 'Dolores Taller Collection' (unprocessed). UCBA.
Wittner, Lawrence S. 1997. *Resisting the Bomb: A History of the World Nuclear Disarmament Movement, 1945–1970*. Palo Alto, CA: Stanford University Press.
Wolf, Diane L. 1996. *Feminist Dilemmas in Fieldwork*. Boulder, CO: Westview Press.
Wolf, Naomi. 2002. Forward to 2002 edition of *The Beauty Myth* New York: Harper.
Wyn Jones, Richard. 1999. *Security, Strategy, and Critical Theory*. Boulder, CO: Lynne Rienner.
——. 2005. On Emancipation: Necessity, Capacity, and Concrete Utopias. In *Critical Security Studies and World Politics*, edited by K. Booth. London: Lynne Rienner.
Yoder, John Howard. 1996. *When War is Unjust: Being Honest in Just-War Thinking*. Maryknoll, NY: Orbis Books.
Young, I. M. (1994) Gender as Seriality: Thinking about Women as Social Collective. *Signs: Journal of Women in Culture and Society* 19 (3): 713–38.
——. 2003. The Logic of Masculinist Protection: Reflections on the Current Security State. *Signs Journal of Women in Culture and Society* 29 (1): 1–25.
Youngs, Gillian. 1996. Dangers of Discourse: The Case of Globalization. In *Globalization: Theory and Practice*, edited by E. Kofman and G. Youngs. London: Pinter.
——. 1999. Virtual Voices: Real Lives. In *Women@Internet: Creating New Cultures in Cyberspace*, edited by W. Harcourt. New York: Zed Books.
Yusuf, Huma. 2009. In Pakistan, Clinton Fails to Charm Professional Women. *Christian Science Monitor*, October 30, www.csmonitor.com/World/Global-News/2009/1030/in-pakistan-clinton-fails-to-charm-professional-women.
Yuval-Davis, Nira. 1997. *Gender & Nation*. London: Sage.
Zalewski, Marysia. 1994. The Women/"Women" Question in International Relations. *Millennium: Journal of International Studies* 23 (3): 407–23.
——. 1996. "All these Theories yet the Bodies Keep Piling Up": Theorists, Theories, and Theorizing. In *International Relations: Positivism and Beyond*, edited by S. Smith, K. Booth, and M. Zalewski. Cambridge: Cambridge University Press.
——. 2000. *Feminism after Postmoderninsm: Theorising through Practice*. London: Routledge.
——. 2006. Distracted Reflections on the Production, Narration, and Refusal of Feminist Knowledge in IR. In *Feminist Methodologies for International Relations*, edited by B. Ackerly, M. Stern, and J. True. Cambridge: Cambridge University Press.

——. 2007. Do We Understand Each Other Yet? Troubling Feminist Encounters With(in) international Relations. *British Journal of Politics and International Relatiosn* 9 (2): 302–12.

Zalewski, Marysia and Jane Parpart, eds. 1998. *The "Man" Question in International Relations*. Boulder, CO: Westview Press. Second edition published in 2008 as *Rethinking the Man Question : Sex, Gender and Violence in International Relations*. London: Zed Books.

Žarkov, Dubravka. 2007. *The Body of War: Media, Ethnicity, and Gender in the Break-up of Yugoslavia*. Durham, NC: Duke University Press.

Zehfuss, Maja. 2002. *Constructivism in International Relations: The Politics of Reality*. Cambridge: Cambridge University Press.

Zucchino, David. 2010. Drone Pilots Have a Front-row Seat on War, from Half a World Away. *Los Angeles Times*, http://articles.latimes.com/2010/feb/21/world/la-fg-drone-crews21–2010feb21.

Index